# Feeding Barcelona 1714-1975

## Public Market Halls, Social Networks, and Consumer Culture

### MONTSERRAT MILLER

LOUISIANA STATE UNIVERSITY PRESS

BATON ROUGE

Publication of this book is made possible in part by support from the
John Deaver Drinko Academy at Marshall University.


Published by Louisiana State University Press
Copyright © 2015 by Louisiana State University Press
All rights reserved
Manufactured in the United States of America
LSU Press Paperback Original
FIRST PRINTING

DESIGNER: *Mandy McDonald Scallan*
TYPEFACE: *Whitman*
PRINTER AND BINDER: *Maple Press, Inc.*


Library of Congress Cataloging-in-Publication Data are available at the Library of Congress.

ISBN 978-0-8071-5646-9 (pbk.: alk. paper) — ISBN 978-0-8071-5647-6 (pdf) — ISBN 978-0-8071-5648-3 (epub)
— ISBN 978-0-8071-5649-0 (mobi)

The paper in this book meets the guidelines for permanence and durability of the Committee on Production
Guidelines for Book Longevity of the Council on Library Resources. ∞

# Feeding Barcelona
## 1714-1975

*To my family, on both sides of the Atlantic*

# Contents

*Photographs follow page 108.*

# Preface

> If the Sagrada Família, for all its contradictory significance, does its best to play the part of the Eiffel Tower, Big Ben, or the Empire State Building, it is not, by any means, the site foremost in the minds of the city's residents. For the residents, such places as markets, schools, churches, cafés, bars, shops, and parks, sites for everyday life and its practices, tend to overshadow more recognizably monumental structures, whose role in everyday life should not be discounted either.
> —BRAD EPPS, "Space in Motion: Barcelona and the Stages of (In)visibility"

Public food markets in Spain, as in some other Mediterranean countries, remained crucial urban shopping venues throughout the twentieth century. With respect to Barcelona specifically, there were forty-one municipally operated food market halls open six days a week on the eve of the 1992 Summer Olympic Games. With one for every 44,000 inhabitants, Barcelona had more markets per capita than any other city in Europe.[1] A curious source illustrating the enduring twentieth-century importance of markets in Spanish visions of what cities should consist of is Antonio Jiménez-Landi's English-language children's book, *A First Look at a City in Spain.* In this seemingly insignificant tome that appeared in 1961, Jiménez-Landi invited young readers to invent their own city, recommending that they first "draw a plan of it" and then choose where to locate "the most important buildings," which were "the Church, the City Hall, the School, and the Market Place."[2] Here we can see a certain resonance of the author's progressive Institución Libre de Enseñanza education.[3] The social body is represented by the city as a concept that is cast as rational and improvable through planning and design. The structures of authority, religious and secular, have their central place, but so too do buildings that provide public services, here embodied in their most basic form through schools, where minds were to be developed, and markets from which food supplies would flow to feed the population of the ideal city. Jiménez-Landi's little book testifies to the ongoing presumption in twentieth-century Spain that market halls remained the most appropriate public institutions for the regulation of food retailing. It also helps to explain the thinking that underpinned the ongoing municipal construction of markets in Barcelona over the long run, where the city council inaugurated seventeen new food market halls in the century leading up to the outbreak of the Spanish Civil War in 1936. Then during the nearly four decades of Franco's rule, it inaugurated twenty-two additional structures. Since the transition to democracy, a handful more have opened and a couple of markets have closed. But the vitality of the system remained remarkable. Commitment to public market-hall construction and municipal management in Barcelona thus constitutes important twentieth-century continuities that were seemingly immune to regime change.

The geographically dispersed, or "polynuclear" model of market-hall location designed to serve individual neighborhoods, the ongoing commitment to municipal management and regulation, and the tenacity and adaptability of food vendors in the face of changing circumstances all contributed to the development of an urban system in Barcelona that has allowed consumers in what Joan Busquets calls the "compact city" to continue shopping for food on foot.[4] As such, Barcelona did not experience the emergence of the "food deserts" that have all too often characterized late-twentieth-century cities in other parts of the world. Because Barcelona is broadly recognized as a premier market city, it is worth examining what made that system work in a period when other cities were abandoning the model as the basis for provisioning their populations. The premise of this book is that how, where, and from whom we buy our food matters. It has been so in the past, and it remains today a quality-of-life issue.

There is no question that the ongoing resilience of Barcelona's food markets has shaped the nature of everyday life in the city, particularly for women. As Manuel Guàrdia and José Luis Oyón assert, market halls were more than just viable economic institutions; they were also extraordinarily ebullient in terms of neighborhood-based sociability.[5] Late-twentieth-century residents of the Sants neighborhood of Barcelona who described themselves as *gent de barri* (neighborhood folk), for instance, defined that identity as one that involved socializing in their market hall with vendors and other customers and talking with neighbors in the food shops near where they lived.[6] These habits of sociability were deeply intertwined with the dissemination of consumerist values. When women stopped to talk in markets, they exchanged pleasantries and various bits of information but also could observe the purchases that their neighbors were making. In my fieldwork, I overheard thousands of such conversations. They would often tell one another, "Since it's Thursday, I'm making rice. I have to get the shellfish from Enric's stall," or "Yesterday I made an *estofat* [stew] that turned out so well my husband almost licked his fingers!" The sharing of recipes and assertions of pride in cooking and in consumer acumen were as much a part of the neighborhood sociability taking place in markets as was the exchange of gossip, humor, and discussions of family fortunes.

One of the first things that I learned about Barcelona when I began to visit as a child was the importance that women of my mother's generation accorded to their daily trips to the neighborhood market. *Anar a la plaça* (going to the plaza), as they called it, was both duty and pleasure; it was an opportunity to chat with neighbors while fulfilling basic domestic responsibilities. My grandmother, I was told, typically stopped at least ten times to talk with neighbors along the block and a half trajectory from her flat on the top floor of a modernist building located on the corner of Bailèn and València streets to the cavernous La Concepció metal market hall where she shopped six days a week. My grandfather never set foot there, except during the Civil War, when exigencies demanded as much. In terms of consumers, the neighborhood market was mainly a feminized consumer space. The routines I observed thirty years later when I first became familiar with La Concepció still bore scant relevance to the supermarket-based shopping patterns that dominated back home in the United States. Rather, *anar a la plaça* involved standing in line at specific stalls, long drawn-out conversations with market vendors and with other consumers, and the privileging of quality in interpersonal exchanges and punctilious selection of small quantities of edibles over speed and efficiency.

Members of my extended Catalan family, in the United States and in Barcelona, have been as crucial to this book's conception as to its completion. As far back as I can remember and an ocean away from their home—when that really meant something—my mother, Maria Teresa Miller, and my aunt, Rosa Maria Martí, fed me and my siblings on a regular diet of stories about their childhood interrupted by the Spanish Civil War and about coming of age during the first decades of the Franco regime. The primacy in this study of the markets and of women buying and selling food comes fundamentally from their accounts of hunger and from the heroic imagery they cast of my grandmother's acumen in acquiring scarce provisions amidst the violence of war and dislocation. My family in Barcelona, including my uncle Lluís Martí, my aunt Maria Ramón, and their six children—Jordi, Maria Lluisa, Xavier, Ricard, Marc, and Teresona—all served, beginning in the late-1960s, as able and patient tutors in my quest to understand their culture and their city. It was at the Martí dinner table and on trips to La Concepció Market with Tieta Maria, in fact, that I was first able to witness the subjects and processes with which this book is concerned. Housewifery, which my Tieta Maria practiced with amazing skill, involved negotiating her neighborhood market as a task she relished, six days a week. Her trips to the market took place only when the family flat had been thoroughly cleaned and she had spruced herself up with a dot of makeup. Then she descended, with joy, determination, and a small change purse that contained her daily allotment of pesetas, to engage in a dozen or more affable conversations with vendors and neighbors before hauling her market basket up the long staircase home and transforming her bounty into a satisfying meal. In a sense, this study is a kind of ode to my late Tieta Maria, as my first and most important embedded informant, and as a woman of great optimism, generosity, wisdom, and humor.

My aim here is to explain how and why Barcelona's remarkably enduring public market-hall system developed as it did. Placed within the context of a dramatically expanding urban framework and a flourishing consumerist food culture, this book examines twentieth-century vendors' lives and work patterns before and during the four-decade-long period of Franco's rule. Ultimately, three themes dominate this history. The first is the ongoing survival of food vendors' small-scale retailing enterprises in a period otherwise characterized by increasing capitalization and the growth of larger-scale business concerns. The second is a surprisingly high level of female entrepreneurship in the food-market sector at a time when women faced broader legal and cultural impediments to independent initiatives in the commercial economy. And the third theme is the ongoing intensity of sociability patterns centered in the market halls of the city and surrounding neighborhood-based food retailing in general.

In the pages that follow, I offer a scholarly and a personal narrative. Though addressing historical questions and relying upon historical methods, this study also draws significantly from other approaches, especially ethnography and participant observation. Yet it does not purport to represent a formal ethnographic analysis in any sense. Rather, it reflects the growing interdisciplinarity of the humanities and social sciences in the last half-century while rejecting synchronic theoretical models of timeless structures defining power relations, beliefs, or systems of symbols. Where illustrative, the book includes some brief reflection upon my family history and my own personal experiences. In the main, however, it sticks to an exploration of the archival and ethnographic sources and to an examination of change and continuity over the long term.

Stall registry books (Llibres de Registre) constitute one of the important sources of information for this study. Although most of the volumes I consulted are held in the central offices of the Institut Municipal de Mercats de Barcelona (IMMB), some of the registries for the oldest markets in the city were not deposited there when I was conducting my research. Consequently, I was able to secure permission to collect data from registries held in individual market directors' offices at La Boqueria, Santa Caterina, Sant Antoni, La Llibertat, and L'Abaceria Central. At several of these markets, and most especially at Sant Antoni, I was also allowed to consult boxes of administrative records that covered a broad swath of the twentieth century. Since that time, most of these documents have been consolidated in the IMMB offices. The Administrative Records of Sant Antoni Market (appearing in the notes as ARSAM), however, were discarded at some point in the late 1990s and thus are no longer consultable as an extant collection. Readers should be aware that when these records are cited in the chapters that follow, I am, in virtually all instances, referencing photocopies of those documents, which I have in my personal collection and would be more than happy to share with any interested scholars who may wish to inquire.

The conclusions that I draw have been shaped by the personal testimonies of a great many individuals with whom I met, spoke, and/or formally interviewed while visiting and studying the markets of Barcelona over the course of several decades. Vendors of all types and circumstances, consumers, passersby, errand boys, municipal administrators, inspectors, security guards, clerks, secretaries, custodians, cleaning women, nearby shopkeepers, waiters, café owners, and a cook or two from all across the city have helped to structure this account. While beginning the formal portion of the research in the summer of 1990, the longest-sustained period of field work extended from September 1991 to July 1992, when I collected the bulk of the tape-recorded oral history interviews upon which some of the chapters of the book depend most extensively. More than a dozen subsequent trips ranging from two weeks to three months in length have involved more intense archival research alongside continued ethnographic work and participant observation in the markets and surrounding spaces. The unstructured oral histories took place in market directors' offices, in vendors' stalls, in their homes, and in the processing workshops located adjacent to where they worked selling food. Less formal interviews took place in myriad places. I was invited to breakfast with market men on innumerable occasions, eating marvelous and sometimes unimaginable foods in order not to offend but also to prove my gustatory mettle. While working on the project I was also a market customer, mainly shopping in and around La Concepció, where I was able for years to keep a small apartment nearby and cook for family and friends. Market women more often offered me recipes, advice, and occasionally a generous weight on whatever I was purchasing.

The issue of discursive context is here, as in all historical analyses, a vital one to consider. Catalan is the indigenous language of Spain's autonomous region of Catalonia, of which Barcelona is the capital. It is not a dialect, and in many respects the language is thriving, even though there have been some concerted efforts in the name of state-building since the War of the Spanish Succession to restrict and, even in some ambits, prohibit its use. The historical relationship between the Catalan and the Castilian languages (the latter being what we refer to in English as "Spanish") remains a contested one. Among Barcelona's market vendors and consumers in the twentieth century, there appears to have long been a pattern of linguistic exchange that was bilingual and based on expediency and ability, with mixing and code-switching within single conversations. I followed the same approach in my ethnographic work; the vast majority of the oral histories used in this study were conducted in Catalan, the others in Spanish. Despite the vehement polemics about language use that are a feature of contemporary Spanish politics, Barcelona remains today a bilingual city. I have opted, for the convenience of readers, for bilingual usage throughout the book. For the most part, place names appear in Catalan. But because this edition is aimed at an English-speaking readership, I have used Spanish where familiarity with places and terms facilitates understanding. Las Ramblas, for instance—an avenue that so many travelers know and appreciate—are not referenced in the proper Catalan as *les Rambles*, which in my estimation would herein only confuse or confound. Likewise, English-speaking readers all know what the term *plaza* means and so therefore I only use the Catalan term for the same sort of urban public space—that is, *plaça*—with respect to specific places and to directly quote the references and common expressions of informants. Also, the terms *Spanish* and *Castilian* are used interchangeably to denote the same language. In addition, some readers may be perplexed by what appear to be missing diacritical marks in specific words, but this is due to the fact that Catalan has its own pronunciation and spelling rules that differ from those of Spanish; for example, *abacería* in Castilian versus *L'Abaceria Central* in Catalan.

Finally, it must be clear that what I posit in the chapters that follow is only one version of the history of Barcelona's markets—my version. The potential for further exploration from a variety of fields remains tremendous. My hope is to stimulate new discussions and contribute to the work that is already underway from several quarters and varying perspectives in Barcelona and elsewhere on this subject of food markets, women's work patterns, and the impact of both on urban life. There are certainly many practices and facets of experience related to Barcelona's markets that remain elusive. Speaking with the adult children of retired vendors from La Concepció Market as we cross paths in the neighborhood and conversations with the children of shopkeepers who have pursued professions other than that of their parents remind me of this and of the paucity of records documenting the lives of ordinary food retailers in the city. This project has, by necessity and by the sheer magnitude of frustration and personal expense, monetary and otherwise, dealt a forceful blow to the romantic-utopianist visions of Barcelona to which I clung as a child growing up in rural Appalachia. The love for the city remains, but the research has imposed greater degrees of realism, or so I would like to believe. Others may disagree. The critical reading and the kind help of a great number of informants and scholars notwithstanding, I accept full personal responsibility for any and all errors that may remain in the text.

I could begin to tell this story at any number of points in time, from the origins of Barcelona's oldest marketplaces to a present-day account of the liveliness one might experience at a given stall in La Boqueria. All have their place and their merits. But one particular vignette set on the eve of the declaration of Spain's Second Republic in 1931 serves as an especially telling episode. Through it, we can see the complex relationship of Barcelona's market vendors to the state, cultural contradictions in the popular response to market women's work, and an encapsulated opportunity to consider the themes this book will take up. After reflecting on the significance of market-related civic pageantry in chapter 1, chapter 2 steps back in time to trace the medieval and early modern history of Barcelona through the lens of its provisioning system. Chapter 3 examines the circumstances that explain how and why municipal authorities moved to construct a market-hall-based food-retailing system over the course of the "long nineteenth century." Chapter 4 considers the various ways in which market shopping and home cooking were embedded within the context of turn-of-the-century consumerist culture. Chapters 5, 6, and 7 then offer a closer look at Barcelona's food markets in the twentieth century. After considering the political economy of food retailing in Barcelona in the decades preceding the outbreak of the Spanish Civil War in 1936, chapter 5 analyzes the formal commercial and administrative networks that emanated from the city's market halls. Chapter 6 then examines the market-based informal social and commercial networks in which women figured so prominently before and during the course of the war. And lastly, chapter 7 assesses changes and continuities through the course of the four-decades-long dictatorial regime of General Francisco Franco, and takes up the connections between market shopping and expressions of Catalan culinary identity.

# Acknowledgments

The research for this book has been generously supported by the National Endowment for the Humanities, the Program for Cultural Cooperation Between Spain's Ministry of Culture and United States' Universities, and the West Virginia Humanities Council. Marshall University's Department of History, its College of Graduate Studies, its College of Liberal Arts, and the John Deaver Drinko Academy also provided significant support for the research and writing process. The work to revise the manuscript has been sponsored by the Spanish Ministerio de Ciencia e Innovación's HAR2011-26951 research project, "La reconstrucción de la actividad económica en la Cataluña contemporánea: trabajo, demografía y economías familiares." While conducting earlier phases of the research, I received support from the History Department at Carnegie Mellon University, from a Spanish Ministerio de Asuntos Exteriores/United States Fulbright Commission Fellowship, and from the American Association of University Women. I am grateful to all those granting institutions and to the officers and independent reviewers working with them for believing in the viability and significance of the project.

Most crucially, Daniel Holbrook, my fellow historian, husband, and best friend, has made it possible for me to complete this book in that he has served as a brilliant and insightful sounding board and has exhibited unending patience with, and sincere appreciation for, my obsession with studying Barcelona's markets. If there is any justice in this world, he will receive his due recompense. I am also profoundly thankful to Alisa Plant, senior acquisitions editor at Louisiana State University Press, for believing in the project and for giving me the time to revise and expand my manuscript, and to Catherine Kadair, for skillfully guiding me through the production process. I am grateful, as well, to the anonymous reviewers for LSU Press for providing me with invaluable criticism that greatly improved the final product, and to Margaret Dalrymple for her detailed and patient copyediting.

A great number of scholars have offered advice, commentary, and assistance with this work. Above all else, I am indebted to Peter Stearns for the breadth of his historical vision and for his crucial mentorship. I must acknowledge, as well,

Richard Maddox, Judith Modell, and Donna Harsch for their skillful contributions to the completion of the study that was the starting point from which this project began. While at Carnegie Mellon, I was also assisted and generously encouraged in a number of ways by David Miller and Joel Tarr and by the community of scholars who were part of the Department of History during my years as a graduate student there. I would like, in addition, to thank all those individuals who read and commented on my work over the years, including Michael Miller, Tim Haggerty, Mary Yeager, Jonathan Morris, Susan Strasser, Marta Vicente, Luis Corteguera, Carla Rahn Phillips, David Ringrose, Pamela Beth Radcliff, and Aurora G. Morcillo. Colleagues at Marshall who have offered invaluable support include Alan Gould, Steve Riddel, María del Carmen Riddel, Frances Hensley, David Duke, Sarah Denman, Donna Spindel, Leonard Deutsch, Joan Mead, Christina Murphy, and David Pittenger. I have had the great fortune to work with some remarkable students at Marshall, including Kara Dixon Vuic, Julia Hudson Richards, and Charlton Yingling, all of whom have gone on to become professional historians and have contributed significantly to this project through their inquisitiveness, research assistance, and inspiration. I owe Phillip T. Rutherford special thanks for having read, commented on, and helped to refine the narrative arc of the final manuscript. I want to thank my old friend Michael Neiberg, as well, for helping to propel me forward with unfailing encouragement and sage advice.

I am also indebted to the assistance and advice of a community of scholars in Barcelona, including Albert Carreras, Paloma Fernández, Lídia Torra, Àngels Solà, Cristina Borderías, Mercè Renom, and Nadia Fava. Manuel Guàrdia and José Luis Oyón in particular have encouraged me and shaped my thinking about Barcelona's public-market system in profound ways. I am also sincerely grateful for the assistance, advice, and friendship extended to me by María José Balcells, Caterina Toscano, Imma Vega, and Maria Mercè Ramón. Clearly, the book would not have been possible without the professionalism of the archival staffs working in a wide range of collections around the city. I am especially indebted to the librarians at the Arxiu Històric Municipal de la Ciutat de Barcelona—Patricia Jaca, Àngels Solà, and Manel Alfaro; to Maria Pont Estradera and Núria Sagala Costa at the Arxiu Històric del Cambra Oficial de Comerç, Indústria i Navegació de Barcelona; to Maria Pilar Gómez at the Biblioteca de Catalunya; to Quima Clapes and Josep Obis at the Deposit Pre-Artxivatge de l'Arxiu Municipal Administratiu de Barcelona; and to Jordi Serchs at the Arxiu Municipal del Districte de Gràcia. I also appreciate the assistance of Elena Carrasco at the Gremi d'Empresaris Carnissers i Xarcuters de Barcelona i Província. The first of the two maps in the text includes cartography that is owned by the Institut Cartogràfic de Catalunya, available at www.icc.cat.

Market vendors who sat for tape-recorded oral history interviews, and to whom I owe a great debt of gratitude, include: Carmen Valls Roig, Francesca Orriols Palmada, Lluís Casals, Maria Cararach Vernet, Antoni Llaquet Carrera, Semi Colominas Aluja, Francesc Camps Torres, Carme Giner Folch, Asunción Conejero Moreno, Maria Teresa Fernández Mitjans, Carmen González Morales, Ramón Illa Viñas, Joan Mani Burgada, Rafel Martí Fiol, Mercè Miró García, Antoni Vinyals Adrian, Maria Marqués Ruiz, Joan Belada Pario, Núria Manadé Ginestà, Sacramento Bosquè Meabilla, Francesc Barceló Duran, Joana Calvet Terrado, Francesc Colominas Aznar, Antònia Condeminas Vendrell, Joaquim Esteba Esteve, Claudi Estaban i Sicart, Joana Grillé Fornell, Antoni Jover Barceló, Amparo Lloret de Aguiar, Pere Malla Vila, Josefa Nogueroles Casas, Tomàs Sancho Roman, Martí Pla Mirosa, Robert Olius Olius, Antonia Peña Martín, Enriqueta Pons Coll, Maria Teresa Costa Pons, Rosa Sanaluja Cot, Antònia Mestres Tuyet, Isabel Colera Magrans, Buenaventura Maurí Pla, and Ricard Rivero Batlle. All these individuals worked as vendors and led lives bound up with the fortunes of the markets. Though each had his or her own unique story to tell, their accounts provided me with crucial insights about the larger patterns defining what could be termed a market-based subculture in the city.

In addition to the vendors providing formal interviews, there have been a number of individuals in Barcelona and within the world of the markets who have supported my research endeavors. Foremost among them have been Adolf Cabruja, Ana Ortanovez, Francesc Puigdomènech, Joan Bonastre, Xavier Trull, Joan Damià, Joan Aymerich, Jordi Tolrà, and Jordi Maymó. The late Manel Ripoll, Salvador Capdevila, and Òscar Ubide, especially, taught me much and exhibited great patience in waiting for the book to be completed. Other dear friends and family in Barcelona who have patiently and generously schooled me in late-twentieth-century Catalan food culture include Marc Martí, Àngles Homs, Xavier Martí, Neus Homs, Pep Salat, Jordi Salat, and Antonio Santolaria. I am grateful, also, for the assistance generously provided to me by Marcel Martí, Gerard Martí, and Mimica Curtó. Jordi Martí, my eldest cousin, deserves special mention for having made the resources of his library and studio available to me and for sharing his tremendous knowledge of Catalan and Spanish history over a lifetime's worth of late-night conversations. I must acknowledge, also, the most basic influence of my late father, John H. Miller Jr., a native West Virginian, World War II Pacific Theater veteran, and enthusiastic Hispanist who taught Spanish at Marshall University and at Michigan State. First and foremost, my father had the good sense to go to Barcelona and marry my mother. But he also knew a great deal about Catalonia and served, alongside my late uncle Lluís Martí, as an excellent first teacher and historical tour guide.

In the United States, key friends and family have helped me proceed with this project in too many ways to list: Marc Miller, Teresa Bailey, Bill Chambers, the late Carolyn Perry Chambers, Don S. McDaniel Jr., Ana Bahr, Niles Riddel, Kathy Nora, Bob Dibble, Dave Holbrook, Eve Aspinwall, Lis Silliman, John Silliman, Greg and Joy Stowers, Teresa Izzo, and Dan Davis provided support on emotional, logistical, physical, and financial levels. In addition to his diligent and patient work in preparing the first of the two maps that are included in this book, Everett Perry deserves my sincere thanks for his friendship over the years and for helping me to put my personal frustrations and challenges in perspective. Worth noting, as well, is that through the better course of this effort I have also benefitted from being a "parishioner" of Huntington, West Virginia's own Mediterranean shopkeeper par excellence, Julian Saad, who represents the contemporary viability of some of the commercial and social strategies long-practiced by Barcelona's market vendors.

And last but certainly not least, this book has definitely been a family enterprise and to a great extent a family quandary of long duration. I have asked my children, Bryan Chambers, Lenna Chambers, Elizabeth Chambers, and John Holbrook to give up too much of my time and attention in order to work on it. They have done so mostly, but not always, with patience and understanding. In their sacrifice and price paid, they have contributed more than I intended to ask. The same can be said of my mother, Maria Teresa Miller, and her sister, Rosa Maria Martí, who have supported me unfailingly and provided decades of crucial child care, domestic help, and encouragement while always looking forward to the day when they could see the book published.

A final word of thanks is due to the West Virginia Humanities Council and to the Faculty Merit Foundation of West Virginia for their financial assistance and recognition of my research and pedagogical endeavors.

WEST VIRGINIA HUMANITIES COUNCIL

*Feeding Barcelona*
*1714-1975*

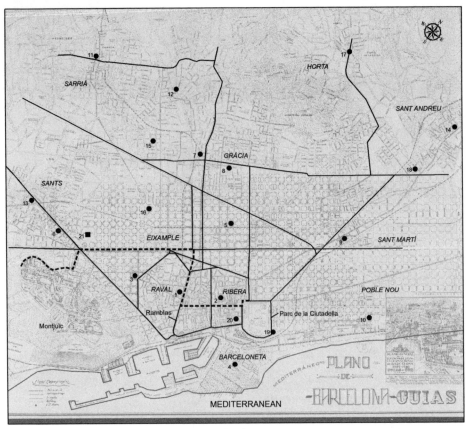

Barcelona's markets and the Market Cavalcade route in 1930. *Map by Everett D. Perry. Background image © Institut Cartogràfic de Catalunya.*

| | | | | |
|---|---|---|---|---|
| 1 Boqueria | 7 Llibertat | 13 Sants | 19 Wholesale Fish |
| 2 Santa Caterina | 8 Abaceria central | 14 Sant Andreu | 20 Born Wholesale |
| 3 Sant Antoni | 9 Clot | 15 Galvany | 21 L'Escorxador |
| 4 Barceloneta | 10 Unió | 16 Ninot (open air) | Slaughterhouse |
| 5 Concepció | 11 Sarrià | 17 Horta (open air) | - - -1930 Cavalcade |
| 6 Hostafrancs | 12 Sant Gervasi | 18 Sagrera (open air) | route, Montjuïc to |
| | | | Ciutadella |

## CHAPTER 1

# There Were Royals among Them
### A 1930 Market Queen Vignette

In the spring of 1930, eighteen-year-old Francesca Orriols Palmada, a third-generation lamb vendor, was elected to serve as the Queen of Barcelona's Santa Caterina Market. The experiences that surrounded her reign would command primacy of place in her recollection of a life spent selling food in her family's market stalls.[1] Maria Cararach Vernet, a third-generation beef and veal vendor at Santa Caterina, explained that there had been much excitement surrounding the municipally organized festival that prompted Francesca's election. The vendors, she said, came together to construct an elaborate float to join those of the other markets in the Grand Cavalcade that wended its way through the streets of Barcelona and presented the city's twenty-one Market Queens to the public.[2] Maria's father, Salvador Cararach Biot, who later served as president of Barcelona's butchers' guild, was one of the chief organizers of Santa Caterina's participation in the 1930 festivities; he tended to the minutest details of the market's preparation for the events, including Queen Francesca's wardrobe and even the purchase of her undergarments.[3]

The gown that Francesca Orriols wore in the cavalcade was made of white tulle with a silver bodice, train, and embellishments. Though she did not win the citywide election as Queen of all the Market Queens of Barcelona, Francesca represented Santa Caterina with honor and dignity, attended the Grand Market Ball, and for months thereafter was whisked away by night in municipal cars to attend parties and events. She got to fly in an airplane and, bedecked in a black lace mantilla and red carnations, went with the other Market Queens to watch the great matador Manolete perform in the bullring. More than a half century later, the old-timers in Santa Caterina Market still gestured in the direction of Francesca's stall, referring to her, with respect and pride, as "La Reina del Mercat."

For her part, Francesca was quick to assert that while there may have been some other minor elections later on, she was the one and only Queen of her market.[4]

Francesca Orriols's identity had been shaped by what was an ongoing and significant early-twentieth-century civic celebration of food retailing through the city's municipally owned and operated markets.[5] Indeed, municipal commitment to Barcelona's market hall-based trade in food had long been explicitly reflected in a range of cultural expressions.[6] The city promoted most holidays through the markets in some fashion or another, usually with decorations and special offers, as a means to enhance sales. Markets were also used as sites for concerts and dances in municipal celebrations of key holidays such as Christmas and the festival of Corpus Christi.[7] Individual market directors in Barcelona were authorized in 1910 to collect money for and organize their own holiday celebrations with vendors, though the city council maintained the right to veto float designs and events.[8] Differences of opinion on these matters is evidenced in an October 1910 petition to the president of the city's Comisión de Hacienda (Treasury Commission) signed by La Boqueria and Sant Antoni market vendors complaining about how their respective directors had spent holiday funds.[9] Evidently, the terms for celebrating market holidays could be contested ones.

That market pageantry had garnered significant popular enthusiasm in the city during the first decades of the twentieth century is evidenced by the Fructuós Gelabert Badiella (1874–1955) 1914 documentary film, *Cavalcada dels mercats de Barcelona*, which shows crowds lining the streets to witness the parade of the vendors.[10] Gelabert was a pioneer of Spanish film who shot a wealth of movies documenting both popular culture and industrial landscapes. His choice of the Market Cavalcade as a subject reflected his own experiences and proclivities. Nine years earlier, Gelabert, already by then a fashionable man and renowned filmmaker who enjoyed considerable press attention for his work, had surprised those around him by proposing marriage, in what seemed to some an inappropriate social match, to Teresa Bonvehí, a young woman from Barcelona's industrial Sants neighborhood who worked in her parents' La Boqueria Market fruit and vegetable stalls.[11] Gelabert clearly had an eye for not only market pageantry, but for market maidens as well. In the republican and democratizing political culture of early-twentieth-century Barcelona, market women had become cultural icons, the youthful among them objects of desire.

Under the Primo de Rivera dictatorship (1923–30), market-based cultural expressions were altered. The use of the Catalan language was prohibited in market administration, replaced as in public life by Castilian (or what English speakers simply call "Spanish"), and the extension of provincial and national controls over Barcelona's markets reversed the trends of the previous half century's growing municipalization of food retailing. Though communication in Catalan among vendors and customers remained widespread, the new regime demanded that market employees manifest "patriotic love and loyalty" to the nation-state and attend a range of ceremonies designed to build Spanish nationalist allegiances. Municipal market personnel and market vendors were increasingly called upon to explicitly support the regime by participating in civic celebrations and collaborating in promotional schemes.[12]

We see this clearly in 1929. On February 20, Barcelona's Lieutenant Mayor Enrique Barrie y Zafra, whose charge it was to oversee provisions in the city, issued a circular detailing how market vendors and municipal personnel were to prepare for Barcelona's long-awaited Expocición Internacional. Not only were vendors required to neaten up their stalls in order to present their wares in "the most appropriate and showy" manner possible, market women were ordered to improve and standardize their dress. All female vendors selling beef, veal, pork, and related meat articles were to wear "perfectly clean" white cotton dresses. Those who sold vegetables and other produce were to wear dark blue-and-white striped bibbed aprons with matching smock sleeves. Tellingly, the circular included no specifications for how male market vendors were to dress, their appearance apparently representing a less significant concern. Focusing on market women and the visual effect of the food they sold, Lieutenant Mayor Barrie emphatically warned that he would accept no excuses for noncompliance with his efforts to showcase each of the city's fifteen retail food market halls as a "visible setting of fitting and complete hygienic, artistic, and aesthetic organization that will attract the attention" of those expected to visit the city.[13] In preparing for the 1929 Expocición Internacional, food markets, and female vendors in particular, were mobilized and sanitized as part of a larger effort to bring prestige to the city and to the Spanish state.[14]

By the time that Francesca Orriols was elected Queen of Santa Caterina Market a year later, the political context had changed, though her account of the events included no reflections on the larger processes or meanings within which that year's pageantry was bound. Rapidly deteriorating economic conditions associated with the onset of the global depression and growing social conflict had led General Primo de Rivera to step down from power at the end of January. Replaced by the more liberally inclined Dámaso Berenguer, his *dictablanda* could not forestall the groundswell of dissatisfaction with the monarchy of Alfonso XIII (r. 1886–1931).[15] In the spring of 1930, the king was caught between a rock and hard place, held responsible for the abrogation of the 1876 Constitution through his complicity with the dictatorship and incapable of mitigating the downward economic spiral and intensifying social unrest that Spain faced. Suddenly, public opinion had become a much more urgent concern.[16] With the survival of the monarchy itself in question, the king set out for Barcelona to participate in festivities that honored one of the few populations whose ideological alignment was not yet clearly staked out against him.[17] Usually billed as the Festival de Primavera, the city renamed the one-day event that year, calling it the "Exposición de Barcelona de 1930" to enhance its prestige and to serve as a postscript to the Exposición Internacional, which had closed six months earlier. With a variety of scheduled activities to be held in the scarcely broken-in exhibition spaces on the mountain of Montjuïc and in other venues, the visit was an opportunity for the king to tap into the popular culture of the city in a vain attempt to generate ongoing support for monarchical rule. Accepting the invitation of Barcelona's mayor, Joan Antoni Güell i López,[18] Alfonso XIII, the royal family, and a retinue of nobles made plans to travel to the city at the end of May.

Barcelona's Festival de Primavera dated to the earliest years of the century.[19] With virtually no religious content or emphasis, these municipally sponsored celebrations included concerts, theatrical performances, exhibits of arts and crafts, and sporting matches. As Temma Kaplan and Stéphane Michonneau have shown with respect to other religious and official civic commemorations, we can see that the Festivals de Primavera followed carefully designed scripts meant to symbolically legitimize the power and perspectives of ruling elites.[20] But they also had popular elements appealing to broad audiences. A key part of the festival had long been the showcasing of the city's market halls as institutions deeply embedded in the political and popular culture of the municipality. Yet unlike the nineteenth-century ceremonies commemorating markets as physical monuments, these early-twentieth-century municipal rituals explicitly recognized and venerated the population of vendors as a specific and legitimate urban constituency. In so doing, they directly reinforced the relationships of mutual dependence between market vendors and municipal authorities that defined a significant sector of the political economy of food retailing in the city.

As had been the case in some earlier years, the 1930 festivities involved the election of Queens from among the ranks of young female vendors in each of the city's markets. Each market chose its own Queen through procedures whose details remain obscure. One observer, though, described their selection as a "delicate and laborious" process because of the "great abundance of beautiful young women" who sold food in Barcelona's markets.[21] Once selected, the Market Queens were dressed in white gowns and paraded through the streets of the city in processions that celebrated youthful feminine beauty and the promise of agricultural fecundity alongside urban social order and efficient political control of the food supply.

Despite the tense political and economic context of the time, the 1930 events in Barcelona that celebrated springtime and the promise of alimentary abundance were particularly elaborate, fitting the prestige conferred by a royal visit. The civic celebration that year included a program of films, sardana dancing, and even the final match of the Copa de España that pitted the Athletic Club of Bilbao against Real Madrid, which was attended by 65,000 spectators in the Montjuïc Stadium. Alongside these popular attractions, the *Diario de Barcelona* announced a "fantastic parade" to show the city its Market Queens, comprised of "22 floats, 60 cars, and a court that included more than 1,000 vendor attendants."[22]

The cavalcade began at 4:00 p.m. on Sunday, June 1. It was led by mounted Guardia Urbana and included no less than five military bands. The market floats were followed by vendors on foot, and then by a parade of cars, "artistically adorned with flowers," carrying each of the Queens. That night, the Grand Market Ball in the Palacio Nacional overlooking the city from Montjuïc constituted the culmination of the day's events with the "Proclamation of the Queen of all the Queens of the Markets."[23] Mayor Güell later reported that no less than twelve thousand people attended the ball.[24] Another observer noted that the night was characterized "by the great abundance of beautiful faces and by the boisterous gaiety of the young people"[25] The Market Queens, seated on stage in magnificent chairs, were flanked by an orchestra and a band that played for the thousands of vendors and their families in attendance. According to the *Diario de Barcelona,* the "congenial visage of the luxuriously adorned Market Queens" was admired by all.[26]

Francesca Orriols, representing Santa Caterina in the pageant that night, and serving for us as an embedded informant, recalled the nervousness among the contestants as they waited for the ceremonies to begin. She noted especially that the Queen of La Boqueria Market, Antonia Morral Moragas, expected to win.[27] After all, she was both beautiful and representative of the city's most prestigious and profitable market. La Boqueria vendors had even constructed four different, elaborate floats to accompany their Queen in the parade. They were entitled "Fame," "Fruit," "Aviculture," and "Allegory of the Queen of the Cavalcade." Yet surprisingly, it was not La Boqueria's contestant who won the ultimate crown that night. She lost the election by one vote. Instead, young Lola Capdevila Pons, a vendor from Horta's open-air market, was chosen from the pool of candidates.

Francesca Orriols remembers that the outcome of the election was understandable; La Boqueria's Queen was a bit too sure of herself, while Lola Capdevila was more modest, attracting the judges' votes for her simple beauty and comportment. In determining who was to serve as Queen of all the Market Queens, tractability was valued over grandeur and reputation. The humblest Queen from one of the city's smallest markets was elected to "reign" over the others.

Just before midnight, the announcement was made that Spain's still sitting and sovereign king, Alfonso XIII, his family, and a retinue of nobles were approaching the palace to honor the Market Queens with a royal visit. Entering the ballroom at 12:30 a.m., Don Alfonso, Doña Victoria Eugenia, with *infantes* Don Jaime and Doñas Beatriz and Cristina, were met with a "prolonged and affectionate ovation."[28] The royals congratulated each of the contestants and chatted with them briefly. The king posed for a photograph with the celebrated market maidens and, according to one account, honored Lola Capdevila, as Queen of all the Market Queens, with a dance.[29] In the presence of royalty, Barcelona's young Market Queens were reified as symbols of virtue, beauty, and civic splendor. Yet the encounter also featured an irony, which those involved could not at the moment fully grasp. As we now know, a groundswell of support for republicanism would drive Alfonso XIII into exile in less than a year's time. Thus Lola Capdevila's reign as Queen of all the Queens of Barcelona's markets would technically last beyond that of the king of Spain. In some ways, it could not have played out as a richer republicanist fantasy.

This historical vignette provides a glimpse of the complexities involved in the practice of food retailing in Barcelona at a particular moment in time. It raises important questions about women's work in small commerce and about the nature of Barcelona's long-term commitment to a public market-based system of retail food distribution. These questions can be explored through an analysis of vendors' work, social, and family lives, and through an examination of the place of markets in Barcelona's political economy and in its physical and symbolic landscape. But the Market Queen vignette also serves a second purpose, which is to illustrate the key concerns of this book. In the 1930 civic pageantry we see several themes: urgent public attention to food as a crucial material and symbolic commodity; contradictions between popular gender iconographies and the actual lived experience of female vendors; ceremonial ritualization of the political economy of food retailing; the embeddedness of markets within urban public space; and the celebration of a particular type of food system that invites broader historical comparisons of how industrial cities have arranged to provision their inhabitants.

## Food as Crucial Material and Symbolic Commodity

In the same issue of the *Diario de Barcelona* that announced the 1930 Market Cavalcade and Ball, there was a short article reporting that the Spanish National Economic Ministry had announced a royal order "decreeing the freedom of salt cod commerce."[30] The new policy did away with price controls and stripped the municipality of its power to regulate trade in this important commodity through shop licensing. It opened the way for the establishment of new salt cod shops that would compete with the stall businesses operating under license to retail the commodity within the city's municipal markets. Reflecting growing national intervention in urban food policy in the period, it was intended, presumably, to create more competition and thus lower the cost of a vital source of protein for the popular classes.[31]

So while the king and the mayor were lauding the pulchritude of the young Market Queens, tensions underlay the public visage of unity and mutual respect that they sought to convey.[32] They most certainly agreed on the necessity to tame and control vendor behavior in the markets through the policing of social practices that could disadvantage all but the most seasoned consumers. And clearly they understood their mutual debt and dependence. The king had appointed Güell mayor of Barcelona earlier that year, and he had ennobled Güell's father in 1918. As host to the king's visit, Mayor Güell was offering Barcelona as a platform from which to foment loyalty to the beleaguered Spanish monarchy. But the king and his government were also compromising the mayor and city council by increasingly dictating from above the details of municipal provisioning policy, and by infringing upon what had been established as municipal purview. Grasping at straws, the king was playing a vain game of one-upmanship in hopes of winning favor among the poorest consumers who ate salt cod because they could not afford more expensive sources of protein.[33] It was perfectly clear to both king and mayor that managing the urban food supply was an urgent concern. Though peacetime subsistence crises had ended late in the last century, the maintenance of adequate caloric levels among the urban population and of access to affordable food across the social spectrum remained keys to the legitimacy of any public authority claiming a monopoly over the use of force. As Pamela Beth Radcliff and others have noted, consumer protest was an intensifying current in Spain during the first decades of the twentieth century. Working-class women especially mobilized around issues related to the access and affordability of provisions and were "willing to employ coercion and violence to achieve their aims."[34] Salt cod policies, while perhaps esoteric to the fate of the monarchy, were certainly connected to the maintenance of urban order.

Beyond testifying to ongoing political concerns with the provision of food as a crucial material commodity, the 1930 market pageantry in Barcelona can be read as a performance that drew on a bank of symbols attached to food, its sources, meanings, distribution, and consumption. We can see this particularly in the floats that vendors from each of the city's markets designed and built for the cavalcade. Twenty-two in all, the *Diario de Barcelona* described the themes of all but four in its coverage of the event. Galvany, San Gervasi, La Llibertat, Sant Antoni, and La Concepció markets prepared floats representing images from Catalan history and literature that might have made the king wince.[35] These were counterbalanced by the Encants used-goods market's float representing a royal throne, and by Santa Caterina's float, whose theme was the "Palacio Nacional." La Barceloneta, Sagrera and Horta, El Ninot, La Boqueria, and the Central Fish and El Born wholesale-produce markets all presented floats with food-specific themes. Of these, five focused on protein-rich foods, especially fresh fish, but also game and aviculture. On one level, their designs reflected the symbolic meaning that foodstuffs have held in all cultures since what Felipe Fernández-Armesto terms the second (of his eight) food revolutions, that which involved the paleolithic realization "that food is more than sustenance."[36] Food consumption and cultural beliefs remain so deeply intertwined that their disentanglement proves daunting. But more concretely, these vendor floats reflected shifts in eating habits between 1870 and 1935, when protein consumption per capita increased dramatically in the city, and poultry and fresh fish became more broadly associated with health, prosperity, and refined taste.[37]

The *Diario de Barcelona* deemed that the two best floats were those presented by El Ninot and the Central Fish Market. El Ninot's float celebrated the hunt as a source of food for the urban population. Featuring huntsmen in medieval costume on horseback and hunters on foot with rifles slung over their shoulders returning with game, the imagery reasserted the male role as provider of protein. While wild boar, jugged hare, red deer, and partridge had once been common elements of the Catalan rural inland diet, such fare did not figure significantly in the eating habits of Barcelonans in 1930, when only a small fraction of the city's market-stall licenses permitted the sale of wild game, and hunting had become a sport.[38] Various types of fowl and rabbit, which were key sources of protein at that time, were farm-raised. The Porvenir's vendors called upon nostalgic imagery from times long past, but these images still buttressed and celebrated the continuing role of men in provisioning the city through their work in production, transport, processing, wholesaling, and stocking retail market vendors' stalls, which were so often, but not always, worked by women.

The Central Fish Market's participation in the cavalcade also affirmed the importance of the male conquest of nature in providing protein-rich foods to the city. They began with a fishing vessel, manned by rowers, and by male vendors with lifesavers bearing the Central Fish Market's emblem. Behind the vessel was a group of virile fishermen carrying an enormous anchor, as if to serve as the city's own ballast. What followed highlighted the collaboration of women in the male-directed enterprise of delivering fresh fish to consumers' tables: fishwives and daughters with a series of nets mimicked the act of mending as they walked the length of the parade route. Taking up the rear was a delegation from the ranks of the market's vendors; both men and women carrying baskets of fish called out the quality and freshness of the wares to the public gathered to witness the spectacle. The chain from sea as source to market as point of distribution for consumers was represented in just a few short, oversimplified stages with men positioned, literally, at the helm while women served in supportive roles and as beneficiaries of the process.[39]

When we consider the context of the global depression and the popular insecurities that the crisis generated with respect to food access, these representations assume more urgent meaning. With upwards of 60 percent of most household incomes devoted to food acquisition,[40] civic pageantry proclaiming male commitment to protein provision could have been read by the public as a comforting narrative. Mechanical refrigeration, expansion of the Spanish rail system, the growth of the canning industry, and "legislative changes in the second half of the nineteenth century" contributed to the transformation and growth of the Spanish fishing industry and to increasing consumer preference for fresh over salted fish.[41] The growing public demand for fresh fish was mirrored in vendors' choices of float design and parade participation: three markets chose the fishing industry as their theme in the cavalcade.[42]

Still, the overarching theme of the celebration was fecundity and abundance, or what could be understood as a public festival of food pornography in which the consuming public could see and watch but not taste and touch what was on display. At the apex of the day's events was the celebration of beautiful young women, who, like ripe fruit ready to be plucked, held the promise to serve as the primordial givers of the first protein foods through the milk of their own breasts, but also as historic food processors, food preparers, and in Barcelona's markets, the dominant sex in retailing to the consuming public.

## Gender Iconographies and Lived Experience

Indeed, the 1930 Market Queen elections involved explicit municipal reinterpretation of broader gender iconographies that were in some ways inconsistent with the city's own policies and practices. Female market vendors had long been associated in Barcelona's popular culture with bawdiness and independence. Markets were, after all, boisterous and busy places with a particular smell and visceral carnality that could challenge bourgeois sensibilities. The idiomatic expression "parlar com una peixetera"—that is, to speak like a fishwife—was a jibe and not a compliment.[43] Articles in the municipal market codes intended to regulate vendor language illustrate the extent to which women working in these commercial venues were perceived as tending toward vulgarity. Yet communication between the buyers and sellers of food remained something of a performance, even an art form beyond the bounds of administrative control. The 1928 market code specifically prohibited the distinctive form of speech that linguists term "vendor calls" and "vendor spiel," but to little effect.[44] The Central Fish Market's float, ending with vendors exhibiting their distinctive calls to the public as part of the spectacle, indicates how female market salesmanship, expressed through specific linguistic practice, was just one of many picturesque components on display that year. Like the Catalan nationalist-themed floats, they constituted an element of the cavalcade's script that the city council did not succeed in directing.

The unruly market woman appeared as a character in the popular republicanist Catalan theater of the late 1920s. Just three years before the Market Queen elections of 1930, Alfons Roure's theatrical work, *La Reina del Mercat*, starring the immensely popular Assumpció Casals in the role of Tresina, had opened at the Gran Teatre Espanyol.[45] Foul-mouthed, widowed, and frankly sexual, Tresina nonetheless elicited the sympathy of audiences because of the cultural prejudices she suffered as a consequence of her work as a poultry vendor in one of Barcelona's markets. Roure built the play's conflict around the engagement of Tresina's daughter to marry the son of a prominent physician. Viewing the union as a social embarrassment, the young man's parents demanded that Tresina give up her market stall to assume a more domestic, and thus presumably more genteel, existence. After rounds of high-pitched verbal combat with her daughter's future in-laws, Tresina ultimately relented by giving up her market stall and her economic independence. In Roure's work, Tresina's character was constructed to possess a profane beauty and sexual appeal that paralleled the carnal sensuousness of the food for sale to the public in the city's markets. In contrast, Barcelona's real-life 1930 Market Queen contestants were young, single, and virginally garbed in white. A new, more sanitized Market Queen reigned in municipal pageantry. The image was a more malleable and controllable one than that depicted in Roure's production.

That such transparent manipulation would have been enthusiastically embraced by the vendors themselves is not surprising. The veneration of Market Queens and their presentation as virtuous young ladies in a broader civic state offered a welcome antidote to more diffuse social and cultural insecurities. If we return once more to Francesca Orriols, Santa Caterina's Queen, we can see that she brought honor and recognition to her market and to female vendors more specifically, and was rewarded for doing so with a lifetime caché of respect. Yet as a female market vendor, she still occupied a contested cultural space whose tension and ambiguities appear in the way she constructed her life story.[46] As she tells it, she did not like cutting and selling lamb and would rather have been a secretary than a food vendor. When she first started working in her grandparents' stall, she ducked down behind the counter and hid at the sight of school friends passing through the market. She felt embarrassed within her social cohort by the work that her family did.[47] Though she was elected Market Queen and showered with the attention and admiration of many, she imagined a different life for herself, in an occupation that may have been more socially acceptable from a bourgeois perspective. Market vendors had long worked at the bottom of the commercial hierarchy and been classified by urban theorists in the mid-1800s as part of the working classes.[48] But by the early twentieth century, many vendors aspired to upward social mobility and some kind of middle-class social and economic status. Market Queens such as Francesca Orriols, who enjoyed commercial success and commanded enormous local respect, might sometimes dream of more genteel work in a pink-collar profession.

However they cast themselves in memory, or were cast in theatrical works and in municipal pageantry, the representation of market women in Barcelona's popular and civic cultures reflected their ubiquitous presence among the ranks of the vendor population and within the formal political economy of food retailing in the city. Ildefons Cerdà's 1867 analysis of Barcelona's markets holds that 90 percent of the city's vendors were women.[49] Other calculations of particular market specializations, such as those by Àngels Solà Parera, show similar percentages of women operating their own enterprises in the mid-nineteenth century.[50] We can also see, with a larger data set, that from the late nineteenth century to the outbreak of the Spanish Civil War in 1936 at least half, and sometimes as much as 60 percent, of all municipal market-stall permits were issued to women. The vast majority of them operated small businesses in their own right, worked throughout their life-cycles, and balanced marriage, motherhood, and domestic responsibilities with formal participation in retail commerce. These women worked alone, with clerks, and with family members of both sexes, and not primarily for men or as widowed heirs to a husband's business, as was more often the case in the artisanal trades or other larger commercial enterprises.[51] In a period during which increased gender-segregation characterized numerous sectors of the economy, the markets of Barcelona constituted one important exception to that general pattern. Though men were clearly moving into market-based food retailing during the first decades of the twentieth century, women's entrepreneurship in the municipal markets remained widespread on the eve of the Second Republic.[52] This was the case despite the fact that female vendors, like so many women from a range of other occupations and social stations, could often feel the circumscription of the contested cultural ground within which they lived and worked.

A focus on Barcelona's market vendors offers rich opportunities for the exploration of the gendered nature of small commerce in food. Here we see the strong presence of women as independent business owners in an area of the tertiary sector that catered directly to other women and in venues grounded squarely in quotidian neighborhood life. We also see women passing stall titles through family lines to form market dynasties, or *sagas*, that frequently extended over three or more generations.[53] The fact that female market vendors typically married but continued their work outside the home allows us to examine gender divisions of labor within the family economy, the culture of work, and identity construction in a popular but heretofore unexplored segment of the twentieth-century urban social order.[54]

## The Political Economy of Food Retailing

The 1930 festivities in Barcelona also affirmed the relationship of mutual dependence between Barcelona's market vendors and the municipal corporation that owned and administered their workspaces. Since the turn of the century, food-market vendors had organized to petition for rights that would enable them to take their place in the city's political economy alongside shopkeepers and artisans and among the ranks of the lower middle class, a group historically called the *menestrelia*. This relationship of mutual dependence between vendors and municipal authorities matured and evolved over the first three decades of the twentieth century with the consolidation of the Restoration-era political economy of food retailing. Yet the period was also marked by political tumultuousness, particularly from the

1890s onward when anarchist bombings, work stoppages, violence in the streets, general strikes, and other forms of opposition to political, economic, and religious authorities became more common. Market vendors had committed themselves as a group to the municipal system of control and demanded and received commercial concessions in exchange. Mayor Güell's part in helping to arrange a royal audience at the Market Ball signaled municipal endorsement of the food vendors' claims for dignity, recognition, and protection from unregulated trade. Moreover, in showcasing the city's markets, the mayor was not only seeking to impress the king with the modern, rationalized, and orderly system through which Barcelona fed its population of over one million people; he was also demonstrating the degree to which the municipal and provincial governments had disciplined and mobilized vendors on behalf of the state. In Mayor Güell's festivities, abundance and female beauty in the food-retailing sector represented broader civic achievements as well as narrower political strategies.

As part of the more generalized political repression of the period, there had been a crackdown on market-vendor associationalism under the Primo de Rivera dictatorship but not a significant alteration in the policy of market operation and regulation, even with the issuing of the revised 1928 municipal market code. Vendors continued to depend upon municipal authority to maintain order and safety in their commercial arenas but more urgently to limit and control the competition they faced from ambulatory vendors, unregulated shops, and other extralegal forms of food trade. Likewise, municipal authorities continued to rely upon market vendors to help provision the industrial city, but they also counted on their support for a vision of the polity that defended property and profit-seeking as a counterweight to the increasingly popular collectivist movements of the period. Whatever broader republican and Catalanist cultural and political orientations and sympathies defined the bulk of the market-vendor population in 1930, they had complied with the regime and provided false hopes in some quarters for broader and deeper popular support of the monarchy.

This was the *Diario de Barcelona*'s take on the matter when it announced the arrival of the royal family on June 1, 1930. The paper lamented "the exclusionary atmosphere" that had surrounded the king prior to the dictatorship when he had not been free to move safely among his subjects and address their concerns.[55] Optimistically, the paper claimed that "the cloud had dissipated" and with it "the distress that weighed upon the spirit of those who sincerely professed the monarchic ideal" defining "the Catalan *moyen*."[56] Counting the market vendors among those who would now have the opportunity to come into direct contact with the monarchy so "deeply embedded in the most intimate sentiment of the heart," the paper urged popular restraint in taking up the king's time so that the royal family could also rest and enjoy some leisure during their visit.[57] Even the military attaché at the United States Embassy was impressed by the outpouring of popular support for the king during his 1930 visit to Barcelona, a sign that Ambassador Irwin Laughlin reported back to the State Department as evidence that the monarchy would surely survive.[58] It was as if the king had come to Barcelona to seek the popular legitimacy that he lacked through ceremonialized contact with the common people. Among them were the market vendors of the city and, most poignantly, their young and beguiling Queens.

Though the political economy of food retailing in Barcelona was mainly a municipal concern, it clearly involved complex chains of supply emanating from the larger Spanish agricultural economy and beyond, as well as significant regulatory and symbolic connections to national political authority. The 1930 Cavalcade and Ball were a continuation of a decades-old ritual celebrating market-vendor collaboration with municipal authority to supply the city with food. But in a tense political and economic moment, the festivities were revamped to emphasize the bonds of vendors to the monarchy in a more specific, tangible, and personal fashion.

## Markets and the Evolution of Urban Public Space

Recent work on Barcelona has emphasized the symbolic usages of urban public space by political authorities and economic elites, especially focusing on the city's nineteenth-century reconfiguration through the construction of the Eixample (Enlargement) neighborhood, monument building, and the design of fairgrounds, pavilions, and other structures for two world's fairs—the 1888 Exposición Universal and 1929 Exposición Internacional.[59] Municipal market-hall construction was embedded within the larger process of extending and modernizing the city's technological networks, alongside water, gas, sewage, electrical illumination, telephone lines, and transport systems.[60] But the market halls themselves assumed significant symbolic weight as expressions of the ruling municipal elite's accomplishment in facilitating the supply of food to the popular classes in all of the city's neighborhoods; they were among the few visible monuments distributed across the city's landscape in rich districts and poor alike. The rhetoric used by city officials at inauguration ceremonies beginning in the nineteenth century explicitly emphasized generosity and concern for the masses of ordinary consumers who depended on markets to secure their daily sustenance.[61] Likewise, the vendors who worked within them were periodically summoned from their various neighborhoods and mobilized in the city's main public spaces to perform in ceremonies and events that legitimized Barcelona's new image of itself as a metropolis and as Spain's second capital. Such was the case with the early-twentieth-century Festivals de Primavera, and especially with the Exposición de Barcelona of 1930.

One key study of the cultural and social movements in the city at this time specifically deconstructs both religious and republican processions and parades. As Temma Kaplan argues, "In Barcelona, the physical act of moving through the city marked the plazas and streets with cultural significance and bonded the people who participated. Even those who joined in as audience, viewing the content of the ceremony from the sidelines, became familiar with the content of 'arguments' proclaimed."[62]

The 1930 Cavalcade, neither religious nor republicanist, can be similarly read. In addition to the "arguments" for vendor dignity and the legitimacy of municipal control over market trade, the Cavalcade was a declaration of public commitment to the "common good"[63] that abundance in food supply represented to consumers. Its route was designed to incorporate representatives of the popular classes in a orderly and controlled movement through the monumental spaces of the newly reconfigured city.[64] It involved what Michonneau would call the promulgation of a particular, though contested, "memory policy" in which the interests and achievements of the ruling elites were symbolically represented through urban space as a means of rallying political support for their vision from a wider audience.[65]

Though the 1929 Exposición Internacional was designed to both further and tout the city's modernization, much of its ceremony and imagery followed a politically expedient script intended to legitimize dictatorial rule from Madrid. That the 1930 market procession would begin from the grounds of the 1929 Exposición six months after its closing is no surprise. Starting just above the Poble Espanyol, the Market Cavalcade moved along l'Avinguda Maria Cristina to the Plaça d'Espanya before following the Gran Via to the Rambla de Catalunya, where it moved away from the harbor for one block and then back. Returning to the Plaça de Catalunya, the Cavalcade moved down Las Ramblas and turned left onto Carrer Ferran, where it proceeded to the Plaça San Jaume, the political center of the city and Barcelona's "town square." Continuing, the procession moved along Jaume I to Carrer Princessa, and then left onto the Passeig de l'Industria and the Passeig de Pujades until reaching the Parc de la Ciutadella and site of Barcelona's 1888 Exposición

Universal. Ending at the monument to former Mayor Rius i Taulet, who had organized the earlier fair, the Market Queens laid "large wreaths and flower bouquets
at the foot of the obelisk."[66]

The procession's intended symbolic imagery is clear. On the one hand, it linked
the two great world's-fair spaces in the city, and thus Mayor Güell to his much-
celebrated predecessor. On the other, with its Market Queens venerating mayoral-
ship through their tribute of flowers, it tied the city's vendors to the municipal
regime, representing them as collaborative and domesticated partners in the orderly provision of food to a city fraught with ideological and class divisions. Like
the two great exhibitions, the 1930 Market Cavalcade used urban space strategi-
cally to promote layered allegiances. The design, architecture, fountains, statuary,
sculpture, and layout of both exhibits celebrated the city as the embodiment of
Catalan nationalist achievements and as the wellspring of Spain's progress toward
modernity.[67] Likewise, the market vendors, through the physical trajectory of their
cavalcade and attendance at the ball later that night, found themselves performing
on a monumental urban set bathed in images of Catalanism while engaging in a
carefully orchestrated expression of loyalty to the central state, in this case in the
form of personal reverence for, and contact with, its monarch.

Yet the show of support for the monarchy was no more than a façade, and no
more real a representation than the Poble Espanyol from which the Market Cavalcade had begun.[68] Urban elites could practice "memory policy" through the design
of rituals that interplayed with urban space, but impact was another matter.[69] For
market vendors experiencing cultural and social ambiguity, it was a chance to walk
the red carpet for a day. The vendors' participation in the events and their polite
reception of the king did not dampen their rapid mobilization and enthusiasm in
support of the Second Republic that was declared less than a year later.

More broadly, the 1930 Cavalcade in Barcelona serves as a starting point for the
consideration of a set of interrelated questions about markets and market vendors
not just in one city in Spain, but rather within a broader comparative framework.

## Comparative Issues

It is not clear from the record how many foreign dignitaries attended the 1930
Market Ball as part of the king's entourage or whether any of them may have
watched some portion of the Cavalcade earlier that day. We do know that representatives of the United States Embassy were there, and in addition to being
impressed with the king's popularity they must have also been impressed with

the number of markets represented in the pageantry. The U.S. Department of Commerce had long collected data on the provisioning of European cities and specifically on their market halls and slaughterhouses. Two decades earlier, a Special Consular Report had noted that many retail covered markets in Europe were waning; their demise was taken as a foregone conclusion. In a number of places, wholesale trade was overtaking retail trade inside the covered markets, while other types of food shops and stores expanded in size, number, and form. With respect to Paris, the 1910 report observed that:

> While the secondary markets are well managed and for the most part bountifully supplied, their popularity has declined in recent years, owing to the increased number and enterprise of grocery, meat, and provision stores, which not only handle all kinds of fresh market supplies, but employ business methods which artfully subserve the convenience of purchasers. Whereas the Parisian housekeeper formerly went to market, either alone or accompanied by a servant to carry her purchases, she now prefers to find her supplies at a provision store or a clean, well-kept meat shop, whence they will be sent to her home without trouble or expense to her; or she may even order everything from her home by telephone. In this way a vast number of grocery and large provision stores have been built up, some of which have the extent and methods of department stores. In this way, the public local markets, which practically supplied the kitchens of Paris twenty or thirty years ago, are gradually losing their importance.[70]

The consular report noted as well that some of the covered markets of Paris had been converted to other uses: "The Marché St.-Honoré, one of the largest secondary markets in the central part of the city, includes four permanent brick buildings, covering an entire open square. Two of them are still partly used for market purposes, a third has been leased as a steam laundry, and the fourth is used by the city as an engine house for its fire department. In other markets part of their space under the roof has been leased for garages, storehouses, and other purposes."[71] Everywhere in Paris, it seemed, the retail food trade in public market halls was decreasing. Such evidence suggests an early-twentieth-century shift in Parisian food retailing away from market halls and toward a greater panoply of larger and more modern shops and stores.

Accounts suggest similar patterns in some other European cities. The American consulate in Berlin reported in 1910 that a "gradually increasing percentage of the retail space remains unrented, and they say that something must be done to save the retail space of market halls."[72] In London, despite the modernization efforts that began with the Smithfield wholesale market in 1850, retail sales in the newer covered food markets never took off. American Consul-General Robert J. Were reported that:

> London differs in one very striking particular from perhaps every other important city, in the fact that it has no general retail markets . . . Practically no market of this kind exists in London, all of those authorized being mainly wholesale markets or depots, to which the producer or importer sends his produce for sale to the retail tradesmen, and at these the actual consumer rarely purchases. The only semblance to retail markets which exist in London are the informal markets established by the costermonger in the public streets, which are unauthorized except by custom.[73]

Even in areas of England such as the industrial Midlands and the West, where market halls had figured so centrally in food retailing during the previous century, by 1918 most people believed, as Schmiechen and Carls put it, "that the public market had seen its day."[74] Competition from cooperatives and chain stores had taken their toll, and increasingly people were shifting toward purchasing food from shops of various kinds.

But in Barcelona this was not the case. Between 1910 and 1930, the network of retail food market halls expanded from eleven to fifteen. Trade within these market halls remained almost exclusively specialized in food and, despite episodes of intermittent turmoil resulting from inflation, business was booming for the small market-based retailers right up to the outbreak of the Civil War in 1936. Here we can clearly see that in terms of relative dependence upon food market halls, Barcelona's urban provisioning system had begun to exhibit some real departures from those of Paris, London, or Berlin in the first third of the twentieth century.

This comparative point is a significant one because it raises two key questions. Since most of the studies treating urban industrial food systems focus on Northern European capital cities, analysis of variation remains urgent to construction of a larger understanding. As Peter Atkins and Derek Oddy argue: "An issue here is scale and intensity because one would expect a different functional response at the lower end of the urban hierarchy from that of the largest cities, so recognizing regional difference is an important element . . . as is the identification of temporal disjuncture in the pace of change between cities and between nations."[75]

Barcelona, the most populous city in Spain in 1930, with just over a million inhabitants, was dwarfed by London, Paris, and even Berlin, all of which were significantly larger.[76] Yet the "metropolitan effect" where "the stages in the food chain between farm gate and consumers kitchens grew" had been accelerating in Barcelona since the eighteenth century.[77] With industrialization, the city grew exponentially. Between 1860 and 1931 alone, Barcelona's population quadrupled.[78] As a key industrial center in Spain, its responses as a city to the challenges of food supply warrant analysis and comparison to other cases both within and beyond the Mediterranean region of Europe.

The most significant effort to address comparative questions related to patterns of market-hall construction and operation has been undertaken by Manuel Guàrdia and José Luis Oyón.[79] They identify four generations of retail food market-hall construction in Europe. The first began with neoclassical designs in the major cities of England and France in the late eighteenth and early nineteenth centuries. The next generation followed in the second half of the nineteenth century, with Victor Baltard's Parisian design of Les Halles Centrales serving as the most important new model of iron-and-glass market-hall construction. Spreading to various French and British cities, metal markets were built all across Western Europe in the last third of the nineteenth century. Yet there was considerable variation by region and even within individual nations. Belgian cities embraced market-hall construction, but in Amsterdam and Rotterdam markets continued to held in the open air. England led initially in market-hall building, especially in the industrial Midlands, yet London's markets remained oriented mostly toward wholesale trade. In the third generation of market-building that began at the turn of the twentieth century, construction waned in Britain and France while numerous markets opened their doors to the public in Scandinavia, Central and Eastern Europe, and in some cities of the Russian Empire and the Baltic. During this period, metal construction gave way to reinforced concrete. Then, in what Guàrdia and Oyón characterize as the fourth generation, which began in the post–World War II period, market-hall building continued only in Latin Europe and in the Communist Eastern Block, where supermarket penetration was weakest. While constituting a much-needed periodization framework, the generational model suggests a range of further comparative questions, which scholars have only begun to explore. Among these are questions related to the significance of markets, to the factors contributing to their continued success or demise, and to the ways in which they facilitated female entrepreneurship in specific settings.

### Consumerism, Taste, and Catalan Identities in the Markets and Beyond

Just as it makes little sense to explore the emergence of Barcelona's modern market-hall system in isolation from its broader comparative context, studying twentieth-century vendors without considering the alimentary commodities that they sold would constitute, in effect, an act of analytical disembowelment. We have seen how Barcelona's public markets and the population of vendors who worked in them could be appropriated for political purposes. But it is also important to recognize that on the eve of the declaration of the Second Republic there was a maturing discourse that equated food and the manner in which it was prepared for consumption with emerging Catalanist political identities. There were other changes afoot as well. Early-twentieth-century Catalan eating habits featured considerable change alongside significant continuities. While elements of the medieval Catalan diet certainly endured, what was typically served at the dinner table or taken in restaurants and other eateries had been dramatically altered as a consequence of the Columbian Exchange, and by the impact of the flourishing currents of consumer culture that impacted food taste and home cooking as surely as the demand for nonalimentary goods.

The political transcendence accorded to foodways begs the question of what this putative early-twentieth-century Catalan cuisine consisted of, and particularly whether there was some greater or lesser degree of essentialism involved in the popular diet. Some food writers, such as Colman Andrews, have suggested as much, asserting in 1988 that Catalan cuisine remained "probably closer to its medieval roots than any other modern Western European idiom."[80] Likewise, major Spanish newspapers such as La Vanguardia (published in Barcelona) dramatically increased their reference to a distinctive "Catalan cuisine" in articles published between 1981 and 1995.[81] More recently, heated polemics over the dangers of departing from the "traditional" Catalan repertoire in its internationally acclaimed haute cuisine made front-page news all across Spain.[82] The issue of "authenticity" in early-twentieth-century Catalan cooking thus deserves some scrutiny here.

There are important late-medieval sources documenting what the economically and socially accommodated consumed. Cooks in the service of royals and the high nobility wrote about what they considered the standard of refined tastes and about recipes and preparations that, after significant diffusion, assumed a central place in what came later to be identified by food writers as a distinctively Catalan culinary tradition. The first of these was the Llibre del Sent Soví, dating to the early fourteenth century and authored by an unknown cook from the Catalan-

Aragonese Confederation in the service of the English monarch.[83] Written in Catalan and reflecting clear Islamic influences, it includes 220 recipes featuring preparations and sauces such as the *sofregit* and the *picada,* which remain centerpieces of Catalan cooking today.[84] The second of these "foundational" Catalan texts was the 1520 *Libre del Coch* by Robert de Nola.[85] Mestre Robert, as he was known, served as a cook to the King of Naples. His treatise included recipes for 204 dishes, some of them carrying the adjective *catalana* in their titles, with others describing dishes as *genovesa, veneciana, lombarda,* and *francesa.* Both of these cookbooks had great resonance over time, with elements reprinted in numerous texts. The *Libre del Coch* was translated into Castilian in 1525 and is held to be the first cookbook published in that language.[86] These sources can be viewed in two ways. Some authors see them as representative of Italian and other European culinary influences in Catalonia; more likely, however, they represent the early codification of a Catalan variant of what we now call "the Mediterranean diet."[87]

There is ample research on medieval Catalan foodways.[88] We know, for example, that bread and wine were the two most important elements of the diet, along with meat, fish, legumes, and fruits and vegetables.[89] For those of means, leavened white bread was considered an essential part of every meal. The poor ate dark bread, more vegetables, and less meat and fish, especially that which was fresh rather than salted or dried. Wine was not understood as a complement to other foods but rather as a key element of daily nutrition for everyone, inasmuch as it provided energy in a hygienic form. Red through most of the year but often white in summer months, wine was taken "as much with dinner as with supper, including the gatherings [that took place] on days of fasting, and also outside of meals, at various times."[90] The most common dish for rich and poor alike, though varying tremendously in the quality of its contents, was the pottage, typically in the form of a soup known as *la olla.* A ubiquitous Spanish recipe in the period, the classic Catalan version in its many iterations was *escudella,* with its liquid and solid components.[91] Made from a stock of vegetables and meats, escudella was served in two courses, beginning with a broth and then followed by its constituent boiled vegetables and animal proteins, most often mutton and salt pork. Fish was a crucial element of the diet because of Catalonia's access to the Mediterranean and the religious prohibitions against meat consumption during nearly half the calendar days of the year. On the many fish days, various alternative pottages were consumed, including ones made of spinach, cabbages, lettuces, rice, pasta, or wheat. These were often seasoned with cinnamon and included almond milk. Pasta pottages were typically finished off with grated cheese. Poultry, including capon, rooster, hen, and goose, was the most valued and most expensive of the animal proteins, reserved for the most important religious holidays.

While the primacy of bread, wine, and escudella continued into the early twentieth century, there were notable shifts in eating habits over the course of the early modern centuries. The first and most obvious change was in sugar consumption, which grew dramatically with the expansion of New World production.[92] Along with the passion for sweetness, chocolate and coffee drinking became popular by the seventeenth and eighteenth centuries. Though tomatoes and peppers had begun to transform the taste and color palette[93] of popular cuisine, other crucial crops deriving from the Columbian Exchange—namely maize and the potato—were slower to catch on, the latter of which made its mark in working-class diets more definitively in the nineteenth century. The broadening embrace of these new foods was accompanied by a general improvement in diet and by decreasing mortality rates owing to agricultural advances, though these advances were periodically disrupted by poor harvests, shortages, and price hikes.[94]

Affecting culinary cultures, eating habits, and commercial economies around the world from Europe to China and Africa, new products from the Americas profoundly transformed Catalan cooking. Some of these products became central in two of the four "mother sauces."[95] Allioli and picada[96] remained essentially the same, while the sofregit took on tomatoes and sometimes peppers, and samfina emerged as what might have been the precursor of the dish that in Provence is called ratatouille and in Sicily caponata. The Baron of Maldà (1746–1819), who kept detailed diaries, ate a whole range of things that his medieval predecessors had not.[97] He regularly consumed tomatoes, green beans, squash, and peppers and engaged in ritualized daily consumption of chocolate and sugar-sweetened foods. In his study of the baron's eating habits, Joan de Déu Domènech declares that even some of his simplest suppers can be read as a "monographic exhibition" to the New World in that everything he consumed except the meat, wine, and bread was originally from the Americas.[98]

Though the Baron of Maldà distinguished between Catalan, Castilian, and other foreign dishes when describing in his diary what was served at important banquets, it remains clear that eighteenth-century Catalan cuisine featured much plasticity.[99] Whether one emphasizes the medieval origins of Catalan forms of cooking that drew on Islamic, Jewish, and broader Mediterranean influences evidenced in the Llibre del Sent Soví or in Mestre Robert's cookbook, or if one considers the impact of New World foods in the early modern centuries, it is a tradition of Catalan culinary syncretism that stands out in bold relief. Yet this plasticity with respect to cuisine does not imply an artificial mandate from above to create an "imagined community" of Catalans at that time.[100] The Baron of Maldà was not a Catalan nationalist in any conscious cultural or political sense, and there was no such coherent movement with which he could have affiliated himself had he been so inclined. His sense of what constituted Catalan and non-Catalan foods predated the origins of the Catalan cultural and literary rebirth by several decades. As we shall see, it was not until the mid-1830s that *Renaixença* writers begin to connect Catalan home cooking to a cultural program of identity formation.

By the early twentieth century, however, Catalanist political aspirations had matured, and part of that movement involved a wedding of national identity with foodways. Nearly all home cooking, and thus the bulk of market shopping, was carried out by women performing a crucial part of their domestic work. Their contribution to the body politic was recognized by writers such as Josep Cunill de Bosch, who in his 1923 *La Cuina Catalana* asserted that "food has a great transcendence, as much for the individual as for the collectivity."[101] This understanding, he argued, underpinned the work of Brillat-Savarin and other writers who approached the study of food from the perspective of physiology, psychology, and practice. In his estimation, the corpus of literature treating gastronomy in his day could be summed up by a set of declarative assertions:

Good female cooks make good foods;
Good foods are eaten with pleasure;
Food eaten with pleasure is that which is most beneficial;
Food that is most beneficial is the fittest for maintaining the individual in a healthy state.
Maintaining the individual in a healthy state means that its functions are regular;
Regular functions make the strong races;
The strong races lead all the others and over the long term become masters of the world.[102]

Cunill de Bosch's aphorism was written in a certain tongue-in-cheek tone, but he was still clearly positing the connection between defining and elevating a Catalan cuisine and—in keeping with a certain scatological bent in the culture—with digestive regularity as a state-building imperative.

The influx of new ingredients and the explicit assignation of political meaning to popular foodways were just two of three processes that embued early-twentieth-century Catalan cuisine with syncretism and plasticity. The third was consumerism. There had been a seventeenth- and eighteenth-century cultural shift that involved the growing attachment of a range of personal and social meanings to the act of purchasing goods in the expanded commercial marketplace.[103] Food was central to this process and arguably the first good around which consumerist values emerged. Even in periods of scarcity and crisis, food consumption demarcated social position but also personal identity. Because everyone had to eat, food was a more crucial consumer good than clothing, shoes, furniture, jewelry, and even kitchenware and other semidurables. Even for the poor, consumerist longings often expressed themselves not just in the desire for foods vital to subsistence but in a growing taste for sugar, chocolate, and coffee. Long before the first market halls were constructed in Barcelona, the act of eating had assumed an important new set of meanings that went far beyond issues of basic nutrition and survival.

Because the origins of consumer culture preceded industrialization rather than having resulted from it, a very significant portion of the research on this cultural development has shifted to a focus on the early modern period.[104] While the urban working-class population of Barcelona could little afford to participate in full-blown consumer culture until later on, shifting attitudes toward acquisitiveness in the economic marketplace were not merely a consequence of industrialization's expansion in the array of cheap manufactured goods for sale. Demand led production, at least in terms of chronology. Gabriel Tortella notes, for example, that as in England, the market for cotton cloth in Catalonia "long antedated the industry."[105] Lídia Torras's work on textile shops in Barcelona shows these tendencies and the growth of credit networks quite clearly.[106] Marta Vicente, more recently, has written about the early-eighteenth-century explosion in demand for calico cloth and its embrace by women as a fashion essential, a pattern in keeping with Northern Europe but also extending to Spanish households in the American colonies.[107] By the late eighteenth century, household furnishings, tableware, jewelry, fans, and silk shawls became more common objects of popular desire in advance of full industrialization. Open-air used-clothing and furniture markets, known as encants, grew in several parts of Barcelona where they had not existed before and offered a wide array of second-hand goods at relatively cheap prices. A little later, but still in advance of the full-blown industrialization of the economy, the opening or widening of streets such as Ferran and Princesa in the urban core of the early nineteenth century created new fashionable shopping districts where a wide range of manufactured goods were elaborately presented in window displays and in accordance with innovative retail models.

The early modern diffusion of consumer culture in Barcelona manifested itself to a very great degree in the food sector, inasmuch as we see an explosion of shops selling new foods, the establishment of a cosmopolitan restaurant and café culture, and a dramatically expanding ownership of kitchen- and tableware, including metal forks and spoons, glasses, jars, bottles, tablecloths, napkins, salt shakers, and candelabras, all of which signaled the growing pursuit of refinement in eating practices.[108] The widespread presence in eighteenth-century Barcelona of ambulatory vendors selling chocolate, pastries, shortbread, and sweetened beverages shows the significant expansion of popular desire for sweet foods that provided pleasurable energy even if falling short of signaling meaningful social advancement.[109]

The interrelated developments that John Benson identifies as the defining elements of late-nineteenth-century consumerism apply to early modern Barcelona, though not yet in terms of participation on a mass level. We see a dramatic expansion in the variety of goods available for purchase, growing levels of personal desire to acquire commodities deemed to be fashionable, and the intensification of consumption patterns that challenged existing social distinctions.[110] The values associated with consumerist culture certainly spread more widely through the social order over the course of the second half of the nineteenth century with the expanded availability of cheap manufactured goods and the spread of advertising and the popular press. By the time of the 1888 Expocisión Internacional, Barcelona was vested with an elaborate and mature restaurant culture that, in its most prestigious establishments, reflected a broadening taste for Italian and French cuisines. Processed foods, branding, and pre-packaging all made inroads into the popular diet in the first decades of the twentieth century and were incorporated into cooking alongside older culinary practices. Diary products of various sorts assumed a central place in the diet where they had not earlier, and the everyday consumption of poultry, eggs, and fresh fish dramatically expanded. As we shall see, the arbiters of Catalan taste in the 1920s touted the embrace by home cooks of what can only be termed a European cosmopolitan taste. Clearly, Catalan foodways featured significant changes and continuities, with the flowering of consumerist values shaping the demand for food as much as changes in supply and the imputation of political meanings to cookery. This fact problematizes efforts to define a "traditional" or "authentic" cuisine in that it demonstrates that both were moving targets.

The 1930 Market Cavalcade vignette with which this chapter began was set at a particular moment in time when the onset of the global depression was making a visible impact at the dinner table for many urban residents and new levels of anxiety about the economic and political future of the state were intensifying. Given the municipality's firm commitment to the public market hall-based system as the basis of urban provisioning, it is hardly surprising that the ritualized celebration of markets, and especially of the comforting iconography of innocent and virginal market maidens as food vendors, would have made for such tempting political fodder. In June 1930, the consumerist dream of ever-growing alimentary splendor was in danger. The participants in the pageantry could hardly have imagined that six years later a food crisis of unimaginable dimension and duration would set in. Throughout this period, the most fundamental barometer of a family's economic fortunes could be demonstrated through any number of consumptive acts, but none perhaps more immediately visible within neighborhood communities of women than what was revealed by the splendor or dearth of the market basket.

Significant changes in taste and food culture notwithstanding, the relationship of market vendors to one another, to the municipal administration of the city, and to the pools of neighborhood consumers from which they drew their clientele showed considerable continuity over the course of the twentieth century. Barcelona's market halls constituted central retailing places in the urban landscape with catchment zones of varying sizes that grew or contracted depending upon a range of circumstances. Layered social, economic, and political networks intersected in the food markets in differing configurations that could strengthen or weaken sales in stalls and in nearby shops, bars, restaurants, and taverns. Indeed the successes—and even some notable failures—of markets shaped the social and commercial character of individual neighborhoods in the city. After establishing the historical urban context for public markets in Barcelona and the emergence of the polynuclear system, the chapters that follow will trace these processes in relation to specific market halls, specific market vendors, and the neighborhoods in which they operated.

## CHAPTER 2

## *City of Markets*
### The Pre-Industrial Backdrop

In considering the significance of markets and market vendors in Barcelona, it is worth recalling the importance of food retailing arrangements to the process of urbanization itself. Unlike in villages, where most people combined agricultural production with other types of economic activity, in towns and cities residents were defined by their specialization in nonagricultural tasks. While transforming many elements of society and culture, neither industrialization nor modernity more generally had the effect of altering the fundamental place of food-distribution systems as the basis of urban civilization. Whether we speak of cities in Western Europe since the eleventh century—or, for that matter, Sumerian city-states in the fourth millennium BCE—we can safely say that urban life has been predicated on the existence of an agricultural surplus and upon the operation of an effective system for allocating food to city-dwelling populations.

Though food-distribution networks have taken many forms through history, nearly all have involved some degree of collaboration between religious, state, or local authorities and private individuals selling commodities that they may or may not have produced themselves. Working from markets and shops, urban food retailers have long operated at the intersection of the public and the private. Their economic livelihood involved exchanging food for money with women and sometimes men seeking to bring nutritional sustenance home to their families. When purchasing food, consumers engaged in forms of social interaction that linked individual households to one another, to governing authorities, and to the rural agricultural hinterland— or even far distant lands—where surpluses were produced. Variations in particular arrangements and degrees of complexity over time and according to place notwithstanding, food-retailing networks remain among the oldest and most enduring features of urban life.

The recovery of Western Europe's economy in the Middle Ages was not simply a consequence of the revival of long-distance trade on the part of merchants. Preceding this development, the gradual improvements in agriculture during the tenth century stimulated local market exchange and drew producers to nascent urban centers where growing populations gathered to "consume in common."[1] Markets were crucial to the making of cities, defining their character and the morphology of their growth, attracting the attention of merchants, nobles, and peasants alike. Markets also played a significant role in compelling the development of urban political authorities who focused their efforts on regulating commerce as much as on defense from would-be invaders.

What is also clear is that, like rural fairs, urban markets operated as centers of intense sociability. Their economic and nutritive functions were just one part of the equation. Held exclusively in the open air through the eighteenth century in Barcelona, food markets operated in urban spaces that served multiple purposes, some of which were interwoven with religious festival life. Expanding in number in response to population growth and burgeoning demand as the nineteenth century approached, food stalls filled numerous public squares and lined designated streets and arteries of the city. As such, they shaped the popular character, appearance, smell, and sound of the walled enclave. Serving as central places for the sale of food, markets attracted women in search of the provisions upon which their households depended. But they also involved large numbers of women working as vendors in a range of specializations. Long before the modernization of the system and the construction of the first halls that would enclose and segregate them from surrounding streetscapes, the culture of food markets was already imbued with a gendered feminine character.

### Local Foundations

An urban settlement with its origins in antiquity, Barcelona is situated on the Mediterranean coast of the Iberian Peninsula north of the Llobregat River and south of the Besòs. Until less than two centuries ago, it occupied only a small portion of a larger plain defined by the mountain of Montjuïc and the Serra de Collserola, which separated it from what had been the medieval principality of Catalonia.

Barcelona's postclassical urbanization process was initially a slow one, with its physical dimensions demarcated by what remained of the walls of the old Roman colony, though with a smaller population than its four to five thousand inhabitants at the height of the empire.[2] Still, those who lived in Barcelona in the early middle ages—nobles, clerics, artisans, and servants—all had to be provisioned, and the kitchen gardens common within the walled confines were not sufficient to support the nutritional needs of the population, nor to feed the handful of merchants who traded from there with al-Andalus. As Gaspar Feliu asserts, "commerce . . . was possibly the motor that permitted the rapid recuperation of the city after the ruin produced by the assault of al-Mansur in 985."[3] In any case, we know that around the year 1000 there was a market operating just north of the walled confines, outside the eastern gate of the urb.[4] Although Barcelona was languid in its early medieval development, the fertile lands running along the Llobregat River fed the population that constituted the "germ of today's city."[5]

In keeping with the eleventh-century revival of urban life that took place all across Europe, Barcelona and its markets grew in symbiotic unison. The city's political prominence followed suit. From a dynastic union effected by the 1137 marriage of the Count of Barcelona, Ramon Berenguer IV, to Petronella, daughter of King Ramon II of Aragon, the Catalan-Aragonese confederation was born. Though Catalonia and Aragon each retained their legal traditions and political institutions, Barcelona, known as the City of the Counts, became the seat of royal administration. The newly conjoined polity emerged as one of several Christian kingdoms situated along the northern axis of the Iberian Peninsula that combined state-building aspirations with the Reconquista crusading ventures against the Muslims as their *raison d'être*.

Yet Barcelona's political and urban ascendency within the Crown of Aragon would not have been feasible without recourse to adequate provisions and the food markets that served as their mechanisms for distribution. In the century leading up to the dynastic union, the burgs located outside the old Roman walls grew in terms of population, specialization, and function. Jaume Sobrequés notes that by the eleventh century the agglomeration of humanity both inside and beyond the walls had grown to include some fifteen thousand souls, and that in the burgs "traders, artisans, and mariners had their own churches, workshops, markets, and shipyards."[6]

The Catalan-Aragonese confederation, with its territorial expansion into Muslim-held lands and remarkable commercial success in Mediterranean trade in the thirteenth and fourteenth centuries, should not prevent us from recognizing Barcelona's historical and fundamental basis as a viable urban entity in much more localized contexts of dependency—the commercial/ agricultural link between city and hinterland. As Felipe Fernández-Armesto notes in his admittedly disdainful though nonetheless quite good history of the city,

> Barcelona's urban identity developed in the Middle Ages in the same way as that of many of Spain's inland centres of civilization: as the market of a small region, the court of a small principality, the magnet of a numerous clergy, and the preferred place of residence of an aristocracy flush with returns from rural investment and the profits of war. Not until the twelfth century does evidence of Barcelona's commercial take-off into an era of large-scale, long-range trade begin to accumulate.[7]

As Fernández-Armesto puts it, "this was a history more reminiscent of Burgos than Venice."[8]

To a large extent, it was markets stocked with local goods that fueled Barcelona's growth as a city. The professional soldiers who comprised a feudal order capable of hauling in Islamic booty could not have functioned had there not been sufficient surplus of food flowing from the hinterland to allow them to specialize in political intrigue and the art of war. The gains from Mediterranean trade in terms of wealth, institutional development, and culture were tremendous. But success as a political and economic central place within the polity, where city and countryside functioned in a relationship of mutual dependency, preceded these and would continue to remain crucial to Barcelona's viability as an urban center over the long run.

In a broader comparative sense, we can see that whether they were located within or beyond the walls, food markets shaped cities not just physically but politically as well. As Guàrdia and Oyón maintain, "the first function of the recently created municipal governments was precisely the economic administration of the city, and within that scheme, the regulation of markets was fundamental."[9] In the case of Barcelona, the twelfth-century count-kings established control over nearby mills, reformed indirect taxes on grain entering the city, and asserted the right to license bread ovens along with meat and fish stalls.[10] But the pressing need for funds to wage war and the ongoing cyclical outbreak of famine combined in the thirteenth century to encourage the Catalan-Aragonese monarchy to concede greater powers to urban oligarchs.[11] Thus King Jaume I established Barcelona's Consell de Cent, or Council of One Hundred, by decrees dating to 1249 and 1265.[12] Charged with varying tasks, the Consell's duties included "rationalising the consumption of meat and wheat, and the conversion of the latter into flour."[13] The new Consell also undertook the matter of defense, which most urgently involved the repair and extension of the fortifications to include the burgs to the north of the city. Absorbing and enclosing what became the Ribera neighborhood, the city thereafter constituted some 130 hectares. Within this space, market activity intensified, particularly in an area known as El Born, where an avenue along which market stalls selling a range of foods were clustered. Exercising more direct control over what had long been an important center of food sales, urban authorities regulated alimentary commerce by designating various open spaces through the city for particular types of market trade. In the fourteenth century, the Consell increased indirect taxation on cereals, meat, wine, and fish entering the city and created the office of the Mostassaf to regulate trade in the markets.[14]

A new set of walls completed in the fifteenth century to enclose the southern Raval burg that had grown up created the dimensions of the city known today as the Casc Antic or Ciutat Vella. With the addition of these new fortifications, Barcelona gained seventy more hectares of enmuralled space.[15] One advantage of enclosing the Raval was that it included quite a number of still-open areas whose potential for cultivation far surpassed the kitchen gardens that had long been tended by women to supplement relatively monotonous diets. The bulk of the market produce feeding the city came from the rural hinterland, and especially the fertile Llobregat Delta, but access to some additional food reserves in times of siege posed a notable strategic advantage. With these much-enlarged fortifications in place, the city was divided roughly in half by Las Ramblas, a crooked avenue that followed the course of a stream once flowing just outside the remnants of the second defensive walls. Bringing Las Ramblas into the city set the stage for its development as one of the key commercial and social areas within the urban landscape. In absorbing the avenue, the city also swallowed the thriving open-air food market that would become known as La Boqueria. The stalls along the section of Las Ramblas near what is called the "Pla de la Boqueria" date back to at least the twelfth century, when growing numbers of peasant women from the surrounding countryside had begun to sell fruits and vegetables there. In the early thirteenth century, a representative of the king authorized the first butchers' stalls nearby, and the market expanded in size and scope.[16] La Boqueria eventually came to rival El Born as the city's most important open-air market.

## Changing Commercial and Political Fortunes

Even before Barcelona's third set of walls was completed, major political, economic, and demographic developments had altered the course of the city's history.

Commercial success in maritime trade was accompanied by dramatic territorial expansion. Military conquests of Muslim-held territory, dynastic unions, and the extension of feudal relations of dependency had transformed Barcelona into a Mediterranean empire whose holdings included Roussillon, the Kingdoms of Valencia, Mallorca, and Naples, plus Sardinia, Sicily, and for about sixty years, the Duchy of Athens.[17] Underpinned by the *Ordinances de Mar* (a legal code governing maritime trade) and the Consolat de Mar (a trading association that had as many as seventy overseas consuls), Catalan economic ascendency in the Mediterranean transformed Barcelona into a cosmopolitan city. Its Llotga trading house was built in the last decades of the fourteenth century, as was its Drassanes shipyard. Barcelona's wealth in this period resulted from both its central place and its network functions. Although historically dependent on the city's hinterland for food, merchants were increasingly able to ship wheat in from Sicilian, Sardinian, and southern French ports while developing a wide range of complex long-distance trading ventures. Thereafter, regular access to imported wheat supplies would make the city less vulnerable to shortages and more able to guarantee bread at accessible prices in times of crisis.[18]

However, Barcelona's Mediterranean prominence had its limitations. Often compared to Genoa and Venice,[19] its port was inadequate and suffered tremendous deficiencies until the late sixteenth century, by which point Catalonia had lost its position of commercial, political, and military dominance in the Mediterranean. Even in its heyday, shipping from Barcelona could not rival either Venice or Genoa in terms of tonnage. Peter Spurford writes that around 1400, the combined merchant fleets from Barcelona, Valencia, and Mallorca "were only slightly exceeded in numbers by the combined merchant fleets of Genoa, Savona, and other Ligurian ports." The difference was in the size of the ships: the most common size of the Catalan boats was "300 *botti* (around 200 tonnes), whilst the most common size of the Genoese boats . . . had a tonnage of 800 *botti*."[20]

In any case, the period from 1349 to 1410 was difficult because the plague and provisioning crises of varying sorts generated social and economic unrest, which intensified municipal involvement in provisioning. Grain imports to Barcelona were largely handled by private merchants until late-fourteenth-century shortages led the Consell to concentrate more effort on acquiring strategic supplies, regulating trade, and supervising sales.[21] These developments help to explain the fifteenth-century consolidation of the Consell's control of the provisioning process. Urban and peasant revolts and pogroms against the Jews complicated the picture.

Commercial decline set in and was soon followed by demographic contraction. Then a new political challenge emerged: the last count-king of the House of Barcelona died in 1410 without a legitimate heir. His successor was elected through a process engineered by Pedro de Luna, the antipope whose lot the Crown of Aragon had supported. All efforts to advocate for the illegitimate grandson of the last count-king proved vain, and the Castilian Fernando de Antequerra from the Trastámara dynasty took the throne in 1412. While Catalonia's historic legal traditions and political institutions, including its parliament, remained intact, the shift in dynasty marked the beginning of a process that ultimately subjugated the principality to Castilian interests, and eventually to its direct political control.

In sum, Catalonia's late-medieval decline can be accounted for by a series of factors.[22] Having lost its privileged political leadership within the Crown of Aragon, its interests decreased in priority within a Castilian state-building program that was accelerated by the marriage of Fernando and Isabel in 1469. A steady incursion on its historical independence began, accompanied in the shorter term by social upheaval resulting from rural unrest and culminating in a Catalan civil war between 1462 and 1472. While Barcelona had been better positioned to endure earlier crises because of its ability to import grain from distant ports, during this war it was cut off from those markets, and a severe depression gripped the city as a consequence of wheat shortages.[23] To that were added the stressors represented by the 1478 imposition of the Inquisition and the 1492 expulsion of the Jews. At the same time that Castile was taking up long-distance trade in the Atlantic and assuming broader European leadership and obligations, Catalonia was turning back to investments in its hinterland and giving up the risky trading ventures upon which so much earlier success had been based.

Yet despite periods of demographic contraction that had re-occurred for centuries as a consequence of subsistence crises, war, and disease, Barcelona remained urban in its cultural orientation and continued to develop a strong civic identity underpinned by constitutional law and self-governing bodies. As James Amelang writes, while early modern Barcelona was "not as prosperous a city as it had been in the late Middle Ages . . . it nevertheless continued to dominate a dynamic regional economy."[24] Moreover, in functioning "as capital of the Principality of Catalonia, one of many territories comprising the Spanish monarchy, Barcelona played an unusually active role in peninsular and even international politics."[25] During these centuries, a new urban patriciate consolidated its place within the city's social order. Traditional aristocrats, landed gentry, university-trained lettered professionals, and newly ennobled individuals formed a self-conscious urban ruling class that coalesced around a set of common cultural values presumed to define what were termed "honored citizens." Inasmuch as this ruling class was to some degree permeable, and thus offered hope to the lower classes for upward social mobility, it also served to bolster greater levels of social and political stability in the city.[26]

In the seventeenth century, with a population of some 40,000 to 50,000 people, Barcelona's provisioning system was firmly structured to generate revenues through indirect taxation and to uphold the "moral economy," according to what Luis Corteguera has called in the case of Barcelona more specifically, "the common good."[27] Food was retailed mainly by stall-keepers plying their trade throughout the city. The main marketplaces were open-air centers of exchange. They were located along El Born in the Ribera neighborhood, which was by then operating in the shadows of the monumental gothic church of Santa Maria del Mar, and along Las Ramblas, centered on and extending from the Pla de la Boqueria. Fruits, vegetables, poultry, and eggs were also sold in smaller open-air markets located in various plazas in the city. Markets involved gatherings of private individuals seeking to generate profits from their trade while remaining under the watchful eye of municipal magistrates, their deputies, and, where applicable, the corporate power of the guilds. In times of food supply crisis, municipal authorities were expected to step in and alleviate distress. We see this in 1651 when war, plague, and famine combined to plunge the city into disorder.

On the heels of a peasant uprising that began in 1640, the Principality of Catalonia launched a war of independence from Castile. The rebellion expressed resentment toward growing royal interference in Catalan governmental bodies and represented an attempt to resist efforts by Philip IV's chief minister, the Count-Duke of Olivares, to increase taxation in order to offset the costs of Spain's involvement in the Thirty Years' War.[28] Catalonia's 1641 secession and declaration of allegiance to the French sovereign, Louis XIII, formed part of a broader uprising against Castilian state-building programs, which ultimately resulted in the re-establishment of an independent Kingdom of Portugal. After a long-drawn-out struggle that included the imposition of direct French rule in the Principality, Catalonia's aspirations for independence were quashed in the Castilian siege of Barcelona of 1651–52.

Among the crises taking place during the war was the outbreak of the plague in Barcelona beginning in early 1651. First affecting Valencia in the south, the plague crept northward. Soon thereafter, the plague began to affect the Empordà and then spread south toward Girona; Barcelona was caught between its pincers. Food supplies were dramatically interrupted as all but two of the city's gates were closed in June 1650. The Barcelona tanner and diarist Miquel Parets wrote that "famine struck Barcelona in August . . . Thus the city government had to help distribute bread, as the bakers did not have enough, and the dearth was so great that everyone feared there would be a riot."[29]

In the face of such a threat, the authorities intervened. The prospect of a food riot was not a trivial concern; less than four decades earlier, a similar uprising had involved a mob of four thousand and an attack on the house in the Ribera owned by the municipal official in charge of overseeing food supplies.[30] A repeat performance was avoided in 1650. Parets noted that "things improved after the city took the dough from the bakers and baked bread at the Customs House."[31] This was the standard pattern, as James Amelang explains: "At the worst moments of subsistence crises, city governments took over direct control of the baking and distribution of bread."[32] Municipal grain reserves were held and ovens maintained to facilitate public intervention in the market at crucial junctures, such as the one unfolding in the face of the advancing contagion.

During the crisis, Barcelona was cut off from inland sources of grain supply. Here its privileged position on the Mediterranean proved crucial. While the plague raged through the city in the spring of 1651, there had been virtually no rain. Parets recorded the following in his diary:

> Since it was time for the wheat to sprout open, the drought frightened everyone. Seeing that things were already so bad, everyone feared that they would become even worse next year . . . Wheat couldn't be found at any price, not even at 25 or 30 pounds per *quartera* from good friends. The city of Barcelona would have suffered greatly had it not been for two voyages made by a large ship built in the city two years ago. This ship made two trips to Livorno and brought back nine or ten thousand *quarteras* of wheat each time, and were it not for this boat Barcelona would have suffered greatly.[33]

Perhaps what is most interesting in Parets's account of the 1650–51 crisis is the degree to which he remained informed of both the outlines and the details of the municipal provisioning system. As a humble artisan, his voice is among the few detailed accounts we have depicting popular perspectives on the crucial question of food supply in early modern Barcelona. He wrote about how authorities resolved certain problems but also was highly critical of them for failing to fulfill their traditional roles in safeguarding the supply of food within the framework of the moral economy. According to Parets, "the provision of food during the plague was badly organized both in the pesthouse and in the city. Many died in the pesthouse for lack of food who would not have died had things been better organized."[34] Food-supply issues and the public management of food distribution formed a central theme of his narrative. They were clearly among the most paramount of his concerns. Parets's account reflects a growing popular consciousness that had developed in Barcelona over the question of fairness in the marketplace for food. Urban unrest resulting from bread-supply issues was most directly tied to a sense of injustice. Most people saw hoarding, profiteering, and speculation as more important causes of price hikes than bad harvests.[35] And they were well-warranted in doing so. Not only was fraud among bakers rampant, a portion of the principality's meager grain supply was often diverted to other ports by merchants operating under royal patent who sought to profit from elevated prices elsewhere. There was also the fact that La Seu, Barcelona's Cathedral de la Santa Creu i Santa Eulalia, only in part because of its beneficent works, was one of the largest grain purchasers in the city. Through its various entities, and like the Inquisition of its own accord, La Seu sold surplus bread from its ovens that redounded to the personal profit of its highest-ranking authorities.[36]

The crisis of 1651 ultimately passed and the war was settled in favor of Castile, though in accordance with a peace that upheld the principality's historic constitutional rights and privileges as part of the bargain. Thus Catalan law and its institutional structures of government remained intact, and the principality entered into what scholars have called a "neo-foral" relationship to the Crown during the second half of the seventeenth century.[37] It was much more definitively the outcome of the War of the Spanish Succession, in which the Catalans opposed the Bourbon inheritance of the Habsburg throne, that brought about a seemingly inexorable political interruption.

Constituting the last armed stand against the Bourbon ascension to power, the 1714 siege of Barcelona came to a bloody end with house-to-house combat and massive physical devastation to the Ribera neighborhood, within whose heart the city's Born marketplace was located. This ushered in a new period. The eighteenth century deserves particular attention because of the change in government institutions and bases of authority, crucial shifts in economic and social patterns, and significant demographic developments. The shape and the contours that the retail provisioning system took in Barcelona thereafter were inextricably interwoven with these developments.

*Inside the Bourbon Walls*

Barcelona's defeat by the armies of Philip V in the War of the Spanish Succession (1701–14) led to the construction of a new set of fortifications with pentagonal bulwarks. They added little territory, at least for civilian use, but expanding the city and defending it from future attack were not the motives behind their design. These walls and the star-shaped citadel to which they were connected were built by the conquering Bourbon military rationalists with the aim of imposing control over a city that had proved so troublesome to subdue. In essence, they were punitive rather than defensive. As the physical manifestations of Philip V's suspension of Catalonia's historic liberties and self-governing institutions, these fortifications became hated symbols of Castilian political centralization.

The Bourbon castration of Barcelona's municipal government was indeed severe. Barcelona's historic Consell de Cent had been comprised of representatives from five estates: the nobility, the military, honored citizens, merchants, and shopkeepers/artisans/artists. The Bourbons shut all but the nobility out, suspended the Consell, created what came to be known as the *Ajuntament*, and ruled the city through a military Corregidor and twenty-four aldermen appointed directly by the king. The Nueva Planta decrees (1707-16) also did away with the Catalan Generalitat and its parliament, the Corts. Other punitive centralizing policies included closing the University of Barcelona and relocating it to the inland market town of Cervera, which, along with the imposition of a foreign language, Castilian, in administration, justice, and then later in teaching, all lent a powerful blow to the culture of the city.[38] Yet—of great import to the operation of Barcelona's markets later on—Catalan civil law was left in place.

Within Barcelona's Bourbon walls in the early eighteenth century were a series of narrow winding streets, with many principal ways leading toward the urban nucleus and La Seu, located more or less in the center on a slight rise that had been the heart of the Roman urb. Behind the cathedral and between it and the port were the town hall and the Generalitat buildings in the Plaça de Sant Jaume. Though there were some Renaissance structures, Barcelona's public architecture at the outset of the eighteenth century was mainly gothic, reflecting the heyday of

Catalan commercial power in the Mediterranean. The bulk of the city's buildings at this time were artisanal workshops attached to residences, though scattered throughout were numerous palaces, churches, and convents, as well as public squares, large and small, which were equipped with fountains from which urban dwellers drew their water.[39]

Though the eighteenth century was marked by Barcelona's military and political subjugation within the Spanish state, the imposition of Bourbon rule coincided with a period of significant dynamism in Catalan social and economic structures. After prolonged commercial decline in comparison to levels of the late middle ages, Catalonia was poised in the late seventeenth century to undertake a sustained economic thrust—delayed by the War of the Spanish Succession—and eventually, an indigenous industrial revolution.[40] The stimulus for economic growth came from the Catalan countryside where wine, spirits, almonds, and hazelnuts had become increasingly more profitable commodities. Then the growth in long-distance trade in these agricultural products increased traffic from the port of Barcelona and stimulated both shipbuilding and local exchange. These developments facilitated the ability of urban artisans, shopkeepers, and the surrounding free peasantry to gain strength in relation to the remnants of the Catalan nobility.[41] Over the course of the eighteenth century, the social structure of the city underwent a transformation characterized by the erosion of the power of the guilds, the growth of capitalist production, the expansion of middle-class groups, and the emergence of a nascent industrial proletariat.

As in England, industrialization in Catalonia was based upon the growth and mechanization of the textile industry and driven forward by the availability of new markets.[42] The textile boom in Catalonia can be dated to the 1730s and was initially characterized by a concentration in the production of cotton cloth and silks. Inside the walled city, workshops sprang up throughout, where bleached cotton cloth was woodblock-printed in operations usually employing forty workers or fewer. With the weakening of the formerly powerful guild system, the narrow winding streets of Barcelona became lined with small diversifying and specializing manufacturing enterprises whose profits fueled the emergence of a new bourgeoisie and set the stage for the industrial revolution of the next century. When Charles III in the 1770s opened up direct Catalan trade to ports in the Spanish colonies, textile production intensified and the agricultural base of the region became even more intensely viticultural. Exports of brandy, aguardiente, and *indiana* cloth to Cuba, Santo Domingo, and Puerto Rico became highly profitable, and merchants reinvested the capital accumulated from that trade in machinery for textile production. By the 1790s, Catalonia boasted the largest concentration of dyers and weavers outside of Lancashire;[43] by the end of the century, more complex mechanization of the city's textile industry was underway. However, interruption resulting from the French Revolutionary and Napoleonic wars, followed by new levels of political instability at the center of the Spanish state, delayed the adoption of steam-powered, factory-based textile production in the region until the 1830s.

As in other peripheral regions of the Iberian Peninsula, the eighteenth century was a period of rapid population growth in Catalonia.[44] With respect to the city of Barcelona, the initial demographic increase was due mainly to short-distance migration to work in the burgeoning textile sector. According to 1717 census data, the city was comprised of 57,709 inhabitants.[45] After centuries of demographic stagnation, the population within the city walls took off, increasing dramatically in the second half of the eighteenth century. Many of the new textile firms were located where there was more available space in the Raval, on the other side of Las Ramblas from the "compact medieval"[46] core. With laborers unable to find housing in the older portion of the city, the increasingly populated Raval began to take on the characteristics of an industrial slum. In the years between 1717 and 1787, the population of Barcelona reached nearly 100,000.[47] Having grown to its horizontal limits, the city in the last thirty years of the century grew upward.[48] In 1772, only 13 percent of all residential buildings in Barcelona went up four stories or more, but by the 1790s, 72 percent of residential buildings did. In the last quarter of the eighteenth century, 80 percent of all construction in Barcelona consisted of adding new floors to old buildings and of chopping up existing floors to create new rooms. Living conditions in the city worsened as population pressure inside the walls intensified. Outbreaks of cholera and yellow fever plagued Barcelona, and shortcomings in the system of provisioning manifested themselves in episodes of popular protest, such as the bread riots, known as the *Rebomboris del Pa*, which took place in 1789.

## Bread and Social Order

Barcelona's 1789 Rebomboris del Pa were part of a series of popular upheavals that took place in Spain and elsewhere in Western Europe in connection with rising cereal prices in the second half of the eighteenth century.[49] Sparked by a municipal edict announcing an increase in the cost of bread, the uprising began on February 28, a Saturday. City authorities had been hearing complaints about the scarcity of *moré*, the darkest and cheapest type of bread, sold from special market stalls used as distribution points in periods of scarcity.[50] Congregating in and around La Boqueria and El Born markets, a crowd of some eight thousand people demolished the bread stalls before moving on to assault the municipal bread ovens.[51] After the mob set fire to the building, the city's ruling captain-general, Francisco González y Bassecourt, sent out troops to quell the uprising and save the bread ovens from complete incineration. Once dispersed, the rioters reconvened near the house of the city's main grain contractor, Torras and Company, which they threatened to set ablaze. Clashes with soldiers followed, and after some members of the crowd were arrested, the riot seemed to have ended by midnight.

But the following day, a Sunday, the revolt intensified, with larger crowds gathering at several points in the city. In front of the captain-general's offices in the Plaça del Palau, the protesters demanded an audience with him and the leaders of the municipal hierarchy, many of whose homes they had already sacked.[52] Rioters also congregated once more at the grain contractor's house, this time successfully forcing their way in and destroying much of its contents. Another group assaulted La Seu, broke through the locked doors of the cathedral, pushed past and insulted the bishop, occupied the campanile, and sounded the bells to alert the city to join the uprising.[53] In the streets and squares, mounted soldiers wielding sabers clashed with protesters armed with stones. The demands were specific: the release of those imprisoned the day before, a reduction in the price of bread to the previous year's level, and the lowering of taxes on meat, wine, and olive oil.[54] What had begun as a bread riot morphed into a broader uprising in protest against rising food prices with an extension of the movement to other Catalan cities, including Vic, Sabadell, and Mataró.[55]

The municipal authorities quickly conceded on Sunday afternoon, announcing a reduction in prices, which ultimately quelled the protest. City authorities organized the more popular aldermen, some nobles, and guild leaders to patrol the streets, and with order restored, food sales resumed at noon the next day. Though the cavalry retreated to the Citadel, its artillery remained pointed toward the city, and the street patrols continued for days thereafter. In the weeks and months that followed, authorities expelled foreigners and blamed *gentes viles* for having plotted to spread rumors and organize the uprising.[56] By March 4, between twenty-five and forty individuals had been rounded up and detained in the Citadel prison.[57] Ultimately, one woman and five men from among the rioters were hung by the military for their part in the upheaval. Still, city authorities downplayed the gravity of the episode in their accounts to Madrid, an effort that proved vain in that the captain general in charge of Barcelona was immediately relieved of his duties and replaced by Francisco Antonio de Lacy.

The 1789 Rebomboris del Pa represented a fairly typical expression of *ancien régime* subsistence protests.[58] The uprising was spontaneous, coalesced around specific grievances within the market for food, and lacked ideological content.[59] The rich and powerful were targeted, but selectively so. Nobles, guild leaders, and aldermen served as intermediaries, offering the rioters assurance that their demands would be met. As Irene Castells asserts, "the revolt did not intend to disrupt the social order . . . it was largely spontaneous and essentially addressed at achieving short-term objectives."[60] Though this revolt occurred less than six months prior to the bread riots that set off the French Revolution, it was markedly different in that Barcelona's emergent bourgeoisie sided with the authorities, collaborating in the effort to restore order. While denouncing the extent of the repression that followed, elites took a conciliatory attitude toward the rioters, intensifying their contributions to charity efforts that were designed to forestall a repetition of the episode. The pre-riot social order survived the uprising intact.

Setting aside the authorities' scapegoating of foreigners and "vile persons," we do not know who did and did not participate in the uprising, except of course that both men and women were among the protestors. Female organization of and participation in such episodes was common in pre-industrial Europe, and in this case one woman was executed for her purported leadership in the affair. The participation of significant numbers of women may help to explain the subsequent reconciliation between the rioters and the city's elites.[61] The aldermen in particular would not have wanted to identify themselves in opposition to the women's collective ire in defense of the common good, and the one woman who was executed received a modicum of mercy in that, unlike the men, she was interred in La Seu.[62]

The gendered social nature of the uprising also followed patterns characteristic of other European pre-industrial food riots. Typically, the protests were started by women, and as they intensified, men joined in. When and if matters became violent, women's direct participation in the action decreased.[63] Contemporary accounts of the 1789 Rebomboris affirm this with one asserting that women started the uprising and another attributing agency in the first phase of the protests to female servants.[64] Mercè Renom's important study of the episode holds that "in fact, the mobilized women and the men with whom they shared the actions had in common the same place among the lowest social rungs" of the urban hierarchy.[65] Those from the middling stations did not engage in public street protests but rather expressed their grievances instead through written petitions and other types of formal redress, albeit ones that were often driven by fear of the disorder they saw unfolding from the marketplaces of the city.[66]

Renom distinguishes between the *clam*, the *avalot*, and the *motí* as differing levels of protest.[67] The *clam* involved individual women expressing dissatisfaction with a particular market transaction because of price, weight, quality, or incivility on the part of a vendor or vendors. A *clam* was typically resolved through the intervention of a male authority figure in the employ of the municipality in a dispute that usually pitted two women against one another. These were common and help to explain the necessity of close direct municipal regulation of the markets. An *avalot* involved groups of consumers who presented themselves to city authorities to decry injustices in the market. The *motí* erupted when the matters at hand were not redressed and violence broke out. The three levels of protest can be understood as gradations on a continuum of popular dissatisfaction, with male participation increasing as *clam* gave way to *avalot* and moved on to *motí*, which was the case in 1789.[68]

The broader causes and the consequences of the 1789 Rebomboris del Pa are also significant. In the pre-industrial agricultural complex, Catalonia could only produce about one-third of the wheat that its population consumed. The rest had to be imported, typically by sea, from other parts of Europe.[69] While the government of Carlos III debated the merits of liberalizing the grain trade, Barcelona's municipal government remained much more interested in maintaining control in order to forestall popular revolts. Bread, after all, was at the heart of the diet and the most crucial source of calories for the growing sector of the population whose household economies depended upon wage work in the textile and related industries. With the 1765 liberalization of the grain trade, bread production in the city's *pastim* ovens had begun to be passed more fully to the city's private bakers. The 1789 crisis was aggravated by the combination of several bad harvest years in the countries exporting wheat to Barcelona and by an economic downturn brought on by the falling price of aguardiente, the distilled spirit that was one of the region's main agricultural exports. The episode served to highlight the explosive effect that rising food prices could have in the increasingly more densely populated city.

After the Rebomboris had been put down, the wholesale wheat market was closed from March 4 to June 15 while the city restocked its strategic grain reserves. Any parties with wheat stores in the city had to register with the municipal government. Bakers were subjected to new levels of suspicion for having abundant bread to sell to the moneyed, yet a shortage for sale to the poor.[70] These were emergency measures and the traditional mixed economy in grain was gradually restored until war with France and the subsequent bread crises at the end of the century brought the municipality back into de facto if not de jure control.[71]

During that crisis, the city took charge of production and distribution, and the only bread available was made from flour comprised of a mixture of wheat combined with ground maize, broad bean flour, and barley. Only the infirm in the city, by medical prescription, could acquire white bread.[72] Here we see why the liberalization of commercial activities that ultimately took effect in 1834 allowed free trade in food, drink, and fuel—*with the exception of bread,* a commodity too central to the diet and too closely linked to the maintenance of urban social order to risk subjecting it to the vagaries of the free market.

## The Tradition of Municipal Control

This late-eighteenth-century urgency underlying municipal intervention in food sales was of course not in and of itself new in Barcelona or elsewhere.[73] Though the Church retained certain privileges in the provisioning system and butchers were authorized by royal patent to ply their trade, the practice of municipal responsibility, authority, and control over the sale of food in Barcelona was clearly established by the fourteenth century when the Consell de Cent issued regulations governing the provisioning of bread, wine, meat, and fish to the city.[74] The regulatory thrust in this case was directed toward controlling prices, limiting the export of foodstuffs to areas outside the city, and abolishing vendor practices that favored one customer over another.[75] Municipal officers known as Mostassafs enforced these rules, along with prohibitions on the sale of meat from animals that died from disease, drowning, or attacks by wolves.[76] Guilds, too, acted to control provisioning by establishing regulations for butchers and other corporately organized food retailers and by sanctioning those who did not adhere to established standards. Market vendors in Barcelona had long been required to fly a banner showing the city's arms as proof that they had paid their stall rents and were in the authorities' good graces. Later, these banners also indicated the type of goods for sale to the public. Harsh punishments for those who violated rules reflected the ambiguous place of food retailers in the urban polity.

While the municipality's official aim was to defend the interests of the members of the urban polity, the regulation of provisioning constituted a crucial source of funds because through the early modern centuries "most of the city's revenues derived from indirect taxes on consumer goods."[77] The fiscal importance of municipal control over the provisioning system had a long history. Indirect taxes on wine dated to 1330 and on meat to the second half of the fourteenth century.[78] Along with taxes collected on fish, they accounted for 80 percent of the city's tax revenues.[79] In seeking to achieve its twin objectives of fiscal health and social order, the municipality periodically requisitioned wheat supplies, set prices, subsidized crucial commodities such as the dark bread of the poor, and created administrative structures to regulate the open-air markets.[80] Most of these policies survived the imposition of Bourbon rule into the second decade of the eighteenth century.

Though the 1716 Decrees of Nueva Planta abolished Catalonia's political institutions and created new structures to govern the city, municipal controls over key commodities such as bread and meat were kept in place.[81] Food retailing from markets and shops continued under municipal license, regulation, and control, though administrative supervision was taken over by aldermen known as the Regidores Almotazenes, who replaced the earlier Mostassafs. The Almotazenes were in charge of regulating weights and measures along with commercial trade in food within the city and its immediate hinterland. Municipal ordinances continued to favor producer-vendors over urban-dwelling retailers for fear that reselling increased prices. This is clearly evident in the military corregidor's 1752 ordinances, which reflect tremendous concern for ensuring that all food supplies be made available to the public for sale and with preventing food stocks from being used for speculative purposes.[82]

Barcelona's vibrant commercial economy in the second half of the eighteenth century contributed to a proliferation in the number of food market stalls and shops. Markets were open seven days a week, expanding alongside growing numbers of butchers, who acquired their stocks from the slaughterhouse in Sants or from one of the smaller privately owned operations.[83] Many of the new butchers and bakers established themselves in the crowded Raval area of the city, where the location of shops had previously been less concentrated. In addition to being driven by higher levels and new types of demand from a growing urban consumer base, the expansion of the food-retailing sector in this period resulted from increases in local and long-distance sources of food supplies and from changes in the commercial economy of the surrounding countryside. Along with the foreign wheat and salt cod that entered Barcelona through the port, the city's markets were stocked with growing quantities of fruits and vegetables produced along

Spain's Mediterranean coast. In Catalonia and Valencia especially, the fruit and vegetable sector of the agricultural economy underwent intense commercialization beginning in the eighteenth century. The process of economic change in the countryside increased food surpluses that served to feed Barcelona's growing population and to expand levels of exports of foodstuffs from Spain to European markets. The commercialization of agriculture also drew greater numbers of peasants from Barcelona's immediate hinterland through the city's gates to sell their wares.

The bulk of Barcelona's perishable food was retailed through open-air markets, where nearly all of the specialized purveyors held stalls. In addition to the key centers at El Born and at the Plà de la Boqueria on Las Ramblas, Barcelona's markets had long operated in a variety of public squares that were adjacent to churches, including the Plaça Nova next to La Seu and in the square in front of and alongside the Church of Santa Maria del Pi. Open-air markets had also grown up in the Plaça del Pedró in the Raval, as well as in the Plaça de Sant Augustí Vell in the Ribera. In yet other locations, such as the Plaça dels Àngels, wholesale markets like the one there that specialized in bread flour, also featured some retail fruit and vegetable vendors. While most markets sold a range of foodstuffs, some, such as the fish market, were more specialized. The city's fish vendors were concentrated in stalls along Peixeteria Street in the Ribera.[84] Barcelona's eighteenth-century demographic expansion was supported by, and reflected in, the growth of its open-air food-market trade and by its physical extension in the streets and squares of the city.

As population pressure intensified over the course of the eighteenth century, trade in Barcelona's open-air markets grew and the stalls that increasingly extended outward from them blocked traffic and added to the general state of congestion in the already crowded city. We can see this tendency clearly along Las Ramblas, where the avenue's increasing social prestige met up against a veritable explosion in market trade. Food stalls along Las Ramblas spread from their original heart at the Plà de la Boqueria both toward and away from that center in the final decades of the eighteenth century.[85]

Although Las Ramblas became a paved thoroughfare in 1776, accounts describe the late-eighteenth-century clustering of vendors there as chaotic.[86] In the summer especially, the smells from the meat vendors' stalls posed a particular problem.[87] In 1796, municipal authorities imposed a new set of regulations that divided the avenue into specific areas according to market stall activity.[88] Moving up Las Ramblas, away from the sea, one encountered, first, the flower vendors. Next were the fruit and vegetable vendors. They were followed by poultry, meat, game, and then fish. Across from the latter group were salted meat, salted fish, pork, and butchery stalls.[89] The growing complexity in these arrangements mirrored the situation at El Born Market, where greater numbers of stalls, arranged by specialty, extended further than ever before along the winding streets of the Ribera.

The urgency of guaranteeing ample supplies of food kept municipal authorities in the business of controlling trade in the hinterland within distances up to seven leagues from the city's walls. The earlier referenced 1752 regulations had confirmed the longstanding practice of mandating that the bulk of all victuals produced in the area surrounding Barcelona would be barred from export. There were special exceptions for commodities, such as aguardiente, that were destined for the Americas, but oil, wine, vinegar, fruits, vegetables, fish, meat, pork, poultry, ash, soap, wood, and coal could only be exported beyond the city's hinterland when supplies exceeded demand. Regulations specified that producer-vendors could enter the city gates and sell at the markets in areas that set them apart from the retailers whose prices were almost always higher and whose motives were more often suspect. The complex set of regulations established fines for infractions and awarded one-quarter of the merchandise confiscated in cases of violation to the person accusing the vendor of breaking the law. Where vendors had the temerity to engage municipal authorities in verbal defiance, public ridicule and incarceration were the penalties. The degree to which elaborate and extensive market control was such an urgent municipal concern indicates that food supply issues in general, and markets specifically, remained on some level and in some respects ungovernable affairs.

These challenges help to explain why Bourbon authorities moved to reform Barcelona's municipal government in 1766, creating something approximating a bicameral system. Thereafter, the Ajuntament was led not just by noble alderman appointed for life by the king, but also by a body of "third-estate" guild representatives charged to help oversee provisioning in the city. Differences between them were resolved by the captain-general, who answered to the monarchy's high court, the *Real Audiencia*.[90] Such reform highlights the contradictory nature of economic policies under King Carlos III's reign (1766–88), which generally leaned toward greater degrees of liberalization. A year after restoring guild representation in Barcelona's municipal government, the monarchy declared freedom of commerce for bakers and breadmakers, thus forcing Barcelona to give up its control over the production and sale of the most vital of all foods. The policy undercut public perceptions of the city's commitment to the "common good" and underpinned the ire that was expressed in the 1789 Rebombori uprising.

## The Popular Uses of Market Space

Along with their nutritive role in sustaining urban life, Barcelona's early modern markets were important social and cultural spaces. Held in the open air, their operation was interwoven with that of the city itself, forming part of the fabric and rhythm of quotidian life. Markets attracted not just buyers but gawkers, hawkers, and gossips. In fact, they were more often sites for popular comedic spontaneity than flashpoints for confrontations over the weight, price, and quality of food. According to the folklorist Joan Amades, El Born attracted people of all ages, with gangs of youthful pranksters developing around them. In a general sense, markets contributed to the fair-like atmosphere characterizing commerce in the city. A great many fixed shops opened up onto the street, and various types of peddlers, both male and female, roamed throughout the walled enclave, selling a wide range of items, edible and otherwise. It is not surprising therefore that upon visiting Barcelona at the end of the sixteenth century, the Swiss traveler Thomas Platter was "struck by the personal relations and the intensity of use in public space."[91]

For many centuries, all of the city's social strata intersected in markets in one form or another. This was particularly true of El Born, which was one of Barcelona's most frequented public areas in the early modern period. As Amelang notes, "local ceremonial and festive life . . . gravitated toward less-encumbered areas," among them those spaces designated for market activity in El Born and Las Ramblas.[92] The social admixture characterizing these marketplaces was dictated by religious and civic calendars. In its default mode, El Born operated as a center specializing in the sale of fruits and vegetables, "replete with all the picaresque details attending 'low life' in a port city."[93] But in addition to this function, it was the main site for public Carnival celebrations and for an annual glass fair at New Year's, as a space where the aristocracy organized jousts and tourneys, and as a key location where the Church held ritual acts of faith. As an urban space, El Born served multiple functions at once economic, social, and cultural in nature. The same can be said for La Boqueria Market, whose stalls extended along growing stretches of Las Ramblas. The realignment and improvement of the avenue had conferred greater social prestige worthy of the throngs of opera-goers attending the Liceu and enjoying the amenities designed to attract the city's upper crust. A broader social nightlife took off in the environs of Las Ramblas in the eighteenth century, drawing in gentlemen, artists, and rabble-rousers in search of cabaret entertainments. Indeed, people of all stations intermingled along Las Ramblas at various times of the day and night. Joan Busquets describes the promenade as "a central spot where the representation of urban life and commercial and institutional activity have been staged side by side."[94]

Yet while Barcelona's eighteenth-century markets expanded in scale, the elite of the city began to physically withdraw from them. This shift in behavior was part of the consolidation and redefinition of a new patriciate, a process several centuries in the making, and one that Amelang sums up with the phrase "retreat to the balcony."[95] A century before, urban notables began to disengage themselves from the popular festival life of the city. Jousts, tourneys, and other patrician social gatherings began to take place more often in enclosed private spaces. In abandoning social engagement in the city's marketplaces, Barcelona's elites effectively reinforced the popular character of these urban spaces, though without giving up direct public control over their administration.

This widening social gulf had linguistic manifestations. Even before the Bourbon program to suppress the use of the Catalan language in public life, Barcelona's "honored citizens" had begun to Castilianize themselves. First in their publications and then later in their speech habits, they increasingly equated the use of the Catalan language either with a narrow audience limited to the principality or with the vulgarity of common people and women.[96] In Amelang's words, "Crucial to the elite's adoption of Castilian was the identification of the Catalan vernacular with the 'lower' classes . . . If the lower classes were restricted to the use of Catalan, those wishing to distinguish themselves as patricians were perforce obliged to use Castilian and/or Latin as well. The ruling class apparently did not always regard familiarity with Catalan as demeaning. However, it firmly associated *exclusive* use of that language with the plebeian order."[97]

Some writers even "relegated Catalan to comic uses, like the theatrical mimicry of women's gossip."[98] Marketplaces in Barcelona, which were enmeshed in the everyday lives of the popular classes, and especially those of women, remained public spaces in which Catalan persisted. Over the longer-term history of the Spanish state's attempts to marginalize the language, markets operated as unregulatable linguistic zones. Though the administrative language after 1714 was Castilian, the form of communication used between vendors and their customers was negotiated on a case-by-case basis among individuals who, often in the eighteenth century, were only fluent in Catalan. Municipal authority stepped in, to be sure, to regulate unruly speech, as in moments of conflict over trade, but otherwise the familiar use of Catalan remained nearly ubiquitous. With the exclusive use of Castilian mandated in government, law, and education, markets became ever-more-important sites for the popular perpetuation of the indigenous language, as did neighborhood commerce more generally, along with family life.

## Women in the Markets

Whatever shift in elite social attitudes and linguistic habits took place over the course of the early modern period in Barcelona, its markets remained crucial sites for the most popular forms of social exchange among neighborhood women who had in common the responsibility of purchasing food and cooking for their households. Food shopping coupled very old forms of urban sociability with the most fundamental type of economic exchange. Markets were meeting places for women on both sides of the commercial equation—as consumers, certainly, but as vendors as well.

Women especially worked as fish vendors, and their elaborate displays of rare species served as both advertisement for their more standard wares and as curious attractions to those wandering through the market for amusement.[99] That women constituted a significant presence among the retailers of fish is documented in municipal records dating back to the last quarter of the fourteenth century. The 1375 Barcelona *Reglamento de la Pescadería* uses both male and female pronouns throughout to stipulate the fines that fish vendors would be sanctioned with for selling without the authority of the Mostassaf.[100] Yet the 1717 tax rolls for Barcelona list thirty-one individuals as members of the fishermen's confraternity, and not one of them was female. Still, we know that in keeping with traditional arrangements, female family members took charge of the retailing end of family fishing concerns.[101] Marta Vicente has documented this pattern in citing female fishmongers in eighteenth-century Barcelona bequeathing their market-stall licenses to one another, typically within family and kinship lines.[102] In fact, Barcelona's 1752 provisioning ordinances explicitly stipulated that the wives, daughters, and widows of fishermen—along with servants and other family members who resided in their households—were the only individuals permitted to sell their catch to the consuming public and that all such retailing was to take place in designated areas at the city's marketplaces.[103] Similar restrictions were imposed by municipal ordinances on egg vendors. Men holding licenses to sell eggs could only be substituted in their stalls by their wives or their children.[104] Though butchers and bakers were typically male guild members who plied their trade along with other family members,[105] women, both urban-dwelling and rural, participated extensively in food retailing on their own through their work as market vendors. The 1752 ordinances suggest that a wide-ranging number of food market specializations, especially fruits, vegetables, poultry, eggs, and fish, were all but monopolized by female vendors.

Issued in the Castilian language of administration, these mid-eighteenth-century municipal ordinances generally used the male pronoun and masculine forms, but they also explicitly referenced women in numerous articles. For the most part, the aim was to ensure accountability on the part of those who sold food by holding an individual and his household responsible for observing municipal regulations with respect to price, weight, and quality. But the ordinances also singled out *revendedors* and *revendedoras*—that is, resellers both male and female—as problematic participants in the city's food-retailing economy and as subjects of scorn and suspicion for speculating on the price of food.[106]

Overall, Barcelona appears to have followed a general northern Iberian pattern of extensive female involvement in early modern food-market trade. As James Casey asserts, there was a real distance between the gender ideology that recommended encloistering for even the unmarried daughters of peasants, versus the lived experience of many women appearing in the "chronicles of Spanish cities of the Golden Age as market vendors and bakers and servants in inns—a wide variety of trades where they were constantly in touch with the public. In 1548 Pedro de Medina noticed the contrast as he moved north from his native Andalusia into the Old Christian lands of Castile, that the women got 'tougher' (*recias*). In some parts they worked in the fields, reaping grain (at most Andalusian women would pick olives) and travelling to market to sell their produce."[107]

Such evidence suggests that Barcelona was one such place in Spain where women's work in commerce was common, albeit often in the least remunerative, most marginal, and least documented sectors of the economy, within which market work squarely fell.

Barcelona's history as a city was bound up with that of its marketplaces. Managing the supply and sale of food was one of the municipal government's most urgent ongoing concerns. In times of plenty as well as in times of dearth, the city's population depended upon its markets as points of distribution for much of the food that it consumed. In crises such as that represented by the plague in 1651 or the shortage of grain in 1789, social upheavals resulted from interruptions in supply and spurred greater levels of public intervention in market trade. The dramatic densification of the city that accompanied its eighteenth-century economic take-off had the effect of intensifying the urgency of food-supply management as the size and number of markets expanded. With this growth came greater opportunities for women to engage in commerce, though largely still from within the structures of the family economy. Long operating as centers of sociability, Barcelona's pre-industrial marketplaces were key public spaces in which women's participation as buyers and sellers of food was a highly visible element of the urban economy. As such, the markets of the city operated as central places for the arrangement of both sustenance and popular entertainment, and as centers for intense interaction with the state, through its representatives charged with maintaining order and control. The construction of market halls in the next century had the effect of segregating a significant portion of the city's trade in food from the plazas and the streets where it had so long taken place. But the new modern market halls, and the system that they came to comprise, further reinforced the degree to which these centers of exchange acted as commercial and social central places within a city that was fast becoming a Mediterranean industrial metropolis.

## CHAPTER 3

# *Mirrors of Urban Growth*
## Market Building through the Long Nineteenth Century

In the nineteenth century, Barcelona's municipal regimes faced challenges paralleling those experienced in many of Europe's other industrializing cities. Among the pressing issues were how best to adjust the food system to accommodate dramatic intensification in population density and how to re-conceptualize provisioning in the context of explosive growth in urban scale. Beginning in the 1840s, varying municipal governments adopted and adapted market-hall models from leading industrialized nations. Once Barcelona spread beyond its Bourbon walls, fanning out to occupy a much larger portion of the plain that had long served as its most proximate market garden, the city began to follow a course of market building and operation that became more characteristic of the western Mediterranean region of Europe.

The first fundamental shift involved relocating existing open-air markets into covered or semi-enclosed spaces. These first new markets formed part of the public effort to minimize violent popular unrest. The second shift involved municipal construction of a revolutionary new type of metal and glass market hall and the assumption of control over similar structures that had been built in the annexed towns. By the end of the nineteenth century, Barcelona had established a rationalized and uniformly regulated system. It was at this juncture that the municipal goal of providing market halls as public services in each of the city's neighborhoods gained traction, becoming the gold standard for Barcelona's governing authorities over the long run.

The process of market building in Barcelona, as elsewhere, involved multiple objectives. Initially conceived as responses to growing street congestion and the intensifying demand for food, after 1871 market projects reflected new approaches to urban design that embodied hygienic and egalitarian visions. They also reflected broader trends toward the municipalization of city services and the monumentalization of public space. Enclosing the city's street markets in much more clearly defined physical spaces enabled municipal authorities to pursue a program of sanitization that, among its other concerns, took aim at female market vendors in an effort to tame and control what was presumed to be an unruly element within the social order.

## The Origins of the Nineteenth Century

The efforts to impose new levels of municipal control over food retailing cannot be separated from the larger endeavors to reshape urban space within the crowded confines of the walled city. Several municipal projects in the eighteenth century reflected early concepts of rational urbanism in municipal thinking. One such effort was the design and construction of a new neighborhood called La Barceloneta with a uniform grid street layout on a spit beyond the city's walls at the northern end of the port. The idea was to design an area of uniform residences to house the more than six thousand fishermen and sailors who had inhabited the portion of the Ribera destroyed after the War of the Spanish Succession in order to build the massive Citadel. Work began on La Barceloneta in 1753. As part of the plan, a centrally located plaza was set aside to serve as a public market square. Though the end result of the project was built up and crowded far beyond the original intent, the carefully ordered streets, intersecting at right angles, represented a complete departure from the winding, confused layout of the walled city to which it was connected. The construction of La Barceloneta reflected new trends in municipal design that sought to define urban spaces for specific social functions.

The widening and straightening of specific streets, such as Carrer Argenteria and Carrer Nou de la Rambla, and the expansion of key public areas such as the Plaça del Palau—ultimately becoming Barcelona's largest square inside the Bourbon walls—also reflected growing concerns with rational urbanism.[1] So too did the improvements made to Las Ramblas after 1776. Having passed from a muddy riverbed on the city's periphery to the principal artery in the center of town, the new paving and widening of Las Ramblas reflected the avenue's growing social prominence as the site of lavish new palaces built with profits from trade with Latin American ports. Though the addition of a central walkway made more room for the expanding population of vendors and improved the conditions under which they worked, it seems clear that municipal authority viewed the growth of the open-air marketplace along Las Ramblas as something of a nuisance, and even an outright affront to the dignity of the avenue itself—this despite the market's strategic importance to underpinning social order by helping to keep the population fed.

That the reconfigured Ramblas brought prestige to the city and that its benefits to market vendors were secondary is evidenced by events in 1802. For the first time in a century, Barcelona was chosen as the site for a Spanish court function. In that year, the royal family staged a double wedding in the city; the fact that one of the grooms was heir to the Spanish throne added to the significance of the events surrounding the visit.[2] In preparation for the arrival of Carlos IV's court, municipal authorities undertook a flurry of activities. The local nobility and artisans alike embraced the opportunity to make improvements in hopes that the events would build the city's reputation in the eyes of the Court and in accordance with Barcelona's renewed commercial success. Accordingly, municipal authorities moved to clear out some of the unseemly commercial elements from Las Ramblas along which the royal family would pass and upon which one of the main viewing stands would be situated.

Toward this end, the city relocated the butchers' stalls from Las Ramblas to a nearby garden belonging to Carmelite friars.[3] Authorities apparently disguised other stalls along Las Ramblas in an effort to make them less offensive.[4] This move is significant because it signaled the emerging conviction on the part of the municipal government that the dense configurations of market stalls along Las Ramblas were becoming aesthetically discordant with its new vision of the city's grandeur. Having become the center of social life for the city's dominant classes, the noise, smell, and squabbling characterizing the marketplace were not compatible with the avenue's new social status. The events of 1802 are thus noteworthy because they presaged one of the solutions to the perceived problem of overcrowding and disorder in the city's open-air markets. The thought on the part of the city was that markets could be moved and regrouped in newly designated places where they would cease to offend emerging bourgeois sensibilities. Moreover, such spatial segregation held the promise of facilitating municipal control of a food-retailing system that had grown dramatically over the course of the previous century. The impediments to adopting such a policy, though, were several, including the fact that the vendors were loath to relocate for fear of losing their clientele. More significantly, space limitations within the city made the relocation of open-air markets a very difficult proposition.

Significantly, these developments were taking place within the context of a period marked by great uncertainty. The unfolding of the French Revolutionary process in 1789 and over the years following introduced a series of challenges. The upheaval interrupted grain supplies to Barcelona, and the city experienced another major food riot in 1793. As in the Rebomboris del Pa four years earlier, collaboration between municipal authorities and guild leaders successfully put down the uprising without shattering the social order. Then the Napoleonic invasion of 1808 ushered in a more profound crisis. Barcelona was occupied by French troops until 1814, and its economic orientation was disfigured by the exigencies of the Peninsular War. When Spanish liberalism burst onto the political stage in Cádiz in 1812, the Barcelona committee that coordinated the fight against the French made a futile plea to the national Cortes for the restoration of the principality's historic liberties and governing institutions suppressed by the imposition of Bourbon rule at the outset of the eighteenth century.[5] Vain hopes of returning to a neo-foralist relationship with the Spanish state aside, more pressing challenges unfolded after the French had been driven back across the Pyrenees. The consolidation of liberalism and constitutionalism would prove long and complicated; political and social stability would be even more difficult to achieve.

Once released from captivity in France, Spain's restored monarch, Fernando VII (r. 1814–33) moved immediately to abrogate the Constitution of Cádiz.[6] In so doing, he reestablished absolutism, reauthorized the Inquisition, and reasserted that sovereignty rested in *his* hands rather than those of the people. Fernando VII's reign coincided with a period of severe economic stagnation, during which time Spain lost the bulk of its colonies to the Latin American independence movements, and thus most of its American markets as well.

Liberalism, especially among the ranks of army officers who had played so central a role in its definition and advancement during the Peninsular War, simmered for seven years before it boiled over in its first successful *pronunciamiento*.[7] In 1820, Colonel Rafael de Riego led a military uprising that forced the king to accept the 1812 Constitution and adhere to its provisions for governance through ministries accountable to an elected national Cortes. Riego and his followers were emboldened by their success. Their swift movement to transform Spanish political culture and open the way toward such measures as freedom of the press made it all the more urgent that Europe's greater forces of reaction coalesce to bring an end to the experiment known as the Liberal Triennium. And so it was that the forces of Louis XVIII of France, with the full diplomatic support of Britain, Austria, Russia, and Prussia, invaded Spain in April 1823. In six months' time, Louis XVIII's forces were able to achieve what Napoleon's army had not succeeded in doing in seven years. So the liberals were again driven from power and exiled.

Yet with absolutism re-imposed, the textile sector of the Catalan economy entered a period of recovery. After a brief lag, the processes of industrialization in Barcelona accelerated. In the late 1820s, mechanization of the textile industry intensified. By the 1830s, industrialists in Barcelona had five hundred spinning jennies of the Crompton pattern in operation, running sixty thousand spindles; steam-powered textile production spread rapidly in the decades that followed. Other types of manufacturing industries, such as soap-making, paper-making, flour-milling, and metallurgy, also grew and became mechanized.[8] As Busquets reminds us, "the pioneering countries in this innovative experience, known as the 'first-comers,' must include Catalonia, once again represented by the protagonism of its capital."[9] The city's working-class population expanded rapidly in response to these developments, with consequent problems of long hours, low wages, and poor housing and hygienic conditions following apace. It was at this point that visitors to the city dubbed Barcelona the "Manchester of Spain."[10] As elsewhere, adjusting the food-supply system to meet the needs of early industrial society emerged as a formidable challenge.

In these decades, Barcelona's open-air marketplaces formed an arc along one side of the city's core, extending from Sant Antoni Gate in the Raval to the Citadel in the Ribera.[11] In this swath of space within which the bulk of open-air food trade took place, there were seven epicenters: the Plaça del Pedró, the Pla de la Boqueria, the Plaça Beat Oriol, the Plaça Nova, the Plaça del Rei, the Plaça del Àngel, and El Born. Connected to or near these were specialized fish and meat markets. In addition to these epicenters, there was the Plaça de Sant Miquel food market in La Barceloneta, which stretched out beyond the walls into the port area. There were also the various stalls that comprised the Encants Públics, which sold everything from household goods and kitchen wares to used clothing and furnishings.[12] In essence, the city was mined with markets that wound along streets and around corners, interlacing like ribbons from one end of the arc to the other and beyond.

The congestion posed by the growth in the number of open-air food-market vendors gave authorities added incentive to consolidate their control. Each had a director, an agent known as the *Repesador,* to control weights and measures, and several guards to maintain order.[13] The municipality continued to set prices, monitor the exactitude of weighing devices, and, as in previous periods, attempted to ward off shortages.[14] In 1826, new municipal regulations set standards for the uniformity of market stalls and brought the city into the business of equipping individual vendors. Not only did the city build rows of identically covered stalls for fish vendors along Carme Street, extending from Las Ramblas, but it also estab-

lished a system that allowed all the vendors in the area to rent chairs, scales, aw-
nings, and other equipment from the municipality. Subsequently, rows of uniform
stalls with wooden bases and metal frames were built by the city for the butchers
at El Born Market.[15] In an attempt to hold individual licensed vendors accountable
for abuses in the weighing of goods sold, the 1826 regulations also involved greater
municipal efforts to control who was actually working in each stall.[16] Compliance,
though, proved difficult to secure. Nine years later, a public notice in the *Diario
de Barcelona* warned that regulations with respect to weights and measures in
markets and shops would be strictly enforced.[17]

As in a range of other areas, uniformity and rationalization were becoming increasingly important aims of municipal policy. But enforcement remained an ongoing challenge. In the 1830s, municipal authorities were admonishing vendors to
refrain from activities supposedly offensive or disruptive to the sensibilities of the
city's most refined inhabitants.[18] Regulations prohibiting the heating of prepared
foods at stalls, like those controlling the emissions from soap and candle factories,
reflected the municipality's ostensible concern for the olfactoral comfort of its citizens in a crowded city. With congestion growing, vendors were continuously chas-
tised by market guards for not adhering to the rules about blocking streets.[19] Police
especially pursued unlicensed ambulatory vendors who paid neither taxes nor stall-
permit fees. It is no wonder that people living nearest the marketplaces complained
about the noise emanating from the burgeoning open-air centers of food trade.[20]

In the meantime, there were dramatic shifts on the national stage that altered
the city's political landscape after 1833. With the death of Fernando VII, the crown
passed to his daughter, three-year-old Isabel II (r. 1833–68). The succession was
welcomed by liberal generals who saw the regency of the Queen Mother María
Cristina as a new opportunity to rid Spain of absolutism once and for all and to
participate in the re-formulation of the polity along the lines of the 1812 Constitution of Cádiz. Yet the forces of reaction were by no means ready to throw in
the towel. Rejecting Fernando VII's last-minute revocation of the Salic Law that
prohibited females from inheriting the crown, an apostolic, conservative, and
explicitly foralist movement coalesced in support of the late king's brother, Carlos. Bitterly opposed to both the revocation of the Salic Law and the secular and
centralizing vision of the liberal military officers who were sure to exercise great
influence in her government, the opposition to Isabel II's succession sparked what
would be the first of a series of Carlist civil wars. Especially popular in the northern regions, Carlism remained a significant variable in Catalan politics for the rest
of the century. Alongside this new violent dynastic division, vehement rivalries

within the liberal movement pitted moderate generals against their progressive counterparts in competing cycles of *pronunciamiento* intervention in government through the full length of Isabel II's thirty-five-year reign.

On the ground level—that is, in the streets and squares of Barcelona—yet another dynamic complicated the picture. Republicans, radicals, utopianists, nascent industrial working-class groups, and the lumpenproletariat coalesced periodically to form what historians term the "urban mob." Often an ill-defined population, they began in the mid-1830s to engage in more frequent, spontaneous, and direct violent action on an independent basis, in conjunction with, or in opposition to, any number of groups more formally engaged in the struggle for political control. One such episode of mob violence against industry, the Church, and military authorities governing the city created new space that spurred the reconfiguration of Barcelona's open-air markets.

### Enclosing the First Markets

Barcelona's municipal market-hall system began to take shape in the late 1830s within the fortified urban core. The initial shift away from open-air market trade to food retailing from within physically defined and delimited urban spaces was made possible by the sacking of ecclesiastic properties in waves of mob violence that broke out in 1835. Among the incinerated convents were Sant Josep along Las Ramblas and Santa Caterina in the Ribera. Not long after their razing, these two properties underwent a conversion from sacred to secular commercial use and were designated by authorities as the sites for the city's first enclosed market projects.

In keeping with the general pattern of revolutionary outbursts in the period, the 1835 upheavals, known as *bullangues,* took place in the summer, when the heat and the spread of illnesses related to it intensified popular frustrations. Underpinning the uprising was intensifying fear about the inroads being made by reactionary Carlism in the nearby town of Reus, divisions within the liberal movement, the dislocation of workers in the textile industry as a consequence of mechanization, and especially by rising food costs. Wheat prices had doubled in the two years leading up to the bullangues and the working classes were suffering from hunger.[21] The outburst opening the way for the first markets began in the city's bullring on July 25, 1835, Saint James Day, when the crowd, unhappy with the matador's performance, stormed the arena and beat the last bull to death. From there, the mob turned its attention to the Church, an obvious target for its support of Carlism and its control of significant property in what was by then a terribly overcrowded city. The sacking and burning of seven major convents and monasteries took place alongside the murder of friars and nuns, while a completely outnumbered garrison stood helplessly paralyzed before the explosion of rage. By July 27, the wave of arson extended to the Bonaplata "El Vapor" textile factory, which despite efforts of the militia to protect the structure was burned to the ground in an attack of Luddism.[22] The city's statue of Fernando VII was pulled down and smashed as an act signifying the end of tolerance for absolutism. The violence continued for more than a week. Before it was quelled, the military governor, General Pere Nolasc de Bassa, was shot and defenestrated, that is, "flung dead or dying over the balcony" into a crowd of demonstrators. Then the rioters dragged his body through the streets of the city "to be burned on a pyre formed of the files of the commissariat of police."[23]

Even after the uprising was put down, widespread anti-authoritarian spirit persisted into the autumn of 1835. On October 7, when an alderman attempted to clear a group of female vendors from blocking part of Las Ramblas with their stalls, the market women responded defiantly. They told him that he had no authority and did not represent anyone because he had been appointed to his seat by decree rather than having been popularly elected. As Rosa M. Garcia i Domènech noted, the market women's response reflected the context of a changing political culture in the city, but also the fact that "vendors did exactly what they wanted to do from time to time."[24]

A year later, through what was known as the *desamortización de Mendizábal*, the government confiscated Church lands held in entail all across Spain. In Barcelona, 80 percent of the ecclesiastic properties, including those destroyed in anticlericalist violence, went up for sale. The sixteenth-century Convent of Sant Josep was one that suffered the ire of the 1835 urban mob and was then purchased by the city. Efforts to move food retailing off Las Ramblas, begun with the royal visit of Carlos IV in 1802, had been renewed by municipal authorities in 1823. But Church resistance to the incursion of food vendors into the gardens of the convent was strong, and the market along Las Ramblas was not easily displaced. The city government finally secured the keys to the burnt convent on January 3, 1836, and by March 24 full-scale relocation of the vendors into the Sant Josep property began.[25] By June 7 there were 340 stalls in the new market, which was popularly called La Boqueria, and officially, Mercado de San José.[26] The market soon became one of the most important and emblematic food-retailing institutions in the city. Along with the relocation of the stalls to the new space set off from Las Ramblas, a prolonged debate ensued over the nature and dimensions of the structure that was to enclose the vendors.

Nearer to the city's historic ecclesiastic and political nucleus, the gothic Convent of Santa Caterina had also gone up in flames in the 1835 violence and then been acquired by the city through the *desamortización* auctions.[27] Though no market had been located there previously, authorities moved to construct one that would absorb a number of small markets and ambulatory vendors operating along the various streets and in squares of the Ribera neighborhood and in the Plaça de Sant Augustí Vell. Santa Caterina thus became a central node within what was becoming a tri-polar market system in the first half of the nineteenth century. Consolidated from the seven earlier epicenters of market trade, Santa Caterina became, alongside La Boqueria and El Born, one of three concentrated points for retail food distribution in the city.[28] The designation of the first two of these spaces for the construction of covered or enclosed markets represented an important step in the rationalization and modernization of the food system in Barcelona. Undertaken before extramural expansion, these projects constituted the first phase of the modern market-building process in the city. Yet they were distinct from what would come later, in that these first two structures exhibited an architectural incoherence resulting from the adoption of multiple and sometimes contradictory plans for construction over time.

The initial design of La Boqueria involved a large rectangular plaza providing covered space for vendors—excepting those selling fruits and vegetables—along arched porticoes that formed its perimeter. But this soon proved insufficient, and a series of plans to provide more covered space were adopted by the city in the decades that followed.[29] Through most of the nineteenth century, La Boqueria was equipped with what can only be described as partial, even makeshift, coverings. The exception was the fish department, which was located in the center of the plaza and protected by a metal roof structure, one of the first such projects built in that period.[30] So La Boqueria Market was initially enclosed but only covered in a provisional sense. By the 1840s, it accommodated 650 stalls of various kinds, 43 shops, and more than a hundred fishmongers' tables, which made it the most important market in the city.[31] It was not until 1914, though, that its extant metal roof, made by La Maquinista Terrestre y Marítima, was installed.

Santa Caterina Market, a somewhat more coherently planned structure, was also slow in coming to fruition. The foundation stone was laid in 1844, but in 1846 the city adopted an expanded building design.[32] At the market's inauguration in 1848, the construction was only three-quarters complete. Even so, at that time

Santa Caterina already had room for 208 fruit and vegetable stalls, 72 fresh fish stalls, 40 poultry stalls, 24 salted fish shops, and 14 grain and bread shops. But it took builders fifteen more years to finish their work.[33] Upon completion, Santa Caterina's rectangular structure with the large covered interior patio resembled, on a smaller scale, the Parisian market of Saint-Germain, an architectural model copied in various European cities.[34] Still, Santa Caterina was slow to take off as a successful commercial venture because Ribera consumers mostly continued to prefer shopping at El Born's open-air marketplace, which had for so long operated as the neighborhood's central provisioning space. Santa Caterina was only able to surpass its nearby rival in terms of the size of its vendor population in the mid-1860s, by which time it had attracted 532 vendors, as compared to El Born's cadre of 384.[35]

These first two market projects had the effect of further institutionalizing the ground gained by urban retail vendors over the previous decades. By the 1850s, stalls had largely passed into the hands of urban dwellers, and rural producer-vendors had been relegated to a more marginal role. One implication of this was that wholesale trade in produce began to expand as a distinct layer of the market system, and increasing numbers of middlemen became involved in the business. With the guilds stripped of what remained of their traditional power by the Spanish government in 1834, food retailing fell under the authority of the somewhat more liberalized Commercial Code of 1829. Within this context, and in order to meet the rising demand for food, the markets of Barcelona began to attract new groups to the lower ranks of the city's commercial classes to work as vendors.

As in other European cities, the construction of the Santa Caterina and La Boqueria markets involved strategies for resolving problems associated with adequately provisioning the population with food under conditions of growing urban density in the early industrial era. Public authorities were driven to improve the system of provisioning in order to ward off popular unrest; the fact that covered markets brought much-needed revenue into the municipal treasury provided further impetus for their building. Yet market halls in and of themselves were not an innovative concept. In many European cities since the thirteenth century, specialized and usually wholesale market halls had been built to accommodate trade in cloth, grain, glass, and other goods. Barcelona itself had the Llotja stock exchange/trading house where cereals and a range of other commodities had been wholesaled since the fourteenth century. It was not the concept of the market hall but rather the idea of building such structures for food retailing that represented an organizational, administrative, and commercial innovation.[36]

By not undertaking the process until after 1835, Barcelona was late in pursuing this model. Retail food-market halls had begun to be built in England and in
France in the late eighteenth century.[37] James Schmiechen and Kenneth Carls
trace the pattern of retail market-hall construction in Britain, finding that "the
increased building activity in [the] 1770s and 1780s was probably a result of
the increased food supply and population—or even a response to food riots—it
speeded up even more after 1801 and through the 1820s and 1830s."[38] Likewise,
eight retail market halls had opened in Paris in the second half of the eighteenth
century before more concentrated and intense efforts to build a fully fledged
system were undertaken under Napoleonic rule.[39] In the early nineteenth century, Paris completed four new market-hall projects, among them Saint-Martin
(1811–18), Les Carmes (1813), and Saint-Germain (1816–25).[40] Across France, 253
market projects in 122 cities were undertaken between 1801 and 1851. The Parisian masonry markets of the first third of the nineteenth century, with Italianate
ornamentations, were the key inspirations for Barcelona and many other cities.[41]
La Boqueria's underlying design used an architectural language imitative of the
French market styles, though with its own eclectic romantic neoclassical lines.[42]
Santa Caterina, as we have seen, was even more explicitly imitative. But as Oyón,
Guàrdia, and Fava argue, these first two structures in Barcelona, not finished
until midcentury, were all but anachronistic by the time they were completed.[43]
The vanguard in Britain and France had by then become metal and glass markets
reminiscent of train stations and world's fair pavilions. Barcelona's municipal authorities embraced this new model only in the second phase of the market-building
program that took off in the last quarter of the nineteenth century.

## Markets as Symbolic Capital

From their outset, Barcelona's new market-hall structures reflected a strengthened
commitment to the already well-established regulatory tradition of public control
over food supply. Yet the rhetorical scripts followed at the ceremonies marking the
construction and opening of La Boqueria and Santa Caterina markets also indicate
that the liberal public authorities acting in defense of Isabel II and the Queen Regent María Cristina had embraced a vision that appropriated and exalted markets
as a new form of symbolic capital.[44] Political authorities at both the local and the
national level, in fact, pointed to the new markets as physical manifestations of the
larger efforts to rationalize the economy, and they organized rituals around them
that were designed to legitimize liberal rule. We see this when on March 19, 1840,

Barcelona's highest-ranking political, military, and religious figures gathered at La Boqueria for the official groundbreaking of the newly relocated and reorganized market. While the ceremonies included a procession from the town hall to the market that resembled the public rituals associated with religious holidays, the task at hand involved legitimizing the re-appropriation of Church property for secular use.[45] As part of the groundbreaking, authorities buried a cache of coins, including gold Mexican pesetas that linked La Boqueria to Spain's imperial past and forecast the future riches that the market would generate for the city.[46] Because mob violence had opened up the space for the new market, such efforts to build popular legitimacy were urgent. Naming the new market after the convent would prove a vain proposition, but its exaltation as a symbol of the benefits to the public that could accrue from liberal commitment to imposing order and rationalization in the food-retailing sector were more tenable. The public ritualization of the space served to integrate food-market trade more firmly within the emerging liberal political culture of the period. We can also see the symbolic power that Barcelona's market halls were assuming for the young and fragile liberal state in the groundbreaking and inaugural ceremonies held for Santa Caterina Market. Here too the municipal rituals celebrating the new market took place in the wake of new rounds of unprecedented urban mob violence.

In the early 1840s, a range of diverse social and ideological groups in Barcelona, joined by their opposition to the free-trading anglophiles in Madrid, staged a series of revolutionary uprisings. Like the others of the period, these popular upheavals were triggered by rising prices of wheat and other basic foodstuffs, and thus by the spread of hunger in the city. In these decades, protests against the dreaded *consumo* excise tax on basic necessities became more common among industrial laborers.[47] Worker distress in response to mechanization, low wages, urban crowding, and strains on the food-distribution system were all linked. The combination of problems made the maintenance of order a serious challenge for urban authorities.

The planning and construction of Santa Caterina in the early 1840s took place within the context of a specific set of political circumstances. In their contest for power, moderate and progressive generals each sought to exert control over the Queen Regent's government during the years of Isabel II's minority. One particular figure, General Baldomero Espartero, who had made his reputation fighting the Carlists on their own guerrilla terms, seized power in the summer of 1840. As a progressive-liberal, his rule was initially welcomed by a throng of eighty thousand in the streets of Barcelona. But the political romance was short-lived; support for

Espartero crumbled as soon as he moved to endorse free-trade proposals that ran contrary to the protectionist policies advocated across the socioeconomic spectrum in Catalonia, and especially by the bourgeoisie of Barcelona and the nascent workers' associations.

Throughout his two-year tenure as regent for the young queen, General Espartero faced the seizure of power by republican and egalitarian committees in Barcelona.[48] In October 1841, angry mobs attacked the Citadel and demolished part of the fortress's walls in an act of widespread ire against Espartero and against centralism itself. Once the garrison had restored order by force of arms, unrest continued to simmer. Just over a year later, a much more serious uprising broke out. Sometimes called "the Revolt of the Pastrycooks," it was initially led by what Fernández-Armesto describes as "a service industry proletariat . . . in rebellion against its bourgeois masters as much as Madrid."[49] Fueled by the republican press, the appeal widened to produce "an old fashioned riot converted into a political movement by an unholy alliance of which protectionism was the only shared policy."[50] The urban mob was joined in throwing up and manning barricades by Carlists, moderate-liberals, Catalanists, members of the petite bourgeoisie, and other unlikely bedfellows. The insurrection went on for weeks and was only quelled when Espartero's forces rained cannon fire upon the city from Montjuïc, destroying some four hundred buildings in the conflagration.

Still, General Espartero's hold on Barcelona remained tenuous at best. By the summer of 1843, new levels of unrest intensified as rounds of attack and reprisal were exchanged between the garrison and the revolutionary committees' popular militia. This newest phase of the egalitarian anticentrist uprising was known as *La Jamància*. Its name was generally attributed to the enthusiasm that the hungry showed for swelling the ranks of the popular militia not so much out of ideological commitment but rather in order to gain access to rations.[51] The revolutionaries took control for a period of eighty-one days between September 2 and November 20, 1843, during which time the city's elite and its political administration retreated to the nearby village of Gràcia. Meanwhile, the military repeatedly bombarded the city from the fortress on Montjuïc and awaited the arrival of troops from Madrid.[52] In the interim, another *pronunciamiento* put an abrupt end to Espartero's progressive-liberal regime. Under the leadership of General Ramón Narváez, the moderate-liberals declared that thirteen-year-old Isabel II had finally come of age, and they seized power on her behalf.[53] Still, the uprising continued in Barcelona.

Connections between the Jamància and the stress on the urban provisioning system were explicit. The name *Jamància* itself, the songs of the revolutionaries, street theater, and even the militia uniform proclaimed the urgency of the food question to all those involved. On November 5, one diarist recording the events noted that not much had happened that day, except that the revolutionaries had come out to sing the "Chirivi," which was among the many hymns expressing popular sentiments. One of its verses went as follows: "To Cristina and Narváez / and to all the moderates / inside of a fry pan / we'll cook the whole lot up."[54] Likewise, in a dramatic piece dating to the uprising, republican workers discussed their demands with a factory owner. Xich, the laborer, declared: we want them to lower the cost of "the meat, the bread, the wine, the tobacco. We want liberty and an end to indirect taxes [on food]." The factory owner answers: "How, then, will all the expenditures of the state be paid?" Bernat, a second worker, retorts: "Let the rich pay it all, we have to eat."[55] In his reflection on the *Jamància*, Guillem Martínez asserts that "in effect, this revolt was filled with hymns and songs in which everything was eaten: the enemy, their projectiles," etc.[56] He adds that "everything was eaten except that which was usually eaten"—in other words, "there was hunger."[57] Even the Jamància militia uniforms, such as they were, stood as a testament to the centrality of food in the uprising. Their red *barretina* freedom caps were decorated with human skeletons stamped from tin; from their chests they hung a frying pan that presumably provided some protection but more ostensibly served as a symbolic endorsement of the song that called for the moderate forces of reaction, including the queen mother herself, to be cooked up and eaten by the revolutionaries.[58]

Using fresh troops from Madrid, General Narváez's moderate-liberals regained control by the end of the third week in November 1843. As Fernández-Armesto writes, they "marched in to bludgeon the city."[59] Not coincidentally, less than a year after order had been restored, authorities organized ceremonies to mark the groundbreaking for the new Santa Caterina market hall. The date of the event was set for October 10, 1844, to coordinate with and to celebrate Isabel II's fourteenth birthday, in whose honor the market was initially named.[60] In doing so, the ruling moderate-liberals used the occasion to help build the case for the legitimacy of centralized control over municipal government from Madrid. Among those in attendance were the highest-ranking military and political authorities, all the foreign consuls to the city, and other persons of distinction. As part of the ceremony's conclusion, the group shouted *vivas* to Her Majesty, to the constitution, and to the queen mother, now removed in public rhetoric from both frying pan and fire.[61]

How all this was received by the popular classes of the Ribera neighborhood is another question, especially given the fact that the physical havoc wrought by cannon fire upon the urban landscape by the victory of the generals ruling from Madrid remained so clearly visible. Such circumstances added urgency to the market ceremonies and to the careful crafting of the rhetorical script. Not surprisingly, the moderates drew upon old forms of loyalty to the Church and to the Crown in hopes of rebuilding support for both in an urban polity that had expressed vehement anticlericalism and anticentralism. Still, it must have been the first time in history that a royal birthday celebration was held at the site of a convent that had been burned to a crisp in a fit of popular urban rage. As in the case of La Boqueria's groundbreaking four years earlier, there is no evidence of commemoration for the victims of the violence in the ceremonies. What was venerated instead was the promise of a more orderly and rationalized system of food retailing. The moderates seized upon the concept of the retail market hall as a sort of provisioning panacea and as symbolic capital to underpin the legitimacy of their rule. Given the still-looming threat of Carlism and the rising power of the urban mob in the political process, opportunities to call attention to the achievements of the state could hardly be passed up.

The inaugural ceremonies that marked the official public opening of Santa Caterina Market four years later were infused with similar rhetoric and imagery. On August 15, 1848, while much of Europe north of the Pyrenees was caught in the century's most significant wave of revolutionary violence, and in the midst of a second Carlist War that questioned the legitimacy of Isabel II's rule, dignitaries again made their way from the town hall to an elegantly draped platform in a procession led by the municipal band. Before the public assembled at the doors of the market, Mayor Domingo Portefaix y Páez emphasized the benefits that Santa Caterina represented to the popular classes of the city, adding that the public should not lose sight of either the aesthetic or the practical concerns that had been embodied in its construction.[62]

Beyond standing as monuments to the government's ostensible commitment to the well-being of the citizenry, the construction of La Boqueria and Santa Caterina marked the point at which authorities began to adopt the view that market halls could serve as physical rallying points around which to conduct rituals designed to reinforce loyalty to liberalism at the municipal and national levels. The ceremonialization of market construction, and especially the inclusion of religious devotions and expressions of loyalty to the Crown, were emblematic of the wider usage by the state of old familiar symbols of authority to legitimate newer forms of liberal rule.

Thus, by 1848 Barcelona's provisioning system had undergone the first phase of its nineteenth-century transformation. Food retailing began its move off the city's streets into more highly regulated physical structures, which in turn had begun to assume new political significance. These interrelated processes continued to gain momentum in the years after 1854, when the Bourbon fortifications were razed and Barcelona was finally able to stretch its boundaries across the wide plain that had for so long separated it from its surrounding villages and from the ring of hills that lay just beyond.

## *The New Metropolis*

The problems of maintaining order in the face of simmering popular unrest had intensified in Barcelona over the course of the 1840s and early 1850s, when the population swelled to 175,000 and pressure within the city's walls reached astonishing levels. With 859 persons per hectare in 1859, the city's population density, "one of the highest in Europe,"[63] was nearly ten times that of London and more than twice that of Paris and Madrid.[64] Barcelona had become a veritable powder keg in which political uprisings, social unrest, and worker protests were easily triggered by the challenge that the poor faced in acquiring adequate levels of food. Thus Engels's famous commentary on the intensity of class conflict in nineteenth-century Barcelona was that it had "seen more barricade fighting than any other city in the world."[65]

Even with the opening of La Boqueria and Santa Caterina markets, significant numbers of food vendors continued to clog the streets and plazas in various areas. While La Boqueria housed 808 vendors in the mid-1850s, Santa Caterina had 291; together they afforded space for only 61 percent of the licensed vendors in the city. The still open-air El Born alone could account at that time for an additional 549, or 30 percent of the city's vendors; the Pedró and La Barceloneta open-air markets combined included another 153 stalls.[66] Given that ambulatory vendors accounted for significant additional commerce in food, the need for new market halls remained evident to the urban planners of the period.[67] At the same time, the main impediment to extending the market-hall model of food retailing in Barcelona remained the lack of available space within the city's walls.

Barcelona's fortifications had long been hated symbols of Bourbon centralism. With industrialization, they became the targets of intense polemical debate. The walls were viewed by Progressive Liberal pamphleteers, hygienists, clerics, and residents as a noose that strangled expansion, fomented epidemic disease, and prevented Barcelona from realizing both its potential and its destiny. Still, the moderate-liberals, who dominated government during the reign of Isabel II, clung tightly to the model of Bourbon centralization. They continued to view the fortifications as necessary for the preservation of order in Barcelona, adamantly defending them as civil and military necessities. Such an impasse clearly limited the extension of the retail market-hall model and afforded few viable solutions to the growing problems of overcrowding, inadequate housing, and poor hygiene. As long as the government in Madrid held the fortifications to be sacrosanct, the municipality's endeavors to reconfigure urban space beyond the walls remained severely limited.

The turning point came in the summer of 1854 when a series of factors converged to begin the process of demolishing the walls. In late June, a military *pronunciamiento* of revolutionary proportions set off popular uprisings in numerous cities, including Barcelona. In an attempt to restore order, Isabel II brought progressive General Espartero back to power. Joined by prominent moderate leaders in key cabinet positions, Espartero formed what was termed a liberal-union alliance to draft a new constitution, which among other measures would provide greater degrees of municipal autonomy and the direct election of mayors.[68] To a much greater degree than the moderates, the progressives relied on the support of a broad range of urban groups and were less committed to centralization in a strict sense.[69] Progressives were also influenced by the English hygienicist movement and thus tended to view Barcelona's walls as posing a grave danger to public health as well as to social order.

Radical enthusiasm for the prospect of change served to ignite new rounds of violence in the streets of Barcelona. On the night of July 14, 1854, Luddite attacks targeted eight factories. Military reprisals followed, with rounds of public executions on Las Ramblas. Thereafter, textile workers went on strike to demand a range of reforms, including wage increases, shorter hours, and a prohibition on the new *selfactinas* (mechanical spinning mules), whose increasing adoption reduced the need for human labor in the mills. Adding to the crisis, cholera struck the city in late July; as the death toll mounted, the elites fled to the countryside. By the end of the month striking textile workers had negotiated a settlement, but they could not return to work because the captains of industry had closed their factories and left town.[70]

Mounting levels of hunger among a population that had gone without wages for weeks created a dangerous scenario. Municipal authorities began distributing food rations in the form of soup.[71] But as Antoni Nicolau and Albert Cubeles argue, the more urgent question remained what to do with the population that had stayed in Barcelona, who could not return to work, and were threatened by the epidemic; "deactivating that bomb" meant devising a plan to provide employment and sustenance without generating further debate. "And, if there was one question that nobody in Barcelona debated, it was that of the walls."[72] The desire to see the fortifications destroyed cut across class lines in the city; bourgeoisie, shopkeepers, and artisans saw the walls as an impediment to commercial growth, while the work-' ing classes expected that their destruction would make cheaper and more plentiful housing available to those of limited means. So on the morning of August 7, five days before news of the official authorization from Madrid arrived, authorities converged on Las Ramblas to announce that the long-awaited demolition of the walls was about to commence.[73] The announcement was met with popular jubilation. Upon hearing the news, thousands streamed out of their homes and workplaces to attack the walls with pickaxes and hammers. The city then moved immediately to hire brigades of unemployed men. By the beginning of October, the social tension and the cholera epidemic had all but passed. Though the demolition itself took more than a decade to complete, plans to expand the city and to implement concepts of rational urbanism on a massive scale were already under way.

The civil engineer Ildefons Cerdà's *Plano de Reforma y Ensanche,* which served as a blueprint for the urbanization of the area between the old walled city and the surrounding villages, was not initially met with much in the way of popular support.[74] Earlier, the municipality had held a public competition to select the best design for the layout of the expansion, and Cerdà's plan lost out to that of Antoni Rovira i Trias. When the moderate-liberals again seized power in 1856, the central government shelved Rovira's plan, and Cerdà's was imposed instead by royal decree. The move was fundamentally a show of moderate political muscle, which had the effect of reminding all concerned that Barcelona's aspirations for greater municipal autonomy would be strictly curtailed. Yet despite its imposition from Madrid, Cerdà's plan for what was called the *Eixample* eventually gained widespread acceptance. Today it is hailed by such towering figures in the field of architecture, urban planning, and design as Joan Busquets as "a paradigm model for new towns built in southern Europe" and "a pioneering work in modern urban development theory."[75]

Busquets writes that Cerdà was influenced directly by Claude-Henri Saint-Simon and that his "generation of engineers and architects began to realise that . . . the new urban planning science had to include a social component."[76] They were working, as well, in a period shaped by ideas set forth by the utopian-socialists Charles Fourier and Robert Owen, when the problems of intensifying class conflict generated new proposals.[77] Cerdà's theories were built around three basic components: hygienism, circulation, and the aim of extending the city in a homogeneous and egalitarian fashion across the plain of Barcelona. His design for the Eixample called for nine hundred octagonal blocks of development and included provisions for a wide array of city services.[78] It differed in some very fundamental ways from the model for nineteenth-century urban growth laid out by Haussmann in Paris in that it left the old city untouched and proposed the design of a vast new urban space in which all the social classes could find healthy and affordable housing.

In this way, Barcelona began to assume the shape of what Busquets calls the "compact city," which became a prototype for Mediterranean urban development.[79] In his words, "Cities in the south of Europe have quite specific formal characteristics and processes of historical foundation; the density and compactness of their urban form and their evolution by means of extension rather than remodeling sets them apart from the European cities of the north."[80] In Barcelona, the project for expanding the city into the plain provided a blank canvas upon which basic infrastructural systems and structures could be drawn before the rest of the picture was filled in. When the municipality first called for Eixample development plans, they specified that they be designed for broad public access to churches, schools, markets, baths, fountains, and laundries.[81] Cerdà embraced these principles in that his plan called for city services distributed in a polycentric hierarchy of zones, districts, and sectors. Each ten-by-ten-block district was to have its own market hall, every twenty-five-block unit its own school, and every block one hundred trees. Cerdà envisioned a uniform city in which social distinctions would become irrelevant. Streets were to be of identical width, chamfered blocks of identical size, artistically adorned buildings uniform in height, and no area of the new city socially distinct from another. Cerdà's Eixample was intended to create a vast urban space where industrial workers, lower-middle-class groups, and the bourgeoisie could live side by side in social harmony. If Cerdà's project had been fully implemented according to plan, we would have to look no further for an explanation of why Barcelona ended up with so many food-market halls.

### The Market System Emerges

The razing of the Bourbon walls and the development of the Eixample neighborhood presented municipal authorities with new challenges. The first phase in the transformation of Barcelona's food-retailing system had involved municipal responses to growing urban density. The second phase, extending from 1854 to 1898, involved efforts to cope with growing urban scale. Barcelona's population more than doubled from less than 200,000 to more than half a million in this period, and its urban morphology changed in some very drastic ways.[82] In developing the vast Eixample beyond the old Bourbon walls, and then in annexing nearby towns and villages, Barcelona became a metropolis with a much larger number of neighborhoods, each with a distinct character and orientation. As part of the development plan, municipal authorities moved to construct a series of market halls to serve consumers who had moved into the new areas, though not as many as Cerdà had called for.

The building of the Eixample proceeded slowly through the 1860s. But in the decades that followed, speculation and disregard for the plan led to development well beyond what Cerdà originally envisioned. Urban rents had long been an important source of wealth for elites, and the opening of new space in Barcelona posed rich opportunities for exploitation. Eventually, Cerdà's blocks, which were meant to have 67,200 square meters of built-up space, had on average 294,771.61 square meters instead.[83] The utopianist vision of a socially integrated city was lost in the process. The construction of a railroad, completed in 1863, linked the old city core from the newly built Plaça de Catalunya with the nearby village of Sarrià but divided the Eixample into two increasingly differentiated districts. The most affluent bourgeoisie settled to the northeast of the rail line, concentrating near the broad and prestigious Passeig de Gràcia. This area, known as the Right, or Dreta Eixample, featured numerous works of Antoni Gaudí and his generation of aesthetic innovators, and today it constitutes what has been called "a virtual museum of art nouveau architecture."[84] To the southwest of the railroad, a mixed residential and industrial zone developed that became known as the Left, or Esquerra de l'Eixample. Cerdà's plan failed to anticipate the problems of implementation, especially how to limit real-estate speculation. This was particularly apparent with the fate of the proposed inclusion of open park areas running through the middle of each of the Eixample's octagonal blocks.

While Cerdà's ambitious aims were never fully realized, Barcelona's municipal governments nonetheless demonstrated considerable commitment to one important element embodied in the civil engineer's vision of the new city—social services should ideally be distributed evenly across the urban landscape, and like schools, municipally operated food-market halls should be understood as basic components of the public infrastructural network. Broader municipal support for this concept certainly predated Cerdà and was embodied in the initial call for Eix-ample proposals. Yet from the beginning of the 1870s, new energy and enthusiasm was invested in developing a citywide food market-hall system based on the French designs of Victor Baltard, the architect of the Parisian Halles-Centrales.[85] Accord-ing to Guàrdia and Oyón, Baltard's project represented a "Copernican shift" in European market-hall architecture.[86] Including ten pavilions covering twenty-two acres, the Halles departed from earlier British iron market halls featuring façades that obscured their structures with adornments and stylistic distractions. Built in 1854, the Halles more closely resembled the new iron and glass train stations and world's fair pavilions, such as London's Crystal Palace. Baltard's market halls fea-tured height and transparency and were designed for the rationalized movement of people through them. Baltard-type metal markets with visible structures were imitated in Italy and became widely popular in Spain after 1868.[87] The process of adoption and adaptation in Barcelona involved architects and engineers visiting European capitals to study metal market-hall construction and design. Various foreign parties and firms, mainly from France, likewise formulated proposals for the development of a network of metal market halls for Barcelona in those same years.[88]

In May 1871, municipal architect Josep Artigas issued a crucial report recom-mending improvements for Barcelona's markets to the city's Public Works Com-mission. Artigas analyzed the central role that La Boqueria and Santa Caterina had assumed within the city's food-retailing system and called for the development of a "solid and consistent network of markets."[89] Thereafter, municipal policy began to reflect sincere commitment to implementing the Parisian polynuclear model. Designed to facilitate food-shopping proximity, the vision departed from what had become the pattern of market-hall building in much of Britain, Central Europe, and Scandinavia, where consumers travelled into city centers to purchase their provisions. In contrast, the Parisian model—embraced in France more broadly, but also in Budapest, Vienna, and a half-dozen cities in Spain—privileged the advantages of having a central market with neighborhood and district markets situated more or less evenly across the urban landscape.[90] The Parisian system set a high benchmark: in addition to the Halles' ten pavilions that combined wholesale and retail space, the city built thirty-two other metal markets to serve individual neighborhoods. Within such a context, consumers shopped closer to home, along-side neighbors, and from individuals with whom they were more likely to develop personal relationships.

In a much more coherent architectural program than that which characterized the first efforts at market building in Barcelona, five grand new metal market halls were erected between 1876 and 1888. These markets dramatically extended the food-retailing infrastructure of the burgeoning metropolis and played on Baltard's designs. The first two, El Born and Sant Antoni, were located on the outer edge of what had been the walled city, opening in 1876 and 1882 respectively. In 1884, La Barceloneta's market hall was completed. Both La Concepció and Hostafrancs were inaugurated in 1888 and, like the others, assumed their position within the ranks of city's monumental complex. It was a veritable flurry of market building according to a new style and approach that increasingly embraced light, ventilation, and movement. In Madrid, the commitment to and process of building metal market halls ran several years ahead of Barcelona, although there private ownership was more extensive and the municipality exerted much less influence in terms of design and management.[91]

The first metal market hall in Barcelona was built to house El Born's vendors. Work on the market began in 1874 and involved collaboration between the architect Josep Fontserè i Mestre and the engineer J. M. Cornet i Mas. The structure was built adjacent to the old open-air El Born Market, enclosing an area of 7,893 square meters.[92] Designed with a visible iron structure, the market featured glass-shuttered windows and skylights, along with a ceramic roof comprised of green, yellow, blue, and white tiles. It included four naves. The largest was flanked by two smaller parallel ones whose extension was interrupted midway by a fourth that sat perpendicular to the others. In the center, an octagonal cupola adorned the roof and allowed for additional light and ventilation. El Born followed the architectural style of Baltard's markets: it was functionalist but also included a variety of decorative elements in iron and local materials.[93]

Barcelona's second metal market hall was built just beyond the old Sant Antoni Gate and was designed to serve the growing population of the Left Eixample. It absorbed the open-air food vendors still selling in the nearby Plaça del Pedró, which the municipal architect, Josep Artigas, had in 1871 proclaimed to be incongruous with the standards to which municipal markets in a city of Barcelona's importance should adhere.[94] Designed by Antoni Rovira i Trias and built by the veteran engineer of El Born, J. M. Cornet i Mas, Sant Antoni was inaugurated in 1882. Occupying a space of 7,741 square meters, it was nearly as large as El Born and shared some of its design elements.[95] Comprised of two perpendicular naves of equal size arranged as a cruciform, the market was crowned by an octagonal cupola at its center. As Pere Joan Ravetllat and Carme Ribas observe, the market reproduced "in both geometry and scale, the alignment of a street crossing," and its cupola "replicates a typical intersection in the Cerdà grid."[96]

In quick succession over the course of the six years following Sant Antoni's completion, three more metal market halls went up. La Barceloneta, La Concepció, and Hostafrancs markets were all smaller in scale and conceptualized as food-retailing centers that would serve narrower neighborhood-based clienteles. In the case of La Concepció, a certain irony unfolded over time in that the market both fit the ideals underlying Cerdà's aims more closely than any other in the city but also defied them with impudence. The block on which La Concepció sits was designed to be a nucleus of social and cultural services for the neighborhood. In addition to the market and a church, a public school and the municipal music conservatory were located there. But contrary to Cerdà's vision of an Eixample that minimalized social differences, La Concepció became such a highly prestigious market that few among the popular classes—unless dressed in a maid or chauffeur's uniform—would presume to go shopping there. Some even called it the "aristocrats' market."[97]

After the first five metal halls opened, the city was vested with the beginnings of its polynuclear system, which included a total of seven markets, including the older La Boqueria and Santa Caterina structures. Then, between 1897 and 1921, Barcelona acquired additional market halls through the annexation of nearby towns that had grown up on the plain outside the city's walls. These areas located along the periphery of the Eixample were gobbled up in a deliberate program of metropolitanism. Barcelona's municipal government thus inherited and took over the management of four pre-existing metal market halls including Gràcia's La Llibertat[98] and L'Abaceria Central,[99] Sant Martí de Provençals' El Clot and La Unió, and later, that of Sarrià.[100] Ongoing growth drove the additional construction of market halls in the newly annexed districts, with Sant Gervasi, Sants, Sant Andreu, and Galvany market halls inaugurated as food-retailing centers between 1912 and 1927. Most of the markets built after the turn of the century were constructed at least partially of reinforced concrete and thus departed from the style and structural bases more common in the last quarter of the nineteenth century. More significantly, in continuing to extend the city's network of markets, Barcelona broke from its earlier pattern of imitating developments in Northern Europe. While market-hall building in France, Britain, and Germany slowed after 1900, and markets in many cities closed, construction continued in Barcelona, through much of Spain, and in the broader Latin European region.

## Monuments to Industrialization

Barcelona's city council pursued market-hall construction in the last quarter of the nineteenth century, as in the preceding decades, for various reasons, including political expediency. At inaugurations, authorities stepped up rhetorical efforts to use food-market halls as symbolic capital. On the occasion of both El Born's 1876 and Sant Antoni's 1882 inaugurations, they pointed to the completion of market projects as evidence of the growth of the domestic iron and steel industries, a sector of the industrial economy whose development had been impeded by the lack of good coking coal in Spain. Both built by La Maquinista Terrestre i Marítima,[101] these market halls were hailed in public ceremonies as a triumph in the history of the nation's metallurgical capabilities.

When El Born's market hall was officially inaugurated, Spain was just emerging from an eight-year period of upheaval. Amidst a financial crisis and popular uprisings all across Spain, the queen had fled the country in 1868. After shopping around for a monarch, the generals had agreed upon Amadeo de Savoy, son of Italy's King Victor Immanuel, who after just one year declared Spain ungovernable and left. He has been called the only monarch in history to have gone on strike. Following Amadeo's departure, another popular uprising led to the declaration of a republic. But this too crumbled into cantonalism within a relatively short time.

The December 1874 restoration of the Bourbon monarchy under Isabel II's son, Alfonso XII, was a turning point, particularly in that it brought a halt to the incessant pattern of military intervention through the use of the *pronunciamiento* uprisings that had defined the reign of Isabel II. While still involving alternating cycles of political power, heirs of the moderate and progressive-liberal camps produced a system that was more stable than the regime of the generals preceding it, but one with notable weaknesses nonetheless. At the very inception of the Bourbon Restoration, with El Born's market hall still not fully completed, inaugural ceremonies were set in motion so that the new regime could monumentalize the structure and declare it a symbol of modernity and official commitment to the commonweal.[102]

The rhetorical script of El Born's inauguration emphasized the bond between the municipal and the national polity. Linking the new market to the nation-state at its highest levels, the events were scheduled for November 28, 1876, to coincide with the occasion of the young monarch's nineteenth birthday.[103] The ceremonies began with a procession from the town hall and the usual ritualized displays of pomp and power. Speaking from a platform festooned with velvet and gold cloth and the municipal coat of arms, Mayor Don Manuel Girona's speech was charged with Spanish nationalist rhetoric. The mayor declared that the new El Born Market had been conceived, designed, and built by Spaniards. The civil governor, Casto Ibáñez de Aldecoa, representing the king at the ceremony, added that the construction of the new market illustrated the vitality of Spanish industry. He extended the king's congratulations to the municipal corporation for having built the market and then led the crowd in a round of *vivas* to His Majesty. Thereafter, the bishop blessed the structure and, seizing upon the occasion, wed it to the prevailing Restoration-era visions of modernity. He declared that the Church always associated itself with "true progress" and that the market's destiny was to operate as a "font of wellbeing for those who sought sustenance for their families"—a goal in keeping with the moral aims of sanctified religious work.[104]

The next day, the *Diario de Barcelona* proclaimed that these events would be "remembered always in the annals of the city." Lauding the new El Born Market for the positive impact it would have on the surrounding Ribera neighborhood, the newspaper predicted that its opening signaled "a new era for our markets, so badly appointed until today and unworthy of a population that carries the title of the second capital of Spain."[105] Building on the inauguration's nationalist rhetoric, the newspaper declared that the grandiose new market hall demonstrated that Spain need not rely upon foreign technical help in large-scale iron construction. That by 1876 progress had more explicitly become understood as involving industrial accomplishment is reflected both in the structure of the El Born's new market hall and in the official rhetoric that celebrated its inauguration.

Ceremonies marking the inaugurations of the other nineteenth-century metal market halls in the city followed similar rhetorical scripts signaling an emerging consensus that such structures were key civic institutions as well as components of the city's public-service infrastructure. In this way, market-hall inaugurations rhetorically brought Catalonia into the increasingly integrated Spanish national economy of the late nineteenth century.[106] We see this also with respect to the September 1882 opening of Sant Antoni Market. In his speech at the inauguration, Barcelona's Mayor Francesc de Paula Rius i Taulet stressed the importance of the market to the well-being of the residents of the district, praised the director of construction for his use of all-Spanish materials, and declared, in the name of the king, that the hall was ready to open for business.[107] These ceremonies also expressed an idealized "double nationalism" of the sort that Michonneau describes as the underlying message of much of the monumental complex constructed for Barcelona's 1888 Exposición Universal.[108]

Over the course of the nineteenth century, Barcelona's municipal governments came to embrace the view that building retail food-market halls constituted an important infrastructural investment that could bring prestige to both the city and the nation. This was occurring at a time when the economy and the state as a whole lagged behind those of national neighbors north of the Pyrenees. So while covered markets segregated some commercial activities by moving them off the streets and squares where they had for so many centuries operated, they nonetheless enhanced the integration of food-market activities within the larger urban and national political cultures of the period. Greater levels of municipal involvement in food-market trade were accompanied by civic enshrinement of the institutions in which food was sold. The symbolic importance that municipal authorities attributed to markets laid the ground for vendors who retailed from within these structures to stake their claim for greater commercial rights in the century to come.

### Gender and the Sanitization of Urban Space

The expansion of the market-hall network in Barcelona mirrored the larger physical and demographic growth of the city. Though increasing urban density and expanding urban scale underpinned public control, the symbolic capital that new market halls often assumed provided additional incentive for municipal investment. But market-hall construction also reflected a more than century-long process of social and spatial segregation. In writing about Barcelona's markets, anthropologist Danielle Provensal asserts that the movement of stalls from the open air into enclosed structures was a symbolically loaded act connected with romantic concepts about the separation of biological functions from social ones. She equates the elimination of stalls from Barcelona's streets and squares to the separation of dining rooms from sitting rooms in upper-class Victorian homes.[109] Guàrdia, Oyón, and Fava likewise explicitly link market-hall construction to the "progressive medicalization of urban space," a broader Western European process that went along with the general municipalization of market management in many cities.[110] They also consider some of the ways in which Michel Foucault's interpretations are relevant to the emergence of Barcelona's public-market system, especially with respect to the concept of the panopticon.[111] Though the new metal market halls were not round, they were certainly designed to increase the visibility, transparency, and policing of vendor transactions with the consuming public.[112] In this respect, Barcelona's markets were analogous to modern hospitals, public schools, and prisons, within which gender constructs were paramount considerations.

With respect to Paris, Victoria Thompson explicitly links market-hall construction to emerging bourgeois ideologies that emphasized the division of the sexes into separate spheres.[113] If women were to occupy private and domestic ambits while men took charge in the public arena, then it hardly made sense to continue to allow female market vendors to clog up the streets of the city. This was especially the case, Thompson notes, because market women were suspected of selling their bodies on the side.[114] Moving them off the street and into enclosed structures can be understood as a strategy for controlling and containing unbridled female sexuality. Selling from within Les Halles, Thompson argues, transformed Parisian market women into more respectable participants in the commercial economy of food.

In Barcelona, as we have seen, women had long been engaged in market work. That the new market-building initiatives involved an attempt to sanitize not just the physical streetscape but the behavior of female vendors is reflected in the 1898 municipal code governing food trade in these institutions. Article 30 specified that vendors would have the obligation to use "good forms and fine manners in their relations with one another" as well as with the public and the municipal employees of the market.[115] Elsewhere, the term *billingsgatry* was coined to describe market women's legendary verbal feistiness.[116] In fact, Barcelona's market code, while explicitly recognizing women as independent and accountable holders of stall titles, was replete with articles that addressed comportment, cleanliness, and even the physical appearance of market vendors, who were forbidden to work stalls if they were physically disfigured in any way. Reading between the lines, we can see significant municipal concern with taming and sanitizing market women's discourses and bodies.

Yet there were decided limits to the efficacy of social control through public markets. Municipal administration of market halls could not guarantee their success. Market women built bonds of trust and loyalty with their female clientele and in some cases were loath to change their habits. We see this in the slow take-off of Santa Caterina Market, which competed with the old El Born open-air market. In 1856, nearly a decade after its official inauguration, Santa Caterina housed only 16 percent of the city's market stalls, while El Born still accounted for 30 percent.[117] It was not until a decade later that Santa Caterina finally eclipsed its open-air rival in the Ribera neighborhood.[118] Then when the grand new El Born market hall was completed, it was left with a smaller cadre of vendors to house.

Still, the process of moving those traders indoors appears to have evinced regret on the part of the neighborhood's artists, some of whom began to fixate on open-air markets precisely as they were beginning to disappear from the streetscape.[119]

The construction of a polynuclear system of public markets serving individual neighborhoods in Barcelona had various implications. Among them was the fact that the new market halls became more clearly defined physical spaces for the engagement of women—as both buyers and sellers—in a very public and popular segment of the commercial economy. On the one hand, markets operated as central place nodes for female sociability; on the other, the regulatory system through which they were managed imposed increasing levels of social control over the female vendors who worked in them.

These developments—the construction of market halls, their monumentalization in civic ceremonies, and the new efforts to sanitize and control what was largely a female economic enterprise—help to establish a deeper context for understanding the emergence of the early-twentieth-century Festival de Primavera traditions in Barcelona. Culminating in the 1930 festivities featuring the market ball and vendor pageant attended by King Alfonso XIII, the annual events showcasing the markets and electing queens from the ranks of its young female vendors reflected deep historical ironies. After working for decades to clear market vendors from the city's streets, authorities developed a proclivity for summoning them back out of the market halls in which they worked and parading them publically in ritual processions that offered images of domestification and submission to elite control.

## For the Love of Food
### Consumer Culture in the City and Its Markets

The late-nineteenth and early-twentieth-century construction of Barcelona's market hall system coincided with the maturation of consumer capitalism. Indeed, trade in and around the markets during this period flourished within the context of changing food tastes and new discourses about women's responsibilities as consumers. Building on clear early-modern antecedents, we can see how, by the turn of the century, market vendors, like neighborhood shopkeepers, benefitted from a much broadened enthusiasm for pursuing food fashions. While embracing various commercial innovations, female market vendors also perpetuated older practices of transmitting knowledge through carefully constructed forms of oral discourse meant to guide consumer decision-making with respect to shopping and culinary practices.

### Scale and Scope

In a number of ways, Barcelona's metal market halls were large-scale retail outlets analogous to the era's new department stores. They offered physical displays of abundance with commodities organized according to strictly regulated schemes. Carefully managed by an expanding cadre of professionals, they were open public spaces that invited consumers to admire goods and to browse among options. They responded to elevating levels of desire among groups seeking to assert their place in the changing urban social order, and they trumpeted modern forms of materialism by enshrining the act of shopping within architectural spaces that emphasized beauty and grandeur.[1] Yet in Barcelona specifically, where department stores were smaller and somewhat slower in emerging than in cities such as Paris or London, fashionable restaurants and the principal cafés located in the city's center represented the only large-scale, highly capitalized commercial alternatives to Barcelona's market halls as sources of food.[2] The fact that the latter depended much more on a neighborhood-based clientele contributed to the consolidation of a commercial subculture in everyday food shopping that drew on personal relations and locational convenience. Here we can see the significance of the Parisian market-hall model's implementation in Barcelona; the creation of a polynuclear system encouraged the development of neighborhood retail clusters in and around the markets, which were sustained by a steady and regular stream of customers seeking to provision their households on foot. As such, Barcelona's market halls operated in a more direct symbiotic relation to a range of small-scale commercial enterprises, such as grocers and specialty shops, but also inns, taverns, and neighborhood eateries. Such establishments usually acquired a good portion of their food stocks from nearby markets, which allowed vendors to earn a living not just from selling what was needed for home cooking, but also to some extent from the growing popularization of public eating and drinking.

The late-nineteenth century maturation of consumerism involved cultural values and economic choices that were not incompatible with the survival of small commerce.[3] Emphasis on the grand scale of Europe's nineteenth-century department stores, on mail-order catalog companies, and on the emergence of chains and multiples has overshadowed the scant attention given to small firms, which historians have too often presumed to be doomed to a long, slow process of strangulation from the outset of the twentieth century.[4] In fact, this was not so everywhere.[5] In Barcelona, a vibrant consumerist culture nurtured food shopping through decades in which market vendors consolidated their position within the commercial order of the city. Market-stall businesses were neither anachronistic retailing enterprises nor insulated firms immune to failure. The most successful vendors embraced changes in taste and food-shopping habits, engaged in innovation in terms of advertising and display, and thus constituted consumerist retail institutions of a particular sort.

The ongoing appeal of markets as food-shopping venues was more than a matter of locational convenience. Their success was reinforced by the visual presentation of abundance and variety that they offered to consumers entering through their doors. Markets were able to offer images of modern plenty in large part because of the standardization and rationalization that accompanied the municipal bureaucratization of retail provisioning. A key element of the regulatory thrust involved establishing a balance among food specializations in order to ensure broad variety in each of the city's markets. Consumers could expect, under one roof and in one location, to be able to purchase nearly everything they might need or desire to feed their families. The growing variety of food available for sale in the markets was a direct consequence of increased agricultural yields, the expansion of commercialized agricultural concerns, and the revolution in transportation resulting from the railway and the steamship as technological innovations. Coinciding with the expansion in supply, the nature of demand was reshaped by medical discourses emphasizing the importance of protein consumption, and by cookbooks and magazines that promoted refined middle-class tastes. Indeed, late-nineteenth-century Spanish markets were in no way screlotic retail institutions.[6] They were capable of qualitative modification in response to consumer demand. Like those of Valencia and some other cities, Barcelona's markets were especially well connected to the rail system, the bulk of whose cargo was agricultural. As such, they offered the most desirable foods from local sources, from Spain, and from the global agricultural market.[7] Thus situated, we can see that the city's market vendors were positioned to profit not only from growing demand but also from changes in the nature of demand that involved greater intermingling of necessity and consumerist desire for food.

## Feeding the Fairgoers

Beyond department stores, market halls were structurally and symbolically related to other large-scale buildings enshrining the consumerist benefits of industrial society. Specifically, market halls shared various features with nineteenth-century world's-fair pavilions. Alongside new expressions of Catalan identity and industrial and artistic achievements, we can see the triumph of consumerism when Barcelona celebrated its first world's fair, the 1888 Exposición Universal, on land adjacent to the Ribera neighborhood where Philip V's much-hated citadel had once stood. Metal market-hall construction projects in the city and the efforts to prepare for the 1888 Exposición Universal were in fact directly connected. Building the new Ciutadella Park that was to serve as the Exposición's fairgrounds was part of the reconfiguration of urban space made possible by the razing of the Bourbon fortifications.[8] Two metal markets, Hostafrancs and La Concepció, inaugurated in the same year that the Exposición opened, were hailed by developers, along with the other constructions that included the Arc del Triomf and the Columbus statue at the base of Las Ramblas, as part of the city's new monumental complex.

Architecturally, the new markets of the period resembled exposition halls in terms of scale and form and in their use of cast iron and glass; both were indebted by way of design to London's famed Crystal Palace, built for that city's Great Exposition of 1851.[9] Metal markets and exposition pavilions even had the potential to function interchangeably. Shortly before its opening, Sant Antoni Market was used by La Sociedad Económica as the venue for a modest exhibition promoting Catalan industrial advancement.[10] A decade after the much larger 1888 Exposición closed, one of its pavilions was repurposed as a wholesale poultry market, which took up 5,444 square meters of that structure's interior space.[11] One might even say that metal market halls and world's fair pavilions were architectural cousins, belonging to the same family as train stations and sharing the common purpose of efficiently managing masses of humanity moving through physical space.[12]

Barcelona's 1888 Exposición Universal, like all world's fairs, was designed to convey a series of messages related to progress. In this particular case, glorification of the principality took precedence over promotion of the Spanish nation-state and thus reflected a vision advanced by the half-century-old Catalan cultural *Renaixença* movement.[13] In the Exposición's rhetorical script, the grandeur of Spain was largely cast as the consequence of Catalan ingenuity and leadership. It was packaged in what Michonneau describes as a carefully crafted memory policy of double patriotism, one that posed so little offense to centralism that it did not preclude the royal family, the Queen Regent, and the infant King Alfonso XIII from travelling to the city to participate in the Exposición's opening ceremonies.[14] But if world's fairs can be read as texts,[15] we can see layered meanings in Barcelona's 1888 Exposición; among the messages conveyed was the idea that eating away from home and leisure had become intrinsically linked for a broad segment of the populace, and that through food consumption, individuals could express refined taste as a form of cultural sophistication and upwardly oriented class identity.

Running from April until December of 1888, Barcelona's Exposición Universal drew in nearly half a million visitors. Arrangements for feeding the fairgoers were built into the plan in a two-pronged strategy. First, a series of small establishments and various booths offered light foods and beverages for sale. Among these were the Quiosc Cafè del Parc, the Quiosc de Cervesa i Sorbets, the Quiosc de Begudes, the Cafè Rus, the Cafè Turc, and the Glorieta Barcelonesa.[16] These enterprises indicate that the organizers expected visitors to want access to drinks, both hot and cold, caffeinated, alcoholic, and even frozen, along with sweets and snacks, as part of their fair experience. The Exposición Universal was designed to impress a mass international audience, inspire awe, and stimulate the senses, including those related to taste and smell. Though the fair's success fell short of projections, it would be safe to say that for most of those who attended, a small treat may well have been the only item they could afford to purchase—an ephemeral commodity which once ingested became part of the self, ideally leaving a pleasing memory behind.

Beyond the smaller purveyors offering light food and drink to those of more modest means, the second element of the food-provisioning strategy of the Exposición involved the construction of two massive eateries, both of which were designed by the modernist architect Lluís Domènech i Montaner. In their dimensions and their design, they advertised abundance and luxury as intrinsic features of the bourgeois dining experience. The first of these was a 1,400-square-meter building of exposed red brick with iron structure and ornamentation that came to be known as the Castle of the Three Dragons. It served as the Exposición's hallmark Cafè Restaurant.[17] Just below its neogothic towers, the building was decorated with blue and white ceramic tiles in the form of shields, each one featuring an image of foods. The representations included a peasant girl squeezing a lemon, a woman drinking champagne, a lady eating pastry, a cook preparing chocolate, a friar drinking chartreuse, and a monk distilling wine. The café was housed on the first floor, the restaurant on the second, and private dining rooms were located in both the towers that flanked the facade.[18] Open to the public and including an expansive shaded terrace for patrons wishing to eat and drink outdoors, it was advertised as "le plus grand et le plus luxueux de la ville."[19]

Over the course of just four months, the Exposición's Cafè Restaurant served as the venue for a series of opulent banquets. Organized by both public and private entities, the first of these was held for the foreign and domestic press covering the fair.[20] Other fêtes, involving as many as six hundred guests seated at banquet tables, were held in honor of members of the Spanish royal family; the king of Portugal; the politician, historian, and architect of the Restoration system, Antonio Cánovas del Castillo;[21] and the Orfeó Bilbaí, as winners of the Exposición's choral society competition.[22]

The Cafè Restaurant's kitchen featured large windows for light and ventilation. A nearly eight-meter-long stove accessible from both sides, seven ovens, a hot-water tank, large plate warmers, and three electric dumbwaiters were among the modern appliances with which it was appointed. The cuisine, the wine, and the flowers were reputedly of the finest quality. All of this culinary fanfare had been subcontracted out by the city council to Guillem de Grau i Arnau, a mercantile agent who paid 200,000 pesetes for the exclusive right to purvey the Exposición's food.[23] The Cafè Restaurant itself was run as a branch of the subletter's prosperous and fashionable establishment located near the Liceu Opera House on Las Ramblas, in what had become the center of the city's nightlife.[24]

The other massive eatery designed by Domènech i Montaner for the 1888 Exposición was part of an even larger and more improbable project known as Gran Hotel Internacional. It was erected as a temporary structure on the Passeig de Colom; measuring 150 meters in length and 35 in depth, the hotel occupied a space of 5,250 square meters and went up in a record-setting fifty-three days.[25] Including three million floor tiles, 800,000 quintiles of cement, and five hundred tons of iron and glass, work proceeded round the clock until completion. On one level, the hotel included suites with servants' quarters; on the others were double and single rooms. Its first-floor lobby and patio featured a series of shops, including some selling umbrellas, gloves, tobacco, books, and newspapers; a telephone office; concierge; and all the modern conveniences that the late-1880s fashionable European tourist would expect.[26]

The hotel's restaurant was also designed to befit a world's fair city. It included a banquet hall with an enormous round table that could accommodate 250 guests, a restaurant with seating for a hundred people, and two family dining rooms.[27] The kitchen was presided over by Monsieur Bourgeois (no less), who was contracted for the job from Monte Carlo. He had come to Barcelona with his own tableware and an "expert and refined" staff in tow.[28] According to Néstor Luján, the stoves brought in to M. Bourgeois's kitchens at the Gran Hotel Internacional were of such tremendous dimensions that they could be used to grill up to four hundred *bistecs* in one fell swoop.[29]

The building and operation of the Café Restaurant and the Gran Hotel Internacional, along with the smaller cafés serving the fairgoers, stand as evidence of the intensification of consumer culture in late-nineteenth-century Barcelona, and they indicate the increasingly important place of food within that value system. The scale of these operations show that food and drink in forms that went far beyond simple nutritive needs—that is, preparations designed to be pleasing in taste and appearance, and in social and cultural meaning—had become commodities of mass consumption.[30] In order to attract a broad audience, the fee for a day's admission to the Exposición Universal was set at one peseta. The smaller and cheaper stands and kiosks selling foods broadened the access to public eating for a wider segment of the urban social order.

## The Popularization of Public Eating and Drinking

After centuries of development, the practice of eating in public places for pleasure and for prestige firmly established itself as part of the landscape of mass commercialized leisure in Barcelona and other Western cities by the late nineteenth century. The preparations for the 1888 Exposición had in fact stimulated much in the way of renovation and expansion in the city's hotel and restaurant infrastructure.[31] Eating publically as a way to display social rank became an activity that especially characterized a broad swath of the city's expanding middle classes. But even the popular classes embraced the trend, though obviously patronizing less pricey outlets. Food had clearly come to constitute a vehicle for what Thorstein Veblen termed "conspicuous consumption."[32] According to Veblen, individuals in consumerist societies make purchasing decisions as much on the basis of how they might appear to others as they do upon the rationally determined intrinsic value of what they purchase. Thus eating away from home was more than just a matter of convenience for many; whether taking place in grand establishments or more humble venues, consuming food in public places could involve gustatory pleasure but also bragging rights. Conversely, eating and drinking away from home could generate scorn or ill-repute, especially for women entering the wrong sorts of establishments.

We can see some debate in the travel literature over the extent to which this was the case in the early twentieth century. Karl Baedeker warned in 1913 that unaccompanied ladies should not go into cafés in Spain unless there was a special room for them.[33] In contrast, Mrs. Villiers-Wardell, in her 1915 *Spain of the Spanish*, made clear that she felt free to eat out wherever she pleased. About Barcelona specifically, she wrote that "a specialty of the city is the *taberna*, which has no connection with other establishments of the same name in the Peninsula! The taberna of Barcelona is an airy restaurant, elegantly and artistically furnished, where immaculately dressed waiters serve an excellent meal at an incredible price. Rice and fish, the famous Catalan stew, fresh fruit, bread and wine may be enjoyed for the sum of one peseta, or about nine pence-half penny and the choice of dishes is long and varied."[34] One is left to wonder where these particular taverns were located and the degree to which they were as exceptional as Mrs. Villiers-Wardell was as a traveler in her time.

Issues of gender aside, the turn of the century in Barcelona was a period in which eating out in swanky places had become all the rage for the affluent, the artistic, the intelligentsia, theatergoers, celebrities, and successful gamblers. Néstor Luján refers to this time as the golden age of great Barcelona restaurants.[35] He points to a number of establishments, including the Gran Restaurant de France, also known as "Justín." There, guests dined on French dishes at tables set with fine linens, Limoges porcelain, and silver utensils. Around that time, the restaurants in the Italian-owned Hotel de las Cuatro Naciones and the Hotel del Oriente on Las Ramblas gained fame, along with the Café de las Siete Puertas, the Restaurant de Paris, and the Pompidor in the Plaça Catalunya.[36] Rivals included the restaurant in the Hotel Grand Continental, also located on Las Ramblas adjacent to the Plaça Catalunya, where Catalan and Spanish dishes were served alongside elaborate and sophisticated continental cuisine. Other fashionable Barcelona eateries of the day were Martin, Chez Pince, Maison Dorée, Glacier, and El Suizo, the latter of which was part of a larger chain with establishments in other major Spanish cities.[37]

Many of the upscale restaurants were located on or near Las Ramblas, the city's most prestigious avenue, though one along which a cross-section of the social order mingled to pursue both livelihood and leisure, and where La Boqueria Market generated massive traffic in terms of buyers, sellers, and wholesalers of food.[38] Centered on the city's vertebral axis that Las Ramblas represented, bourgeois fine-dining habits were anything but lost upon those whose acquisitive powers paled in comparison. Given that an important component of consumer culture involves imitation of one's social superiors, the emergent but largely diffuse lower-middle classes were especially eager to imitate bourgeois habits and had begun to dine out more frequently in a range of less prestigious establishments and more modest cafés. The fact that workers were less well-positioned to do so contributed to growing class tensions.

We can see evidence of the diffusion of consumerist attitudes toward food through the commercialization of snacking as a part of popular courtship rituals. The folklorist Joan Amades tells us that Sant Pere Més Baix Street, which was located in the Ribera near Santa Caterina Market, was the site for numerous late-nineteenth-century establishments offering light afternoon repasts, or what are known in Catalan as *el berenar* and in Castilian as *la merienda*. With supper served later in the evening than in many other cultures, the afternoon snack was an old practice in Spain and much of the Mediterranean. According to Amades, the city's *menestralia* petite bourgeoisie gathered at the small snack shops along Sant Pere Més Baix, especially on holidays and days off from work:

> In winter they served chocolate, cream, curd, custard and syrup with hot water. There were braziers and also small charcoal pans for the fingers on the tables. In the summer, the tables were placed outside, under an awning . . . It was common [for customers] to eat figs, strawberries, and cherries and to drink fresh *orxata*[39] accompanied by *anis*. It became nearly obligatory for enamored couples who went out to walk and court on Sun-

day afternoons to go and *berener* in one of these places. Among the diverse [such establishments] located on this street, Ca la Pona, Ca la Teta, and Ca la Sinforosa enjoyed popularity.[40]

Food and drink, the most basic of all consumer goods, had become an important part of popular commercialized leisure practices, and of courtship patterns specifically.

For its part, the industrial proletariat, particularly males among that class, had long frequented taverns and the like, socializing in venues where imbibing alcohol often predominated over the consumption of food. In addition to wine drinking, distilled spirits had become common, and then around the time of the Exposición, beer-drinking became broadly popular. In the mid-1860s, there were some 168 taverns in Barcelona, three times as many of these establishments as cafés.[41] The physical expansion of the city in the second half of the nineteenth century was accompanied by an equally dramatic rise in the number of public drinking establishments, including *cerveseries*.[42] The popularity of branded pilsner beer such as that marketed through advertising by the new A. K. Damn and Sons' brewery as of 1876, reinforced the trend. In 1896, just before the annexation of the surrounding municipalities, there were some 131 *cerveseries* in the city.[43] There were an additional 699 *tavernes*, 54 *bodegues*, and 124 *bodegons* operating at that time.[44] Though full meals were not served in all, some sort of prepared foods were typically available in these establishments.

The ubiquity of public eating and drinking shows up in the work of the great Catalan journalist, essayist, and memoirist Josep Pla. Coming to Barcelona as a student during the World War I-era, he later wrote extensively about changes and continuities in the culinary culture of the city and the region.[45] Recalling his student days, Pla described developing a lifelong habit of eating out for breakfast. Among the four or five foods in the city that he claimed had "no rival—from the culinary point of view"—was the ham "sandvitx."[46] He was smitten as a young man by the high quality of bread in Barcelona, "fine, tasty, light, and airy," and especially by new forms such as the small, soft-crusted *panets de Viena*. Pla notes that their popularization coincided with the introduction of meat-slicing machines that facilitated sandwich-making and generated widespread enthusiasm for their consumption as a novelty breakfast food.[47] Pla developed a powerful affection for *panet de Viena* sandwiches and a glass of cold beer as the ideal breakfast, taken away from home, adopting it as a practice he pursued during the whole of his life. A critic of light morning meals, Pla was anything but a glutton: he advocated measured eating and the importance of family meals, especially in the evening, as crucial to the well-being of society. Still, his food memoirs show the unquestioned acceptance of the practice of eating some part of the day's food in public places, at least for men, and the excitement that gustatory novelty could elicit among students experiencing the big city for the first time in the opening decades of the twentieth century.

The significance of these developments lies in the fact that alongside an explosion in the availability of retail establishments specializing in a wide range of semidurable manufactured goods more typically associated with consumerism, turn-of-the-century Barcelona had become a city peppered with enterprises patronized by masses of people seeking to eat and drink publically for convenience, pleasure, leisure, and for the prestige associated with the ability to do so. While it is difficult to conceptualize any time in the past when only elites enjoyed eating and asserting their social status on the basis of the food they could afford, this period marked a tremendous broadening of social access to the conspicuous consumption of food and drink in a general sense.

These trends coincided with the consolidation of middle-class culture in a city that Jesus Cruz asserts was "the most eminently 'bourgeois'" in nineteenth-century Spain.[48] Social entertaining at home became more widespread, in connection, of course, to the reconfiguration of domestic space in bourgeois apartment houses. In the Eixample district's new residential buildings, kitchens were increasingly constructed as separate rooms specifically designed for food preparation but not consumption, save in the case of servants. Kitchens were equipped with coal-fired cast-iron stoves and a whole range of new utensils, including those made of aluminum and stainless steel. Glass and porcelain tableware also became much more common. The emergence of the dining room was an architectural expression of bourgeois culture that facilitated public social entertaining in spaces that were separate from the private areas of the home.[49] As such, they reflect the growing domestic embrace of consumerist attitudes and behaviors toward food.

The pursuit of fashion through public eating and home-cookery trends were intertwined. We can see an illustration of this connection through Pla's literary work. In his *Un Senyor de Barcelona*, the protagonist, Rafael Puget, dines at the Restaurant del Café Continental with his wife and then marvels at her ability to replicate and even improve upon the fine Parisian cuisine served there. Pla's characterization of Puget's wife, with her "innate sense of cooking" and acute sensibility for refined culinary styles, suggests how women acted as agents for the diffusion of new tastes. What was consumed in haute-bourgeoise restaurants could be deconstructed and then, through careful market shopping and home-cooking skill, reconstructed for refined consumption in the private sphere.[50] By the turn of the century, eating, whether in public or at home, had assumed much greater meaning, becoming more intrinsically associated with lifestyle choices, shifting class arrangements, and with expressions of good taste. And to a great extent, the source of all this food was the city's market halls, institutions that symbolized modernity in their own right and offered visible displays of alimentary abundance at the center of rich neighborhoods and poor.

These intensifying consumerist trends involved a broader diffusion of early modern values attached to food and drink across the social spectrum but were not exclusive to Barcelona. Madrid and other major Spanish cities embraced consumer culture apace, and in keeping with a wider European pattern that was more evolutionary than revolutionary. The late-nineteenth-century boom in fine-dining restaurants and the explosion of cafés, as well the construction of new modern market halls, characterized Spain's largest urban centers and was mirrored to a lesser extent in provincial capitals.[51]

## Diet and Social Rank

The nineteenth century was a period of considerable social fluidity during which a new class system took shape. Guild structures gave way to a more liberalized economy, and the embrace of the factory system of production created a burgeoning industrial proletariat. The profits from both manufacturing and commerce dramatically broadened the ranks of the middle classes. Yet Barcelona was a highly polarized city in social terms, and such distinctions were clearly visible in diets, and were certainly connected to the revolutionary uprisings that periodically broke out. As one author puts it, "the Eixample was an extraordinary gesture of confidence in an era disfigured by the extremes of poverty and prosperity, urbanity and violence."[52]

While more people in mid-nineteenth-century Barcelona were eating pastries and chocolate on Sundays and frequenting cafés in the afternoon and evening hours, the diet of the poor in Barcelona remained simple and insufficient. It consisted mainly of bread and wine, legumes, potatoes, salted fish, and with some luck, cheap variety meats such as tripe on Saturdays. Indeed, large numbers of Barcelonans lived in such abject poverty that they had to resort in times of crisis to Church and municipal charities in order to acquire their daily bread.[53] In his study of Barcelona's poor at mid-century, Ildefons Cerdà found that prevailing salaries could support a single worker but that those wages, when extended to maintain a family of four, translated into a diet of mainly bread, potatoes, legumes, and oil, with scant amounts of salted fish, an alimentary regime that involved ongoing hunger.[54] The debate over workers' diets is an old one that will not be resolved here because research on the question remains insufficient. Yet other sources confirm Cerdà's grim portrait of the early-industrial-era diet in Barcelona. Ramon Simó i Badia, a "self-educated" factory worker, and the physician Jaume Salarich both focused on working-class diets and living conditions. Their work suggests abysmal levels of nutrition similar to those that Cerdà calculated.[55] Evidence points to the conclusion that in the mid-nineteenth century, factory workers faced worse living standards in Barcelona than in most other industrial settings.

The poor diets of nineteenth-century wage-laborers help to explain the growth of working-class movements, which by the era of the Exposición Universal were beginning to coalesce around anarchist ideologies. However diffuse it was in this period, anarchism's appeal was strengthened by the intransigence of capital in addressing low wages, long hours, and poor working conditions, and by the polarization of income that accompanied the industrial process. Working-class housing was increasingly concentrated in parts of the old urban core, especially the Raval, but also parts of the Ribera, La Barceloneta, and in peripheral factory districts including Sants and Sant Martí, all of which were served by public market halls by the end of the nineteenth century. Beyond those areas, shanty-town settlements formed, and even more abject poverty defined the lives of those who lived without the benefit of connection to the city's network of infrastructural services, including such basics as water, sewage, paved streets, and municipal food markets, open-air or otherwise.

Such dire conditions contributed to the coalescence of anti-capitalist, republican, and democratic movements in poor neighborhoods. It is not surprising that a good part of the concern for the abysmal state of worker diets was cast as a threat to industry itself. The physician Pere Felip Monlau, known for his stirring polemic in favor of razing the walls encircling the city, argued that worker productivity rates were adversely affected by low-protein diets.[56] Monlau pointed to the superiority of English factory workers' output over those of France, Belgium, and Spain as a consequence not of character and inclination, but of higher meat-consumption levels.[57] Comparative considerations aside, the initial phases of industrialization had generally eroded worker diets for a number of reasons. The new factory systems offered only wage-based pay without replacing guild practices of compensating workers partly through food. Factory wages were also more precarious, in that workers often faced dismissals and layoffs that plunged them into conditions of near-famine.

Yet the tradition of paying rural workers with food continued in the countryside into the early decades of the twentieth century.[58] The heartiness of rural diets can be traced through medical reports from a number of Catalan towns in the Restoration-era.[59] Generally speaking, we can see that rural alimentary habits adhered to a pattern of five meals per day, all of which were accompanied by bread and wine. The rhythm of eating followed a solar schedule, beginning at four or five in the morning in summertime and extending to eight or nine at night. Escudella was typically the main dish at midday, though its meat content varied depending upon the acquisitive power of individual households. Supper was based fundamentally upon varieties of vegetables, including potatoes and legumes and often included salads. Both fruit and dairy consumption reflected local sources of production and varied according to differences in agricultural specialization.

In examining the range of physicians' reports on the popular diet in rural Catalonia during the Restoration era, Llorenç Prats finds that apart from those receiving public charity in food, there was not much in the way of generalized hunger. The poorest segments of the rural population were restricted by their means to the most vegetable-based diets; the wealthiest ate a more varied range of foods and especially consumed more protein.[60] Significantly, coffee drinking and chocolate consumption had spread widely through rural Catalonia by the turn of the century. The alimentary problem that physicians addressed as a public health concern at that time was not one of insufficient caloric intake. The principal concern was rather lack of protein and heavy drinking, the latter caused by the use of alcohol as a source of energy and often involved the consumption of wine or aguardiente as the first food of the day.[61]

Returning to the urban context of Barcelona, we can see significant dietary improvements in the decades leading up to 1914, in keeping with a trend that characterized Europe more generally. Periodic famines ceased to break out after the mid-1860s, and though Spanish agriculture in general lagged in terms of productivity, Barcelona's food supply expanded, in part as a consequence of the emergence of the national market and the industrialization of food processing.[62] Specifically, per-capita consumption of animal protein in Barcelona increased dramatically, and distinctions between urban and rural diets became less pronounced.[63] In 1881, the annual consumption of meat per person in the city stood at 32.4 kilos. By 1914, it had reached 52.1. Milk, which prior to 1900 was considered "mainly as medicine for the sick," grew from 13 liters a year per person in 1888 to 60.9 liters by the eve of World War I.[64] Likewise, the 98.7 eggs consumed per person per year in 1900 in Barcelona increased to 135.1 by 1914. There were shifts as well in the types of meat most often consumed, with mutton giving way to veal and lamb, along with the growth of fresh pork and kid as dietary staples. Generally speaking, meat from adult beasts ceased to predominate in the diet of the city's residents while meat from younger animals took precedence at the table.[65]

Roser Nicolau-Nos and Josep Pujol-Andreu argue that over the long run increasing income per head helps to explain these dietary shifts. They write that between 1870 and 1895 wages in Barcelona rose "60 percent in spending power with respect to bread. Then they deteriorated slightly in the closing years of the century, and between 1900 and 1914 they remained at about 50 percent above the levels that had existed up to 1871."[66] But these authors also assert that rising income offers only a partial explanation. Developments in the structure of the agricultural economy, in technology, in the science of nutrition, and in tastes and habits also help to account for these seismic dietary changes.

A cluster of factors led to greater consumption of meat in general and specific types of meat in particular. The Catalan agricultural economy had long specialized in viticulture, olives, fruits, and nuts—all crops that were consumed locally but also had significant export value. Much of the land not under cultivation was unsuitable for grazing livestock, and therefore meat from local sources was limited. As had long been the case, a significant portion of the principality's food had to be imported from other parts of Spain, from Europe, and beyond. By the end of the nineteenth century, the railway network, the steamship, and improved roads all facilitated livestock transport to the city, acting to dramatically improve supply. The extension of municipal control over livestock slaughtering at the end of the nineteenth century helped to rationalize distribution to the city's retail food markets, which in turn facilitated growing access to meat across diverse urban neighborhoods. Concomitantly, as Nicolau-Nos and Pujol-Andreu explain, "First, the import of improved English, French, Swiss and Dutch breeds for meat and milk production improved the national herd's genetic profile. Second, the supply of feed and fodder also increased, as a result of: (a) the spread of more intensive crop rotation and new means of production (seeds, fertilizers, ploughs, harvesters and threshing machines); (b) an expansion of the area under irrigation; and (c) the intensification of internal trade in agricultural products."[67] The introduction of mechanical refrigeration facilities in the slaughterhouses and retail market halls in the early twentieth century also contributed to the expansion of the fresh meat supply available to urban consumers.

With respect to milk and eggs, nutritional science, firm concentration, technological innovation, and new tastes played crucial roles in increasing consumption. Medical concern continued to center on the issue of animal protein, which physicians equated with "health and bodily strength."[68] Doctors urged the public to include milk and eggs in the diet as rich sources for protein, vitamins, and minerals. Large-scale poultry concerns began to appear in the periphery of the city, expanding the supply of eggs and then of chickens to the city's markets in the first decades of the twentieth century. The most important of these was Lluís Martí Codolar's Granja Vella, a diversified farm located in what is today the Barcelona neighborhood of Horta, which by 1913 was operating 150 incubators and producing some 100,000 chicks per year.[69] The *Revista Oficial de la Sociedad Nacional de Avicultores* declared it to be the largest in Europe.[70] The growing supply produced by the Granja Vella and other industrial poultry concerns contributed to a decrease in the price of chicken relative to other proteins such as veal. In 1902, veal in the city sold for 2.3 pesetes per kilo, while chicken sold for 3.8. By 1916, veal was selling for 5.5 pesetes per kilo, while chicken sold for 4.5.[71] Inflation and price fluctuations notwithstanding, poultry had become more affordable and began to make a regular appearance in the escudella soup pot. Eggs, selling for 2.7 pesetes a dozen in 1916, remained the most economical option for women following the medical advice of the day to increase their families' protein intake.[72] The ongoing program of municipal market-hall construction, and the proliferation of egg stalls within them, facilitated distribution and contributed to the growing popularity of egg-based dishes, including the now-famed *tortilla de patatas,* as supper food.

The dramatic growth in milk consumption in this period also illustrates the complex relationship between changing tastes, social conditions, and technological innovation in production and processing. Whether from cows or goats, milk played almost no role in the Barcelona diet until the second half of the nineteenth century, save in the case of its use as medicine.[73] The growing consumption of milk thereafter was linked initially to the popularity of chocolate. While in the mid-nineteenth century hot chocolate rarely included milk, by 1916 it had become a common breakfast food, especially for school children.[74] We see growing consumption also in the establishment of a new type of retail outlet specializing in milky drinks; the early-twentieth-century *granges* of Barcelona specialized in the service of what were known as *suïssos*—that is, hot chocolate topped with whipped cream made on the premises.[75] The addition of milk to coffee, common in Madrid, was not customary in Barcelona until the 1920s.[76] Nor was cheese making a significant tradition in Barcelona and its environs.[77] Long understood as having medicinal value in the treatment of coughs and colds, milk consumption among adults was highest in the winter months when such ailments were most common. Among the factors that contributed to the embrace of fresh milk as a near-universal breakfast food by adults was the establishment of the eight-hour workday after 1919. The shorter shifts in workshops and factories reduced the time that workers spent eating breakfast and involved an embrace of milk and bread as quick morning foods.[78] The growing demand for milk in Barcelona transformed some nearby areas in the hinterland into large-scale dairy concerns.[79]

The embrace of the new science of bacteriology in milk production was initially limited to the emphasis on maintaining sterility in the large firms.[80] Sterilized and glass-bottled milk was introduced on a limited basis as a consequence of demand for distribution through the municipal maternal hospital and milk depot for infants, the Casa de la Lactància, which opened its doors in 1913.[81] In 1925, the industrial production of pasteurized and sterilized bottled milk was introduced with the branding of Letona by the Viader family, which also marketed butter, cream, and condensed milk. Perhaps Letona's key innovation, though, was the development of a cold chocolate milk preparation called Cacaolat, which was patented in 1932. Cacaolat was an immediate success, establishing itself as a nutritive drink for children on the basis of certification by Barcelona's municipal laboratory on August 3, 1933.[82] Its branding led to a shift in taste and the embrace of cold sweetened milk as a highly desired food of mass consumption.

The branding of yogurt in Barcelona followed a similar trajectory. Yogurt was unknown in Spain until the physician Isaac Carasso, an immigrant from Salonica, drew upon Elie Metchnikoff's Nobel Prize–winning studies on phagocytosis and, using cultures from the Pasteur Institute, developed a formula made from fresh cow's milk. Carasso was driven to produce yogurt as a medical treatment to address the common intestinal disorders he saw among children in Barcelona. Carasso opened a yogurt factory in 1919 and marketed the product in honor of his son, using the diminutive for Daniel, "Danone." Employing the public network of streetcars, Carasso developed a system for home-delivery in glass jars. Though the Carasso family moved to Paris in 1929, and then to the United States because of the German occupation of France during World War II, its brand and the taste for yogurt continued to grow in Barcelona over the long run, with other firms such as Letona moving quickly into the yogurt market.

The success of Letona, Cacaolat, and Danone reflect the broader commercial development of food branding. Until the era of the 1888 Exposición, most advertisements in Barcelona were black-and-white typographic ones, which appeared in newspapers and magazines.[83] As Eliseu Trenc and Pilar Vélez note, such ads typically touted the benefits of particular brands of "alcoholic beverages, women's perfumes and cosmetics, and miracle cures."[84] Thereafter, several factors converged to transform the potential of branding and its promotion through commercial art. Population growth in Barcelona created a massive new readership, especially among the petite bourgeoisie. Women began to enthusiastically buy magazines in order to keep up with the latest trends and to follow serialized novels.[85] The technological embrace in the 1890s of three-color chromolithographic printing capable of producing bright images on a large-format press further stimulated the poster industry.[86] Marc Martí Ramon has connected these technological developments to the new concern for firm image that led to the organization of poster competitions in 1897 by numerous companies, including Xocolata Amatller, Codorniu "champagne," and Vicente Bosch Anís del Mono.[87] Evidence from the turn-of-the-century print industry—magazines, newspapers, and especially commercial posters—document a veritable explosion in food and drink branding, with the notable contribution on the part of some of the great Catalan illustrators of the period in helping to generate demand for specific commodities.[88] In the extant commercial art of the turn of the century, we see advertisements for a range of food brands and companies. As Hans Teuteberg argues, branding is one of the characteristics of mature food consumerism. Its introduction and growth signaled mass emotional attachments between producers and consumers that emphasized taste and nutrition in ways never seen in the pre-industrial era.[89]

Not all of the foods claiming a larger place on the plate lent themselves easily to branding. Potatoes became a basic food for a wide segment of the population, but they, like bread, were not branded in this period. Pasta constituted a more interesting case. It reflected both change and continuity in the urban diet while suggesting further relationships between particular food fashions and social rank. The growing consumption of pasta, like potatoes, supplemented bread as a source of carbohydrates. Pasta was an early-modern staple for the well-accommodated and thus it had a longer history within the syncretic body of Catalan cuisine. By the late 1700s, there were at least twenty-five pasta-making firms in the city.[90] The pasta industry was concentrated near the Convent of Santa Caterina and around the nearby Church of Santa Maria del Mar. In addition to making spaghetti and macaroni, Barcelona's pasta-makers produced an elaborate array of shapes; angels, human figures dressed in the fashions of the day, letters, stars, bows, and miniature snails all enhanced the appeal and prestige of this food product. Noodle-makers displayed their original creations in the doorways of their shops, and neighborhood children delighted in keeping track of the new forms available for sale.[91] Over the course of the nineteenth century, pasta became one of the most common elements of the urban diet in Barcelona, and its point of sale shifted from producers to market vendors and also to grocers, for whom trade in the product represented an important element of that food-retailing specialization. By 1905, the median daily consumption per inhabitant of pasta in Barcelona was 73 grams, and only bread, potatoes, fruits, and vegetables figured more prominently in urban diets.[92] Though mostly sold in bulk, the branding of pasta by producers such as El Pavo and Sauri supported old culinary habits while encouraging new consumer preferences for particular shapes, forms, and makers. Here we must return to the escudella as the dish that was most typically served at the midday meal and the main vehicle through which pasta travelled to the stomachs of consumers.

Rich and poor alike ate versions of escudella. Served in two courses, it could be humble or grand, depending upon what went into the soup pot. Catalan proverbs illustrate this point: "Molta verdura i poca carn, escudella per matar la fam" (lots of vegetables and little meat, escudella to kill hunger); "L'escudella manté el cos i la butxaca" (escudella maintains the body and the pocketbook); and "Bona olla cada dia ens arruïnaria" (a good soup pot every day would ruin us). These serve as just a few of the many phrases speaking to the economic elasticity of the dish.[93] By adding pasta to the broth that was served as a first course, escudella's caloric value increased, and this of course made pasta a more appealing commodity for those concerned with issues of economy. But because pasta could be manipulated into so many different shapes, its consumption also became, for some, a matter of keeping up with new food fashions in a manner that easily lent itself to more traditional forms of cookery. The incorporation of different types, quantities, and specific brands of pasta in escudella to substitute for or complement more expensive meats established new standards of consumption within a broad swath of the social order. The variety and uses of pasta in escudella could be read as a barometer of both economic means and taste.

Barcelona's social fabric was indeed a complex and fluid one at the turn of the century, as were the commercial and consumptive behaviors that people engaged in with an eye toward asserting class position. The well-accommodated economic elites who increasingly allied themselves with the city's traditional nobility and the burgeoning ranks of an often abysmally poor industrial working class occupied polar extremes in the city's social hierarchy.[94] In between, there was a growing and variegated middle class. The contrast between the material circumstances of these social groups was a bold one, expressed through food consumption as much as through access to other forms of consumer comforts. So in considering food and social rank, we must bear in mind that there was much in the way of variation and that what foods were eaten, where they were consumed, and from whom they were purchased depended upon a range of factors and circumstances. We know that all the groups comprising the end of the nineteenth century "middle classes" ate more higher-quality foods and ate out more often than their working-class counterparts. But there were differences, also, that transcended social class. Women tended to eat less food, and to eat in public less often than men. Children also consumed less food than adults, exercised little power over food choice, and participated in the pursuit of food fashions through the intermediation of their parents and relations.[95] And, particularly significant to this discussion, women's participation in food consumerism manifested itself more often in the choices they made at neighborhood markets and shops and in the preparation of new dishes at home for their families.

### New Discourses on Housewifery and Cooking and Older Traditions of Orality

Until the industrial era, the bulk of the evidence documenting culinary practices in Europe reflected elite tastes and habits among royalty and members of the nobility. Most of the sources were written by men and aimed at a male audience of cooks who dominated the ranks of the most prestigious private and commercial kitchen staffs. Spain, and by extension Catalonia, was no different in this regard.[96] The two treatises generally held as the foundational works on Catalan cuisine, *Sent Soví* and the *Libre del Coch*, fit this bill. But neither was designed as a guide for home cooking, nor explicitly directed to a female audience.

The first modern Catalan cookbook aimed at a literate middle-class audience was *La Cuynera Catalana*, which appeared in the form of four serial pamphlets beginning in 1835. With its subtitle, *Useful, Easy, Sure and Economic Rules for Cooking Well*, its anonymous author was also most surely male, though significantly its title used the feminine *cuynera* rather than the masculine *cuyner*. Reprinted numerous times until the early twentieth century, it was a product of the Catalan cultural and literary Renaixença and constituted one of the first nineteenth-century books published in the indigenous language of the principality.[97] Not surprisingly, it referenced dishes as being specifically Catalan, alongside certain recipes denoted as having Castilian, Italian, Dutch, French, Tatar, and other origins. The fact that it was published in Catalan rather than in Castilian, and that it enjoyed such ongoing commercial success, certainly testifies to the quotidian use of the language, especially among women, who did the bulk of the cooking in Barcelona's private kitchens. Still, the book addressed a male audience, presenting itself as a guide for the proper operation of middle-class patriarchal households in which men had a serious vested interest in the economy and nutritional health of its members. Reflecting lower literacy rates among women and the practice of men reading aloud at home, La Cuynera Catalana emphasized the place of fathers at the head of the table, presiding over their families at mealtime, and presumably receiving the largest and best portions at every meal. Rules for entertaining were also addressed, including the admonition that conversation not stray toward political matters.

Male intermediation aside, La Cuynera Catalana was clearly a piece of prescriptive literature meant to guide women's behavior, reinforcing habits of economy in the fulfillment of wives' most basic roles as cooks and caretakers. Female responsibilities to ensure the health and well-being of their families, and to shop for, prepare, and serve food, were nearly inviolable precepts in Catalonia as elsewhere. Only upper-class women escaped such obligations. Even so, in 1859 Fernando Bertrán de Lis admonished "that the well-educated woman 'ought to know how to do everything incumbent on her sex without need of help . . . all type of domestic labors, from overseeing the pantry to even preparing the food by herself from time to time.'"[98] The servant- and cook-employing bourgeois class audience to whom La Cuynera addressed itself held wives as ultimately responsible for everything that came into the kitchen in terms of supply and everything that came out of it as prepared food. Widely disseminated, the book served as a measuring device for both men and women to judge the success of their household's alimentary operations.

Still, La Cuynera Catalana should also be understood as a codification of broader knowledge and practices otherwise transmitted and developed orally over time, and not merely as an expression of Catalan cultural artifice. Its recipes did not spring from whole cloth. Cooking practices, food-related customs, and culinary preparations designed to address health and beauty were typically only recorded in noble households, though cookbooks penned by women began to be published in English and in German in the eighteenth century. In Italy, France, and Spain, female-authored cookbooks did not appear until later.[99] Otherwise, such knowledge was passed down and amended from one generation of women to the next through oral discourse that took place mainly at home and within marketplaces and shops.

The emerging nineteenth-century literary corpus on Catalan food did not substitute for or undermine the longstanding oral transmission of knowledge that shaped women's everyday culinary practices.[100] One essential element in the socialization of young women was the knowledge of how to shop for the best food at the best price, a skill that could only be honed in direct contact with the market vendors and shopkeepers selling what was needed to prepare the day's sustenance. The Catalan proverb "*al moli i el mercat, envieu el més espavilat,*" which translates as "send the most quick-witted to the mill and the market," suggests not just the cunning reputation of vendors but the importance of savvy as a consumer attribute. "Saber comprar"—that is, knowing how to buy—involved building relationships of trust and mutual personal dependency with specific vendors and shopkeepers. Failure to do so could result in disastrous misunderstandings of various sorts, potentially requiring municipal intervention to resolve the arguments that might ensue. The nature and contours of the relationships of trust and familiarity between buyers and sellers of food were not codified in the cooking manuals of the day. Nor were the conversational exchanges between customers and vendors that went beyond neighborhood gossip and so often focused on recipes, techniques, and preparations.

The structure of food retailing in Barcelona's market halls and the principles according to which it was managed by the municipal corporation underpinned the ongoing importance of oral discourses about food among women. In all but the peripheral working-class shanty areas, every neighborhood in the city had its own central place, or nucleus, for food shopping in the form of a municipal market. In all these centers of exchange, the sale of alimentary goods overwhelmingly dominated. The municipal licensing system that authorized the retailing of a very limited range of goods in each stall, and imposed severe sanctions for violations, reinforced the long-standing specialization of the food-market trade. The municipal licensing system meant that in order to provision their households, consumers would have to shop from a number of stalls of varying types on a regular basis. Buyers had to build relationships, of an economic nature certainly, but also of a cordial social nature as well, with a set of market-based retailers.

As Clifford Geertz long ago asserted, the most valuable commodity in the marketplace is always information.[101] Consumers' sense for which vendors were trustworthy and which might render aid in time of dearth was certainly crucial information to possess, but so too was knowing which vendors offered the best advice in terms of cooking and economy. Reconstructing this market-based oral discourse before the earliest decades of the twentieth century is for the most part impossible, yet there is evidence of it nonetheless. We know that market women were wont to call out their wares in an age-old form of advertisement. The cacophony of their calls to attract customers was such that municipal regulation sought to contain it after 1898. Late-twentieth-century interviews with vendors show that verbal exchanges about price, quality, and especially recipes were common elements of market conversation with consumers and ones that the vendors themselves understood to be historic in nature. Nearly all of the vendors who offered me their personal testimonies touched upon or even emphasized the importance of culinary advice that generations of vendors in their families had dispensed to their clients. Intertwined with the art of salesmanship, or what vendors called "saber vendre" (knowing how to sell), the reputation for dispensing good culinary advice constituted a form of commercial capital.

While market trade in food tended to perpetuate personal bonds between consumers and retailers, it is noteworthy that vendors' commercial strategies were not necessarily static ones. In fact, there was much in the way of innovation in Barcelona's markets in the first decades of the twentieth century that responded to technological change, new products, and new expectations in terms of hygiene and the aesthetics of shopping. Some of the changes were mandated by municipal authorities. Others were initiated by the vendors themselves. Electric lighting was introduced in the markets in the first years of the twentieth century. Over the course of the next decade, individual vendors were required to install electric meters and pay for their own usage.[102] Sant Antoni vendors had begun to install telephone lines in their stalls nearly a decade before.[103] By 1911, the city was specifying that new fish stalls be made of brick and tile, with vendors securing municipal authorization to improve their stands and bearing the cost of the construction.[104] Other common upgrades in the first decades of the twentieth century involved the installation of water lines, marble countertops, stall enclosures with grates that could be locked at night, and elaborate decorative signage denoting the name of the vendor and the type of goods sold.[105] The most lucrative stall businesses undertook the most far-reaching improvements. Sometimes project proposals were denied by municipal authorities on the basis of their extravagance and the unfair advantage that would accrue to the vendor over those selling the same goods nearby.[106]

While vendors were not allowed to post advertisements inside the markets, they could buy ad space in newspapers, a practice becoming more common by the early 1930s. By then, Anton Alsina, who sold salt cod from Stall 907 in La Boqueria, claimed in an ad in *La Publicidad* that he offered the best in "taste, modernity, and hygiene."[107] Likewise, in her ad for her La Boqueria Stalls 39 and 40, Madrona Moragas asserted that she sold the "best and most appreciated fruits from our land, national, and foreign" sources.[108] Other market-stall ads touted home deliveries, service to hotels, restaurants, and schools, and decorative fruit baskets for gift giving and special occasions. When newspapers featured articles about markets, vendors bought advertising space on those pages. L'Opinió's coverage of the opening of the El Ninot market hall in 1933 was accompanied by five stall advertisements that reflected the vendors' embrace of consumerist values. Rosa Mauran's ad for her El Ninot butcher Stalls 100 and 101 announced the sale of "first class beef and veal, specialty in fine meat from Girona," and "delicate awards and gifts for her distinguished clientele."[109] When two years later L'Opinió ran an article on La Concepció Market, subtitled "The Importance of This Market," twelve vendors bought ads to appear in that issue. The ad with the most copy was for A. Valls's "Interesting Provisions and Fruits," sold from La Concepció Stalls 496 and 497. It read, "Italian pasta, chocolates, coffees, cheeses, and butters of the best brands. Fresh pasta every day. Presenting this ad will give you a ten percent discount on all articles except milk and sugar."[110] The ad suggests that A. Valls was a small-scale entrepreneur who, like other vendors attempting to increase their sales, engaged in innovations of various forms. The emphasis on brands, on quality, and on taste and selectivity that shows up in newspaper advertisements indicate vendor eagerness to capitalize on the broader currents in food consumerism that had become a deeply embedded part of the culture by the first third of the twentieth century.

Yet in some ways, market vendors were at a disadvantage in comparison to neighborhood shops in terms of promoting new food fashions. The bulk of the branded, processed, and pre-packaged food trade was conducted by the growing numbers of grocers operating from shops that were often located in the immediate environs of the city's markets. Still, some brands pushed for greater presence in the markets. Municipal authorities increasingly allowed markets to be used by food companies to promote their products. We see this in the case of Sant Antoni Market in the 1920s and 1930s, where Lechera Montañosa condensed milk, Tex-Ton, Maggi, Caldox bouillon, and Gal·lo and Bonzo flan powder promotions were held, with free samples distributed to the public.[111]

Consumerist values typically emphasize the importance of pursuing the new and the fashionable. But the discourses on housewifery that were expressed through cookbooks and women's magazines emphasized a syncretic blend of new and old dishes, with forms of escudella maintaining primacy of place as the fundamental midday recipe. La Cuynera Catalana offered twenty-one ways of preparing escudella, touting both its nutritional and economic advantages. Other cookbooks, such as Doña Eladia M. de Carpinell's classic turn-of-the-century Carmencita o *la Buena Cocinera,* also stressed the importance of escudella, offering Catalan and other Spanish regional variations.[112] Escudella-making remained central to women's daily routines in the early twentieth century, so much so that some poultry vendors even tested the resolve of inspectors and directors to control market trade by selling small bundles of vegetables they were not authorized to offer so that housewives could more conveniently acquire all the escudella ingredients at once, without having to shop at multiple stalls.[113] Beyond its function as a practical manual for cooking the classics economically, Doña Carpinell's *La Carmencita* can also be read as one of the first female-penned guides to refined, modern, and cosmopolitan food fashions. Carpinell's explicit aim was to guide its readers in preparing Catalan, Spanish, Cuban, American, French, and Italian dishes in order to "satisfy all tastes and fill all needs."[114] In a sense, this was in keeping with the spirit of the *Libre del Coch* and *Sent Soví.* Syncretism in cooking, presented as a modern aesthetic, was further consolidated as a Catalan alimentary tradition in the first decades of the twentieth century.

We can also see this in the culinary advice proffered by the Institut Cultural i Biblioteca Popular de la Dona from its founding in 1910 to the outbreak of the Spanish Civil War in 1936. Catholic and socially conservative in its orientation, the Institut targeted a female audience, offering lectures, typing and business classes, cooking courses, recipes, clothing patterns, and a range of guidance for the proper management of the home.[115] The Institut began to publish a weekly magazine in 1925 called *La Dona Catalana.* Its staff of mainly male writers promoted modern home economics and the education of women as tasteful consumers. Each issue included an advice column and four pages of a serialized novel.[116] *La Dona Catalana* was also filled with advertisements for a vast array of products from radios to Maggi bouillon, to depilatory creams, and even Kotex sanitary napkins.[117] Written in Catalan and connected to the politics of the Lliga Regionalista Party, it had a mainly middle-class readership and advocated an explicitly conservative political Catalanist message.[118] The magazine rejected and even ridiculed feminist discourses that might encourage women to overlook their essential domestic responsibilities.[119] With respect to cooking, *La Dona Catalana* emphasized demanding standards of culinary sophistication.

Among its main concerns, the Institut had a department devoted to home economics and provisioning, along with its own restaurant. In addition to its cooking classes, it published suggested weekly menus and recipes, offering reflections on particular ingredients and their health values. Through publication of *La Dona Catalana,* the Institut promoted a cuisine deeply infused with cosmopolitan taste alongside more familiar regional preparations. On the cosmopolitan side of the equation, suggested dishes included *Mouselina d'Espinacs a la Francfort, Ous Florentina, Glace Vaticane, Coliflor a la Polignac, Consumé Monte Carlo, Salmó a la Vendòme, Poularde a l'Eduard VII, Patates a la Chester, Croquetes a la Italiana, Tonyina Bordalesa,* and so forth. Yet some of these appeared on menus alongside recipes for things like *Perdiu a la Catalana, Arròs a la Parellada,* and *Rovellons a la Casolana,* all of which were older Catalan dishes.[120] Not surprisingly, many of the recipes involved significant quantities of milk, butter, and eggs, and potatoes were dressed up and sophisticated in numerous preparations. Branded and processed products, such as Maggi bouillon and Opson rice flour, along with canned salmon, French mustard, English cheese, and Japanese tapioca, were held among the many must-have ingredients. *La Dona Catalana* acted as an agent for the infusion of ever-more-sophisticated cosmopolitan dishes and preparations into what was being defined from above in this period as modern Catalan taste.

The crime novelist and esteemed food writer Manuel Vásquez Montalbán waxed lyrical on the impact of this culinary cultural initiative, especially in terms of its direction by the Swiss chef and pedagogue J. Rondissoni.[121] Teaching cooking courses aimed at generations of future housewives in the interwar period and devising the recipes and culinary content of *La Dona Catalana*, Rondissoni emphasized the construction of menus that balanced taste, dietary science, and economy. Not everyone agreed with his approach, which had little relevance to working-class women or to those embracing anarchism and/or feminism. In effect, Rondissoni's regime imposed higher standards of culinary skill upon women and greater expenditures of time in shopping, cooking, and keeping abreast of all the new dishes. *La Dona Catalana* reads as an exemplar of broader Western tendencies in the new science of home economics that first flourished in the 1920s. Above all, the prescriptive message in the genre dictated a domestic regime that implied "more work for mother," as Ruth Schwartz Cowan has so firmly established.[122]

Yet within the pages of the magazine itself, there were respectful registrations of objection to Rondissoni's syncretic fervor. The April 9, 1926, issue included a letter addressed to the "Sr. Director de La Dona Catalana" from one Antonieta la Cuinera, a female cook in the service of a Barcelona family that was "well recognized for its importance." Antonieta explained humbly that her father, rest in peace, had been a fisherman and that from him she had learned "la cuina a la marinera." Thereafter she had mastered French and English cooking, which she claimed to practice with skill. Still, she bemoaned the cost of *La Dona Catalana's* culinary paradigm, reminding the magazine's direction that not everyone with means had inherited their wealth or embraced the new cosmopolitan tastes assumed intrinsic to the bourgeois class. The self-made, she pointed out, preferred the cooking of their childhood rather than that of foreigners (or "*foresters*," as she put it). Antonieta asked, "why, senyor Director, instead of publishing just the cooking of complicated foods, do you not leave a little space in our important magazine for recipes that are simple, without complicated preparations or new tastes that are not always digestible?" She explained that she had talked the matter over with fellow readers, all of whom agreed. Then she volunteered on behalf of herself and others to contribute indigenous Catalan recipes, asserting that "we have our own cooking, fully ours, healthful, extremely economic, and above all simple and practical for housewives that do not dispose of the time to immerse themselves" in the food fashions dominating the pages of the publication.[123] There is no evidence that her plea was heeded.

On the one hand, Antonieta la Cuinera's letter represents the kind of opposition to new fashions and to heightened consumerism that one finds in response to nearly all material change. On the other hand, her letter offers more insight. Antonieta was calling for a codification of what she understood to derive from the oral culture of Catalan cooking, one whose techniques were developed and disseminated through families, private kitchens, shops, and public marketplaces. Her reaction to Rondissoni's penchant for complicated cosmopolitan recipes represented an early expression of what would become a more vociferous debate later on.[124]

In all fairness, Rondissoni's pedagogic devotion to uplift the taste of Catalan housewives should not be cast in total opposition to the codification of oral culinary traditions deriving from home cooking or market shopping. Part of his work involved developing updated and more exacting versions of Catalan "classics." He also included a detailed month-by-month guide to the seasonal availability of market foods in his *Culinaria,* published in Spanish in the early years of the Franco regime and then reprinted many times over since 1960.[125] Rondissoni, like so many other authors of cookbooks addressed at Catalan audiences, was a syncretist. He drew on Escoffier while synthesizing especially French and Spanish culinary traditions. But he also embraced new products, promoting brands such as Maggi bouillon in what he touted as the latest in haute cuisine, and he developed recipes that could be prepared using the new technological devices of his era, including pressure cookers and electric frying pans.[126]

There is further insight to be gained by returning briefly to two of the most notable twentieth-century Catalan food writers—Manuel Vásquez Montalbán and Josep Pla. Neither were chefs; rather, they were eaters and chroniclers of taste. Vásquez Montalbán was much more of a sybarite. He praised Rondissoni for attempting to broaden the culinary horizons of Catalan housewives beyond rabbit with allioli and white beans with sausage.[127] In so doing, Vásquez Montalbán exaggerated and oversimplified what women were serving to their families in the first decades of the twentieth century. Though it was a prescriptive source, and thus has its limitations in representing actual practice, La Cuynera Catalana as it was published and re-edited over the course of the nineteenth century vividly illustrates a much broader set of culinary tastes already popularized in the decades when Barcelona's polynuclear market-hall system took shape. It included, for example, myriad recipes for poultry, game, beef, lamb, and mutton dishes, an entire section on fish, crustaceans, and bivalves, and a wide variety of vegetable and legume preparations. More concretely, we can see the breadth of what housewives incorporated into their cooking by the early twentieth century in the wide range of products sold from the city's markets, a clear indication of significant variety in popular cooking practices. Unlike Vásquez Montalbán, Josep Pla valued simpler foods that formed what he understood to be a rich corpus of Catalan culinary tradition. In addition to the panet de Viena ham sandwich that he praised as one of the four or five unrivaled foods in Barcelona at the end of the second decade of the twentieth century, he wrote about the virtuosity of white beans and sausage, baked salt cod, and coffee made using a cloth barretina filter.[128] His food memoir glorifies home cooking and suggests that he might have preferred to eat from Antonieta la Cuinera's kitchen rather than from Rondissoni's. Pla wrote that with respect to food, Catalonia was "a country of copiers." In keeping with Antonieta's pleas to the directors of La Dona Catalana, Pla bemoaned the tendency to imitate foreign recipes of extreme complexity that produced "absolutely uncertain results."[129] Though Pla showed no appreciation for the syncretic nature of what he called "our old family cooking," his curmudgeonly opposition to changing tastes and habits illustrates the close and contested relationship between food and collective identity.[130]

A long academic tradition treats food as a system of symbols, as an expression of culture, and as a class-specific but also regional type of language.[131] The fact that consumption, habits, and tastes have changed over time shows that the system of food symbols is not a closed one; rather, it has responded to a multiplicity of external forces. In the case of Barcelona, factors altering food options and preferences over the long term emanated from the city's shifting fortunes and strategies within the Mediterranean, Atlantic, and global trading networks. Food habits in Barcelona have also been shaped by the geographic reality of the city's coastal location and the ecosystems and agricultural exploitation of its hinterland. Religion, technological and organizational change, public policy, medicine, and the construction of sometimes competing cultural discourses produced by its dominant social classes also shaped culinary practice. The tension that is reflected in the debate over how middle-class Catalan women should prepare food in the industrial era and what weight "tradition" (however constructed) should carry in the face of change and innovation foreshadows contemporary disputes that blend health concerns with the urgency of using food as a cultural marker of national identity within, and distinct from, that of the Spanish national state. The continuous tendency toward syncretism, with its origins in the classical period, is undervalued and under-recognized in the vast literature on Catalan foodways. Historical analyses that take a synchronic snapshot of Catalan cuisine at any given point in time risk failure to grasp the significant and continuous process of cultural construction.

Like many other European cities, Barcelona faced complex challenges in adjusting its provisioning system to keep up with the explosive growth in urban density and scale that accompanied the industrialization process. The commercialization of Spain's Mediterranean agricultural economy, new technologies, and growing levels of trade from the port of Barcelona expanded the array of foods available to retailers and consumers alike, while new municipal projects designed to redefine and reinvent urban space transformed both the city and its food system. The nineteenth-century metal market halls, like the reinforced concrete structures inaugurated in the early twentieth century, functioned as neighborhood commercial epicenters. Deeply embedded within the currents of modern industrial mass consumerism in food, the trade that took place within them was neither archaic nor static. Yet against this backdrop of maturing consumer culture, there were still significant continuities; small-scale enterprises continued to dominate the food sector, and as we shall see, widespread female entrepreneurship in market-hall-based retailing remained paradigmatic. The prescriptive cacophony of the new discourses on housewifery and cooking notwithstanding, market women and their female clients were situated at ground zero in the dissemination of new trends in taste.

Barcelona's food markets functioned within the context of the emergence of consumerism. Consumerist attitudes toward food were constructed and reconstructed with every retail transaction within the city's markets, with every meal prepared and served at home, and with every bite taken, pleasing or otherwise. Ultimately, what vendors sold in the city's markets, and what women brought home and cooked, served as crucial a determining force in the construction of Catalan cuisine as did privileged tastemakers who dominated the city's restaurant culture, wrote cookbooks, or by those who formulated policy or developed new supply chains and technologies of production.

Women buying and selling shellfish at La Boqueria Market , ca. 1929–1932. *Photo by Josep Dominguez, image courtesy of Arxiu Fotogràfic de Barcelona.*

Aerial view of Sant Antoni market showing the tremendous scale of some of Barcelona's late-nineteenth-century public food retailing structures. *Image courtesy of Arxiu Fotogràfic de Barcelona.*

Butchers' protest demonstration in front of Barcelona's city hall, March 30, 1936. *Image courtesy of Gremi d'Empresaris Carnissers i Xarcuters de Barcelona i Província. Photo reproduction by Gerard Martí Huguet.*

Conxita Cortada Segarra, a life-long fish vendor at La Boqueria Market, who worked alongside her husband Jaume Barcardí, here posing for photograph taken by a tourist, ca. 1940s. *Image courtesy of Imma Vega Barcardí.*

## CHAPTER 5

# New Political Economies
## Municipal Control and Associationalism in the Markets before the Civil War

Barcelona became a major European metropolis in the first decades of the twentieth century, with a population that reached beyond the one-million mark by 1931.[1] Along with the continued absorption of surrounding villages, immigration from other regions of Catalonia, as well as from Valencia, Aragon, and elsewhere in Spain, drove this demographic expansion and helped to create a city whose scale and rate of growth were comparable to those of Madrid and Naples in Southern Europe, and Liverpool, Manchester, and Brussels in the North.[2] What had been for so long a relatively small walled enclave had grown into a sprawling city. Against a backdrop of simmering social-class and ideological conflict, a host of urban problems resulted from this explosive growth. Republicans, regionalists, and monarchists alike, vying for control of Barcelona's Restoration-era city council, faced the common challenge of bringing administrative coherence and city services to urban residents in disparate neighborhoods and districts. The rationalization and control of food retailing were an important part of this process, and one that contributed to urban integration and the fundamental viability of the industrial metropolis.

In maintaining a commitment to market-hall building and operation at the base of its provisioning strategy, the municipality directly and deliberately contributed to the ongoing success of the population of vendors engaged in small-scale retailing. By 1931, there were over seven thousand stall enterprises operating from the sixteen marketplaces in the city.[3] Individual and family economy-based opportunities to earn a living through selling food expanded as the city grew and as the retail apparatus became more elaborate. The codification of a uniform set of municipal market regulations in 1898 established the bases for the continued economic viability of the system. But the success of Barcelona's markets was equally due to the agency of the vendors themselves. Through forming new associations designed to fill the vacuum left by the abolition of the guilds, through petitions for change and redress of grievances, and occasionally through more direct confrontation, Barcelona's market vendors helped to define a regulatory environment that was based upon shared principles of fairness. The new political economy of food retailing that took shape during the first decades of the century emphasized the municipal obligation to limit the competition that market vendors faced, while favoring the development of an associational milieu through which food retailers of all varieties negotiated the terms of their trade. In broad outline, the system put in place by 1923 remained in force not just through the years of the Primo de Rivera dictatorship, but through the Second Republic and much of the Franco regime.

## A City of Monikers

The turn of the century was a socially and politically tumultuous period in the history of Barcelona. Tensions between the working classes and factory owners and between regional and national elites were building as the economy reeled from the twin blows of lost colonial markets and viticultural devastation resulting from the spread of the phylloxera plant louse.[4] The labor movement, long libertarian in its ideological orientation, had all but rejected the socialist Unión General de Trabajadores's (UGT) organizational efforts emanating from Madrid and was moving headlong toward anarchist allegiances. In the 1890s, a series of anarchist bombings was aimed at elites and the representatives of authority. The most famous of these were two that exploded in 1893 within the Liceu Opera House, killing twenty people. A second wave of bombings that began in 1902 targeted popular public spaces, including the flower vendors on Las Ramblas and, in 1907, 1908, and 1910, La Boqueria Market itself. Generally attributed to "agents provocateurs," these acts gave Barcelona "an international reputation as 'The City of the Bombs.'"[5]

In the first decade of the century, a new branch of the labor movement emerged under the demagogic leadership of Alejandro Lerroux. Attracting workers and members of the lower-middle class who had migrated to Barcelona from outside Catalonia, Lerroux formed the Radical Republican Party, through which he fomented centralist, populist, and anticlericalist sentiments.[6] In the summer of 1909, a convulsive uprising gripped the city during what is called "The Tragic Week." Sparked by a military conscription of the poor to fight in Morocco, mobs sacked and burned eighteen churches and forty-nine other ecclesiastic properties with an anticlericalist vehemence not seen in the city since 1835.[7] Ongoing general strikes and the looming threat of violence directed at economic and political elites further strained social tensions. After holding a workers' conference in Barcelona in 1910, anarchists formed the Confederación Nacional del Trabajo, or CNT, trade union. By 1919 it had six hundred thousand members across Spain.[8] Because Barcelona was the nation's leading urban center of anarchist activity, it became known in this period as "La Rosa del Fuego" (The Rose of Fire).

Though Spain was neutral during World War I, the production of textiles, machinery, and other commodities for the belligerents set off both shortages and vicious rounds of inflation that especially affected the cost of food. Consumer protests, often involving women, became a recurring theme.[9] Labor unrest intensified with major strikes in 1917 and 1919, and street fighting between the CNT, rival conservative unions, and company thugs devolved into what was called *pistolerismo*.[10] As Temma Kaplan reminds us, "between 1920 and 1921, more than 230 people were shot in the streets of Barcelona alone."[11] In these years leading up to the imposition of the Primo de Rivera dictatorship, violent social strife was at a fevered pitch. The degree to which government or other provocateurs fomented the disorder as justification to suppress the CNT remains unclear. But by the early 1920s, some observers began to call Barcelona the "Chicago of the Mediterranean."[12]

All of these monikers reflect E. J. Hobsbawm's estimation that Barcelona was Western Europe's most revolutionary city in the opening decades of the twentieth century.[13] These sobriquets speak to volatility, to change, and to danger. Nadia Fava and Manuel Guàrdia emphasize the role that a public "sense of insecurity" played in the development of Barcelona's market-based food-retailing system over the long run.[14] They assert that by the early twentieth century, "the problem was no longer hunger caused by a lack of grain supplies," but rather, food scarcity resulting from "an increase in prices and in the cost of living for the workers in relation to their salaries."[15] Control over the food trade through the markets became all the more urgent a concern in a city that had become known for its revolutionary fervor.

## Regenerating the Public Market-Hall System

Yet not all revolutions challenge private property; they come in various forms— technological, scientific, demographic, and so on.[16] Spain at this time was experiencing a revolution of a different sort, one that transformed the collective psyche as it sought to grapple with the regret and humiliation following the loss of the last of its colonies in the Pacific and the Caribbean. All of the intellectual, cultural, social, and political movements of the era featured some greater or lesser obsession with "regeneration"—that is, revival, the path forward, and/or the repair of wounded pride. Regenerationism, of course, served diverse agendas. Among the Catalanist political variants of regenerationism, the formation of the Lliga Regionalista Party in 1901 was the most significant. Catholic, bourgeois, and conservative in its orientation, the Lliga presented itself as an alternative to the corrupt national political system of the Restoration, which featured rigged elections and the regular rotation of government between predominating Liberal and Conservative parties. First scoring a series of victories in municipal elections, the Lliga was able to achieve administrative control over the province of Barcelona in 1908, and to use it, as Enric Ucelay da Cal explains, as "a power base from which flowed all manner of cultural initiatives."[17] Capitalizing on the broad appeal of Catalan nationalism, the Lliga played a crucial role in breaking *caciquista* control over Catalonia, even though mayors and civil and military governors continued to be appointed from Madrid.[18] Though a host of new political parties emerged in Barcelona in the first decades of the century, the Lliga was the most influential. Along with Lerroux's Radical Republicans and other smaller regionalist parties, the Lliga dominated the city council between 1901 and 1923.

For all those who governed in the volatile and populous city that Barcelona had become, regeneration remained central. If Barcelona was to rival Madrid as the nation's preeminent expression of metropolitan modernity—and the race was on—the annexed municipalities had to be integrated rationally and city services had to be extended and systematized.[19] The inextricable link between food supply and social order was evident to all. Shortages of food and fuel and rising prices had sparked most of the popular uprisings of the nineteenth century. As the twentieth century began, issues related to food access continued to constitute a potentially explosive problem. Given the soaring cost of living and the provisioning crises associated with the World War I era, ongoing intervention in the food-retailing system remained an urgent item on the municipal agenda. In their efforts to dampen social unrest, municipal authorities in Barcelona stepped up sanitary inspections of food, restructured wholesaling, and intervened to impose price controls. The city council also amended the regulatory codes governing markets and sought to integrate them more effectively with the shops, taverns, cafés, and eateries that surrounded them. These efforts to bring about integration and systemization in the food sector reflected regeneration in a crucial area of urban planning; ultimately, they had the effect of reinforcing older mutual dependencies between small-scale retailers and municipal authorities.

CONTEXT

The liberalization of the Spanish economy took place in stages with a notable weakening of the power of the guild system over the course of the second half of the eighteenth century. In Barcelona specifically, the conquering Bourbon administrators reorganized guild structures after 1716 in accordance with some of the centralizing economic principles of Jean-Baptiste Colbert, Minister of Finance under Louis XIV.[20] The guilds were stripped of their effective political power until 1766, even though they still controlled historic trades and forms of production. Pere Molas Ribalta's crucial study of Barcelona's eighteenth-century guilds shows that the new Bourbon policies set the stage for a gradual process of decay and that the number of guilds in the city, and the number of workers included in the system, decreased as the economy expanded.[21] New types of trade and new technologies of production tended to flourish outside the eighteenth-century guild structure. Still, Spain was late in comparison to many other European nations in stripping the guilds of their effective power. After the Cortes of Cádiz made initial efforts to liberalize the economy in 1813, the guild structure was revived under Fernando VII's reign. Then in 1829, Spain adopted its first national commercial code, the *Código Comercial*, and in 1834, the guild system was formally abolished under the regency of María Cristina. The new law set forth freedom of commerce in all varieties of food and drink, except bread.[22] The liberalization of commerce facilitated the expansion in the ranks of butchers, fishmongers, and other vendors who acquired stall permits and filled the vast interior spaces of the new markets dotting the urban landscape. The development of the Eixample and the gradual liberalization of the real-estate market worked together to underpin this process.[23] Article 1 of the 1858 *Ley de Inquilinatos* promulgated by the Spanish Cortes gave the owners of urban buildings the legitimate right to freely rent properties according to lease agreements.

Yet the new political economy of food retailing that took shape in Barcelona in the decades leading up to the outbreak of the Civil War in 1936 was not based upon a model of laissez-faire capitalism. After the passage of the 1887 Law of Associations that guaranteed the right of free assembly, the city's food retailers, both inside and beyond the markets, began to create a new generation of associations designed to exert political influence in defense of their trades within the expanding municipal bureaucracy that governed provisioning. Though partially suppressed during the years of the Primo de Rivera dictatorship, these food-retailing associations matured during the Second Republic, forming part of what Javier Casares Ripol and Alfonso Rebollo Arévalo describe as a sort of guild revival they term *cuasigremialismo*.[24]

## THE REGULATORY INTEGRATION OF
## THE FOOD MARKETS AFTER 1898

The municipal governments of the Restoration era justified ownership and management of food-market halls by including them within their paradigm of the city's modern public-service infrastructure. Ongoing annexation between 1897 and 1929 altered the city's physical and social morphology while posing a host of new problems for municipal authorities seeking to extend and consolidate administrative control. Each of the city's new peripheral districts came into the metropolis with some pre-existing infrastructure for the retail distribution of food. Some, such as Gràcia and Sant Martí, were already vested with modern metal market halls before annexation. Authorities in other areas, such as San Gervasi, San Andreu, and Sants, had not undertaken such initiatives. Rather, they had open-air or partially covered markets, which in the years after annexation the city moved to more fully enclose in new structures. Continuing its program of new construction, the municipality inaugurated five new market halls between 1911 and 1927. By the declaration of the Republic in 1931, the municipality was operating fifteen retail and three wholesale food-market halls according to a standardized system of rules and regulations.[25]

The regulatory codes adopted to govern the operation of Barcelona's food-market system struck a balance between fomenting profit-making enterprises that would generate revenues for municipal coffers and defining them as realms subject to municipal intervention in the name of the public good. Though some control rested at the provincial and national level, the city's legal authority over the expanding network of market halls was well established by the early twentieth century. Supreme Court rulings of January 13, 1903, and May 5, 1905, as well as the Sanitary Commission's instruction of January 4, 1904, all "clearly and unmistakably" promulgated "as a general and indisputable principle that the provisioning of the population falls within the legal authority of the Municipalities."[26]

In the case of Barcelona, two distinct levels of bureaucratic control emerged. Operating under the direction of the mayor and the city council, Barcelona's Treasury Commission (Comisión de Hacienda) regulated food sales through its Bureau of Provisions (Negociado de Abastos) and a corps of municipal inspectors. Beneath these authorities, a second level of bureaucracy operated to administer each of the individual markets. The 1898 code specified that municipal markets would be staffed by a director, a rent collector, a verifier of weights and measures, and also a team of uniformed porters, janitors, and doormen, known collectively as *mozos*.[27] Municipal veterinarians charged with certifying the safety of the food for sale were also assigned to inspect market halls.[28] Testing food safety in the Municipal Laboratory began in 1905. In 1911, the office of the Director General de los Mercados was established to create another level of control.[29] In addition to the broader goals of collecting rents and taxes and warding off popular unrest, the 1898 code and its subsequent amendments also reflected municipal commitment to the defense of public markets as the city's preeminent food-retailing centers. In so doing, the city committed itself to protecting the commercial rights of vendors working inside the markets and to limiting the competition they faced within each of the structures.

Barcelona's 1898 market code strengthened the rights of urban-dwelling retail vendors while legitimizing and institutionalizing the long decline of rural-dwelling producer-vendors from the city's hinterland. Though some producers were permitted to continue selling their wares along the outside of the city's market halls, the urban-dwelling vendors inside were accorded permits that were increasingly more stable and valuable.[30] The 1898 code specified three types of stall licenses for vendors inside the market halls: fixed-stall permits (*puestos fijos*) that were auctioned off by the city and required vendors to pay monthly rents for their space; provisional stall permits (*provisionales*) that were temporarily held by vendors and required weekly payments of rent; and a third type of permit, designated in the code for itinerant vendors (*ambulantes*), that involved daily payment of rents.[31] In the first two decades of the twentieth century, stall concessions underwent a process of standardization with fixed-stall permit-holders coming to predominate over provisional and itinerant licensees. In 1905, the Treasury Commission ordered that all market vendors who held provisional stall titles for more than two years had to undergo a process of legalization and become fixed-permit holders.[32] On February 4, 1915, the Treasury Commission declared the expiration of all the remaining provisional stall permits in the city.[33] The administrative history of Sant Antoni Market suggests how this pattern played out in the city as a whole.[34] By 1919, all but 4 of the 726 stalls at Sant Antoni were held through fixed licenses, in the hands of vendors paying a set monthly fee and tending to stay in their stalls over the course of several decades.[35] This process of market-stall title rationalization enabled municipal authorities to exercise greater control over food retailing in the markets of the city. Market directors were ordered by the Treasury Commission to keep registries with the names and addresses of all the vendors, while individuals working in the markets were expected to familiarize themselves with and adhere to the complex rules governing this form of commercial exchange.[36]

These municipal policies were underpinned by several motives. One was purely pecuniary. The city operated food-market halls in part to generate funds for public coffers. The *Gaceta Municipal de Barcelona* in January 1915 reported that the city had spent 367,295 pesetes operating markets during the previous month and took in from them 1,383,100 pesetes in revenue through rents, taxes, and fees.[37] The defense of consumer interests was a another motive. Article 77 of the 1898 code set forth the obligation of market directors and their employees to "ensure the interest of the public and attempt to prevent fraud from being committed for any reason." The code set hours, established standards of cleanliness, controlled weights and measures, and required vendors to use "proper forms and manners" in dealing with the public. All insults and offenses were to be reported to the director for resolution.[38] Market butchers who were physically repugnant to public sensibilities were prohibited from entering the premises. Offal vendors were forbidden to split livestock heads and extract brains in their stalls because it could have "an ill effect" on the public and detract from the markets' "importance and decorum."[39] The code also held individual permit holders personally responsible for all that took place in their stalls by forbidding subleasing or hiring clerks or substitutes to take over operations, except by permission from market directors, and then only in the case of temporary absence.[40]

The 1898 code also set up a system in which every market was allotted a given number of concessions according to strictly set-forth specializations. At least in theory, all urban residents could be assured that they would find an assortment of the necessary staples at a centralized point within their neighborhoods. But beyond broadening consumer access to food, such regulation permitted the city to exert direct control over the growing population of vendors, who were required to remain within the good graces of directors and inspectors in order to operate their stalls. In return for adherence to municipal rules, vendors were insulated by the city from new sources of competition. The political economy of food in Barcelona thus sought to protect both consumer and vendor populations from unregulated market forces. In their affirmation of a reciprocal relationship between the city government and the urban population, these policies served to contribute legitimacy to the structures of authority that constituted municipal rule in the socially volatile and dramatically expanded metropolis.

## CENTRALIZING MEAT SLAUGHTERING AND WHOLESALE TRADE

Rationalizing the markets involved a corresponding extension of municipal authority over meat slaughtering and wholesale trade in food. A long debate over location preceded the construction of the municipal slaughterhouse, known as "l'Escorxador," on land called "La Vinyeta," near what would become the Plaça d'Espanya.[41] Incorporating materials repurposed from the 1888 Exposición, the city's new slaughterhouse was officially inaugurated in 1894.[42] As the surrounding municipalities were annexed at the turn of the century, the pre-existing slaughterhouses were gradually shut down.[43] The process of centralizing and controlling livestock-slaughtering in the city remained difficult, however. Clandestine private operations were pursued with much vigor, and the Bureau of Provisioning developed a system of symbols marking meat from legal slaughterhouses, with the responsibility for keeping the encryption key carefully guarded by the police.[44] Public health issues aside, the incentives for establishing a municipal monopoly over meat slaughtering were tremendous. By 1915, the city was spending 37,950 pesetes per month in its operation of four slaughterhouses and taking in 1,526,121 from them in revenues as a return.[45] In 1927, the Excorxador was expanded with the addition of two new halls, and beef slaughtering in Sant Martí and Sarrià was brought definitively to an end.[46] Nine years later, the city's butchers were calling for additional expansion and upgrades, but all such projects were put on hold due to the outbreak of the Civil War and the rolling crises that followed.[47]

The centralization and rationalization of wholesaling was a similarly lengthy process. Until 1921, the wholesaling of fruits and vegetables took place in stalls designated for that purpose at La Boqueria, Santa Caterina, San Antoni, Sants, La Llibertat, Sant Andreu, Clot, and Horta markets.[48] The municipal government had been working toward rationalizing wholesale trade in food since at least 1906.[49] On the eve of the outbreak of World War I, the city faced increasing pressure from producers and wholesalers to establish a central market where trade could take place in a less chaotic fashion. Writing in the *Revista del Instituto Agrícola*

*Catalán de Sant Isidre* in 1913, J. M. Pujades decried the traffic congestion that wholesalers faced in attempting to reach La Boqueria Market, with long lines of carts forming around midnight and heaps of fruit and vegetable baskets unloaded with a haste that damaged perishable products. Pujades called for the establishment of a central wholesale market for fruits and vegetables located near a rail line and including modern refrigeration and warehousing facilities.[50] The strain upon the provisioning system during the war led to more pleas from the Instituto Agrícola. In May 1916, it asserted that food shortages in the city were due largely to the disorganized manner in which wholesale trade in fruits and vegetables was effected.[51] By November of that year, the Instituto Agrícola had submitted a proposal to Barcelona's Treasury Commission for a central market.[52]

In 1918, the Treasury Bureau began to move forward with a plan to centralize wholesale trade in produce from within the cavernous El Born market hall. The project involved repair and reconditioning the structure to make room for some 250 new wholesale stalls.[53] El Born had been overbuilt and never attracted enough retail vendors to fill its available space. For the better part of two decades before 1921, up to half of El Born was used to house the city's central wholesale fish market.[54] Still, the fixed-license retail vendors working from there opposed the plan to convert the market to wholesaling of fruits and vegetables, and thus they acted to delay the completion of the process until after a new civil governor, General Severiano Martínez Anido, was appointed in 1920. Martínez Anido understood that the heightened levels of labor unrest and social conflict were directly connected to subsistence issues and that El Born's reorganization had to proceed without further delay.[55] As a corollary, the city established a new central fish market in a pavilion left over from the 1888 Exposición on Wellington Street, adjacent to Ciutadella Park, and near what had already operated for more than two decades as the wholesale poultry market. These moves signaled what Guàrdia, Oyón, and Fava describe as a "decidedly interventionist policy of control" by the municipality over both profit margins and prices at the wholesale level.[56]

## CONSOLIDATING THE RETAIL VENDOR POPULATION

On the retail side of the equation by the early 1920s, increased sedentariness in the city's public markets had contributed to the consolidation of fixed-stall vendors as a more definable commercial block and as an important interest group within the municipal polity. For the most part, fixed-stall permits were acquired through public auction as well as through the legalization process that brought older market vendors into compliance with the new policies. Those who had long worked as vendors were recognized by the municipal corporation as having legitimate claims to earn a living in the public markets, and everyone else was offered a chance by the Treasury Commission to enter into the trade on the basis of public auction.[57] The new rules also recognized, as before, that market-vendor work was often a family-based economic activity and that individuals should have the right to pass their stall titles on from one generation to the next. The code thus allowed that upon the death of the fixed-stall license-holder, permits could be legally conveyed through what was known as a "conveyance by demise" (*trespaso por defunción*) from one spouse to another, to children, parents, or siblings, or as designated in a vendor's last will and testament.[58] Where such relations did not exist or the designated family members did not desire to claim the rights, stall titles reverted back to the city and were auctioned off to the highest bidder. These policies had the effect of protecting family-based food-stall operations in the event of the death of individual title-holders while underpinning market vendors' expectations that the city should defend and protect the rights of descendants to earn a living.

In November 1921, the Bureau of Provisioning announced an amendment to Article 17 of the 1898 code that allowed for stall conveyances between living persons (*trespasos intervivos*).[59] Such a provision increased the value of successful market-stall operations and meant that vendors could accumulate greater amounts of capital. Market-stall licenses thus became a form of real property much more similar to fixed shops than they had been before. Still, the rights of descendants were protected. Anyone who stood to inherit a stall could present his or her claim to the Bureau of Provisioning for adjudication, and if the sale of the stall permit was deemed to constitute an injustice, the transaction would be nullified. This rule stood through revisions of the market code, remaining in effect during the Franco-era municipal regimes. Inasmuch as the 1921 amendment to Article 17 allowed the city to collect quintuple the usual rates for this new form of conveyance, we see once again that expanding vendors' commercial rights could serve to enrich the municipal coffers.

### Regulatory Limitations on Competition

The fact that, as in earlier periods, market-stall licenses continued to be highly restrictive also had the effect of protecting vendors from unrestrained competition in the food-retailing sector. Individuals securing market-stall licenses through municipal auctions, through the legalization process, through a conveyance by demise or otherwise, could only sell those items specified in their permits. Entrepreneurial initiatives and broader market forces therefore had limited impact in determining which items were sold by whom. In fact, such narrowly defined market-stall titles were disadvantageous to some vendors who sought to increase sales by offering new and different products not specified in their permits. But the strict application of these rules also protected vendors whose trade did not involve artisanal skills. It would have been easy, for example, for fresh fish vendors to add mussels, clams, and shrimp to their list of offerings because the latter were items that simply had to be scooped into the scales, wrapped in paper, and handed to customers in exchange for the asking price. A shellfish vendor, on the other hand, could not compete by adding fresh fish to the list of offerings because selling fish required cutting, boning, and scaling, all skills that were considered by the market community as artisanal in nature. In order to be executed according to community standards, selling fish required a period of training and apprenticeship. Similarly, poulterers could have easily added the vegetables needed to make the traditional escudella soup to the list of items sold at their stalls (which, as we have seen, some did illegally), but vegetable vendors could not reciprocate because they were not trained in the fine arts of killing, bleeding, and cutting fowl. The market-stall licensing system thus acted to limit commercial expansion and product-line innovation while preserving older models of firm specialization. Though the city did alter the balance among specialties offered in given markets over time, it did so only slowly and infrequently. Even when stall licenses changed hands, new licensees could not expand sales beyond the goods assigned to that stall.

Ongoing tensions surrounded enforcement of the licensing rules. After receiving numerous complaints about violations in May 1910, the Bureau of Provisions scolded market directors and inspectors across the city for assuming the authority to allow vendors to change the goods they sold. Enforcement at the market level continued to be a problem throughout the decade.[60]

Complaints about violations of the rules limiting competition were among the most common themes of both individual and collective vendor petitions to the city for redress of grievances. For example, in April 1923 nine La Llibertat Market vendors petitioned their director to oppose broadening the range of fowl that hen vendors could sell; in August of that same year, four more La Llibertat vendors complained about one particular poulterer in the market selling items for which she was not legally authorized.[61] Conversely, when in 1919 Francisco

Vilaró y Vilaró was permitted to shift from selling mutton to selling veal at La Llibertat Market, his petition expressly set forth that the change in his license would not prejudice other vendors.[62] So while the municipal rules specifying the items that each vendor could sell certainly had the effect of defending consumers by guaranteeing a balance of varied offerings in each market, they also were a way of keeping internal competition among stall-keepers in check.

## MARKETS VERSUS SHOPS

Municipal shop-licensing laws, which were tightened in the 1920s and 1930s, similarly protected vendors and other pre-existing food retailers by authorizing new retail enterprises only where they would not directly compete with markets. As of 1925, no new shops selling items available inside the city's markets could be located within fifty meters of these structures, and most new shops were forced to locate in areas that the Bureau of Provisions considered to be underserved by the existing food-retailing infrastructure.[63] Municipal policy sought to integrate markets and shops and to create a balance between these two forms of food retailing. Regulations governing the sale of breakfasts and refreshments (desayunos y refrescos) serve as just one example of how the city tried to balance the interests of food vendors inside the markets with those of retailers located in fixed neighborhood shops. On July 1, 1914, the Treasury Commission ruled that ambulatory vendors selling breakfasts and refreshments could no longer enter the market halls where fixed stalls designated for the sale of such items had been licensed by the municipality.[64] Two months later, the commission modified this rule slightly by allowing that when vendors placed orders in advance, licensed establishments from the neighborhoods could make deliveries to individual stalls.[65] A decade and a half later, the issue remained a contested one. In September 1930, Florencio Gelabert Figueras complained in writing to the director of L'Abaceria Central about the practice. He had acquired Stall 2, the only one in the market designated by license for the sale of chocolates y refrescos, only to discover that every bar and kiosk in the area was delivering food and beverages to the vendors in their stalls. In his view, the situation constituted unfair competition to market-based trade.[66] We see here that the boundaries between retailers and consumers were not fixed ones. Those who spent their days in Barcelona's market halls selling food generated a demand that supported nearby eateries of various sorts. Vendors were also consumers. The Bureau of Provision's policies reflected the city's eagerness to regulate how vendors and food retailers within and beyond the market carried out their trades in complex relationship to one another.

Shop licenses, like market-stall permits, strictly limited the goods that could be sold to consumers. Municipal statistics for 1902 indicate that there were no fresh fish, shellfish, greengrocer, or offal shops operating in the city. All these foods were sold exclusively through the markets from 3,526 individual stalls (the Bureau of Provisions having issued 441 fresh fish, 68 shellfish, 2,863 fruit and vegetable, and 154 offal market licenses at that time).[67] Other goods, such as bread and milk, were rarely sold from market stalls. Only five of the city's sixteen markets in 1902 featured any milk, and only eight had any bread available for sale. There were 597 bakeries in the city at that time and only 43 bread stalls; likewise, there were 102 *lechería* shops selling milk, and only ten stalls citywide that offered the product from within the confines of a market. Certainly, shop licensing was less restrictive than market-stall licensing. The 1902 *Anuario Estadístico de la Ciudad de Barcelona* lists sixteen types of licenses for retail food shops; with respect to markets, it listed fifty-eight types. The single largest category of retail food shops were licensed as *abacerías* and *comestibles,* terms that referenced the dramatic expansion of the grocery trade beyond the markets by the early twentieth century. These represented 1,128 out of the 3,741 retail food shops in the city, just over 30 percent of the total. Inside the markets, conversely, *abacería* and *comestible* licenses made up only 5.4 percent of all the stalls.[68] While growing in overall importance, neither grocers' shops nor their counterparts in the markets could legally expand the lines to include such basic items as eggs, bread, meat, poultry, fish, milk, or fresh fruits and vegetables.

Each shop license specified a particular retail niche within which the Bureau of Provisions acted to limit competition by attempting to space new firms out across less densely commercialized areas. The complex rules governing shop licensing and the minimum distances between the food shops that competed with market stalls were made more stringent over time, with butchers and fresh fish vendors earning the greatest protections by the late 1920s. After August 5, 1927, no new butchers were authorized to open within 250 meters of the public markets in the Eixample and within 150 meters of the public markets in the rest of the city.[69] After June 30, 1929, fresh fish shops were authorized to open, but only where they were located at least 700 meters from the markets.[70]

The urban commercial geography that such a system created sharply contrasted with that of the pre-industrial city where groups of specialized retailers had often located along specific streets that bore their names. Almost as restrictive as the defunct guild order, the municipal provisioning system had become rationalized on the basis of the assumption that each food retailer, whether working from a public market or a private shop, had the right to draw upon a predictable share of the neighborhood clientele. The concept of fair competition for both food retailers and municipal authorities alike had developed into one that stressed the even spatial distribution of commerce outside the markets and the balance among vendor specializations within.

There were of course differing opinions and myriad disagreements regarding the implementation of the geographic principles underlying the new political economy of food retailing in the city. Pre-existing shops located adjacent to the markets were grandfathered in, and plenty of extralegal trade took place. Unlicensed ambulatory vendors remained an ongoing issue of consternation. Resources devoted to enforcement varied through time, with the municipal governments of the Primo de Rivera dictatorship accused by established retailers of lacking a sincere will to uphold the rules. By the early 1930s, shops increasingly competed with markets, especially in comparison with the commercial landscape of 1902. Guàrdia, Oyón, and Fava's analysis of tax rolls in 1932 indicate that shops accounted for 40 percent of all fruit and vegetable sales, 26 percent of fresh fish sales, and 21 percent of meat sales.[71] Barcelona's markets were certainly still holding their own, especially in comparison to their counterparts in Britain, France, and Germany, but food sales from fixed shops had taken off dramatically nonetheless. The city's food-retailing geography by 1932 featured two key characteristics: a clustering of shops located near municipal markets; and some strong concentrations of food shops in residential areas located at the greatest distance from markets, thus in parts of the city that were least-served by the municipal system.[72]

## KEEPING MARKET-STALL ENTERPRISES SMALL

The 1898 code governing the operation of the city's markets, and its successor that was issued in January 1928, both explicitly limited competition among vendors through prohibition on the accumulation of stall licenses.[73] Article 19 of the 1898 code specified that no individual could acquire more than two permits in a single market, but Article 9 of the 1928 code went further. It specified that individuals holding two stalls, wherever located, could not bid at municipal auctions for an additional title, and neither could those whose household members held four stalls in one market. The 1928 code also specified that minors could not bid at municipal auctions, nor could those who lacked full civil rights to contract (this prohibition, as we shall see, did not extend to women, regardless of their marital status). Thus efforts to expand the size of market-stall enterprises were strictly limited.

The building of market chain operations within or beyond the structures of the family economy was likewise impeded. Many vendors had long possessed two licenses and were able to operate a single enterprise from a double-sized stall. Married couples or other relations could acquire four contiguous stall licenses in one market and operate their businesses as a single family unit. This was an arrangement that encouraged endogamous marriage within markets, especially among the children of contiguous stall owners. But such efforts to expand stall businesses were effectively restricted by the 1928 code, which limited stall licenses to four stalls per household. Thus larger chain operations similar to those that Marks and Spencer were forming in Britain's markets during this period did not appear in Barcelona. The few chain operations that formed in the early twentieth century sold goods seldom if ever offered for sale in the city's public food-market halls. J. Salat and Sons, for example, had eleven retail shops selling oil and soap in Barcelona in 1910.[74] By 1915, the firm had incorporated as Salat S.A. and had seventeen retail shops in the city.[75] Likewise, Granjas Soldevila, a family-owned and -operated dairy firm, built a chain of more than a dozen separate retail outlets in the early 1910s.[76] But such commercial expansion was a rarity in the early twentieth century. Nearly all food-retailing firms inside and beyond the markets, with the exception of upscale cafés and restaurants, remained relatively small-scale operations.

## TWO EARLY DISPUTES OVER COMPETITION WITHIN THE COMMUNITY OF MARKET VENDORS IN GRÀCIA

Late-nineteenth- and early-twentieth-century disputes involving market vendors in the neighborhood of Gràcia illustrate the extent to which market vendors were often highly sensitive to issues of fairness. Where Gràcia's market vendors believed that public authorities were failing to control what they perceived as unfair competition in the sale of food, they acted to demand redress. Conflicts among food retailers in Gràcia that predated annexation had to be resolved by the highest levels of Barcelona's political administration as the new metropolis took shape and absorbed the village after 1897. In the process of integrating Gràcia's food-retailing system into that of the larger city, Barcelona's provisioning bureaucracy took measures that legitimated the demands of urban-dwelling fixed-license market vendors for protection from competition in the sector.

A closer look at Gràcia is warranted here. Two markets had operated to provision its residents through the final decades of the nineteenth century. La Llibertat Market, of iron-truss construction and elaborate modernist ornamentation, had opened in 1888 near what today is the Plaça Gal·la Placídia on the Via Augusta just above the Diagonal. Like El Born, Sant Antoni, and La Concepció markets, La Llibertat was constructed by the Catalan firm La Maquinista Terrestre i Marítima. La Revolució Market, nearer to the historic center of Gràcia, had operated in the Plaça de Isabel II much longer; it was only partially covered and never fully enclosed. The names of these markets, of course, reflected Gràcia's political inclinations, as well as municipal support for the uprising in 1868 that signaled the ascent of liberalism as the basis for the constitutional regime of the Bourbon Restoration (1874–1931). In this sense, Gràcia's markets carried their own distinctive symbolic loads.

After decades of rapid population growth and the intensive expansion of mechanized textile production in Gràcia,[77] La Revolució vendors had grown too numerous by 1890 to fit into the space allotted to them in the public square.[78] As was often the case in such circumstances, stalls spilled over into surrounding streets. As the century came to a close, a number of the largest industrial concerns began to move their textile factories out of Gràcia to more peripheral areas in the plain of Barcelona where greater space was available. Controversy ensued when in 1891 Gràcia industrialist Francesc Puigmartí undertook to sell the site of his former textile factory, located just one block from La Revolució, to the village in order to build a new and more modern public market-hall structure. Both the provincial government and La Revolució vendors opposed the project from its outset because they saw it as a threat to the two already existing markets in Gràcia, and by extension to the retailers who worked therein. But despite opposition from both above and below, Puigmartí and the Gràcia municipal government persevered in their desire to see the new market constructed. As a way of getting around the impediments placed on the project by the provincial government, the municipality of Gràcia approved a plan in 1891 for the construction and operation of a new market by private investors on Puigmartí's site.[79]

Construction of the new L'Abaceria Central Market proceeded through 1892, and by December the building stood ready to be inaugurated.[80] The new iron market hall featured elaborate decorative elements and three naves: a central one that was to include 28 fresh fish stalls, 9 salt cod stalls, 20 poultry and game stalls, and 144 fruit and vegetable stalls. Two lateral naves were designed to include 93 meat and 20 chickpea stalls. The market's design also incorporated 73 grocers' shops, a provision that certainly reflected new tastes and eating habits at the end of the nineteenth century. The *Diario de Barcelona* lauded the L'Abaceria Central's modern infrastructural elements, especially noting the abundance of light and running water and the marble counters and sinks that would allow for the sale of meat, fresh fish, and salt cod in accordance with the highest standards of hygiene.[81] Under the private management of J. Torrents, Serra, i Companyia, new vendors were recruited to purchase stall concessions.

But both private investors and Gràcia's municipal authorities underestimated the opposition of established Gràcia vendors to the new market's opening.[82] Two days prior to the scheduled inauguration, angry La Revolució vendors and their supporters converged upon the town hall in Gràcia with a petition demanding that the municipality block the opening of the L'Abaceria Central Market on the grounds that it constituted unfair privately organized competition in the public food-retailing sector.[83] After a prolonged and heated debate among officials divided in their support for the threatened vendors, Gràcia's mayor turned the issue over to a special commission for resolution. Fearing an outbreak of violence, he called in the Guardia Civil to restore order.[84] Ultimately, the interested groups reached a compromise that involved the prohibition of fresh fish sales at L'Abaceria Central.[85] Because fresh fish was an important and popular staple, this policy had the effect of compelling consumers to visit both the new and the old markets in order to find a full range of goods for sale. When three years later the civil governor of the province overruled the municipality of Gràcia's prohibition on fresh fish sales at L'Abaceria Central, new rounds of protest broke out.[86] A key part of the negotiated settlement was the commitment on the part of Gràcia's village government not to purchase the new private market hall and to defend and protect the already existing La Llibertat and La Revolució public markets instead. Ultimately, L'Abaceria Central became a public food market in 1912, but only after Gràcia was annexed by Barcelona and the city purchased the structure. Then an agreement was reached to guarantee La Revolució vendors a place therein.[87]

A second episode of conflict in the newly annexed neighborhood of Gràcia is also worth considering for what it reveals about the extent to which La Llibertat Market's urban-dwelling vendors were willing to defend what they perceived as their right to earn a living. This conflict, unfolding in 1898, surrounded the role of rural producer-vendors in the city's provisioning system.

As was the case with other markets in Barcelona, La Llibertat's director was authorized to issue a specific number of licenses to what were known as *pagesos*, or "peasant" vendors, many of whose families had sold at the city's markets for generations. Every day a group of several dozen women traveled to La Llibertat Market by train or by cart, bringing with them bundles of fruits and vegetables from their family's lands in the Vallés region behind Tibidabo Mountain.[88] Beginning at five a.m., these vendors set up crude makeshift stalls around the outside of the market and sold their produce at prices that were usually below those offered by the fixed-license urban-dwelling retail vendors who sold from inside. Because working-class women usually went to market in the earliest hours before clocking in at mills or factories, peasant vendors drew mainly on these consumers for their sales. The more affluent housewives in the neighborhood tended to do their marketing later in the morning, by which point the producer-vendors had packed up and left for the day.[89] The conflict over producer-vendor sales around La Llibertat Market stemmed from disagreement over the fairness of the rules mandating that such activity cease at nine a.m. so that the bulk of the best clientele would be reserved for the retail vendors inside the market. This left the peasant vendors with the option of hauling their leftover stock back home or selling it at the last moment at prices that did not render a profit. The arrangement ultimately generated indignation among the producer-vendors.

The *Diario de Barcelona* reported that beginning on Monday, July 25, 1898, the producer-vendors at La Llibertat moved to test the resolve of the authorities by refusing to pack up at the specified hour and continuing sales until all their stocks were gone.[90] Multiple efforts on the part of the market director and his staff to force them to adhere to the rules proved fruitless. Called to the lieutenant mayor's office, these bold women held their ground, refusing to concede. When they arrived to set up their stalls the next morning, they were met by police brought in to enforce the lieutenant mayor's order cancelling all producer-vendor sales for the day. Arguments ensued, and when some of the women resisted, arrests and detentions followed. This act of defiance was immediately perceived as a threat to the retail vendors inside the market, who believed that the rules of fairness limited the extent to which producer-vendors should be allowed to compete with them by offering lower prices. In addition to confronting the market administration and the producer-vendors themselves, the retail vendors inside La Llibertat Market announced that if the nine a.m. rule was not upheld they would go on strike. Given the social volatility of the populous district of Gràcia, which included some sixty thousand residents, such a prospect portended chaos.

The response of the market administration offers further evidence that urban-dwelling food-market vendors were emerging as a formidable block capable of wielding power within the municipal bureaucracy. The next day, the president of the Treasury Commission, the lieutenant mayor, and three city councilmen converged on La Llibertat Market to seek a solution to the problem that would "satisfy the pretensions of the vendors from the interior and the exterior" of the structure.[91] The negotiated settlement provided for the resumption of peasant-vendor sales outside the market, but only if they adhered to the set closing time. Moreover, those vendors were limited from then onward to wholesale rather to retail trade, and to the sale of goods that were not available for sale inside the structure. The concession made to producer-vendors was that as stalls opened up inside the structure, they would be given first access to them.[92] The looming crisis was averted because the highest levels of authority over provisioning showed a willingness to use force to uphold the retail urban-dwelling vendors' demands.

Still, the population of producer-vendors that traded from around the outside of, and sometimes within, the markets was not driven to extinction in the twentieth century. Some, expanding production, moved into wholesale trade from El Born; most kept their stalls as retail outlets for small family farms. In any case, the peasant-vendors increasingly integrated themselves into the larger system in the first decades of the twentieth century and allied themselves with emerging retailer associations as of 1921. By 1926, a group of fixed-permit vendors at La Boqueria successfully petitioned the mayor for the recuperation of losses that they had sustained when these producer-vendors were moved out of their most proximate environs.[93] Subsequent vendor campaigns to limit competition focused instead, among other issues, on the suppression of unlicensed ambulatory trade.

## The Vicissitudes of Food-Retailing Associationalism

Through the first decades of the twentieth century, market vendors from across the city demanded municipal protection from a range of threats to what they perceived as fair competition in their sector. Their demands took myriad forms. Individual and group petitions for redress of specific grievances were common, but so too was the formation of organizations and associations designed to reassert and redefine the lost power of the guilds. One of the earliest of these was the Sociedad de Venedores del Mercado del Born (Society of El Born Market Vendors), which in 1904 was headed by Francisco Cusell, who not coincidentally was also a representative of the wholesale fish vendors in the city.[94]

El Born Market faced a special set of challenges to commercial success. Inaugurated in 1876, the grand market hall was located in the heart the old Ribera neighborhood just a stone's throw from the Church of Santa Maria del Mar, an area that had long been a center of food trade in the city. Situated in the same neighborhood served by Santa Caterina Market, El Born's retail vendors were hard-pressed to draw customers away from what had become the area's epicenter for food shopping by the 1860s. Because there was unused space in El Born, the city set up its wholesale fish market there. Later, fish wholesaling was moved out of the market to another venue, which caused El Born to decline further. In a February 13, 1904, petition to Mayor Guillermo de Boladeres y Romà from the Society of El Born Market Vendors, Francisco Cusell claimed that it could not escape "the most dim-witted" observer that moving wholesale fish selling out of the structure had dealt "a mortal blow" to the remaining retailers there.[95] Cusell asserted that El Born, already "anemic," had fallen into a "soporific" state "resembling a vacant cemetery."[96]

On behalf of El Born's retail vendors, and with the support of the fresh fish wholesalers, Cusell urged that the municipality take measures to bolster the market's commercial viability. The fresh fish wholesalers, they asserted, should be moved back to El Born because it was better equipped, because it would save the city administrative costs, and because such a measure would, they believed, reinvigorate retail sales. Though the Treasury Commission honored the vendor organization's request and moved fish wholesaling back into the structure, retail sales did not recover at El Born in the following years. In 1921, as we have seen, El Born was refurbished and reorganized to specialize exclusively in the wholesaling of fruits and vegetables. Yet the demands made by Cusell on behalf of El Born vendors in 1904 illustrate the extent to which formal vendor organizations had begun to exert pressure on the city by the first years of the century. Over the course of the next decades, successive groups of vendors from El Born and elsewhere more frequently formed associations to demand municipal intervention in defense of their trade.

Indeed, market vendors created a complex web of commercial networks. A number of markets formed vendor associations in the second decade of the twentieth century, and then several citywide organizations emerged to represent vendor interests.[97] Alongside these associations was an array of organizations designed to advance the interests of specific market trades, with butchers and grocers leading the pack. Before the 1923 imposition of the Primo de Rivera dictatorship, vendors had organized formally at El Born, Sant Antoni, La Concepció, Sants, Hostafrancs, and El Clot markets, and possibly elsewhere.[98] Along with La Concepció's Associació de Vendedors Concessionaris (Association of Vendor Concessioners), which created a well-endowed mutual-aid fund, Sant

Antoni's Asociación de Vendedores del Mercado (Association of Market Vendors) appears to have been among the most vibrant and active. In 1919 it had offices on the Ronda San Pablo 77, a seal, and a letterhead. Upon electing a new board of directors on October 7 that year, it announced the names of its president, three vice-presidents, general secretary, two sub-secretaries, treasurer, vice-treasurer, accountant, and vice-accountant, and an additional ten voting members in a formal letter addressed to Sant Antonio's director.[99]

Mobilization in a number of markets responded to the challenges involved in centralizing wholesale trade in El Born and relocating its retail vendors to other markets. This was most certainly the case with respect to the Asociación de Vendedores del Mercado del Clot (Association of El Clot Market Vendors), which first appears in the historical record in February 1920 petitioning the Bureau of Provisions to keep its wholesale fruit and vegetable vendors there, rather than have them moved to El Born.[100] Other market vendors formed associations near the end of the Primo de Rivera dictatorship. La Boqueria's Associació de Concessionaris del Mercat de Sant Josep (Association of Sant Josep Market Concessioners) was born in 1929, in response to what *La Publicitat* later described as "arbitrary and unjust dispositions of the dictatorial municipality."[101]

Associations and bodies representing broader groups of market vendors also emerged. In March 1913, the Cámara de Vendedores en los Mercados Públicos de Barcelona y su Provincia (Chamber of Public Market Vendors of Barcelona and Its Province) sought the support of the city's Chamber of Commerce in its campaign to halt the retail sale of oranges at the port because these sales prejudiced the fruit vendors among its ranks.[102] Then, amidst heady labor unrest and after several years of intensifying consumer protest over the rising cost of food, Barcelona's mayor Antoni Martínez i Domingo pointed to the "special circumstances that run through the city" and therefore endorsed the December 1919 recommendation of the Federación de Vendedores de los Mercados (Federation of Market Vendors) that Christmas Eve sales end at the regular eight p.m. hour rather than extending late into the night, as was traditional for the holiday in more normal circumstances.[103] Ultimately, it was the Unión General de Vendedores de Mercados de Barcelona (the General Union of Barcelona Market Vendors) that assumed leadership, eclipsing or merging with the earlier citywide organizations by 1921. The Unión General stepped in to negotiate complex issues surrounding the reorganization of El Born Market, attempting to negotiate settlements with the Treasury Commission and the Provisioning Bureau that would be acceptable to all the parties affected by the process. Its president at that time, Francisco de A.

Casamitjana Germà, was a Sant Antoni vendor who had formerly served as head of that market's vendor association.[104]

## INDIVIDUAL MARKET-VENDOR ASSOCIATIONS

Individual market associations embraced the fundamental principles embodied in the 1898 code and were concerned with issues of commercial geography within and beyond the markets. In a number of instances, the Treasury Commission ceded to vendors' demands. At Sant Antoni Market, for example, vendors petitioned in 1910 to change the order and arrangement of stalls.[105] After more than a year of vendor pressure, the commission agreed to move the fresh fish stalls to the center of the hall and to situate poultry, salted fish, and offal stalls in the southern wing of the market where the fresh fish had until then been located.[106] This reconfiguration reflected collective beliefs about commercial fairness.

Stall location was an urgent matter to Sant Antoni vendors. Clearly, most stall enterprises competed to some extent with neighborhood shops and with the newly emerging consumer cooperatives. But because neighborhood fresh fish shops were not authorized until 1929, fish was a commodity that was especially powerful in drawing customers into the markets. The presumption among vendors was that being situated in the market along the path to the fresh fish section constituted something of an advantage. As customers passed other stalls on their way to buy fresh fish, they might buy things that they would otherwise purchase in the neighborhood shops. By securing the relocation of fresh fish to the center of Sant Antoni Market—where the four naves of the structure met—vendors reconfigured the market's commercial geography to better fit their sense of fairness. Thereafter, consumers seeking to buy fish would have to penetrate deep into the market; and because each nave had a door leading out to the streets of the neighborhood, all the market's vendors were given an equal chance of profiting from the boon that fresh fish vendors enjoyed by virtue of not having to compete with shops. Interestingly, the new arrangement situated the fresh fish vendors at the heart of what was designed as a panopticon, originally meant to house the office of the director. At least in retrospect, the move can be read as a sign of the ascendency of vendor power within the system. It also reflects changing alimentary habits underpinned by the development of mechanical refrigeration technologies and by new medical discourses that stressed the nutritional benefits of fresh fish as a source of protein.

Riding on this success, Sant Antoni market vendors then moved to organize more formally and to push for greater enforcement of the rules governing who could sell what in the market. In an October 4, 1911, petition, the new Association of Sant Antoni Market Vendors complained to the Bureau of Provisions that stall-keepers with grocers' licenses were selling eggs.[107] The association held that such violations subjected fixed-permit egg vendors to unfair competition. The president of the city's Treasury Commission recognized the legitimacy of the vendors' complaint and continued to demand greater vigilance by directors in the enforcement of the licensing rules. The fact that the on-site authorities—that is, the market director and his staff—often failed to provide vendors with the protection they demanded drove the formation of quasi-corporatist bodies seeking redress from the city's higher levels of provisioning bureaucracy.

## CONSOLIDATION

The Unión General de Vendedores was born out of an alliance among vendor associations that had formed in the city's seventh municipal district, in which the Sant Antoni, Sants, and Hostafrancs markets were located. It first appears in the historical record in 1921 with two petitions to Mayor Martínez i Domingo dated February 24. The first, which reads as if it had been drafted earlier in the day when cooler heads prevailed, took up the issue of the Treasury Commission's crackdown on weights and measures. It began by endorsing the city's efforts to "cut the root of systematic abuse by unscrupulous vendors," who hereinafter would be obligated to comply with the rules.[108] But then it proceeded to decry the Treasury Commission's policy of allowing individual buyers bringing charges for violations of weights and measures in the markets to claim part of the fine that was imposed upon the vendor. The petitioners asserted that the city had created powerful incentives for consumer fraud and that these had led to incidents in which "unscrupulous" shoppers who, between "leaving the place of sale and reaching the *repeso* [weight verification] office, practice concealment" of some part of whatever they had bought.[109] The temptation to accuse vendors of violations in weights and measures, and thus to claim a share of the fines, was especially intense in the salt cod departments of the markets. There, consumers bought rehydrated *bacalao* from which water continued to drain after it was removed from the desalinization sinks, weighed, wrapped in paper, and sold. Logically, the petitioners explained, the fish could not possibly weigh as much when it was presented to market officials for verification. The petition offered practical solutions to these problems, which included immersing rehydrated *bacalao* in water just prior to official weight verification, and mandating that consumers announce their intention to contest a sale before leaving the stall area where they made their purchase. This would allow a representative of the accused vendor to accompany the disgruntled buyer to the *repeso* office. In plain language, the vendors' association's petition asserted that if the buyer requested that the *repeso* verify weights and measures, the vendor should also have some municipal guarantees against consumer fraud.[110]

The second petition to the mayor drawn up by the allied Sant Antoni, Sants, and Hostafrancs vendor associations the same day was more strident, reading as if it had been written later in the day after heated discussions. It reacted vehemently to the announcement of the proposed municipal budget for 1921–22, which called for a 10-percent increase in market-stall rents.[111] It pointed to stall-rent hikes already imposed in 1911 and 1918 and to vendors' narrow profit margins. The petitioners announced that they would issue "the most firm protest" to the civil governor and threatened action if the rent increases came into law.[112] In response, the Treasury Commission offered a two-week period of public comment in which individual vendors and vendor associations could offer written evidence of specific injustices that would be caused by increased rents. It also offered to re-examine, with vendors and their associational representatives, the taxonomy according to which markets and stall specializations were hierarchically classified, and which ultimately determined the amount of rent due.[113] Both of these February 1921 petitions were endorsed by additional entities whose interests and commercial activities stretched beyond the city's seventh municipal district. These included the older Chamber of Barcelona Market Vendors, two butchers' associations, the salted fish guild, and an association of Llobregat farmers.[114] Both petitions were signed by the head of Sant Antoni's vendor association, Casamitjana Germà, who a few months later was elected president of the new Unión General de Vendedores de Mercados de Barcelona.

## THE EMERGENCE OF THE UNIÓN GENERAL DE VENDEDORES DE MERCADOS DE BARCELONA

If we return to El Born, we can easily observe how the 1921 conversion of that market into exclusive wholesale trade disrupted existing food-retailing geographies. The city's commitment to the defense of retail vendors was evidenced by the fact that the Treasury Commission made accommodations for the bulk of those displaced from El Born to be moved into Santa Caterina and La Boqueria markets. Simultaneously, wholesalers were moved from various markets to El Born. Because vendors in multiple markets were affected by these changes, the new citywide Unión General de Vendedores de Mercados de Barcelona stepped in to assert principles of fairness and to advocate for all those who were adversely affected by the reconfiguration.

On the surface, it might seem that El Born's retail vendors would have profited from being moved out of the market and would have welcomed the opportunity to relocate their stalls in structures where ordinary neighborhood consumers were more numerous. But such was not the case. The policies governing the market's reconfiguration established by the Treasury Commission, and their application by individual market directors and their staffs, left the displaced retail vendors from El Born dissatisfied. The move, they claimed, posed a commercial disadvantage for them and prevented them from competing on an equal basis with other already established fixed-license vendors in the retail markets into which they were being absorbed.[115] In July 1921, the Unión General's President Casamitjana Germà petitioned Barcelona's Mayor Martínez i Domingo on behalf of the displaced El Born retail market vendors.[116] Casamitjana brought to the mayor's attention the fact that El Born's retail vendors had actually been moved twice. First, they were temporarily relocated within El Born itself while a portion of the market underwent renovations to accommodate the new, larger wholesale stalls. Then they had been moved out of El Born altogether. Casamitjana asserted that the Treasury Commission had not fulfilled its promise to compensate the displaced retail vendors for the losses that they had suffered in the process of centralizing wholesale trade in the city. Casamitjana argued that "a fixed market stall is like . . . [any other commercial] . . . establishment in that it depends on its own specific clientele."[117] The relocation of vendors from one market to another, he maintained, entailed the loss of that clientele. The period of transition leading up to the formation of a new body of customers in a new location involved the investment of personal capital and a decrease in profits that "would be unjust if it were not duly compensated for" by municipal authorities.[118] The Unión General believed that the three month's free rent offered by the Treasury Commission to displaced El Born vendors was not a sufficient recompense for their loss. President Casamitjana's petition demanded that the city refund all the vendors' costs related to first moving from one part of El Born to another and then to other markets where they had been assigned. His closing departed from the typical cordialities and simply ended with: "Lo insto por ser de estricta justicia" (I insist on the basis of strict justice).

Such collective action on the part of a citywide vendor organization serves as further proof of the market-based food retailers' beliefs that the municipal corporation owed them protection. In a second petition to the mayor on the same day, Casamitjana decried the unhygienic conditions at Santa Caterina Market, which the city had promised to renovate and improve prior to the relocation there of the displaced El Born vendors. Here Casamitjana demanded that Santa Caterina and its surrounding streets be disinfected and cleaned daily in order to "remediate the deplorable state" of the market, which he called "an embarrassment for Barcelona."[119]

The Unión General de Vendedores de Mercados won some of its battles and lost others. Mayor Martínez i Domingo did not agree to an across-the-board refund of displaced Born vendors' moving costs, though he did take up individual petitions for redress.[120] With respect to conditions at Santa Caterina, however, the Unión General secured renewed commitments from the Treasury Commission to undertake the repairs and impose new sanitary standards.[121] From there, the Unión General moved on to tackle other thorny issues, such as the growth of ambulatory trade in and around Sant Antoni Market. In a less-heated petition to the mayor in August 1921, Casamitjana closed with the typical deference and platitudes.[122] The ambulatory vendors that roamed the environs of Sant Antoni responded with a crude petition of their own, signed by more than fifty men and women asking to be ceded fixed-license stalls inside the market—a plea that proved to be of no avail.[123]

## VENDOR PARTICIPATION IN BROADER
## TRADE-SPECIFIC ASSOCIATIONS

Vendors also joined a range of broader trade-specific associations. This was especially the case with respect to what were deemed skilled, or "artisanal," market specializations—that is, those whose execution required not just knowledge about the product sold, but also apprenticeship in its manipulation and processing. The attempt to create modern quasi-corporatist versions of the old provisioning guilds was ongoing. The Federació Gremial Catalana (Catalan Guild Federation) and its national counterpart, the Federación Gremial Española (Spanish Guild Federation) worked explicitly to foment a corporatist revival in the 1910s.[124] By the early 1920s, Barcelona's fresh fish and salt cod retailers had both created associations to defend their interests within the polity. As we have seen, in 1921 the city's Gremio de Pesca Salada was involved in the effort to adjudicate consumer disputes over rehydrated salt cod weights.[125] Two years later, we see that a new fresh fish vendors' association was weighing in on the details of market administration. In November 1923, the Unión de Vendedores de Pescado's (Union of Fish Vendors) president, Manuel Dardé, wrote a personal letter to Mayor Fernando Álvarez de la Campa to express his opposition to a petition by two mussel vendors at L'Abaceria Central Market requesting municipal authorization to sell fresh fish.[126] The vendors in question were members of the Unión de Vendedores de Pescado, but Dardé asserted that their petition to expand their product line beyond mussels represented a violation of the association's standards of fairness and quality control. Dardé even argued that approving the petition threatened the future viability of the shellfish specialization in the city, posing a danger to vendors and consumers alike. Lying low during the years of the Primo de Rivera dictatorship, the Unión de Vendedores de Pescado re-emerged in 1930 as one of the most vibrant and well-organized trade-specific associations that represented vendor interests in markets across the city.[127]

To a great extent, the process of incorporating market vendors into broader trade-specific associations was distorted and delayed by the 1923 imposition of the Primo de Rivera dictatorship. In the fall of 1924, the individual and citywide market vendor associations were suppressed, and all vendors were inscribed as members into a new Comisión Mixta del Trabajo en el Comercio al Detall (Mixed Commission for Work in Retail Commerce).[128] Administered by appointees from outside the provisioning sector who had been chosen by the Ministerio de Trabajo, Comercio e Industria in Madrid, the Comisión Mixta was not a participatory association. Beyond its two administrative positions, it was comprised of a joint committee of six elected members, of whom three were to be owners of retail businesses and three were employees. It was designed to affiliate those involved in all forms of retailing in the city through a state-organized and -administered body. The Comisión Mixta del Trabajo en el Comercio al Detall was one of several such structures that presaged the fascist-inspired vertical syndicates that would define the corporatist nature of the Franco regime. Still, the Primo de Rivera dictatorship allowed the Federació Gremial Catalana and the Federación Gremial Española, both renamed as *Confederaciónes,* to continue to operate, albeit with official government representation and intervention. References to vendor or trade-specific associations all but disappear between 1924 and 1930 in the administrative record of Sant Antoni Market and in the Bureau of Provisioning's extant documentary base.

## GROCERS: "ULTRAMARINS, QUEVIURES, I SIMILARS"

One trade-specific food-retailing association in Barcelona, though, grew in power and influence under the Primo de Rivera dictatorship. Formed initially in 1883 as the Circulo de Ultramarinos, the association became an umbrella organization representing all those engaged in Barcelona's flourishing grocery trade, including the *abacería* and *comestible* shops and the market stalls referenced in the 1902 municipal statistics.[129] By 1923, it was the city's preeminent trade-specific food-retailing association with experience in successful advocacy at the municipal, provincial, and national levels. Known by then in Catalan, rather than Spanish, as the Cercle d'Ultramarins, Queviures, i Similars, it professed an explicit apoliticism while working within the changing structures of authority. In 1925, the Cercle held an homage to Don Manuel Sorigué i Casas, recognizing him for the various posts he had held and for his work to "restore the guild."[130] Having been elected to the presidency of the Cercle in 1914, Sorigué thereafter built provincial and broader regional and national ties with similar associations.[131] He was appointed to serve on the board of Barcelona's Chamber of Commerce and, as one of three representatives of retail business owners, to the city's joint committee of the Comisión Mixta de Trabajo en el Comercio al Detall. He was also elected to serve on the board of the Confederación Gremial Español and to the presidency of the Federación Nacional de Ultramarinos, Comestibles i Similares. In addition, Sorigué was appointed to the Junta Provincial de Subsistencies (Provincial Nutrition Board) and to various official commissions that dealt with labor laws and other matters related to social questions. In 1922, Sorigué met with the minister of labor in Madrid to discuss laws governing shop clerks. The following year, he took a delegation to speak personally with General Miguel de Primo de Rivera about a rash of fines imposed on his members, a meeting that was later described in the Cercle's historical narrative as a disappointing encounter.[132]

The Cercle had not initially advocated for or defended market hall-based trade in the items that grocers sold. In 1889 it petitioned the city to do away with all stall licenses that permitted the sale of items that would otherwise be sold in grocers' shops.[133] Having failed in that petition, it embraced market grocers within its ranks. As of 1902, as we have seen, 5.4 percent of the city's grocers were operating from market stalls.[134] Through membership in the Cercle, market hall-based grocers could access networks of support for their trade in an association with considerable national influence.

The Cercle's success between 1923 and 1931 appears to have been based upon the leadership acumen of men such as Sorigué and a willingness to both engage and contest the Primo de Rivera–era provisioning bureaucracy. The tone of certain passages in the 1925 homage to the Cercle's former president Sorigué belie the rhetorical strategies it deployed toward that end. Delivered and published for its members in Catalan at a time when suppressing Catalanist political initiatives took high precedence for the regime, the homage incorporated vague disparagements of all forms of revolutionary millenarianism as utopianist fantasies. Eloquently drafted by the Cercle's attorney Josep Castany i Gelats, the homage urged the members to align themselves with authority and to remember that "social peace" took precedence above all else.[135] As had been the case in the rhetorical script for the 1888 Exposición Universal, here Castany i Gelats again practiced the rhetorical high-wire balancing act of double patriotism. He spoke in Catalan of the collective hope "to continue with love for the glorious history of our land in order to follow the ascendant and progressive path that has brought her to the forefront of the people that, like her, constitute the Spanish nation."[136] The sycophancy of this declaration is exposed by the fact that the Cercle joined with a long list of market-based, trade-specific, and citywide food-retailer associations in 1931 to denounce the fundamental misdirection and corruption of the dictatorship's provisioning policies and to celebrate the declaration of the Republic as the "historic hour in which the Catalans will recover our national personality."[137]

### BUTCHERS: "CARNISSERS"

The butchers were a second group establishing trade-specific associations before and during the Primo de Rivera era. In English, the term *butcher* is a broad one that includes those who slaughter livestock and those who break down carcasses in smaller establishments dedicated to retail sales. With the centralization and municipal monopolization of the slaughterhouse in Barcelona, the butchers became a more clearly segmented group. Slaughterhouse butchers were municipal employees; retail butchers, known as *carnissers,* worked from markets and shops. It was the latter group—the retail butchers—from which the trade-specific associational efforts sprang. By 1921, there were two citywide butchers' organizations: the Centre Gremial dels Carnissers and the Associació dels Carnissers. Among the issues that divided them was how to balance the interests of market-based butchers with those of butchers who plied their trade from shops.[138] Whereas shopkeeper butchers were often more heavily capitalized, market-based butchers predominated in the overall number of retail establishments. Municipal statistics for 1902 indicate that 79.11 percent of retail butchers operated from stalls in the city's markets.[139] Data from 1932 show little change, with 79 percent of meat in the city still distributed through the retail markets.[140] After years of schisms and disputes, the city's retail butchers finally consolidated their representative entities in 1929 within the Associació dels Carnissers de Barcelona. After officially registering the association with the authorities, one of the first acts of its new president, Antonio Mir y Vidiella, was to name a well-known La Barceloneta market butcher, Josep Portas, as general secretary.[141]

As Jeffrey Pilcher reminds us, European butchers had a long reputation for contentiousness: "their skills with knives made them particularly feared by officials and citizens alike."[142] Indeed, ongoing disputes taking place within Barcelona's Associació dels Carnissers involved various forms of drama. Divisions within the Junta Directiva led first to the resignation of one member from that body and then to the mass resignation of all the rest, including President Mir y Vidiella. New elections in 1932 ushered in the presidency of Salvador Cararach Biot, a second-generation Santa Caterina butcher who, readers may recall from the opening paragraph of chapter 1, had two years earlier so assiduously seen to the preparation of that market's Queen to participate in the cavalcade and ball attended by the Spanish monarch and the royal family. Commanding great respect from the membership and public authorities alike, Cararach was able to restore harmony within the association. His presidency, along with the position still held by La Barceloneta market vendor Josep Portas as general secretary, showed that the more united iteration of the association was led from the ranks of the city's stall-keepers. When Cararach's term was up in 1934, Antoni Pou Alaya was elected to the presidency. During his tenure, Pou faced new conflict between market-based and shopkeeper butchers on the one hand, and rogue butchers selling meat from unlicensed establishments on the other. That dispute culminated in public protest and in physical violence.[143]

Ostensibly, the issue of contention surrounded the implementation and enforcement of the 1927 municipal regulations governing the operation of all forms of meat sales in the city. Articles 7 and 8 of this new code divided Barcelona into seventeen market zones and gave market directors and their inspectors the power to enter into and denounce infractions in butchers' shops.[144] Promulgated under the Primo de Rivera dictatorship, the new regulations were enthusiastically endorsed by the Associació dels Carnissers, within which vendor interests predominated. Yet there was an almost decade-long lag before municipal authorities moved to implement the policy.[145] With across-the-board endorsement by vendors for greater enforcement of the rules designed to limit competition during the Republic, in March 1936 municipal authorities ordered market directors and inspectors to identify those butchers' shops that were unlicensed or in violation of regulatory norms. As butcher shops were fined and even closed by municipal authorities, tensions mounted. Those who had been sanctioned demanded amnesty and converged before city hall in the Plaça San Jaume on March 24.[146] The press described the protest as a tumultuous one, with the aggrieved butchers and their clerks attempting to use brute force to enter the municipal palace.[147] The massive doors of the city hall were closed to keep out the angry crowd. Police intervention initially diffused tensions, and representatives from among the protesters were selected and allowed to enter the palace with the expectation of presenting their demands to Mayor Carles Pi i Sunyer. Moments earlier, though, representatives of the Associació dels Carnissers, including its president, Antoni Pou, had also entered the building. When the two groups met in the hallway leading to the mayor's office, a scuffle ensued. In the process, President Pou was *agredit* (assaulted), *abofeteado* (punched), and *atropellado* (knocked down).[148]

The assaulted President Pou was a man who bore no resemblance to the old caricature of the knife-wielding, aggressive premodern butcher, though perhaps his assailants did. Pou was neither physically imposing nor coarse and threatening. Rather, he was known for his modesty, his reserved manners, and his patience.[149] Though not seriously injured, the physical altercation that President Pou suffered—at the hands of rogue butchers who did not agree with the market-based interests that the association represented—was taken by the membership as a profound insult. The Associació dels Carnissers was working to legitimate licensed butchers' interests and to collaborate with Republican authorities in maintaining law and order. The assault constituted a setback, but one that served to rally the association's membership and the larger population of market vendors and shopkeepers in their campaign against unregulated trade in food.

Clearly, the spring of 1936 was a tumultuous time in the history of Barcelona and of the Spanish state. The Popular Front had won in the national elections on February 16, and half a million people turned out in Barcelona on March 1 to greet Lluis Companys's release from prison and celebrate his resumption of the presidency of the Generalitat. The outbreak of the Civil War was only a few months off. But the protectionist militancy of the butchers' association more specifically at that time was rooted in longer-term challenges, some of which had little to do with municipal provisioning policy and bore no relation to the larger political and ideological juggernaut that Spain was caught in as the summer of 1936 presented itself.

The butchers were feeling the impact of changes in consumer tastes and habits. Beef had never been a staple in the Catalan diet; its sale in markets and shops was an exception rather than the rule. Mutton had long been the preferred quadruped, along with pork, both of which had their privileged places in the paradigmatic escudella soup pot. The early-twentieth-century shifts in consumer meat preferences and eating habits was toward younger animals, specifically veal, lamb, and kid.[150] In 1881, over 200,000 rams met their maker in the city's slaughterhouses; despite a more than doubling of the human population by 1933, only 55,000 rams were consumed that year.[151] The growth in veal, lamb, and kid slaughtering did not make up for the fact that per-capita fresh meat consumption was plummeting in the city. Between 1914 and 1933 it fell by 28.8 percent.[152] Still, overall per-capita protein consumption rose from 13.2 kilos in 1900 to 18.1 in 1933, a sign of modestly improving diets in an era otherwise marked by labor unrest and periodic food protests.[153] From the turn of the century until the outbreak of World War I, consumers in Barcelona were eating more eggs and drinking more milk, hot and cold.[154] They also more often ate poultry, rabbit, and fresh fish.[155] The growth of the mechanical refrigeration industry and the expansion of commercial poultry and dairy concerns help to explain this. But so too did the articulation of certain bodies of prescriptive conventional knowledge that represented a veritable assault on the composition of escudella as it had been known and even its centrality to the diet. We see this in the culinary program set forth by the Institut Català i Biblioteca Popular de la Dona. It can be traced to other sources as well, such as J. Raventós's 1923 L'Alimentació Humana, which questioned the nutritional value of mutton-based cooking.[156] The fact of the matter was that Barcelona's butchers in the 1930s were for the most part offering a line of goods for which demand was in retreat.

What drew the Associació de Carnissers's most immediate ire in 1936, however, was unbridled and extraregulatory competition in its sector. In the same issue of the association's monthly, La Veu dels Carnissers, in which President Pou's assault was decried, the association offered its comparative analysis of the larger structural problem that butchers in Barcelona were facing. In 1935, Madrid's slaughterhouses had killed the equivalent of 25,291,691 kilos' worth of livestock, which was then retailed in approximately 850 market-stall and retail-shop enterprises. In contrast, Barcelona's L'Escorxador slaughterhouse had that year killed the equivalent of 22,949,882 kilos' worth of livestock, which was retailed in over 2,200 points of sale, only 992 of which were market stalls.[157] The Barcelona butchers argued that such large numbers of retail outlets meant that each individual butcher had a smaller base of consumers and, as a result, a narrower profit margin, which naturally drove up prices. Endorsing the right of market vendors to earn a living, the logical place to begin to address the problem was through closing down the multitude of new shops that had opened without licenses at distances closer to the markets than was allowed by the 1927 code.[158] The Associació de Carnissers believed that these establishments were operated by rogue butchers who showed no respect for the principles of limiting competition through licensing that underpinned the political economy of food retailing in the city.

The case of associationalism among Barcelona's butchers shows that the division between vendors' and shopkeepers' interests is not as clear as it might seem at first glance. The butchers' association represented both groups, so long as they were duly licensed. Individual vendors held important positions in the Associació de Carnissers in part because up 80 percent of the meat retailed in the city came out of the markets.[159] Moreover, there is some evidence that market vendors and shopkeepers were populations that overlapped. At least in Gràcia at the turn of the century, nearly half of La Revolució Market vendors were registered according to addresses indicating that they lived nearby.[160] At that market, and perhaps others, some significant part of the vendor population came from among the ranks of shopkeepers who probably acquired market-stall licenses as a way of horizontally extending their family's retail businesses. Even though interests could diverge, there was some complementarity between the two groups. The growth of trade-specific retailing associations that included market vendors and shopkeepers among their ranks and that sought to defend the interests of both groups shows the fallacy of presuming that they were always locked in competition with one another.

## AN APEX IN FOOD-RETAILING ASSOCIATIONALISM: 1930 TO 1936

We see the growing alignment between market vendors and shopkeepers at an organizational level half a year before the declaration of the Second Republic. On September 2, 1930, at 4:45 in the afternoon, the Unión General de Vendedores de Mercats reclaimed the stage in defense of Barcelona's legally constituted food retailers. Holding an assembly in the Teatro Español, the Unión General convened vendors representing all the markets in the city, along with the leadership of the salt cod, fresh fish, egg, poultry, and butchers' associations. Also present and addressing the assembly was the president of the Confederación Gremial Catalana, Bartomeu Amigó Farreras. The Unión General's then-president Enrique Sánchez began by declaring that the rally "did not have any political character, but rather was purely administrative in that its aim was the defense of the interests of the vendors."[161] But after all the retailers' representatives spoke, it was agreed that the assembled shared a commitment to contest "municipal provisioning policy and the superfluity of ambulatory sales." Taking a defensive tone, the assembled asserted that the rising cost of food was not the fault of the city's legally constituted retailers, but rather that its "origin was rooted in the profound disorder" of the larger economy.[162]

In his capacity as president of the Confederación Gremial Catalana, Amigó Farreras went on to pronounce six points of consensus. First, that the municipality should enforce the 1927 regulations governing the sale of meat, the 1928 market code, and the rules adopted in 1929 for the sale of fresh fish in shops. Second, that there was no rational justification for the ambulatory sale of food in a city like Barcelona. Third, that the city should close all those food shops not meeting the conditions set forth in the codes and move to construct new markets in working-class districts. Fourth, that wholesale markets should be more effectively policed. Fifth, that a more "sane policy" governing provisioning in the city would allow the "guild associations" to collaborate with authorities. And sixth, that any municipal attempts to regulate food prices must take place in consultation with retailers, through their representative associations. President Amigó Farreras concluded by asserting that after "a painful seven-year experience" of seeing various provincial juntas exercise control without demonstrating any "competent deliberation" with respect to inspections or price regulations, any return to the "regime of abuse to which those juntas subjected us, will provoke our angry civil protest."[163] In sum, what resulted was hardly the apolitical assembly that the Unión General asserted it intended to hold at its outset. The positions of the allied market vendors, with full endorsement of the Confederación Gremial, were explicitly set forth and clearly exemplified the rapid erosion of popular support for the enfeebled dictatorship.

One might conclude from the vehemence of this rhetoric that the seemingly enthusiastic vendor participation in the June 1930 Market Queen Cavalcade and Grand Ball that had been held just three months before was an expression of sheer patient political pragmatism and a kind of forced charade. And perhaps it was for some of those involved. In fact, much had run amok between market vendors and municipal authorities over the course of the summer of 1930. In July, the Treasury Commission announced a 25-percent increase in monthly stall rents, and vendors had responded with widespread indignation. The ensuing crisis led vendors to mobilize through revived market-specific associations and, more collectively, through the rejuvenated Unión General de Vendedores, which announced that proposed increases in stall rents would simply not be paid.[164] The reaction of the authorities is unclear. What is not in doubt is that Barcelona's vendors were mobilizing associationally on an unprecedented level by September 1930. Such mobilization involved considerable aplomb in a political context within which there were no constitutional guarantees to the right of free assembly. The revival of broad-based vendor associationalism continued through the fall and winter.

### La Niña Bonita

On April 12, 1931, municipal elections in Spain brought republican candidates to power. Two days later, Spain's Second Republic was declared, and King Alfonso XIII fled the country, never to return. The provisional government that took control of Catalonia adopted the historic Generalitat as its name. Headed by Francesc Macià, one of its first acts was to abolish the provinces that had been imposed on the principality a hundred years earlier, and through whose administration Madrid had wielded power over and contested municipal authority. The "painful seven-year experience" of provincial intervention in market-based and shopkeeper trade in food was brought to an end and the already mobilized food retailers did not miss a beat. Their various efforts at affiliation having been born and bred in the nutritive republican associational milieu of the first decades of the twentieth century, they joined the chorus of enthusiasm for the new government.

One of the first expressions of organized food-retailer support for the Republic came from the fish vendors' association, a group whose remobilization had been intensifying since January 1930. On the front cover of their April 1931 monthly, La Unión, they announced their enthusiastic embrace of the new government. Asserting that while their policy was to distance themselves from partisan issues, at this juncture they could not help but be moved by the great gesture of "public-spiritedness on the part of the Spanish people . . . we feel proud as Spaniards, as Catalans, and as citizens." They declared: "We greet the Republic with fervent reverence, [and as] the most human, the most noble, and the most progressive of all political regimes."[165] The enthusiasm coming from the leaders of the city's fish vendors' association, as from other quarters, was palpable.

Indeed, Republican-era municipal administrations moved quickly to take up the concerns of market vendors and shopkeepers, as well as those of store clerks. Shortly after the Republic's declaration, the Cercle de Ultramarins, Queviures i Similars was faced by the threat of a strike organized by the Centre Autonomista de Dependents del Comerç i de la Indústria (Autonomous Association of Commercial and Industrial Employees), known as CADCI, which sought the extension of Sunday closing to the retail-provisioning sector.[166] The Cercle vociferously opposed Sunday closing, but given the CADCI's strong base of support for the newly formed, and now ruling Esquerra Republicana de Catalunya Party, the new labor legislation was adopted on November 3, 1931, and put into force on February 14 of the following year. Certain types of businesses, such as bakeries, cafés, and bars were exempted, but all the markets were thereafter shuttered on Sundays, and earlier closing times were instituted for Saturday evenings as well.[167] Reactions among the market vendors were mixed, with the strongest opposition coming from those who sold fish.[168]

Also during the first year of the Republic's life, Generalitat president Macià held a conference to "study the social and economic problems facing the guilds."[169] On November 19, 1931, all the provisioning associations in the city, along with organizations representing food processors, joined together in support of a collective statement delivered in the form of a speech and a printed address. Entitled "The Guilds and the Present Moment," it was signed by the Unió General de Venedors de Mercat dels Barcelona, the Unió de Venedors de Peix, the Cercle de Ultramarins, Queviures i Similars, the Associació de Carnissers, and by twenty-four other entities from the sector. Anticipating the drafting of a new statute for an autonomous Catalan state within Spain, the signatories set forth three "basic aspirations."[170] They hoped for constitutional provisions that would establish technical councils to explore economic questions, a defense of commercial property, and reform of the tax code.[171] Significantly, in the preamble that led up to their statement, the signatories offered an assessment of the nature of the guilds in the context of their time. They asserted that the guilds were "the veritable soul of the economy," and that their members formed part of an "estate" defined by the values of tenacity, sacrifice, intelligence, and honesty. Their vision was of a quasi-corporatist/associationalist polity that embraced changing economic and political conditions but that squarely defended the interests of small business.

They pronounced that "the guilds had also undergone a revolution" and were not a "fossilized force, as many claimed."[172] They anticipated a reinvented Catalonia that would legitimate their commercial rights and endorse their dignity within the social order. Among those leading the provisioning-sector associations, and more broadly among the supporters of the Republic, it was a moment of unbridled optimism and firm belief that through self-determination all things were possible. Most could probably not have imagined the complexity of what was to come, the powerful impact of individual and collective agency among those who held other visions, and the obstacles and impediments that their state-building aspirations would face.

All evidence points to the fact that the Esquerra Republicana Party could not have agreed more with the market vendors and food shopkeepers' mixed-economy vision of how the provisioning system should operate. On December 2, 1932, Barcelona's city council announced that no new licenses for grocers' shops would be issued. The only exceptions would be in cases where the proposed shops were to be located at no less than one hundred meters from already existing grocers or markets within the old city center and the Eixample, and no less than two hundred meters in the annexed towns and districts.[173] The proposal for this policy initiative had come directly from the leadership of the Cercle de Ultramarins, Queviures i Similars, and went a long way toward mollifying the grocers who had one year before lost the battle over mandatory Sunday closing in the retail-provisioning sector.[174]

Esquerra Republicana efforts to enforce existing laws limiting competition, and to extend those laws to new categories of food shops, were interrupted by larger political developments. The Republic had initially been governed by a left Republican-Socialist coalition that undertook a series of reforms. By 1934, that coalition had fallen apart, and national elections had brought conservatives to power. The party that won the most deputies, though still falling short of an absolute majority, was the Confederación Española de Derechos Autónomas, or CEDA. But because the CEDA's explicit aim, as Nigel Townson writes, was to "supplant the Republic by an authoritarian regime based on corporatist Catholic principles," the Republic's President Niceto Alcalá-Zamora asked the party that had come in second in the elections to form a government instead.[175] Alejandro Lerroux's Radical Republicans, who despite their party's name were actually quite conservative, thus assumed power, ushering in a period known as the "Black Biennium." Because the Radical Republicans had to depend upon support from CEDA deputies in order to govern, there was growing fear from disparate quarters that the Republic itself was in danger. When three CEDA deputies joined the cabinet on October 4, 1934, that fear was confirmed.

The entrance of the CEDA into Lerroux's government was seen by Generalitat president Lluís Companys as nothing short of a fascist takeover. Companys had agreed with other Spanish parties on the left that if CEDA were to gain power there would be no alternative to a revolt against the disfigured government.[176] Expecting broad support from a national coalition of left Republicans and Socialists, whose withered condition he had failed to recognize, on October 6 Companys took to the balcony of the Generalitat and pronounced the Catalan state within the Spanish Federal Republic. Moving headlong into what was probably the greatest political blunder and misunderstanding in twentieth-century Catalan history, Companys called upon General Domènec Batet, as head of the troops in Catalunya, to place his forces in support of the new Federal Republic of Spain, which he had just proclaimed.[177] But General Batet refused, and after communicating with the government in Madrid, he declared a state of war against the rebellious Catalan government. Within less than twelve hours, Batet's forces entered the Generalitat and took custody of President Companys and his supporters.[178] Immediately thereafter, Mayor Carles Pi i Sunyer faced the same fate. The government of the Generalitat and the municipality were taken over by the military, and by December there were some 3,400 political prisoners in Catalunya.[179]

The catastrophic events of October 6, 1934, halted the Esquerra Republicana's endeavors to further rationalize the city's food-retailing system and to bring markets and shops into full compliance with existing regulations. Military authorities controlled the city government until January 13, 1935, and then power passed to parties whose agendas were otherwise-directed. It was only after the victory of the Popular Front coalition in the national elections of February 17, 1936—which returned the Esquerra Republicana to power over the Generalitat and the municipality—that market and shopkeeper associations could again count on support for more definitive enforcement of the regulations limiting competition in the food-retailing sector.

Soon after returning to power, Mayor Pi i Sunyer's administration committed itself to drawing up new policies governing the sale of food and beverages in the city. Developed in consultation with market-vendor and trade-specific associations, the new regulations left the 1928 market code intact but introduced two key innovations. First, all retailers of food, drink, and coal for cooking were mandated to organize themselves into "guild associations," according to a set list of fourteen specializations.[180] Those guilds would then represent individual retailers in their petitions to the city. Second, a stricter set of minimum distances were mandated separating all types of food shops from one another and from the market halls of the city.[181] Market-based trade was protected through the specification that new shops be located only at a significant distance from established markets. Here we see a more rationalized codification and systematization of various pre-existing rules about the commercial geography of food retailing in the city that were designed to limit the competition that markets and shops faced and to spread new enterprises out to areas not otherwise vested with commercial outlets for the sale of food.

The problem, however, was that from the last years of the Primo de Rivera dictatorship and during the interruption in Esquerra Republicana's control of the municipality that followed the events of October 6, 1934, many new shops had opened without license and in contradiction to these precepts. Back in power in February 1936, the municipal government turned first to closing butchers' shops that were operating extralegally, which is what led to the assault against the Associació de Carnissers's president Antoni Pou inside the confines of the city hall. In fact, there was much dispute about the implementation of these and other Republican-era food-retailing policies. The Chamber of Commerce was much more liberally inclined and opposed new efforts to restrict competition among shops and with markets. In so doing, the chamber positioned itself in opposition to the Confederación Gremial Catalana.[182] What both entities supported, though, were new efforts to curtail the rise of ambulatory trade, which was understood by all the parties involved—with the exception of the peddlers themselves—to constitute unfair competition.[183] The fact that ambulatory vendors paid no taxes and functioned beyond the reach of sanitary inspection only made them more of a target for municipal, shopkeeper, and market-vendor ire.

In the spring of 1936, market-vendor mobilization in defense of policies that limited competition continued to build. We can see this most pointedly in the aftermath of the Associació de Carnissers' President Pou's humiliating assault on March 24. Two days later, the association held a special general meeting that was attended by more than three hundred members. The assembled agreed to join together to protest the act of aggression and to support the municipal order to close rogue butchers' shops. They agreed that on the following Monday, March 30, all the legal butchers working from markets and shops would close their businesses at noon and attend a demonstration to accompany guild representatives who would present a statement to the city council.[184]

News of the planned demonstration spread quickly through the city's markets, and a broad range of vendors turned out to voice their support. The press reported that the Plaça de Sant Jaume (it was actually called the Plaça de la República at that time) began to fill with vendors shortly after eleven a.m. and that groups formed under banners with the names of the markets in which they worked. The doors of city hall were closed as a precaution, and as the crowd grew larger the "nervousness of some was translated into a few small incidents" of aggression that led to arrests.[185] With the guild leaders inside city hall, the demonstrators called for representatives of the city council to address them, a request that was roundly refused on the basis of the assertion that such matters "should be processed and resolved in offices and not from balconies."[186] But city officials did allow the president of the Confedració Gremial Catalana, Amigó Farreras, to step out onto the balcony "to calm the impatience of the protestors" and to ask them to disperse peacefully. After Amigó successfully negotiated for the release of those few people who had been detained by the police, the demonstrators left the square by one p.m. An hour later, Councilman Hurtado met with the press to make light of the incident. While noting the lack of violence among the demonstrators and the unquestionable importance of their mobilization around an issue that so evidently affected "the life and the prosperity of the markets," Hurtado asserted that the protest had been unnecessary.[187] Such flippancy was likely overcompensation for the unease that the sight of a fully mobilized vendor population at the doors of city hall caused. Municipal authorities had long understood the importance of endorsing market-vendor aspirations, but this demonstration drove the point home further.

### Patterns of Continuity in a Period of Instability and Change

Whether one focuses on the larger political history of this period or on the details of market administration and retail policy, it is tempting to emphasize change. Important regulatory shifts certainly had the impact of increasing the inherent value of market-stall titles. The 1923 introduction of the *trespaso intervivos* conveyance was especially significant in encouraging individual vendors to invest capital in infrastructural improvements to market stalls over the long run. But the continuities that defined the first decades of the twentieth century are equally significant.

The first pattern defining the period from 1898 to 1936 is one of ongoing municipal commitment to market-hall ownership, regulation, and management, despite the ideological direction of regime change. This involved the steady construction of new markets that expanded the system, culminating in the inauguration of El Ninot's market hall in 1934—the only one built under the auspices of Republican-era municipal administration. Though the Primo de Rivera dictatorship imposed greater levels of centralization, according provincial authorities more control over provisions through the Junta de Subsistencias, that process had already begun during the subsistence crises of the World War I period, with the creation of a new national Ministerio de Abastacimientos (Provisioning Ministry) in 1918.[188] There was some further erosion in municipal control over provisioning during the life of the Republic, but that only occurred after the outbreak of the Civil War in July 1936, when broader measures were put in place to govern food production and distribution in the context of a multi-tiered crisis. Even the Primo de Rivera dictatorship's circumscription of municipal control was limited in nature. The 1928 market code did not constitute a break from the basic premises set forth in the 1898 edition that it replaced. The real distinction between the Primo de Rivera regime and the Republic's policies was in commitment to enforce existing laws. We can even see a clear adherence to established precepts in the 1929 regulations authorizing the sale of fresh fish from fixed shops. The setting of a seven-hundred-meter zone around each market within which no new fish shops could open was justified on the basis of "attending to the just demands of market vendors."[189] Verifying the estimation of Sant Antoni's vendors nearly two decades earlier, the 1929 regulations asserted that within markets "fish stalls are . . . the magnets that attract buyers." Allowing fish shops to locate near markets would cause them to gradually "depopulate" and thus would complicate municipal efforts to police, inspect, and administer food retailing in a general sense.[190]

Opportunities for graft through municipal market administration also reflect the darker side of this continuity. On September 18, 1934, when the Esquerra Republicana was still in full control of policy, Confederació Gremial Catalana president Bartomeu Amigó Farreras petitioned to halt the activities of a new corps of special provisioning-sector inspectors appointed by the Generalitat. These inspectors would not be paid as functionaries, but rather would be compensated for their work through the right to pocket 30 percent of any fine they imposed. Outraged, Amigó Farreras pointed to the fact that this was a revival of a failed policy; during the Primo de Rivera dictatorship an identical corps had been deployed, but the level of "abuse was so important and so scandalous that the dictatorship itself annulled the body of inspectors that in reality lived at the expense of the country."[191] Michael Seidman might term this arrangement "institutionalized acquisitive individualism." In fact, such practices were longstanding ones.

The second pattern defining the period from 1898 to 1936 is intensifying associationalism, which characterized Catalan and Spanish society more broadly but which market vendors engaged in according to their specific interests and inclinations. As we have seen, market-vendor associationalism underwent a process of consolidation that began before the Primo de Rivera dictatorship and then accelerated as the regime, and the monarchy itself, collapsed. Increasingly tied to related trade-specific entities that included and were sometimes led by shopkeepers, these associations also acted as mutual-aid societies offering group-buying opportunities, savings plans, and accident insurance for their members. These associations also developed important social components, holding banquets, dances, and outings of various sorts. They reflected republican values and employed democratic practices and procedures. As such, they should be considered as having constituted the vehicles through which market vendors participated in civil society during the decades before the outbreak of the Civil War.

## The Woman Question

As market vendors consolidated their social and economic positions within the metropolis and aligned themselves organizationally with shopkeepers, men moved increasingly into the occupation. Still, women held their own and were not squeezed out of market trade. Female entrepreneurship in the markets flourished in early-twentieth-century Barcelona. Separate-sphere gender ideologies assigning private roles to women and public roles to men had only limited relevance to the lives of the thousands of market vendors who worked in the city. Municipal records and ethnographic data show a general pattern of women's work in market stalls that began at an early age and then continued after marriage and through the reproductive years of life. Markets were public spaces, and women's ownership and operation of small businesses within them were ubiquitous.

The larger process of administrative rationalization of the provisioning sector, the growing levels of demand for food in the expanding metropolis, and the integration of new neighborhoods into the municipal system served as catalysts for the formation of a series of layered and intertwined networks. A newly expanded municipal bureaucracy governing food sales in Barcelona was the basis of one of these. The individuals and agencies regulating market-stall and shop licensing, sanitation, supply, and pricing policies made up a political and administrative network of functionaries. This municipal bureaucratic network, however, operated in accordance with regulations set out by provincial and even national authorities who retained some control over food supplies and therefore linked the city to the central government in Madrid. Below this political and administrative network, retailers inside and beyond Barcelona's markets increasingly created citywide networks of shared economic and social interest. In the formal political and regulatory hierarchy, as well as within the food retailers' associations, men played an overwhelmingly dominant role. There were few females in positions of authority within the municipal, provincial, and national provisioning bureaucracies in this period, and women did not assume leadership roles within the food retailers' associations. Yet food shops and market stalls were frequently run as family enterprises and often as independent concerns by married women whose husbands worked in other occupations both within and beyond the provisioning sector. While many men had moved into the expanding trade in market-based retailing, women tended to predominate in terms of direct contact with female consumers in both market halls and neighborhood shops. Though there were women who joined the new retailing associations, they tended more generally to defend their commercial interests on an ad-hoc basis through petitions to redress specific grievances. Both female market vendors and consumers also periodically engaged in more spontaneous and less peaceful forms of protest, such as strikes and demonstrations.

Rather than simply assuming that retailers and consumers comprised two distinct groups whose interests were inherently incompatible, we must recognize that there was much that bound them together. All of the women selling food in Barcelona were also buying it. Thus female vendors did not cease to be consumers. Like most of the population, they too had to pursue careful strategies to adhere to budgetary constraints. So below the male-dominated formal political and commercial networks making up the city's food-retailing system there were also informal consumer/retailer networks dominated by women who shared the quotidian rhythms of selling and buying in the neighborhood markets. These networks were constructed and extended through rituals of familiarity and sociability that defined the nature of food shopping and contributed to the integration of immigrant populations into the burgeoning metropolis. What went on from the bottom up in the food-retailing system was just as crucial to the success of the new political economy that governed the provisioning of the urban population as what went on from the top down, and thus merits explicit and extended consideration.

## CHAPTER 6

# Layered Networks
### Quotidian Life in the Markets before and during the Civil War

Late-nineteenth and early-twentieth-century food-retailing associationalism proved crucial to the ongoing economic viability of small-scale enterprises operating out of both fixed shops and the city's market-hall structures. But so too did other types of much less formal and often more feminized social and commercial networks that took shape and expanded in the decades preceding the outbreak of the Civil War. Centered in socially and architecturally diverse neighborhoods with market halls acting as spatial anchors, these networks involved family and kinship relations among market vendors and shopkeepers, long-term sociability among neighborhood food retailers and their customers, and ongoing links between the metropolis and the rural hinterland from which vendors and shopkeepers often recruited their clerks, servants, and apprentices. Built largely upon familiarity and trust, such networks were the bone and sinew of many women's daily lives, and they linked food retailers directly and personally to consumers. With the outbreak of the Spanish Civil War in 1936, the informal networks that had come to characterize the provisioning system proved crucial to survival in a city plagued by food shortages, aerial bombardment, and internecine conflict.

### Places of Work and Sociability

By the early twentieth century, tens of thousands of women were earning their livelihoods in food retailing through family-economy arrangements, as clerks and apprentices, as shop owners, or as the legal holders of fixed-stall titles in the city's markets. The paradigmatic gendered division of labor within families that assigned food shopping and meal preparation to women meant that the bulk of food purchasers were female. This was still the era of the icebox. In the absence of mechanical refrigeration, women avoided spoilage by purchasing small amounts of food on a daily basis. In carrying out their domestic responsibilities within a commercial system characterized by retailers selling a narrow range of goods, female consumers patronized a series of market stalls and food shops each day. Both contemporary and ethnographic evidence show that daughters often followed the commercial trajectories of their mothers, buying from a particular set of retailers out of a sense of loyalty and trust. Such habits had the effect of reinforcing social and commercial bonds that tied one generation to another. Neighborhood communities of shared interest between female consumers and the women who sold provisions were thus strengthened by a series of factors: the localized nature of small-scale commerce, the licensing system that limited the lines that each retailer could offer, the persistence of gendered divisions of labor within families that assigned food shopping and meal preparation to women, and the necessity to avoid spoilage and waste through acquiring small amounts on a daily basis.

Yet the relationships among women buying and selling food varied widely in accordance with socioeconomic distinctions and other factors. For many in the rapidly expanding middle classes, food shopping had become a form of personal and collective expression that was deeply embedded within the urbanized consumer culture that had matured in the late nineteenth century. The food that women purchased for themselves and their families, where and how they purchased it—as well as the rituals associated with consuming it—were all commonly understood to be markers of social position and of personal identity. Though broad areas within and beyond the old walled city were characterized by poverty and squalor, prestigious avenues and much of the Eixample had come to constitute one of Europe's most elegant urban landscapes. Along Las Ramblas and the main thoroughfares of the new city, the comfortable classes ate luxury foods in restaurants, lingered over cups of hot chocolate topped with whipped cream, and purchased expensive "champagne" and pastries to consume at holiday meals with family and friends.[1]

Charles Augustus Stoddard, the American editor of the *New York Observer,* traveled through Spain in the early 1890s and noted what surprised him about Barcelona. Stoddard wrote, "Unlike the custom in other towns in Spain, the women throng the streets . . . They dress in the gayest of colors, and add to the constant clatter of the town by their vivacious conversation."[2] But Stoddard also offers us glimpses of the gendered nature of consumerism in food and drink in the city when he wrote that

In the principal streets there are many handsome cafes, which seem to be always crowded with men . . . Here in the morning the Barcelonese come to take their chocolate, which is served thick and hot, to read the journals, and to talk politics. All day long the cafes are full of men sipping sweet beverages or drinking wine, and at night the crowd is so great that one can hardly find a place. The noise of hundreds of tongues is increased by the clatter of hundreds of dominoes on marble tables, and finds vent into the street, where it blends with the cries of itinerant venders and the roar of the great city.[3]

While working-class women and servants certainly were present in taverns, the city's most elegant cafés were primarily understood to be masculinized commercial spaces. Within Barcelona's more popular neighborhoods, where streets were mined with smaller and cheaper *cafes-económicos,* taverns, and bars, the geography of food retailing was no less gendered. Where men socialized over coffee, beer, and other alcoholic beverages, women on their own tended to socialize more often in much more feminized commercial spaces. In the market halls and shops, female consumers could exchange pleasantries and bits of gossip while displaying their social status through the purchase of expensive cheeses and cured meats, whole chickens, or the pricier varieties of fresh fish.[4]

Yet again, glimpses of Barcelona's glittering consumer culture at the turn of the century must not obscure recognition of the fact that much of the city's population was comprised of the working poor and that food shopping was essentially a matter of survival for a great many people. Within the ranks of the economically marginalized, women remained on the front lines of the ongoing struggle to acquire enough bread, salt cod, beans, and the barest of soup-makings to keep their families minimally fed. Poor women also faced rising prices, adulteration, and intermittent shortages as ongoing problems. High levels of female consumer acumen were thus important to survival in the industrial metropolis, and given that many women had little choice but to periodically seek out credit, trust and familiarity between retailers and consumers remained as urgent a currency as ever in the early twentieth century. In the juxtaposition between poor and haute-bourgeois neighborhoods, Barcelona's morphology reflected the socioeconomic variegation that characterized its political culture in the first decades of the century. As had been the case through the whole history of urban life, the vast gulf in economic means was expressed as clearly in food consumption patterns as in wages, working conditions, and housing.

The considerable differences between the living standards and eating habits of industrial wage workers and the emergent middle classes certainly served as an impetus for the growth of labor movements in Barcelona and elsewhere in this period. Historians have paid tremendous attention to the ideologies that competed for the allegiance of workers in the city.[5] Likewise, they have carefully traced the emergence of political parties representing the interests of industrialists and other members of Barcelona's elite.[6] Yet a substantial portion of the urban population fell somewhere between the social polarities that distanced the poor from the well-to-do. Along with the growth in the size of the industrial wage-earning population and the consolidation of the new urban ruling class comprised of the city's "good families," Barcelona's early-twentieth-century social history also featured considerable expansion in the ranks of its lower-middle class. Market vendors and shopkeepers, rarely commanding significant wealth or resources in this period, were one of several rapidly expanding lower-middle-class groups. By virtue of their roles in the distribution of food to residents across the social spectrum, and through their power to extend and rescind credit, they played a crucial role in neighborhood life. The bonds that often developed between generations of women buying and selling food in individual neighborhoods had the effect of dampening social unrest and facilitating immigrant acculturation to life in the city through decades otherwise characterized by upheaval, violence, and abrupt regime change.[7]

## Codifying Female Entrepreneurship

In a number of important ways, women's work in Barcelona's early-twentieth-century markets and shops represented a clear continuity of older patterns; women in many parts of the world had long been widely involved in food retailing.[8] In Europe and beyond, food shops of many sorts were typically run as family enterprises, and women were often the ones presumed to have an advantage in selling directly to a mainly female clientele. In numerous civilizations, from Africa to Latin America and the Caribbean, to much of Asia and certainly Western Europe, women traditionally worked in large numbers as vendors in local and regional markets. That women so often worked selling food in Barcelona is thus not in the least surprising.[9]

Barcelona's early-eighteenth-century guilds were dominated of course by men.[10] The 1717 *Manual de la Taxa de Comercio* lists no women as members of the bakers' or butchers' guilds, though certainly many worked alongside their husbands, brothers, and sons in family-economy arrangements.[11] In activities such as urban pork slaughtering in the eighteenth century, specific tasks were generally assigned to women, even though the larger process was dominated by males. Women on their own more often worked in the marginal food commerce, such as peddling and market vending, where overhead costs were lowest.[12] But as Marta Vicente reminds us, these women often paid a high cost in terms of their personal reputations and were seen as vulgar and socially dubious because they worked outside their homes and beyond the direct oversight of husbands and fathers.[13]

Still, significant changes in women's work as food retailers took place between 1714 and 1848. Industrialization, the growing separation of home from workplace, and the articulation of separate-sphere ideologies were once presumed to have had a powerful marginalizing impact on female entrepreneurial initiatives.[14] That perspective is now changing. In examining broader European patterns, Beachy, Craig, and Owens have argued that industrialization presented women with new opportunities in business.[15] With respect to Spain in particular, the work of Lina Gálvez Muñoz, Paloma Fernández Pérez, Cristina Borderías, Àngels Solà Parera, Juanjo Romero, and others has shown that female entrepreneurship in the tertiary sector of the economy, as well as women's work in certain forms of independent production and in wage labor, fluctuated and/or intensified over the course of the nineteenth and early twentieth centuries.[16] Separate-sphere ideologies assigning males to public roles and women to private ones dominated prescriptive discourses but may not have shaped as many women's experiences as was once presumed. In Barcelona, demographic pressure, the spread of consumerist values, the expansion of the food-retailing sector, and the deterioration of guild structures combined to create new commercial opportunities for women. Female participation through the family economy and the official ownership of fathers, husbands, and sons continued as the most common organizational strategy in most fixed shops, but women also increasingly acted as independent entrepreneurs in the city's food sector.

The 1848 tax rolls for Barcelona show that women had come to own 32 percent (33 of 103) of the bread shops, 19 percent (41 of 217) of the butchers' shops, and 13.7 percent (18 of 131) of the pork, ham, and sausage shops—all specialties where men's official ownership had been nearly universal in 1717.[17] Only a small fraction of these women were widows who had taken over their deceased husbands' enterprises. Barcelona's marketplaces, though, whether covered or open-air, were the main commercial venues where women continued to predominate. Here the capital required to open a commercial enterprise was the smallest, and women could use their independent work to supplement income generated by the men in

TABLE 1

Ildefons Cerdà's Calculation of Gender Balance among Vendors in Barcelona in 1856
n=1,801

| Market | Female Vendors | Male Vendors | % Female | % Male | Totals |
|---|---|---|---|---|---|
| Boqueria | 727 | 81 | 89.976 | 10.024 | 808 |
| Born | 494 | 55 | 89.982 | 10.018 | 549 |
| Santa Caterina | 262 | 29 | 90.034 | 9.966 | 291 |
| Pedró | 40 | 5 | 88.889 | 11.111 | 45 |
| La Barceloneta | 98 | 10 | 90.741 | 9.259 | 108 |
| Totals | 1,621 | 180 | 90.006 | 9.994 | 1,801 |

Source: Data drawn from Ildefons Cerdà, *Teoría General de la Urbanización, Reforma, y Ensanche de Barcelona*, vol. 2, *La Urbanización Considerada como un hecho concreto: Estadística Urbana de Barcelona* (Madrid: Imprenta Española, 1867; republished by the Instituto de Estudios Fiscales, 1968), 622. Table by the author.

their families, who often worked in other occupations. The 1848 tax rolls list all of Barcelona's egg stalls (28 of 28) in the names of women, as well as 94 percent (358 of 382) of the city's vegetable stalls, 73 percent (86 of 118) of the fresh and dried fruit stalls, and 47 percent (39 of 82) of the offal stalls.[18] Though women continued to figure as the iconic sellers of fresh fish in the markets, they were less frequently listed as the title holders of these stalls, for two reasons. Most of the city's fish stalls at that time were operated on the basis of daily permits and thus were assessed their taxes on a daily basis. Fresh fish stalls were also most commonly operated as family enterprises with wives and daughters selling while husbands and brothers either fished or bought stock at the port while holding the retail permits that pertained to the enterprise. This anomaly apart, Barcelona's marketplaces had clearly long operated as feminized commercial spaces. While men were involved at many levels in market trade, women dominated in terms of direct contact with customers. A woman entering one of the city's markets to shop in the mid-nineteenth century could reasonably expect to deal mainly, if not exclusively, with other women in the process of purchasing her family's food. Because markets were public arenas serving specific residential areas, they functioned as central places for commercial and social exchange among the female population of the city.

In that market-stall businesses were usually more marginal commercial operations than fixed shops, the place of food vendors within the social hierarchy remained a somewhat ambiguous one.[19] We see perceptions of the marginality of market-based retailing in an 1864–65 commercial registry that claimed to list all of the taxpayers of Spain and its overseas possessions—*El Indicador de España y Sus Posesiones Ultramarinas*—yet included no mention at all of food vendors in Barcelona.[20] Though market vendors paid commercial taxes on an individual basis from 1848 onward, learned minds had long considered them as part of the city's working classes. Idlefons Cerdà was one such individual.

In his 1867 *Estadística Urbana de Barcelona,* Cerdà found that 90 percent of Barcelona's market vendors were female. By Cerdà's count, the total number of vendors represented 3.3185 percent of the working-class population and 1.0965 percent of the urban population. In his whole survey, there were only five other categories of workers in which women figured at or above 90 percent; these were certain occupations within the textile industry, laundresses, seamstresses, hairdressers, and clothes ironers.[21] From Cerdà we can see that market trade constituted an important entrepreneurial option for women in the lowest commercial rungs of the city. We can also see that prior to Barcelona's extramural expansion into the Eixample and beyond, female consumers in Barcelona purchased much if not most of their food from other women in public spaces where females dominated, at the very least, in terms of raw numbers.

With the dramatic growth of the city following the demolition of the Bourbon walls, the construction of the Eixample, and then the annexation of surrounding municipalities at the turn of the century, opportunities to earn a living in Barcelona's food-retailing sector grew tremendously. The rapid growth in the numbers of grocers' shops, as we have seen, was just one example of this. But in addition to these types of enterprises, from which the farthest-reaching male-dominated municipal, provincial, and national networks of food retailing first sprang, it is highly significant that men also moved in larger numbers than ever before into the ranks of Barcelona's market vendors during the late nineteenth and early twentieth centuries.

Because market stalls were so often operated on the basis of family-economy arrangements, records documenting who held title do not tell the whole story. Husbands often held stall licenses but worked other jobs while their wives sold in the markets. Likewise, some women held title, but the work of running the stall on a day-to-day basis was handled by daughters or other female relations. Such varying arrangements notwithstanding, we can see the movement of men into the markets reflected in the 1873 tax rolls for Barcelona, which list some categories of

TABLE 2

Market Stall Fixed-Title Acquisition Patterns, n=13,258

| Market name | Beginning date of municipal registry | Number of permits recorded up to 1936 | Stall permits issued to females | Stall permits issued to males | Female % of total | Male % of total |
|---|---|---|---|---|---|---|
| Santa Caterina | 1863 | 1,905 | 1,159 | 746 | 60.84 | 39.16 |
| Sant Antoni | 1882 | 2,425 | 1,438 | 987 | 59.3 | 40.7 |
| Barceloneta | 1884 | 914 | 539 | 375 | 58.97 | 41.03 |
| Concepció | 1888 | 1,192 | 708 | 484 | 59.4 | 40.6 |
| Hostafrancs | 1888 | 708 | 438 | 270 | 61.86 | 38.14 |
| Llibertat | 1875* | 1,100 | 660 | 440 | 60.0 | 40.0 |
| Abaceria Central | 1892* | 1,263 | 733 | 530 | 58.04 | 41.96 |
| Clot | 1889* | 500 | 291 | 209 | 58.2 | 41.8 |
| Unió | 1889* | 490 | 262 | 228 | 53.47 | 46.53 |
| Sarrià | 1911* | 276 | 139 | 137 | 50.36 | 49.64 |
| Sant Gervasi | 1912 | 178 | 94 | 84 | 52.81 | 47.19 |
| Sants | 1913 | 814 | 471 | 343 | 57.86 | 42.14 |
| Sant Andreu | 1923 | 549 | 307 | 242 | 55.92 | 44.08 |
| Galvany | 1927 | 523 | 285 | 238 | 54.49 | 45.51 |
| Ninot | 1933 | 421 | 218 | 203 | 51.78 | 48.22 |

*Denotes markets whose registries include entries predating annexation and the passage of owner-ship and control to Barcelona's municipal corporation.

Source: Administrative Records Area de Proveïments i Consum (now Institut Municipal de Mercats de Barcelona), Llibres de Registre, and Administrative Records Santa Caterina, L'Abaceria Central, and Sant Antoni markets. Data collected and tabulated by the author. La Boqueria is not included in these calculations.

vendors, such as those specializing in cured meats and milk. Though milk was only rarely sold in markets and represented a new element in the nineteenth-century diet, all ten of the city's milk stalls in 1873 were registered in the names of men. Of the ninety market stalls licensed to sell ham and sausages, sixty-seven were listed in the names of men.[22] Though representing only a glimpse at what was emerging in terms of a new gender balance in Barcelona's markets, these figures certainly show a significant departure from Cerdà's 1856 count. In the golden age of metal market-hall construction, men were attracted in larger numbers to the expanding opportunities in the retail food trade. While there was a good bit of variation by specialty, men continued to move into food-market retailing in large numbers after 1873. By the first third of the twentieth century, they were acquiring just over 40 percent of all the new market-stall titles issued by the city. Though many of these retail firms were undoubtedly run by women, the pattern is significant nonetheless.

Men were drawn increasingly into market-based food retailing from the last quarter of the nineteenth century onward for a number of reasons. The expansion of the sector, its municipalization and rationalization, and the formal organizations and networks that took shape to defend commercial interests all helped to institutionalize market trade and underpin the potential that market stalls had to generate profits. The presence of men as fixed-stall permit holders increased dramatically, but women were not eclipsed or marginalized in the process. A specific set of historic circumstances and legal advantages underpinned the tradition of women's work in commerce as well as its continuity in the face of growing male interest, investment, and activity in the food sector.

In the context of Spanish civil and commercial law, high rates of female proprietorship of municipal market-hall stalls may initially seem difficult to explain. The 1885 Código Comercial specifically stipulated that married women needed their husband's permission to engage in commerce and that husbands had the right to singlehandedly revoke their wives' commercial licenses at any moment they so chose.[23] The Código Civil of 1889 went even further and forbade married women from acting independently in any legal capacity whatsoever.[24] Indeed, most scholars hold that until the late 1950s, married women in Spain functioned under some of the most restrictive laws in all of Europe.[25] Yet market women in Barcelona were effectively exempt from these limitations. Whether single or married, they were able to function as independent legal actors, acquire market-stall titles from city authorities or other vendors, and run small businesses over long periods of time. Nowhere in the administrative records of Sant Antoni Market, for example, is there any evidence of the intervention of husbands in their wives' legal possession of market-stall titles. Lacking in all the extant administrative records of food retailing in the city are any forms for, or references to, spousal authorizations for the acquisition of stall titles by married women or documentation suggesting that any married woman had her stall title revoked by petition of her husband.

In fact, municipal market regulations in Barcelona through the first half of the twentieth century specifically codified female entrepreneurship, recognizing women as legally independent actors. Article 11 of the 1898 market code specified that the full payment price for stall titles acquired through municipal auctions had to be satisfied within forty-eight hours of the sale and that "women will be subjected to the same [terms], regardless of their status, and . . . married women will not be permitted to use as a pretext or excuse to elude their obligations the fact that they may have contracted without the consent of their respective husbands."[26] Likewise, Article 9, Section E of the 1928 market code reaffirmed the right of women to participate in auctions irrespective of their marital state.[27] The legal status of Barcelona's early-twentieth-century market women thus appears to represent something of an anomaly within Spain's juridical system.

There is, though, no real mystery behind the ongoing ability of women to act on an independent commercial basis in the municipal markets of Barcelona, or their expansion into the ranks of food-shop ownership in the city. Within a more specific Catalan historical context, high rates of female proprietorship of stall enterprises and explicit guarantees of commercial rights for married women were actually quite consistent with the inheritance and property laws long operative in the region. Stephen Jacobson's work on this subject offers us perhaps the best understanding of how women's legal status in Catalonia differed from that in most of the rest of Spain.[28] While the Spanish state from the early eighteenth century onward moved to impose centralization, local property laws in "foral" regions such as Catalonia continued in effect even after the promulgation of the Spanish civil code in 1889. As Jacobson explains, the Spanish central state was exceptional within Western Europe in its failure to achieve a "depoliticization of its juridical discourse."[29] In the face of ardent Catalan proto-nationalist resistance to the imposition of a centralized civil code, the Spanish Cortes capitulated, recognizing the former principality's juridical particularism. The fact that the Spanish civil code remained supplementary in "foral" regions such as Catalonia serves as only one of many examples of the limits of late-nineteenth-century centralization endeavors, especially in comparison to Germany and France.[30] Ultimately, the rejuvenation of local property laws in Catalonia and elsewhere only helped to reinforce the extent to which certain of Spain's geographically peripheral regions remained socially and culturally distinct from the interior of the state. In Catalonia, this was particularly evident in the unusual legal rights accorded to women in commerce.

In many ways, Catalan legal traditions held men and women as equals.[31] The property-law system strictly controlled inheritance to single recipients, but under certain circumstances, even where competent sons were available to act as heirs (*hereus*), daughters could be specified by their parents as heiresses (*pubilles*). The assets that women brought into marriage, known as the *dot*, did not become joint property. Rather, they remained under the control of wives until such time as they were passed on to her children or to other designated heirs. Husbands, therefore, did not have legally guaranteed access to the economic resources that their wives brought into marriage nor, for that matter, to assets that wives acquired through business enterprises. Within the Catalan legal context then, women's independent proprietorship of market stalls and shops in the late nineteenth and early twentieth centuries was not in the least a socially or culturally incongruent phenomenon.

### Stall Acquisition Patterns: Women Hold Their Own

There were several different types of market-stall conveyances during this period, with patterns of acquisition changing over time. Between 1898 and 1919, nearly all the fixed-stall permits were acquired at city auctions. But in the 1920s and 1930s, the number of stalls in the city's already established markets acquired through auctions fell, and other forms of acquisition became more frequent ways to gain title. One of these, of course, was the legalization process that involved the city's conveyance of fixed permits to persons who had worked a stall under a temporary license for more than five years. As part of the continuing effort to rationalize and standardize retail food sales, the process was largely completed by 1931 when only 6 of 7,286 market-stall titles in the city remained designated as temporary permits.[32] Equally significant to the consolidation of the vendor population within Barcelona's expanding lower-middle class was the introduction of new avenues for stall acquisition, particularly the right of vendors to sell their market-stall permits on the open market through a *trespaso intervivos* conveyance. This regulatory change contributed significantly to the value of market-stall enterprises in the early 1920s by making market-vendor concessions much more like real property.

One question that arises is whether women entered into market work as title-holding vendors through different avenues than men. At La Boqueria between 1920 and 1925, we can observe that men acquired stall permits at municipal auctions a little more frequently than women. And women acquired their permits by purchasing them from other vendors, and through inheritance, with a slightly higher frequency than men. Such data suggests that daughters tended to inherit market stalls more frequently than did sons. Overall, though, the distinctions in conveyance forms were relatively minor.[33]

Throughout the first three and a half decades of the twentieth century, and across the city's varying neighborhoods, the percentage of market-stall permits acquired by women continued to be greater than those acquired by men. Even though men were moving in larger numbers into food market-based retail trade in food, women held their own. There are, however, some distinctions in male and female stall-permit acquisition patterns by neighborhood and age of structure. In the city's older markets, where women had long dominated, men moved into the sector at a somewhat slower rate. Where new markets opened in the early twentieth century, men gained stall permits in larger numbers. This was the case, for example, with respect to El Ninot Market, which opened in 1933. The new market hall featured wider aisles, larger stalls, and modern refrigeration equipment, all of which were touted by officials as modern advances and as a symbol of the municipal administration's commitment to the well-being of the populace in the heady first years of the Second Republic.[34] Though incorporating scores of open-air vendors who had long been selling near the site of the market, El Ninot's inauguration involved the auctioning-off of hundreds of new stalls, 48.22 percent of which went to males. We also see higher percentages of market-stall titles acquired by men at Sarrià, inaugurated in 1911 (49.64 percent), San Gervasi, inaugurated in 1912 (47.19 percent), and Galvany, inaugurated in 1927 (45.51 percent). Older markets, where the social, commercial, and familial networks among women were more firmly established, were characterized by smaller percentages of men acquiring fixed-stall permits. Yet the key pattern that we see is that while men moved in larger numbers into market-stall work, women were not eclipsed in any real sense and enjoyed expanded commercial opportunities as a consequence of ongoing municipal commitment to market-hall construction.

The real significant gender distinctions in market-stall permit acquisition patterns were in terms of the specific foods that vendors were licensed to sell. Certain market specializations attracted more men than women. The fact that women acquired 63.3 percent of all the fruit and vegetable stall permits (out of a total of 5,329) but only 38.5 percent of the pork stall permits (out of 705) suggests that, apart from issues related to physical strength, initial capital investment shaped gender patterns in market-based food retailing. Pork stall permits allowed the sale of a range of pricey items, including cured hams and sausages, some of which, as we have seen, were branded and advertised and thus constituted particularly attractive items for consumerist expression. Many pork vendors did some of the processing themselves from small family-owned workshops located near their markets. Fruit and vegetable stall operations, where women predominated, required lower levels of investment in inventory, labor, and commercial space. The pattern of stall-permit acquisition in the salted fish specialization is similar to that of pork. Women acquired only 37.3 percent of those licenses (out of 220

TABLE 3

Fixed-Stall Title Acquisition Patterns by Selected Specializations, n=11,225

| License type | Number of licenses recorded up to 1936 | Female % of total | Male % of total |
| --- | --- | --- | --- |
| Salted fish | 220 | 37.3 | 62.7 |
| Pork | 705 | 38.5 | 61.5 |
| Grocers | 395 | 43.8 | 56.2 |
| Fresh fish | 1,170 | 53.8 | 46.2 |
| Fresh meat | 1,838 | 59.6 | 40.4 |
| Poultry, game, eggs | 1,568 | 62.6 | 37.4 |
| Fresh fruits and vegetables | 5,329 | 63.3 | 37.7 |

*Source:* Administrative Records Area de Proveïments i Consum (now Institut Municipal de Mercats de Barcelona), *Llibres de Registre,* and Administrative Records Santa Caterina, Abaceria Central, and Sant Antoni markets. Data collected and tabulated by the author. La Boqueria not included.

issued). Salted fish vendors also engaged in intensive processing activities, mostly related to desalinating cod and deboning *arangades* (a type of salt-cured sardine). Market-stall spaces were often too small to accommodate salted fish processing needs, so many of these vendors had adjacent shops that functioned as additional retail outlets, stockrooms, and work spaces. The fact that women predominated in the acquisition of stall licenses to sell fruits and vegetables, which might be conceptualized as the easiest and cheapest trade to ply, does not suggest that they were in the minority among those acquiring permits to sell goods that involved "artisanal" skill. Women outnumbered men in the acquisition of fresh fish, fresh meat, and poultry permits. Women in fact acquired more permits than men in all the largest specializations.

The differences in stall acquisition patterns notwithstanding, the dominant pattern featured men and women working alongside one another in the city's markets and collaborating on the basis of family-economy relationships to successfully operate food-retailing businesses. Inasmuch as the 1928 market code specifically allowed spouses, children, and other household members of stall-permit holders to legally work behind the counter without special permission, it further endorsed and facilitated long-standing family-economy strategies.[35] The key point is that markets were definitively not commercial venues in which men dominated across the board in stall proprietorship or in entrepreneurial initiative.

## Contested Cultural Identities

As food retailers built formal commercial networks, they increasingly laid rhetorical claim to some sort of middle-class status. We have certainly seen this with respect to fishmongers, grocers, and butchers, at the very least. But just as a rising tide lifts all boats, such organizational endeavors contributed to the greater frequency with which food retailing from the city's markets came to be construed as a more legitimate and more profitable form of economic activity, and one to which men were increasingly drawn. Through their retailing associations, vendors, along with shopkeepers, presented themselves as belonging to a respectable social station that generally rejected the more confrontational tactics of the working classes. But while market vendors experienced a modest but discernable degree of upward social mobility, they were hard pressed to embrace the predominant middle-class gender ideologies that emphasized greater degrees of domestic encloistering for women.

Gender analyses of the development of food retailing in Barcelona serve to illustrate some of the crucial distinctions within the emerging middle classes of the late nineteenth and early twentieth centuries. Female market vendors especially had to modify, ignore, or even reject the prevailing gender ideology of the social class among whose ranks they aspired to be counted. Work outside the home, in the formal economy and in direct contact with the consuming public, was understood among the proper bourgeoisie as socially unacceptable. Yet market women and female shopkeepers tended to remain active in the commercial economy throughout their life cycles. Thus we see that aside from the obvious material distinctions that separated those in the lower middle classes from their supposed social superiors, there were differences in the prevailing gender ideologies characterizing these strata as well.

As we would expect, the main middle class in Barcelona, which widely accepted dictates imposing leisure upon women, tended to look down upon the "grubby" traders whose wives and daughters were compelled to spend all or a portion of their lives working outside their homes. Female market vendors especially suffered from social and cultural derision. Though they may have owned more capital and exercised more independence in their work routines than other lower-middle-class groups such as telephone operators, department store clerks, and office workers, market vendors were often viewed as belonging to a less honorable station. Markets were unseemly to some. Even with the rationalization of the sector and the imposition of stricter hygienic regulations, Barcelona's market halls remained crowded spaces. The types of vegetable, meat, and fish matter of which their stock was comprised gave them a special verdant and carnal odor. The fact that fish vendors and butchers of all manners wore aprons that by day's end were often dirty or even blood-soaked contributed to the impression that market work was somehow beyond the delicate sensibilities of those claiming proper middle-class status. Conscious of their appearance, market women went to great lengths to bleach, starch, and iron their aprons in order to compensate.

The many voices reverberating in the city's market halls distinguished them as performative spaces. Because successful stalls were in great measure marked by vendors' verbal dexterity, market women were sometimes boisterous. Female vendors especially could use distinct forms of speech and a specific tone of voice that was generally deemed inappropriate for respectable women. Municipal authorities, of course, sought to contain these practices, to little avail.[36] Some of this, though much toned down, continues until the present. Recently, a fourth-generation fish vendor, who started working at La Boqueria at the tender age of thirteen, described his wife's abilities in the verbal art to me. Gerard Jolí and Puri Albiol met in the market as children. Once married, they worked their stalls on the basis of family-economy arrangements. As a third-generation fresh fish vendor herself, Puri is a carrier of both family and market tradition. Over an unforgettable breakfast at the Bodega Sepúlveda with some of La Boqueria's leading market men in June 2011, I noticed a clear consensus that Puri's verbal dexterity was a form of valuable commercial capital. Gerard said that his wife was "tremendous" at work. He called her an absolute *crac* who had two personalities.[37] Working from her stalls in the fish section of La Boqueria, she was a verbal force to be reckoned with; at home, she was altogether different. It was like night and day. Gerard spoke of this as a point of pride.

Everyone who has ever shopped regularly in Barcelona's markets understands that they are distinctive sites of neighborhood sociability and places where a certain type of comedy-laced rhetoric is used by vendors to entertain and to persuade. The late and great Manel Ripoll, La Boqueria fishmonger par excellence and former president of that market's vendor association, eloquently explained the importance of the performative art of market-vending. He cast it in a much more positive light, though. He would say that a great many customers patronized certain stalls not just for the goods they offered, but also because this is where they felt most comfortable in going to "confession." Understanding this and offering genuine empathy and good humor to consumers, he told me, was the essence of vendors' ongoing commercial success. Stall-keepers were at once entertainers and counselors. While the economic fate of shopkeepers was also often dependent upon the dexterous use of a certain set of rhetorical forms, they involved less animation, less in the way of theatrics, and certainly less volume than those used by vendors inside the city's market halls. In this respect, shopkeepers could be better positioned to lay claim to the respectable manners and polite discursive practices expected of the middle classes.

The distinctiveness of the market-vendor subculture that now seems quaint to tourists, many city residents, and journalists alike carried with it a set of real pejorative connotations earlier in the century. Market vendors were stereotyped as untrustworthy and crude by municipal regulators and by the press. Market administrators used the adjective "unscrupulous" in reference to vendors in their records.[38] Newspaper articles, such as that printed in the August 7, 1918, edition of *La Publicidad* demanding that "the authority's actions . . . should seek to protect the public against the deception on the part of vendors which may victimize them," were fairly common.[39] As noted earlier, the popular jibe used to denigrate a vociferous woman—"she talks like a fishwife"—still survives. So too does the term *marmenyera*, which literally means retail market vendor, but is also used to describe women who are contentious frauds.[40] This negative cultural image was not lost on the vendors themselves, who in many instances were pained by the stereotypes and sometimes even exhibited shame about the work they did. As we have seen, Santa Caterina's own 1930 Market Queen recalled the embarrassment she felt at working in her mother's stall when her school friends passed by.[41]

### Market Women on Stage

Though market women were often portrayed in civic pageantry and in the theater as radiant young beauties, there was clearly a darker side to their cultural iconography. As market women matured, they were more often characterized as hags and as gossips, and they were derided for their language and their flashy and sexualized appearance. We see this in a number of theatrical depictions. In a 1935 play by Josep Maria de Sagarra, *La Rambla de les Floristes*, La Boqueria's female flower vendors are engaged in near-constant verbal combat among themselves and with their customers and male admirers. The play's protagonist, unmarried thirty-something Antònia, is at once alluring and "very quarrelsome."[42] Likewise, in Alfons Roure's 1928 *La Reina del Mercat*, the beguiling thirty-five-year-old widowed protagonist, Tresina, has a bawdy way about her. She hurls insults at adjacent stall-keepers and comes close to trading blows with another vendor in the opening scene. When a market guard tells Tresina that a city councilman has announced his intention to come see her in her stall, she replies that she is too busy to waste time on him and his sexual advances: "Let him interest himself with what he has at home, which should occupy him plenty, because his wife, they say, is like a rocking chair upon which everyone rides."[43] After the policeman accuses her of lack of respect, she answers that she would react in the same way to the Kaiser if he were to similarly attempt to "tickle her honor."[44]

Published during the Civil War in 1938, Ramon Juncosa's *El Mercat del Guinardo* may never have been performed before an audience. Even though Juncosa held stall-keepers up as victims of capitalist exploitation, the negative cultural image of the female market vendor remained a powerful theme. In his play, a vegetable vendor by the name of Filomena is harassed by an unscrupulous market director and his staff. As retribution for not supplying the director with free vegetables on demand, Filomena is ordered to close her stall for fifteen days. She reacts angrily to the sanction; she insults the director and his representatives, and refuses to comply. As in Roure's work, Juncosa depicts female market vendors as verbally aggressive, with sharp exchanges escalating in the opening scenes. Filomena does not hesitate to take a city policeman by the collar, shake him, and call him a straw doll, a year-round "Carnestotles," and an overripe turnip.[45] She turns to another vendor and says, "If you don't move from here, I'll separate your head from your body with the same facility with which I do a cabbage from its stalk." In arguing with a male customer, Filomena explodes, "I'll rip out your tongue." Her assistant adds, "And she'll cook it in a stew." The customer hisses back, "Insultress, bad woman, wicked . . . "[46]

The defense of personal honor and concerns with social stature are running themes in a number of these theatrical works. In Sagarra's *La Rambla de les Floristes*, Antònia initially responds vituperatively from her stall when a suitor finally gets around to proposing marriage. Then he pleads with her to speak with him "more naturally" and to be less "severe."[47] When Antònia gives up the performative mode, she rebuffs her suitor nonetheless, on the grounds that she has no interest in being looked down upon by his presumptuous relatives: "I have not lost sight of this world and I know the place in that world to which I pertain."[48]

There are similar declarations of personal honor in Roure's *La Reina del Mercat* and its epilogue, *El Casori de la Tresina*.[49] The play's action surrounds the problems that ensue when Tresina's daughter Tecleta becomes engaged to marry Fidel Colom, a young physician who has just finished his medical training. As the plot unfolds, Tresina agrees to give up her work as a poulterer in order for her daughter to marry, but only because she knows that Tecleta is with child and thus the nuptials are urgent. Saving her daughter's honor involves giving up her own. Tresina closes her market stall and disappears into the arms of a shadowy figure with whom she lives in sin in order to survive. But love conquers all in the end. The mystery man turns out to be the director of her market, and the pair has fallen deeply in love. Again, her son-in-law's parents appear on the scene to confront her unacceptable conduct. Tresina defiantly refuses to give up her lover, saying that she had "fallen to save the honor of a daughter." With vehemence, she declares that "even if all of society spits on me, my conscience is tranquil, it tells me I can carry my head high wherever I go!"[50] Ultimately, Tresina re-opens her stall, marries the market director, and takes her daughter and son-in-law in under her roof. The young doctor ends up establishing a medical practice based upon his mother-in-law's market-based social connections.[51]

The venerated actress Assumpció Casals's 1927 portrayal of Tresina was not her first appearance in the theater as a market queen. Ten years earlier, she starred in Josep Burgas's *A La Remei l'han fet Reina* as a salt cod vendor's daughter who had just been elected Queen of La Boqueria Market. The plot surrounds Remei's marriage prospects. She is courted by her presumptuous and spoiled cousin, Ramonet, but her heart belongs to her father's clerk, Peret. Remei is feisty and strong-willed, and at her wits end over Peret's foot-dragging in asking her father for her hand. When Peret jealously urges her to turn down La Boqueria's Market Queen crown because he knows she will be showered in male attention, Remei defiantly replies, "I will be queen [if] only to enrage you. Now more than ever! I will be the queen of the market and the betrothed of my cousin. Mother agrees, she says that by marrying him I could change position . . . I could become a lady." Peret responds to this with scorn: "From *bacallanera* to lady! Don't believe it, Remei: your hands would give you away."[52]

In addition to the sharp tongues and combative nature these playwrights ascribed to their respective protagonists, they also emphasized the degree to which meddling in others' affairs was a common practice in market-based social exchange. Everything seemed to be everyone else's business. The spatial configurations of stalls, featuring rows of vendors crowded together, shaped the nature of social relationships between and among market women and their customers. Barcelona's food markets appeared on the stage as heady environments where feisty women engaged in combative exchange. Here we can see an important distinction in the popular perceptions of women working in food shops versus women working in food markets. Shopkeepers inhabited their own separate and enclosed spaces. To the extent that women in retailing were subjected to social and cultural derision in the early twentieth century, it was market vendors who were more often targeted.

It remains important, though, to remember that early-twentieth-century theatrical representations of female market vendors were subject to differing interpretation by their audiences. First of all, they were comedies that must have seemed funnier to some than to others. They could be read as confirmations of the unseemly and explosive nature of the market subculture and of female vendors' inclinations to defy authority. To others, no doubt, they reinforced popular conceptions about class struggle and about the contempt and arrogance of the socially presumptuous toward individuals from the humbler strata of the urban polity. In a general sense, playwrights used market women as literary devices in service to the larger effort to argue for a new, more egalitarian social order.

## Embedded in Their Neighborhoods

In real life, Barcelona's twentieth-century market women were often quite successful in laying claim to personal honor and dignity within their neighborhoods. Relationships of dependency, credit, personal favors, and kinship linked women retailers to localized urban communities. So too did residential patterns. Both shopkeepers and market vendors frequently lived among those who purchased food from them and thus were tied in complex ways to one another. With respect to shops, we see this most readily. The bulk of the ground-floor commercial establishments selling food in Barcelona included retail space leading to the street and, albeit often cramped, residential space in the interior of the building. Commercial space was frequently separated from residential space by little more than a curtain. Women working in shops usually did double duty through most of the day, cooking meals, nursing and attending to small children in between waiting on customers, though often with help from husbands, female relatives, or clerks. In this respect, late-nineteenth- and early-twentieth-century shopkeepers did not experience the separation of home from workplace that came to characterize the industrial economy more generally. Such continued blending of commercial and domestic space was less common in larger shops that sold luxury goods, in cafés, and in restaurants, though it certainly continued through the pre–Civil War decades in many neighborhood taverns and small eateries.

Embedded residentially within the neighborhood communities from which they drew their customers, shopkeepers operated within complex social and economic networks. Just as neighborhood men often met in bars, cafés, and bodegas to play dominoes and discuss politics, women commonly met at given hours in shops to socialize and strategize. Food shops were crucial arenas for the negotiation of neighborhood honor. Within these venues, women's reputations could be made or unmade, innuendos of sexual indiscretion could be spread, and news of personal fortune or misfortune disseminated. So while female shopkeepers could not fully adhere to the gender ideologies of their social superiors, they could command significant power in the neighborhoods in which they lived. They participated actively in the negotiation of personal reputations, and they supplied a portion of the sustenance that their neighbors of varying social classes consumed at dinner tables with their families. The spatial configurations of food markets, on the other hand, more readily lent themselves to different sorts of social exchanges. Market vendors did not and could not sleep in their stalls. Though there was much chatter, and customers standing in line to be waited upon often talked to one another, the discourse among women buying and selling food in markets was more public. Markets were less amenable places for the careful plotting of strategies to resolve personal problems. While verbal exchanges in Barcelona's food markets were more performative and less private than those taking place in many shops, the lines between home and workplace and between commercial and social relationships were nonetheless amorphous there as well.

Like shopkeepers, many market vendors and customers were neighbors, lived together in the same apartment buildings, drew water from the same fountains, and hung their clothes from the same rooftop lines. Because vendors were so often spatially woven into the social fabric of their neighborhoods, they tended to draw their clientele from among the ranks of their neighbors. As was the case for all food retailers, commercial success to a significant degree depended upon securing the fidelity of consumers who would predictably patronize the enterprise on a regular basis. In a context where food safety and food adulteration issues remained serious concerns, consumer trust, consumer confidence, and consumer fidelity constituted crucial commercial capital. In the city's public market halls, female vendors' abilities to cultivate a body of regular clients were to a very large extent a function of their acumen in navigating neighborhood social networks of women.

## LIVING NEAR THE MARKET: SANTA CATERINA

The case of Santa Caterina serves as an especially illustrative example of market vendors' residence patterns in early-twentieth-century Barcelona. Santa Caterina was located in the Sant Pere neighborhood, an area inside the Ribera, and served as a spatial anchor of informal sociability. Sant Pere's social character had long been intimately intertwined with the growth and mechanization of textile production in the city because many of the first factories were located there. Populated by both bourgeois and artisanal families, the neighborhood entered a period of decline from the mid-nineteenth century onward when many of the wealthy left to take up residence in the Eixample and most of its textile factories were relocated to areas beyond the urban core. Situated a short distance from Barcelona's main train station, Sant Pere's deteriorating housing stock and cheap rents increasingly attracted immigrant populations drawn to the city in search of work in the late nineteenth century. The 1909–13 construction of the Via Laietana, a new broad thoroughfare extending from the Pla del Palau to the Plaça Urquinaona, brought further dislocation.[53] Involving the destruction of dozens of buildings, the Via Laietana provided better access to the old city from the Eixample and from the port, while also more firmly demarcating Sant Pere as a distinct area, separate from the ecclesiastic core surrounding the La Seu and the commercial area above it anchored around Carrer Condal.

While the neighborhood of Sant Pere experienced significant proletarianization in the first decades of the twentieth century, the Santa Caterina market hall remained its retail and its social epicenter and provided a modicum of stability to the area as a consequence. Municipal registries listing vendors who were issued titles for stalls at Santa Caterina between 1869 and 1929 reveal that more than a third resided in domiciles that were within a one-block radius of the market-hall structure and more than half lived in the Ribera portion of the old urban core. With El Born's conversion to wholesale trade in 1921, Santa Caterina emerged as the Ribera's definitive epicenter for the retail sale of food. Santa Caterina Market functioned as a central place in which intense and repeated interpersonal contact among retailers and consumers, who were often neighbors, took place on a daily basis.

That structures such as Santa Caterina acted as loci of commercial and social relationships in neighborhoods across the city by the early twentieth century is evidenced by the varied uses of market space. In addition to its main purpose as a food-retailing center, a portion of Santa Caterina near the rear of the market had long served as a municipal shelter for indigent women, and portions of the building had also housed both fire services and police.[54] While the administration of the city's markets was very clearly in the hands of municipal authorities who jealously guarded their turf, vendors and consumers alike laid claim to markets as neighborhood community spaces as well. Within Santa Caterina itself, vendors

TABLE 4

Residence Patterns as Revealed in Stall Titles Issued for Santa Caterina Market,
1869–1929, n=235

| Place of residence | % titles issued |
| --- | --- |
| Within one block of the market | 34.9 |
| Within Sant Pere but beyond one block of the market | 10.6 |
| Within the Ribera below Princessa Street | 6.4 |
| Elsewhere in the Casc Antic | 6.4 |
| Beyond the Casc Antic | 29.8 |
| Unknown | 11.9 |

Source: Administrative Records, Santa Caterina Market. Data tabulated by author.

organized dances, decorated and celebrated for holidays, and met to undertake group excursions to hike and picnic in the countryside. The expression *anar a la plaça* (go to the plaza) rather than *anar al mercat* (go to the market) is indicative of a popular understanding that these places were public gathering spaces. Vendors' use of the term *parroquia* (parishioners) in reference to their loyal clientele implied a relationship between food retailers and consumers that involved both stewardship and devotion. Though market halls were specifically built to cover and enclose stalls, the space within them was popularly understood by vendors and consumers alike to be an extension of the public square, which in addition to its commercial functions in the neighborhood had important social functions as well.

Santa Caterina vendors recall a strong sense of community in the market in the decades preceding the Civil War. Carme Giner Folch was born in Barcelona in 1906. Her father had emigrated from Aragon and found work in a grain warehouse near El Born; her mother, a native of the city, worked an olive and legume stall at Santa Caterina all of her life. Though Carme attended a municipal school and then began working as a hatmaker's apprentice, her mother wanted her only child to acquire and run a market stall. Arranging a *trespaso intervivos* in 1921 from an old woman who suffered from bronchitis, Carme took over a stall at the age of fifteen that was located in the same aisle as her mother's and that specialized in the same line of goods. Describing the atmosphere at Santa Caterina in the pre–Civil War years, Carme recalled that she had a regular and faithful set of clients. She asserted that there was much gaiety in the market and that servants especially gathered around certain stalls to laugh and to talk.[55] Her memories attest to the way that market halls served double functions. For housewives and servants alike, going to the market was a domestic duty that also offered an opportunity for sociability. The lively and entertaining aspects of market exchange enhanced the appeal of work in them, which helped to offset the early hours, the strain of standing for long periods of time, and seasonal extremes in temperature.

Carme Giner was one of many women who followed their mothers into work at Santa Caterina in the early twentieth century. Francisca Astor Pijuan was another. She was a third-generation fresh fish vendor who in 1919 inherited a fixed permit for Santa Caterina Stall 39, shortly after the death of her mother, Ana Pijuan Morató. The same stall had been worked by her grandmother, Magdalena Morató, for more than fifty years, which probably meant she was one of that market's first vendors. As such, Francisca Astor asserted that market-stall title Number 139 was definitively and irrefutably hers. In a petition to Barcelona's Mayor Antoni Martínez i Domingo, Francisca indignantly reported that the director of the market refused to recognize her rights. Her quandary derived from the fact that at the time she was to take possession of the stall title in her own name she was convalescing from an illness. Following conventional practice, she had turned the stall over to a niece with full permission from the market director to do so. Three months later, though, her niece had to withdraw from market work to care for her ailing mother. So Francisca arranged, again with the permission of the market director, to have another fish vendor, "Trinidad, wife of Segarra," sell from her stall on a temporary basis until her health would allow her to return. Having recovered by December of 1920, Francisca found that Trinidad refused to give up the stall with the justification that the market director had in the meantime conveyed the fixed-stall permit to her.[56] The conflict proved difficult to resolve, and when Francisca determined that she could not achieve a satisfactory settlement with either her stall usurper or the market director, she turned to the highest level of municipal authority to plead her case.

The tone of Francisca Astor's 1921 petition to the mayor is telling. As far as she was concerned, Santa Caterina Market did not belong to the director and he could not speak to her "as if he were the owner."[57] As heir to her mother's and her grandmother's stall, she demanded that the conveyance of her license to Trinidad, who was supposed to be her temporary substitute, be rescinded. This case illustrates most obviously that access to market-stall permits was a competitive business and that market directors acted in some instances to unflinchingly enforce the provisions of the 1898 municipal market code—in this case, Article 19, which forbade substitutions in day-to-day stall operation for more than six months' time. More significantly, it shows that from the perspective of women such as

Francisca Astor, the markets belonged to the vendors who had a family history of working in them and that those who had legitimate rights could claim a defense of the same before the highest municipal authorities, on an individual basis and without the intermediation of male-dominated formal associations representing vendors' rights. Francisca was more than just a Santa Caterina fishmonger. She was a Ribera resident who lived nearby on Carrer del Rec and was something of a neighborhood fixture. As such, she minced no words in schooling the municipal authorities, according to a clear sense of inherited occupational identity, about what was right and just within a community that was hers.

Members of subsequent generations of Santa Caterina market veterans described a powerful sense of community in their workplace. Maria Cararach was born in Barcelona in 1923 and shared detailed memories dating to when she was six years old.[58] Her paternal grandmother had established the stall business cutting and selling beef and veal at Santa Caterina, and her father, Salvador Cararach Biot, who had served as president of the butchers' association, began working there at a young age. Maria followed suit. Not long after the death of her mother, she and her sister joined the family business when they were respectively twelve and thirteen years old. Maria described their customer base in those days as including women who worked outside the home, domestic servants, and wives who had given up paid employment. She said that almost every day they had the same customers and that women bought about 200 grams of meat at a time. The scales were not as accurate as they became later, and customers often wanted a weight that was a touch heavy in their favor. Women still haggled over prices, and faithful "parishioners" could expect to sometimes get a ten-centim discount on their purchase. Maria also remembered the excitement surrounding the 1930 Market Queen pageantry, recalling how vendors came together to construct the parade float upon which the Queen would ride. All this she described within the context of a market culture that featured strong social bonds among vendors and customers. In her youth, she said, there was real love in the market and much friendship among those who passed daily through its doors.

The social networks that linked Santa Caterina vendors together and to the surrounding Sant Pere neighborhood were often forged in childhood and involved young men as well as young women who had grown up near the market. Joan Mani Burgada, a second-generation fishmonger born in 1925, remembered the neighborhood surrounding Santa Caterina in the years before the war as being made up of families that took care of one another. The children of market vendors, he said, often participated in two of the Catalanist civic organizations located nearby—La Penya Cultural de Barcelona and the Germanor Barcelonina. Both organized hiking expeditions and other activities for the youth of the neighborhood. The bonds among the young people participating in these organizations, according to Burgada, were based upon affections "that were a continuity from the market" and helped to develop mutual respect among the children of the neighborhood.[59] These sorts of relationships, in his view, offset the tendency of some vendors to quarrel and use foul language, a problem that he says lingered until after the war. In Burgada's estimation, the social status of vendors had never been a function of the accumulation of wealth, but rather was determined on the basis of refined manners and character; those vendors who had a sense of responsibility and respect for their customers could make legitimate claims to propriety and to community respect. Though Sant Pere was a neighborhood in ostensible socioeconomic decline in the first decades of the century, the ongoing commercial viability of Santa Caterina, the residential clustering of vendors in the market's immediate environs, the varied use of market space, and the complex interpersonal relations among retailers and consumers contributed to a strong sense of community in this part of the old urban core.

The testimony of Santa Caterina market vendors about neighborhood life in the years before the war offers a somewhat later vision from the bottom up of that which Dolors Monserdà (1846–1919) wove into a number of her novels. In La Fabricanta, Monserdà described the Sant Pere neighborhood in which her protagonist, Antonieta, lived, married, raised a family, and built a fortune.[60] Economic and social success, though, meant that Antonieta had to withdraw from day-to-day public participation in the business she has been so crucial in constructing. Still, Antonieta remained grounded in the San Pere neighborhood as a powerful reference point for her life. Monserdà's novels treat the city itself as a protagonist; her plots interweave women's lives with specific urban spaces.[61] Viewed from this perspective, we can more fully appreciate that Santa Caterina Market was more than merely a building or a place of commercial exchange. The market was more analogous to a community, an organic system that was vital to ordinary women's everyday lives.

## LIVING NEAR THE MARKETS IN GRÀCIA

In Gràcia we can see that similar informal social and economic networks emanated from the municipal market halls. The persistence and complexity of the relationships among vendors and between vendors and their customers contributed to the ongoing sense of community through the decades preceding the outbreak of the Civil War.

Though retaining its distinctive physical character based upon a plethora of plazas from which narrow streets extended, Gràcia grew from an urban core of 2,608 persons living on 17 streets and squares in 1825 to include 102 streets and squares inhabited by 13,548 persons in 1850.[62] That year, Gràcia achieved the full municipal status to which its residents would cling until annexation to Barcelona. By the time of its absorption into the city at the end of the nineteenth century, Gràcia, with its 61,935 inhabitants, was the ninth-largest municipality in Spain.[63] Long a hotbed of both liberalism and workerism, Gràcia was characterized by a vibrant civic and political culture. In addition to hiking clubs, choral societies, popular libraries, and cooperatives, there was significant anarchist, socialist, and radical republican mobilization. It is not surprising that Gràcia's cafés and taverns were particularly known as centers of political fervency.[64] Here again, we see that small-scale privately owned enterprises selling coffee, alcohol, and prepared foods assumed multiple functions. They were commercial entities retailing alimentary consumer goods with the aim of generating a margin of profit sufficient to sustain the households that operated them, but they were also intimately woven into Barcelona's civic culture. Which cafés men choose to frequent in Gràcia, as elsewhere, depended upon their ideological and political orientations as much as upon location and access to disposable income for use in this form of commercialized leisure.

Of course, the women of Gràcia participated much less frequently in the political and ideological debates taking place within neighborhood cafés, taverns, and bars. Their culturally prescribed domestic duties kept them closer to home while also affording them the opportunity to socialize as they went about the task of purchasing food in the neighborhood's markets and shops. Mercè Rodoreda's novel *La Plaça del Diamant*, about Gràcia before, during, and after the Civil War, poignantly illustrates this social pattern.[65] Natalia, its protagonist, lost her mother at a young age and faced tremendous hardships, but she could always count on the neighborhood chestnut vendor, who watched over and advised her, and helped her through her difficult ordeals.

Gràcia's veteran market vendors spoke eloquently about the intensive sociability among women that took place there in the early twentieth century. Joana Grillé Fornell, born in 1915, grew up in the shadow of La Llibertat Market, where her parents held permits for four contiguous fruit and vegetable stalls. In 1930, Joana's father died, leaving his widow and daughter to carry on the business. Yet

Joana recalled enjoying her work in the market because the atmosphere was so lively during the years of her youth. The existence of cultural derision toward market vendors seemed distant to her. In fact, Joana took great pride in her work. La Llibertat, she explained, was a prestigious market offering select commodities for sale. Its location near the Via Augusta and Balmes Street made access to it by train convenient for upper-middle-class women who lived in wealthier areas above Gràcia. Joana described La Llibertat as a sort of extended family. Vendors tended to live near the market, and their lives were bound up with those of the women who shopped there daily.[66]

Another vendor who worked in Gràcia's La Llibertat Market before the war offered similar testimony about the powerful sense of community emanating from the structure. Josefa Nogueroles Casas, a third-generation offal vendor whose nickname was "Paquita," was born in 1919 and grew up nearby. Her grandparents had held stalls at La Boqueria and acquired a license to sell offal—primarily in the form of veal tripe, lungs, head, feet, and liver—from La Llibertat when the market opened in 1875. Paquita's mother began selling from one of the family's La Boqueria stalls when she was just eleven years old. Eventually moving over to La Llibertat, her mother married a man she met at Barcelona's wharf and continued working as an offal vendor through the birth of her children, only giving up her work when old age made the long hours and cool temperatures of the market too difficult to bear. Paquita was one of three surviving children when she began to work with her mother at La Llibertat in 1931 at the age of twelve. From that time until her retirement, Paquita built and cultivated a network of relationships with neighborhood consumers that drew upon her family's more than half-century history in the market.

Paquita Nogueroles's memories of a life spent working in La Llibertat attest to the fact that women in food retailing often laid successful claim to personal honor within their neighborhood communities. She described her mother as having been "molt senyora" (a real lady). She noted that her mother's refined manners in dealing with customers placed her among the elite vendors in the market and that upon her death she had accumulated jewelry worth more than three million pesetas. Paquita inherited her mother's sense of propriety and honor, drawing upon it as commercial capital that helped her build what she described as one of the biggest "parròquies" in Gràcia.[67]

Though Paquita Nogueroles did acknowledge contentious exchanges between some consumers and market vendors, such drama, she insisted, never characterized the relationship she had with her clientele. Paquita recounted how she quickly dispatched with ill-mannered shoppers. Witty verbal dexterity was a must, both in terms of avoiding conflict and as a tool for winning over and keeping a loyal clientele. Eager to uphold both her mother's prestigious reputation in the market and her own sense of personal honor, she made sure not to gossip or be perceived as a busybody. Her conversations with "parishioners" revolved mainly around cooking, which enhanced sales, and inquiries about the well-being of her customers' mothers and grandmothers, which reinforced the multigenerational nature of the socio-commercial network upon which she depended. Because much of what Paquita sold was relatively cheap, she tended to do more business during times of economic hardship when tripe and other variety meats were substituted for chicken, fish, or veal. As such, her social role in the neighborhood was crucial. The enduring ties of affection she built with her clientele were evident when she was greeted with the warm physical embrace of shoppers five years after her retirement as she entered the market to offer her personal testimony.

Ethnographic evidence indicating widespread residential embedding of market vendors among their base of neighborhood clients is confirmed by the few extant municipal registries that include vendors' addresses. With respect to Gràcia, the registries surviving are for La Revolució Market and reinforce what individual vendors recount more generally. In the period extending from 1882 to 1912, La Revolució's registries record 240 stall titles, 25 percent of which were issued to persons living within one block of that market. An additional 46 percent lived further than a block from the market but still within Gràcia itself. The process of transferring vendors to the new L'Abaceria Central structure obviously disrupted this pattern, though not dramatically. L'Abaceria Central was just two blocks away from La Revolució. Vendors relocating could remain in their residences and still live close to the new market hall. Whether in the old core of the city, as was the case with Santa Caterina Market, or in newly annexed neighborhoods such as Gràcia, the residential clustering of vendors around the markets in which they worked, like the permeability between shopkeepers' domestic and retailing spaces, acted to reinforce the overlapping commercial and social networks that were the essence of everyday neighborhood life for women.

Markets were central places for female entrepreneurship, consumerism, and sociability. Yet the networks emanating from them extended beyond the neighborhoods they served. This is most obviously the case in terms of the supply chains through which markets were stocked with the food that they sold. It was also the

TABLE 5

Residence Patterns as Revealed in Stall Titles Issued for Revolució Market,
1882–1912, n=240

| Place of residence | % titles issued |
| --- | --- |
| Within one block of the market | 25% |
| Within Gràcia but beyond one block of the market | 46% |
| Beyond Gràcia | 29% |

*Source:* Administrative Records, L'Abaceria Central Market. Data tabulated by the author.

case with respect to both public administration and private associationalism, both of which plugged Barcelona's market halls into broader regional and even national networks. But there were also strong links between specific economic practices in the city's hinterland and patterns of gender-based divisions of labor within Barcelona's markets. This was the case with respect to one particular category of vendors—that is, the rural producers.

### NOT RESIDENTIALLY EMBEDDED: A MODERN PEASANT'S STORY

As we have seen, each of the municipal food markets included a certain number of peasants, or producer-vendors (known as *pagesos*), who lived in the rural hinterland but came to the city daily to sell from cruder makeshift stalls than those of their fixed-permit urban-dwelling counterparts working from inside these structures. Though they were limited by regulation to shorter operating hours, they were nonetheless the most direct carriers to urban areas of long-established rural family strategies. Maintaining a presence through the whole of the twentieth century, they remained an enduring part of the system until much later than we might otherwise expect if we were to adhere to simpler models of retail modernization.

Smallholders who engaged in the production of fruits and vegetables throughout Barcelona's hinterland relied historically upon a division of labor within the family that frequently included the operation of a market stall by one or more of the adult females in the family. Though some of these stalls were located in nearby towns, large numbers of rural women also traveled to Barcelona to sell in one of the city's numerous market halls. Husbands, fathers, and sons of working age, along with whatever day-laborers and sharecroppers were involved in the family-farming operation, worked in the fields and took responsibility for whole-sale transactions, while females engaged in retailing what was left over. As Barce-lona's importance at the top of the central-place hierarchy of the region grew and the number of markets and other retail opportunities expanded, larger numbers of rural women chose to travel to the city to sell surplus fruits and vegetables. The growth of the rail network from the second half of the nineteenth century onward facilitated this trade to a significant extent, though horse and buggy trans-port remained common well into the twentieth century. Some markets, such as Santa Caterina, had more than a hundred peasant women selling wares on a daily basis through the decades preceding World War I. Administrative records from La Boqueria Market indicate that in 1920, 62 of the 1,637 stall titles were held by producer-vendors.[68] Though certainly a significant minority and clearly operating at a certain disadvantage, producer-vendor market-stall permits remained impor-tant and valued assets, which were often passed from one generation to the next. Even where such permits were held by men, it was typically the female members of the household who ran and managed the stalls while male family members stayed in the village to work in nearby fields.

"We are peasants. It is our life," Núria Manadé Ginestà explained.[69] She re-called how four generations of her family had owned and worked a small holding in the nearby village of Sant Joan Despí and how in all four generations the women had traveled daily into Barcelona to sell produce at one of the city's markets. Her story began with her husband's grandmother, who had sold from a stall at the elegant and spacious El Born. When retail sales were abolished at El Born in 1921, the city granted her a new peasant-stall license to sell from the older Santa Caterina market hall that also served the neighborhood. Later, the peasant-stall license passed to Manadé's mother-in-law as part of a dowry package. When Núria married and joined her husband's household, she took over the stall from her mother-in-law, even though she soon gave birth to a child. The arrangement was based upon the presumption that older female family members were best suited for management of the household and for child care and that the younger women in the family, although they might be in the reproductive phase of their lifecycles, should take responsibility for the retail work that involved daily travel to the city.

The basic outlines of this economic strategy proved a viable option for Núria Manadé's family through the four generations that spanned the twentieth century. It even proved capable of absorbing newcomers of distinct backgrounds without much in the way of modification. Núria explained that even before her daughter's marriage, her son-in-law to-be had joined the household in order to "learn how to be a peasant." As a carpenter who had immigrated from the south of Spain to Catalonia, his entrance into the family involved a period of training in agricultural production. By the early 1990s, Núria's daughter had long since taken over the Santa Caterina peasant stall, and she only traveled to the city to help out on the busiest of market days.

In the case of Núria Manadé's family history, we can also see how stall-permit records can be deceiving. The gendered division of labor within this family was a fairly rigid one, with men coming to market to sell only in the rare instances when illnesses prevented the women from doing so. Though it was nearly always the female members of the household who worked the stall, the permit had been passed from Núria's husband's grandmother to her mother-in-law, to her father-in-law, and then her husband. These sorts of cases suggest that many of the stalls held in the names of men, particularly in the rural-producer license category, were more likely to have been actually worked by female members of the family.

## Marriage in the Market

In keeping with the plot lines of various Catalan theatrical productions of the period, female vendors enjoyed advantages within their neighborhood marriage markets. Skills related to food handling and display, the possession of and access to stall permits, and family and kinship ties with other vendors all constituted a certain commercial capital that added to the appeal for men of choosing a wife from among the ranks of market women. Their popular allure was also underpinned by municipal market pageantry and the election of Market Queens.

In the fact that vendors frequently chose marriage partners from within the markets where they worked, we can see that matrimony was also a strategy that vendors used to consolidate stall business operations. When Rafel Martí Fiol emigrated from Mallorca to take over his deceased brother's cheese, ham, and sausage stall in 1933, he was struck by the playfulness of the youth working at Santa Caterina.[70] Like so many others entering into market-based trade in food, Rafel quickly found a wife from among the cohort of young women working within the same structure. Mercè Miró García and Rafel Martí met in Santa Caterina Market, married, worked a stall together their whole lives, and then passed the business on to their son. Their story is typical of many vendors from across the city.

For Mercè Miró and Rafel Martí, affective sentiments and economic pragmatism underpinned one another. Mercè, born in the city in 1911, stopped attending school at a young age. "I did not want to study," she asserted, "I wanted to work."[71] Despite her stepmother's reservations, Mercè secured a position for herself as a butcher's apprentice in a Santa Caterina stall operated by an elderly woman. For the first few years, Mercè learned to cut meat and keep the stall clean and tidy, but she was not allowed to serve customers. Working from seven a.m. to two p.m. daily and dressed in a crisp white apron, she watched and listened to her mistress at work. During these crucial years, Mercè mastered the social relations that were crucial to retail success in the city's market halls. "It takes a certain personality to sell," she explained. *"Take this home with you, it's delicious,"* she said, demonstrating the tone of voice she would have used with a customer.

When Mercè Miró was twenty-two years old, her husband-to-be took over what had been his late brother's stall in Santa Caterina Market. Rafel Martí, still grief-stricken and new to both the big city and to market work, sought solace in the companionship of Mercè, who though still young was by then something of a seasoned market veteran. After a brief courtship, they married. Mercè explained the circumstances of their union in the following words: "When you are bound to fall in love, you fall in love . . . and he, since he knew that I worked with meat, liked me, because he knew I could help him in his stall." The enduring affection between the couple was evident more that fifty years later as they recounted their life stories. But clearly the marriage was also a sound one from an economic perspective. Unfamiliar with the ins and outs of market sales, Rafel gained a partner who knew the ropes. In marrying Rafel, Mercè was able to move to a stall from which she could earn profits rather than just wages and from which she could expect greater security for the future.

Throughout her married life, Mercè Miró worked alongside her husband. During her two pregnancies she continued to sell until just a few days before giving birth. With each child she returned to work after ten days of lying-in. Because Mercè and Rafel lived in a flat very near the market and had help from family, she was able to balance work in the stall with the demands of child-rearing. Her mother-in-law and an aunt joined the household shortly before the birth of their first son, and Mercè described how they would bring him down to the stall for feedings. Such practices confirm again the convenience of living near markets for females of child-bearing age. Residential clustering as near to the points of sale as could be arranged represented a domestic advantage as well as a commercial and social one. The iconic story of Mercè and Rafel's marriage and commercial success at Santa Caterina Market is one that replicated itself all across the city. It was difficult in the last decade of the twentieth century to find a market in Barcelona where vendors were not eager to offer similar accounts.

Personal testimonies provide evidence of common market-vendor strategies otherwise not documented in municipal registries and administrative records. While interviewing vendors both formally and informally, I heard hundreds of stories of endogamous marriage that clearly illustrate a broad pattern within the subculture of the markets. Marriage in the markets took various forms. There were many clerks, both male and female, who married licensed market vendors, their children, or heirs. This represented one of the most common ways through which married couples came to operate stalls as a team. There was also much marriage between fixed-stall permit holders or their children, whether working in the same specialization or not. Typically, when vendors' children wed, the new couple might join either the wife's or the husband's family business. Determining where the new couple would work in the market appears to have been based on which stall operation most needed, or could best accommodate, the extra pairs of hands. The most fortuitous matches involved marriage between the children of competing stalls in a given specialization that were located adjacent to one another. Such unions facilitated stall business expansion and enabled vendors to purchase larger quantities of stock from wholesalers at a better price. Another common form of endogomous marriage involved female vendors wedding men who worked in provisioning-related capacities outside the city's retail market halls, such as the slaughterhouse, or in various wholesaling and contracting businesses.

### Contention and Conflict in the Marketplaces

The extensive evidence of multigenerational bonds that linked food-retailers to one another and to their clients in early-twentieth-century Barcelona must not obscure recognition that conflict in the markets of Barcelona was an ongoing concern. At various times, markets and shops were sites of protest, political mobilization, violence, and even looting. Certainly the commercial associations that male food retailers built most reflected the larger sense in which markets and shops constituted spaces where private interests negotiated the terms of the political economy with the multiply-layered institutional structures of the state. The fact that female vendors frequently filed formal grievances with municipal market authorities is amply documented in the archival record as well. Women tended to directly engage themselves with the state in an effort to shape the implementation of policy on a case-by-case basis, though they sometimes presented petitions signed by other vendors in support of their immediate concern.

## VENDOR RESISTANCE

Vendors in general—both male and female—exhibited broad-based resistance to certain rules and regulations governing market trade. The administrative records of Sant Antoni Market offer ample documentation. Treasury and provisioning bureaucrats generated a constant flow of written orders insisting that the market director show greater diligence in enforcing the rules. For example, the illegal subletting of stalls was widespread.[72] One of the most common forms of paperwork passing through the director's office was related to verifying market women's illnesses that justified their hiring substitutes. Municipal physicians were sent out to visit the women in their homes and to identify malingerers who used illness as an excuse to get around the rules that made them personally responsible for what took place in their stalls. The extant documents detailing Sant Antoni's daily municipal administration also show that vendors throughout the early twentieth century resisted regulations that forbade packaging food in newspaper or reddening the meat with preservatives.[73] Market directors struggled to force vendors to adhere to fixed markups over wholesale prices and to treat all customers alike rather than show preference in the price and quality of the wares that they offered to favored clients. In sum, the whole provisioning bureaucracy was kept busy trying to keep the market vendors in line. The imposition of fines by inspectors and the closing of stalls were ongoing but never, it appears, able to catch up with the broad-based resistance to some of the details of the regulatory codes. Market vendors clearly adhered to their own set of informal rules while also being shaped by the larger process of rationalization and modernization.

## CONSUMER RESISTANCE

As Pamela Beth Radcliff reminds us with respect to Spain in general at this time, "working-class women's sphere of political activity . . . emerged out of the daily networks of female sociability, which were the marketplace and the neighborhood."[74] Radcliff, Kaplan, and others have shown that female consumer protest against price hikes and shortages of food and fuel emerged as a facet of mass politics by the last decade of the nineteenth century. With deep historical antecedents in terms of food-inspired protest, Barcelona experienced a series of such episodes in the early twentieth century. Typically, these protests were spontaneous, small in scale, localized, and directed at specific sites of perceived offense. When protests involved a *clam*—that is, a vociferous public demand by a single consumer or group of women—the vast majority were quickly resolved through the intervention of male municipal authorities. There was a rash of such incidents in 1895 and 1905 when bad harvests drove up food prices.[75] With the subsistence crisis associated with World War I inflation, however, female consumer protests became more common, and in 1918 a widespread uprising against the high cost of living broke out in the city.[76]

The crisis began in the first week of January in response to the rising cost of cooking and heating coal sold from the city's *carboneria* shops. In full recognition that coal was vital to the ability of urban populations to prepare food and warm their homes in the cold of winter, the new national Provisioning Ministry ordered its provincial Subsistence Committees to cap prices. But because wholesale costs were above that set amount, some *carboneria* shop owners refused to adhere to the policy; by January 10 authorities were sanctioning them in Barcelona for price abuse.[77] This set off working-class women's ire and rapidly drove mobilization forward. Women began attacking scattered *carboneria* shops for overcharging, and they forced their way into factories to recruit female workers to join a strike against the rising cost of living. Gathering at the civil governor's building on the afternoon of the 10th, a delegation of women pleaded their case, explaining that scarce resources and ever-increasing costs were adding to the challenge of keeping their families fed. "Desperation grows," they asserted, "because hunger has no hope."[78] The civil governor expressed his sympathies, promised to do what was possible to control prices, and gave candy to the children whom the protesting women had in tow.[79] In the days and weeks that followed, the uprising intensified and the strike widened to include more than 24,000 women and as many as 2,300 men.

The 1918 women's consumer protest involved various tactics. Women raided factories all across the city, and by January 21 they had shut down some 274 of them.[80] They also forced their way into a range of sites where women worked or gathered to sweep up support for their cause; they especially targeted cabarets and department stores.[81] A series of demonstrations and meetings were held in which, shockingly, women denied the men among them the right to address the assembled. As Lester Golden put it, they "took command."[82] Crowds of women returned to the civil governor's building on multiple occasions to demonstrate and demand redress of their grievances, but when authorities ultimately tired of their tenacity, they were greeted with force of arms rather than sweets. Factions emerged among the protestors over various issues, including the use of violence against those who sold fuel and food. The leaders of the movement advocated simply forcing closure, while other elements broke windows, confronted retailers, and looted.[83]

The multiple aims of the uprising all had to do with the economic survival of the working poor. From the problem with cooking-coal prices, the protest extended to commodities such as oil and other foodstuffs, but especially salt cod. Rent control also became a central demand of the protests. Price controls were extended to a range of food categories, including salt cod. But the conflict continued because, as the *carboneries* had done earlier, salt cod shop owners and stall-keepers either refused to sell below wholesale costs or closed their establishments in a work stoppage of their own.[84] Attacks on shops broadened as the uprising unfolded. The tumult ultimately lasted for just over two weeks, spread to nearby towns such as Sabadell, and was only put down when a state of siege was declared on the whole Province of Barcelona on January 25. Reverberating across Spain to other cities such as Alicante and Málaga, the uprising caused serious alarm, especially because it was led and dominated by women.

Significantly, markets did not constitute the main targets of consumer ire. In fact, the protesting women initially used the markets like department stores and cabarets, as points from which to advance female mobilization. The potential of the city's markets to serve as rallying points was clearly manifest in the uprising. As Golden recounts, on January 11 one of the movement's leaders, Amalia Alegre, "posted a manifesto at a market calling upon women to demonstrate peacefully in front of the Civil Governor's Palace and the town hall in protest. Held that same morning, four hundred women attended this first illegal demonstration, which 'formed by magic.'"[85] Golden also writes that domestic servants gathered at El Born on January 24 to "map out strategy," and since women converged there daily, "the police could hardly shut down such meeting places."[86] The 1918 consumer uprising thus demonstrates that Barcelona's market halls could function as places that fomented female solidarity not just among the population of vendors but among working-class consumers as well.

There were, though, a number of confrontations in the markets of the city. On January 15, when the protestors converged to recruit women from Sants, Hostafrancs, Sant Antoni, and La Concepció, those markets closed for the day. When the protestors went to La Boqueria to do likewise, vendors resisted and the protestors retreated. Returning later, the women discovered a cache of cooking-coal stored in the market, and their indignation reignited. Facing a mob of angry consumers hurling accusations about hoarding, La Boqueria's vendors found themselves having to comply with the protesters' demands and thus closed their stalls for the day.[87] There were also confrontations in the salt cod departments of five markets on January 22. After the forces of order had restored calm, the salt cod vendors closed their stalls and paid the civil governor a visit to seek a resolution. They were among numerous vendors and shopkeepers who turned to their associational representatives for intervention in the crisis.[88]

For the most part, the 1918 rioters focused upon suppliers, public authorities, and suspected hoarders, and demanded a redress of their grievances in a way that was disembodied from the specific and competing ideological movements of the formally organized male-dominated unions and political parties. In essence, an important subtext of the uprising was the criticism of male authorities for failing to fulfill their role as protectors.[89] As Joan Manent i Peses later recalled, "more than one policeman or civil guard was given a spanking and thrashing and sent home without his pants and with his alleged manhood exposed in the street."[90]

Most historical attention to consumer rioting in Spain has been focused on the World War I period. But there were certainly other moments when conflict erupted. Chris Ealham writes about how poor consumers came to the defense of unlicensed ambulatory vendors during the Second Republic, when authorities used force to attempt to clear them from the streets of the city.[91] Likewise, Michael Seidman treats the wave of female consumer protests that took place during the first years of the Civil War, when ongoing shortages and rising prices led to increasing numbers of disputes between food retailers and customers. There were, for example, female consumer protests against bread prices in late 1936 and early 1937, though none that compared to the January 1918 uprising. Seidman also argues that there was an element of female consumer protest in the internecine conflict that plagued the city in May 1937; on the 6th of that month, women attacked vans filled with oranges at the port, looting and seizing supplies.[92] He points to such incidents in order to show that heightened levels of female consciousness were just as apt to lead to subversive individualism as they were to organized collective movements.

Yet if we consider the four decades preceding the victory of General Franco's Nationalist forces in 1939, a period marked by much in the way of social unrest and political upheaval, it becomes clear that incidents of female consumer protest in Barcelona were much more the exception than the rule. Despite the visible and periodic episodes of contention, there was much more in the way of consensus underpinning market hall-based trade during these tumultuous years. To posit that early-twentieth-century female food retailers in Barcelona formed direct and ongoing alliances with consumers may appear to run counter to the studies on modern consumer protest in Spain.[93] In fact, no such contradiction is necessarily implied.

The predominant scholarly consensus on women's public protest in early-twentieth-century Barcelona builds on Temma Kaplan's model of "female consciousness."[94] Kaplan holds that the vast majority of women who engaged in demonstrations accepted established gender roles. When mobilizing, they demanded public recognition of their obligation to act as caretakers and defenders of their families' well-being. Kaplan writes that women, not just in Barcelona but also in Spain more generally, and in Italy, Russia, and Mexico, accepted hardships in times of scarcity and inflation as long as public authorities regulated supply. What they did not accept was "hoarding, speculating, and profiteering," which often sparked their anger.[95] The municipal market system in Barcelona was designed and managed to avoid such perceptions, and for the most part succeeded in doing so. The realization that women could mobilize around injustice underpinned the operation of the *repeso* office in each of the city's markets, where consumers could go and have the weights of whatever they had purchased verified on municipal scales. Likewise, regulations that prohibited vendors from occulting their stocks and showing preference for one buyer over another were designed to reinforce the belief that the markets were open to all consumers on an equal footing. Problems and disputes did occasionally arise, but overall they were infrequent. This is especially evident in sources that trace the day-to-day administration of Sant Antoni Market, which allow us to see that consensus nearly always trumped contention. The bonds that market vendors and female consumers formed over the long term, their shared neighborhood experiences, and their common concerns and interests as women seeking to defend the well-being of their households meant that market stalls were rarely looted and sacked in moments of crises. As Joan B. Culla notes, even in the Tragic Week of 1909, the markets operated smoothly and were not subject to attack.[96] Likewise, during the January 1918 uprising, the markets as a whole remained open for business on all but part of one day.

In addition to considering broader conditions and causes, the phenomenon of women's food-rioting in the early twentieth century must be placed within the specific context of the urban provisioning system in which it took place. Historians have thus far failed to consider how and why municipal markets, which were operated according to a public commitment to balancing both consumer and small retailer interests, were less appealing targets for protestors than shops or wholesalers. We also see how government edicts that set retail prices below wholesale costs placed vendors between a rock and a hard place, thus eliciting work stoppages as a form of resistance to provisioning policies. What we do not yet know is how food protests may have been connected to the emergence of consumer cooperatives as alternatives to public markets and private shops. Even those studies focusing on the Catalan cooperative movement do not treat the question of why workers in certain instances preferred or rejected public markets.[97]

## Coping with the Civil War–Era Food Crisis

The outbreak of hostilities in July 1936 marked the beginning of a prolonged and painful food crisis that affected Barcelona's markets and all of Spain. The Spanish Civil War was a conflict that unfolded in slow motion. Its origins can be traced to nineteenth-century political divisions and the seemingly intractable challenges of modernization. The breakdown of the Restoration system and the growing ideological polarization of the first decades of the twentieth century set the stage for the conflict. So, too, did the instability that characterized the Republic after its declaration in 1931. *La Niña Bonita*, as the Republic was known, was first bruised and then battered. The events of October 1934, which led to the arrest of the Esquerra Republicana leadership in Catalonia and the uprising of Asturian miners, spurred a more decisive re-assertion of power from the right of the political spectrum. The Black Biennium Cortes rescinded the Agrarian Reform Law, engaged in harsh repression of left republicans and socialists alike, and drove trade unions underground.[98] In response, the left gradually reunited in what Nigel Townson has called "a flawed and inherently unstable" electoral coalition known as the Popular Front.[99] The inclusion of the Communist Party in the coalition served as one of several pretenses for broad-based conservative commitment to reject their ascent to power. Winning a narrow victory in the elections of 1936, the Popular Front moved quickly to exclude communists and socialists from government and thus lost control of the streets as workers mobilized. The Popular Front's monopoly over the use of force in the countryside also evaporated, and as Townson writes, "landless labourers in the south and west also took the law into their own hands, seizing and settling more land in a matter of months than in the previous five years."[100] On July 17 and 18, 1936, the military launched a failed coup d'etat against the government. The generals were only able to lay claim to about a third of Spain, and neither Madrid nor Barcelona fell to the insurgents. The orchestrators of the uprising, known as the Rebels or the Nationalists, were able to count on the support of most of the military, monarchists, Carlists, the Church, large landowners, the mass Catholic CEDA party, and the fascist Falange, which had formed in 1933. By October 1936, General Francisco Franco (1892-1975) emerged as their leader, and Spain found itself engulfed in a protracted internecine conflict. The Spanish Civil War was both brutal and quintessentially modern in a number of regards. Ultimately upwards of half a million people died on the battlefield, from execution, from disease, and as a consequence of the Nationalists' relentless program of aerial bombardment. Though twenty-seven countries entered into what was mainly a British-orchestrated Non-Intervention Agreement, key signatories—Nazi Germany and Fascist Italy—provided extensive support for the Nationalists. The Soviet Union supplied more limited aid to the Republic at a significantly higher cost. Civilians paid a tremendous price in the conflict for three main reasons. First, violence behind the lines took well over a hundred thousand lives in the Nationalist-held zone where an explicit program of right-wing regenerist "cleansing" targeted workers, intellectuals, artists, trade unionists, and progressives of all stripes for execution and often burial in mass graves. There was brutal violence behind the lines in Republican-held territory as well, including the murder of some six thousand clerics, which understandably sparked international Catholic outrage. Still, the death toll from extralegal violence in Republican territory was much smaller and the executions were largely beyond the control of military and civilian authorities. Second, civilians in Republican-controlled areas suffered enormous physical and psychological costs because the Nationalists subjected them to sustained aerial bombardment, the first such campaigns in the history of warfare. While the Condor Legion's April 26, 1937, bombing and machine-gunning of fleeing civilians in the Basque town of Guernica stands as the most emblematic aerial assault of the war, in fact innumerable Spanish towns and cities were targeted, resulting in ten thousand or more deaths. Third, there was the even more widespread problem of endemic hunger, malnutrition, and related illnesses. The war interrupted Spain's larger food system, posing a range problems that varied by region and circumstance.

The most insightful analysis of food policy during this period is Michael Seidman's *Republic of Egos: A Social History of the Spanish Civil War*. Seidman focuses on the relative successes and failures of the Republican and Nationalist governments in providing basic biological necessities such as food, clothing, and medical care. Though acknowledging the better-known causes of the Republican defeat, he convincingly argues that the Nationalists' superior ability to provision military and civilian populations, its much greater respect for private property, and its success in maintaining monetary stability ultimately proved decisive to the outcome. Seidman concludes that the Republicans were incapable of waging an industrial war against an insurgency with a much stronger and more stable agrarian base.[101]

The attention that Seidman pays to food production and distribution is especially illuminating. From early on in the war, the Nationalists enjoyed an advantage in controlling the bulk of wheat-producing and cattle-grazing areas. The Republicans' initial control over the main olive oil, wine, and citrus-growing regions proved less advantageous in the challenge to keep soldiers and cities fed, despite the fact that these commodities served as vital exports.[102] While the Nationalists moved away from food expropriation more quickly and exercised greater control over soldiers' plundering of the countryside, the Republicans imposed price controls that favored urban consumers but had the effect of discouraging production and encouraging hoarding and black marketeering. Seidman emphasizes the diverging interests of rural versus urban populations on the Republican side and contrasts these with the more effective agrarian and provisioning policies of the Nationalists. He holds that material privations, and especially hunger, were at the center of the Republic's defeat. By the end of the war, cynicism had eclipsed ideology on the Republican side and the social order had devolved into a simple division between those who had access to food and those who did not.

Much of Seidman's larger argument is supported by the evidence documenting food-market operation in Barcelona during the war. Although the military uprising was put down fairly easily in Barcelona, both the municipal government and the Generalitat lost control of public administration as a result. Anarchosyndicalists, communists, and socialist groups seized various degrees of power, and the Esquerra Republicana had to negotiate with them in an attempt to restore public order. The first phase of this process lasted until May 1937, when the civil war within the civil war that broke out on the streets of the city was resolved by excluding the anarchosyndicalist CNT-FAI and the anti-Stalinist POUM from power. Thereafter, and until the end of the war, Barcelona was governed by the Esquerra Republicana with the Socialists and the Communists. This power struggle played itself out in the city's markets.

During the first few months of the war, municipal administrators lost power at the highest level of the provisioning system. By October 1936, the anarchosyndicalist Sindicato de Transportes, which answered directly to a new revolutionary Comité de Abastos, had successfully collectivized the El Born wholesale market. According to their propaganda, they had done so with the assistance of the vendors, whom the revolutionaries referred to as "former owners."[103] The first objective of the collectivizers was to lower prices "so that consumers would immediately note the intervention of working-class forces in the market."[104] The revolutionary rhetoric was new, but the administrative strategies used to control prices and the justification for authority to rule were as old as the market system itself. The transport workers' stated goal of controlling food markets in defense of consumers' interests was a common feature of regimes of varied ideological character. The tactics they chose to lower prices were not innovative; the new anarchosyndicalist authority proposed to collect daily lists of prices, set profit margins for each type of food sold, and publicize information on prices in the press. The revolutionary authorities did not succeed through this system in preventing shortages and dramatic rises in prices, and their power waned in the following months as the Esquerra Republicana municipal administration gradually reasserted control over wholesale trade. Retail markets across the city, however, remained under the almost-exclusive jurisdiction of municipal and Generalitat rule throughout the war. The first phases of the rationing system were implemented in October, the operating hours of markets were shortened, and as the scarcity of provisions intensified, directors instructed vendors to give preference to customers who came with food "prescriptions" for individuals in their households who were certified by a physician to be sick and malnourished.[105]

In November 1937, consumer unease at Sant Antoni Market intensified, and the market director feared that tension centered in and around the fish stalls "will spread with consequences which no-one knows."[106] Two weeks after the director reported his concern to the provisioning authorities, a group of women consumers appealed to him to lower fish prices because "the poor do not have the economic means" to acquire enough food.[107] The angry female consumers then compelled the director to close down the market. With only two guards at his disposal, he had no choice but to comply. The women who took this drastic step believed that if the market did not operate in defense of consumer interests, then it should not operate at all. The next day, additional guards were assigned to the market and the consumer resistance was put down.[108] What happened at Sant Antoni in November 1937 reflected a loss of confidence on the part of female consumers in the ability of the director to guarantee that food-retailing would be operated on the basis of fairness.

The focus on rupture that is at the center of the literature addressing food consumption in Barcelona during the war is useful, if somewhat misleading. Our understanding of the crisis that the war represented should not obscure the broader recognition that in some respects the system of food distribution functioned on the basis of consensus between municipal authority, retailers, and consumers. The war did not threaten public control over trade in food, but rather had the effect of further reinforcing political commitment to balance consumer and retailer interests as part of the larger struggle to persist in fighting the Nationalists. At a time when revolutionary concepts were tested in many public ambits, the basic outlines of the retail-provisioning system, featuring municipal control over markets and regulation of prices, continued. The fact that hundreds of thousands of transactions between buyers and sellers of food took place every day in market halls and shops all across the city, even during the war, is proof that retailers and consumers got along with one another far more often than not. There was widespread hunger and endemic malnutrition, but not as high a death toll from starvation in the city as one might imagine. At the peak of the alimentary crisis in 1938, 286 people died from hunger, a tragic figure indeed, but not a large percentage of the population in a city that at the war's outset included over a million people.[109] Severe shortages of food and contention between consumers and food retailers were an ongoing problem, but it was greatly outweighed by consensus and by a collective understanding that individuals had to devise collaborative new strategies in order to survive. Several markets, including Santa Caterina and La Barceloneta, were damaged in the intense bombing campaigns to which the city was subjected; consumers and vendors alike fled the city for safety, shops closed down, but in skeletal form the pre-existing system persisted.

In the face of food shortages and in retreat from aerial bombing, outmigration to the urban hinterland was significant. But many people remained behind, and in fact the more than 100,000 refugees pouring into the city balanced those who fled to the countryside, which meant that Barcelona's population actually grew over the course of the war.[110] Those who remained behind drew more heavily than ever on the interpersonal relationships of trust that they had established before the war broke out. Everyone had to eat, and women turned first to the markets and shops and to the rationing system in order to acquire food for their families.

In the face of all this, consumers in Barcelona lined up outside markets and shops early in the morning, in desperate hopes of finding food to buy. L'Abaceria Central poulterer Isabel Colera Magrans remembers how during the war the crowds pushed into the market when it opened for the day. She recalls that women sometimes even lost their shoes in the scuffle.[111] Vendors as well as shopkeepers likewise formed queues outside the city's wholesale markets and competed with one another to acquire enough stock to keep their retail establishments in business. Paquita Nogueroles, who was seventeen when the war began, remembers struggling to buy stock to keep her family's La Llibertat Market stalls open.[112] She and five or six other young women would set out for the long trek on foot to El Born's wholesale market at one a.m., where they would stand in line to wait for the pre-dawn opening. Because they were young and attractive, they were able to develop bonds with wholesalers and often have their goods delivered back to the market by cart. Sometimes they would re-sell a portion of their stocks to grocers on the way back to Gràcia. They also bartered vegetables for other goods among their closest neighbors, though not as much with other vendors. They traded ration tickets as currency, and always managed to get fish, bread, potatoes, and a range of other foods to eat.

At Sant Antoni Market, some stalls converted to the distribution of basic rations during the war. In early 1938, there were more than 3,000 children registered to receive cans of condensed milk at the market. At first, shortages prevented more than half of these children from receiving their allotments. By the war's end, things had improved a bit, and 3,983 children were receiving three cans of condensed milk each per week. Other stall conversions were common as well, as vendors sold whatever they could get their hands on irrespective of whether the goods were specified in their permits. Public efforts to distribute provisions aside, acquiring the food necessary to survive during the war often came down to whom one knew, and more important, whom one trusted. Extralegal trade in food was considered a serious crime during the conflict. Policing food distribution was a major concern. Hoarding food in warehouses was viewed as an act of treachery, all the more so because it was so common.

The term that Catalans most often use for black marketeering is l'estraperlo. It emerged from an infamous roulette-wheel swindle that two Germans brought to Spain during the Republic and that resulted in a public scandal exposing both regional and national political graft and corruption.[113] From that point on, trade outside licensed firms was associated with the term estraperlo; everyone who lived through the war in Barcelona had some acquaintance with it, though many refused to engage in it on principle or feared the harsh punishments that could come from participation. My grandmother, Paquita Ferré Mestres, participated in it in her own way. After my family fled to the village of Vilaplana from their apartment and their nearby wrought-iron workshop on Bailèn Street in the Eixample in 1937, my grandmother continued to make weekly treks back to the city and the neighborhood to stand in line for food, using ration tickets that were no longer legal. Only urban residents were eligible for the rationing tickets issued by the city.

She got around this stipulation by pretending that the family continued to reside there as they had before the war. Having acquired some food, she then undertook the risky trip back to the village by train, skirting guards and aerial bombardment on numerous occasions.

Market vendors spoke openly and extensively about the extralegal trade they engaged in during the war in order to survive. But more often than using the pejorative term *estraperlo*, they referred to the *intercanvi*, or interchange of goods, on the basis of barter. Indeed, money all but disappeared in Barcelona in the last year of the war. Both Republican and Generalitat currencies became virtually useless because of their devaluation. Beyond what was distributed through the rationing system, much of the city's food supply was exchanged on the basis of one or another form of black-market trade. Apart from political, militia, and military elites and those who engaged in the highest levels of graft and profiteering, it was those who had long worked in food retailing who were best positioned to survive.

Antonia Peña Martín explained how her experience working in the city's food markets, even as a wage-earning clerk, represented a form of security once the war broke out.[114] By the time the uprising was launched in July 1936, Antonia had already spent a decade working for poulterers at Santa Caterina and La Boqueria markets. She had learned a range of skills related to her trade and had earned the respect of both her employers and her customers. When the war began, she took a position as a domestic servant for a jeweler, joining his wife and their two children as they fled to a country cottage in the Collserola foothills at the edge of the city. From there, Antonia proved extremely valuable to the family for whom she worked. She used her skills in the food-retailing sector to buy, gather, sell, and trade food in a complicated set of arrangements requiring her to move from the rural hinterland to the urban core and back again on a regular basis. As a result, she was able to regularly acquire white bread on the black market so that the jeweler's children could eat toast for breakfast throughout the war. They survived quite well, she insists, through a range of strategies. Sometimes she bought turnips from women in Sant Cugat and sold them on the streets outside La Boqueria Market. Other times, she gathered wild mushrooms and sold them to the Hotel Peninsular. Bit by bit, exchange by exchange, Antonia helped the family for whom she worked survive the Civil War food crisis.

Antonia Peña's story parallels that told by Joan Reventós, who was an eleven-year-old boy living in Sarrià when the war broke out. Joan was part of an extended influential Catalan family that depended on a servant, Raimunda Torrents, for their supply of food. Joan recalled how in his household, "domestic provisioning . . .

became an obsessive subject that filled the better part of the conversations."[115] Torrents had served the Reventós family so loyally for forty years that she retired on a family-provided pension and was living in a small apartment of her own on Lepanto Street when the war erupted in the summer of 1936. The crisis brought Raimunda back to the Reventós household, where she took over managing the intricacies involved in the family's acquisition of food. Joan recalls that "with ingenuity and skill, and thanks to her relations of many years with the personnel of La Boqueria, she constructed a direct provisioning network, [that was] efficient and continuous. She never said how she had acquired the things, but she just as often arrived with a chicken or a rabbit as she did with a bag of legumes or a jar of lard. She even was able to connect, albeit for a short while, with some that were clandestinely making white bread."[116]

Black marketing was widespread, and food retailers and their preferred customers were in a strong position to engage in it. Examples abound of men, women, and children exchanging goods illegally, trading in ration tickets, and smuggling food into the city. Some vendors did not have the stomach for it and had to rely on other family members to carry out the task. Depending on the circumstances, some retailers preferred to trade furtively in apartment buildings, visiting trusted neighbors, friends, clients, and fellow vendors and shopkeepers in their apartments. Others traded illegally more often inside the market halls. Mercè Miró was twenty-five when the war broke out, and she worked in her husband's stall at Santa Caterina throughout the conflict.[117] The streets became dangerous, but "those that were in the *plaça* helped one another," she recalled. Their system operated on the basis of trust and subterfuge designed to avoid the watchful eyes of the market director, the inspectors, and other authorities. The vendors involved would place the goods they wanted to trade in a bundle known as a *farcell*, which was nothing more than the traditional cotton scarf in which peasants carried any number of commodities when they traveled. Mercè and her fellow vendors would surreptitiously pass the *farcell* from stall to stall, adding and withdrawing the foods from it that they had previously agreed, by hushed word of mouth, to trade. That vendors developed a broad range of tactics for black marketing and bartering foods should not surprise.

What is more interesting is that so many market vendors claimed that they did not experience real hunger until after the war. This was the case with Maria Cararach, whose father had influence at the slaughterhouse and was able to continue acquiring meat, which they traded for bread. She said that they stayed in the city throughout the war and never went hungry.[118] Carme Giner told a similar story.

Her father worked in a food warehouse that gave the family access to provisions and prevented them from experiencing hunger until after the war's end.[119] Likewise, Antoni Jover Barceló explained how market vendors exchanged food among themselves in a provisioning economy that involved more black market than legal trade during the war.[120]

These accounts stand in stark contrast to the stories of the Spanish Civil War that I heard growing up in the United States. It seemed as if we talked about wartime hunger at every meal when I was a child. When my mother's family relocated to the village of Vilaplana, they struggled terribly to survive, despite my grandmother's valiant endeavors to trek back to Barcelona weekly so that she too could draw on the social channels that neighborhood women used to acquire provisions. There was food in and around Vilaplana, but my grandmother had nothing to trade for it. Beyond what she brought back from dangerous excursions to the city, the best she could do was to acquire squash, which they boiled with a little flour, wild herbs that they gathered in the countryside (*mastagueres* and *llasconeres*), worm-infested dried fava beans, and six hazel nuts a day for dessert. My mother described the situation as follows:

> Those who have not suffered serious hunger cannot imagine how annoying it is. You almost can't do anything except think about food. You go to bed and dream about food and upon waking your stomach hurts and you wish you were still asleep because you were dreaming of a good rib or a chicken thigh . . . The food that mama gave us was never enough to allow us to even begin to salivate. How she must have suffered in seeing us so hungry!![121]

One is left with the impression that they would have been better off had they stayed in the city and withstood the terror of the bombings. In fact, my mother's sister-in-law, Maria Ramón, did just that. Her family stayed in their apartment on València Street near La Concepció Market. My Tieta Maria, whose mother was a *portera* and thus deeply embedded in the neighborhood network, often told me that she had no memories of hunger at all during the war. The real hardships, she explained, came later.

There is no question that overall Barcelona suffered food shortages during the years of the Spanish Civil War, that food retailing involved conflict, and that hoarding, corruption, and barter were widespread. Yet the caloric deprivation that so many families suffered would have been much worse if the black market trade had not operated so extensively and pervasively. Market vendors in particular were well-positioned to carry out transactions extralegally, to barter foods, and to piece together an adequate and varied diet. Their willingness to do so certainly testifies to the power of what Seidman calls "subversive individualism" as a strategy for survival in a time of crisis. Such activities also reflect longstanding habits of defying and eluding public control over the food trade. But in particular, the success of market vendors in surviving the war through extralegal commerce stands as powerful evidence of the endurance of social networks binding those who sold food together as a group, and individually with the clients with whom they shared bonds of loyalty and trust. The Spanish Civil War disrupted the municipal provisioning system in a number of significant ways, but in a great many instances it reinforced the ties that bound men and women together in informal neighborhood-based social networks.

The political economy of food retailing in the early twentieth century was anything but laissez-faire. Over the course of the three decades preceding the victory of the Nationalists in 1939, the state, at the municipal, provincial, and national levels, imposed regulations on food retailing that were designed to protect consumers and to limit unbridled competition among retailers selling like goods. But such policies alone cannot explain the triumph of consensus over contention in the food-retailing sector. The personal relationships of mutual dependency that linked female food retailers with female consumers on the neighborhood level also did much to mitigate and ameliorate social tensions. Residence patterns that involved market vendors and shopkeepers frequently living in the same apartment buildings as their customers, or at least in the immediate environs of their enterprises, reinforced the social ties linking retailers to consumers on the neighborhood level. If we consider the history of provisioning in Barcelona in terms of a broader sweep of time, we can see that despite notable episodes of violence during infamous moments of social and political rupture, women's informal networks at the very base of food retailing generated significant levels of consensus between the purveyors and the consumers of food. This observation applies even to the tumultuous years of the Civil War, when food supplies were interrupted and the monetary system in the city collapsed into barter and black-market exchange.

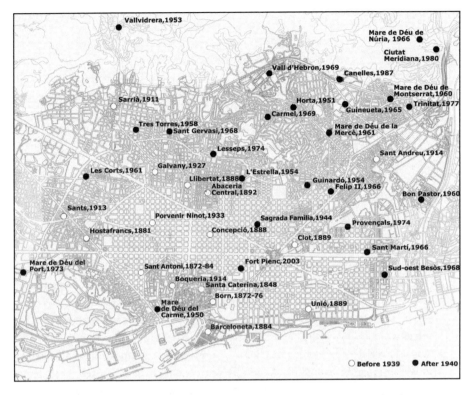

Barcelona's market halls in the early twenty-first century. (Note: El Born has been converted into a Centre Cultural and museum, and the date given for La Boqueria refers to the inauguration of its current metal roof.) *Map by Nadia Fava, courtesy of Nadia Fava, Manel Guàrdia, and José Luis Oyón.*

CHAPTER 7

# And Time Goes On
## Market Vendor Life and Work under Franco

As the Spanish Civil War entered its final months in the winter of 1939, Barcelona lay prostrate and wounded. Intensifying bombardment and the advance of the Nationalist lines drove a torrent of refugees toward the French border into exile. With significant portions of the city in ruins, the calorically deprived and exhausted population that stayed behind offered almost no resistance as Nationalist troops entered the city on January 26, 1939. Though trepidatious of what defeat would imply at the hands of their new masters, few residents expected that more than a decade would pass before food supplies and per-capita alimentary consumption levels would reach their prewar benchmarks. Ultimately, both demographic pressure and major shifts in policy from the early 1950s onward served as motors for significant expansion in the commercial infrastructure for food retailing through public markets and private shops. Yet while the Franco-era municipal governments in Barcelona showed much in the way of initial commitment to the food-retailing model prevailing in the city since the mid-nineteenth century, they eventually changed course and pursued some different strategies. Furiously building new market halls and authorizing new food shops in emerging working-class and immigrant neighborhoods, the city moved to increase food supplies in the late 1950s by sanctioning the opening of both supermarkets and privately owned and operated small-scale indoor markets known as *galerías comerciales*. The addition of new types of food-retailing enterprises introduced a set of ironies and tensions into the political economy of provisioning in the city that were especially portentous in terms of their legacy.

### Coping with the Extended Twentieth-Century Food Crises

The 1940s were lean years in Barcelona, as in all of Spain. Market vendors who lived through the period describe the difficult struggles they faced in acquiring

stock to sell in their stalls. Semi Colominas Aluja, a Santa Caterina salt cod vendor who had begun market work in the 1920s for an uncle and then fought on
the Nationalist side during the war, described some of the strategies that retailers
were forced to pursue in the postwar period. Semi maintained that there was less
food available for sale after the war than during it. In response, some salt cod
vendors, he explained, organized enterprises in the Canary Islands to fish for an
inferior and "vulgar" species known as *pardo*, which was salted and then shipped
to Barcelona for sale in the markets. The "Moorish" laborers hired to fish for
*pardo*, Semi recalled, were paid one peseta a day and allowed to eat the fish heads
removed before the salting process.[1] Rosa Sanaluja Cot, daughter of l'Abaceria
Central Market butchers, recalled the circumstances she encountered when she
began at the age of seventeen, at war's end, to work in her parents' stall. Because
of meat shortages, there were times when they went for weeks without selling
from their stalls.[2] Food scarcity in the immediate postwar period constituted a
significant constraint to vendors' work and to consumers alike.

The first five years after the war were the bleakest in terms of food supply.
Bread, oil, beans, rice, sugar, salt cod, coffee, chocolate, potatoes, pasta, and
chickpeas were all distributed through rationing while the black market continued
to flourish.[3] Yet the rationing system alone could never provide for consumption
levels matching those of 1936. In 1944, rationing supplied Barcelona consumers
with only 4.4 percent of the beans, 16 percent of the salt cod, and 44.2 percent of
the potatoes that they had eaten at the war's outbreak. Bread was the largest commodity supplied through rationing, but here too the system fell far short in providing for the per-capita consumption levels of the prewar period, reaching only a
dismal 54.7 percent by 1950. A series of foods long central to the diets of Barcelona residents were never included in the postwar rationing system. Milk, eggs,
meat, fish, and fruit were sold at government-set margins over wholesale prices.
But dramatic inflation put these goods beyond the reach of most working-class
families—by 1950, milk had risen 563 percent over 1936 prices, eggs 675 percent,
veal 769 percent, pork 1,000 percent, fish 300 percent, and fruit 800 percent.[4]

Such dire circumstances brought changes in culinary habits. The traditional
two-course midday meal that began with escudella became a much thinner broth,
served as a single course accompanied perhaps by a bit of salt pork. Meat, when
available, was often frozen or canned. Salted herring became a major staple. As
Francesc Barceló Duran recalled of the postwar years at l'Abaceria Central Market, everything that is thrown away now as useless was sold then and considered
edible.[5] For its part, the government promoted single-course meals, the *plato*

*único,* and distributed inventive recipes for newly introduced foods such as sweet potatoes: steamed, grilled, sweetened, in sauce, and folded into eggless omelets.[6] Ingenious food substitutions such as almond-based cheese and corn-flour flans appeared to fill the gap left by the scarcity of more customary alimentary commodities.[7]

There was widespread hunger in the first decade after the war ended. Food budgets for individual families in Barcelona rose to represent nearly 70 percent of total income.[8] The results were catastrophic. Ailments deriving from vitamin deficiencies, lack of protein, and caloric insufficiency assumed epidemic proportions among the working classes. The lost productivity that this implied generated considerable discussion at the national, provincial, and municipal levels while leading some factory owners to supplement workers' incomes with extra supplies of inexpensive foodstuffs.[9] The legitimacy of the Franco regime hinged on its ability to shepherd economic recovery; its failure through the 1940s to manage the basic food supply testified eloquently to the shortcomings of the autarkic model upon which that recovery was premised.

One of the many ironies of twentieth-century Spanish history lies in the juxtaposition of Second Republic wartime agricultural policies with those of early Franco regime, both of which were dismal failures. During the war, the Republic sought to control spiraling food costs through the imposition of caps on wholesale prices. The policy acted as a disincentive for production, and/or as a rational pretext to hoard or trade on the black market. Food shortages were the result, as was the inability of the Republic to keep its troops properly fed. In the Nationalist zone, soldiers and civilian populations, both urban and rural, fared better in comparison. A free market in grain and advancing military control over the largest-scale olive oil and meat-producing regions of Spain forestalled the types of shortages and the breakdown in the legal economy for food faced by those on the other side of the conflict.[10] Yet upon victory, the Nationalists immediately changed course, inexplicably imitating failed Republican policies by setting wholesale price caps on a broad range of agricultural commodities, including wheat.[11] The result was nearly the same as under Republican authority—dampened production, hoarding, and reinvigoration of black-market trade in food.[12] Thus, as Seidman suggests, we should recognize that the agricultural policies of the early years of the Franco regime involved much continuity with those of the Second Republic and a profound departure from the successful strategies of the Nationalists between 1936 and 1939.

## Rationing and the Black Market

At war's end, there was widespread expectation that at the very least, material conditions would improve for beleaguered civilian populations and that food supplies would quickly increase. Such was not the case. Though the Franco dictatorship's rationing system, put into place in May 1939, set forth minimum levels of per-capita consumption of bread, salt cod, and legumes, the state was never able to arrange for more than one-third to one-half of those levels.[13] In an effort to make up for such dramatic shortfalls, the regime charged its Auxilio Social with the task of operating soup kitchens to distribute meals to the most destitute. In the province of Barcelona during 1939, the Auxilio Social provided a monthly average of 1.5 million meals; seven years later, the monthly average for the province was still 700,000.[14] Widespread hunger persisted, and consumers had to look beyond the state, the public markets, and the private shops in order to acquire enough food for the survival of their families.

Along with the fundamental outlines of agricultural policy, the ongoing vibrancy of black-market trade represented a second continuity between the war and the postwar period. The persistence of hoarding and of black-marketeering was a consequence of rationing, shortages, and official price-setting at the wholesale and retail levels.[15] We see this most clearly with respect to bread. Carme Molinero and Pere Ysàs offer an eloquent explanation of the link between agricultural policy and urban black marketing in the early years of the Franco dictatorship. Wheat farmers, required by law to sell their flour to local state-directed syndicates, could count on the collaboration of officials who, for a price, would overlook the fact that weights fell short of the legally set levels. These farmers then clandestinely sold what they had held back from the syndicates to urban bakers, who in turn produced bread that could be distributed on the black market at elevated prices. Such opportunities to circumvent state controls led to widespread participation by bakers in some forms of black-market trade, which took place furtively alongside their legal activities within the rationing system. The availability of flour on the black market also led to the establishment of a considerable number of bakeries that operated on a completely clandestine basis.[16] What remains clear is that the ability of consumers to acquire bread beyond the dismal quantities allowed by the rationing tickets was wholly dependent upon informal social networks of trust between family, friends, neighbors, and acquaintances.

Black marketing in the 1940s was widespread. Based mainly on food, *l'estraperlo* extended to such commodities as cotton, wool, gasoline, coal, and minerals, involving some 10 percent of the gross domestic product of Spain between 1939 and 1954.[17] The creation in September 1940 of the Fiscalía de Tasas to police widespread trade in food through extralegal channels did little to forestall the accumulation of great fortunes on the part of numerous businessmen, and even mayors and city councilmen from Cornellà de Llobregat, Olesa de Montserrat, Santa Coloma de Gramanet, and elsewhere.[18] The persistence of the practice serves as evidence of broad-based official corruption in the provisioning bureaucracy at municipal, provincial, and national levels. Notorious cases notwithstanding, the efforts of the state were devoted almost entirely to punishing small-scale black marketeers. In Borja de Riquer's and Joan Culla's estimation, the truth was "that only the minor traffickers were detained and sanctioned while the large and most widespread complicitors that surrounded them remained always within absolute impunity."[19] Major efforts, for example, were directed at detaining individuals who bought directly from rural producers and then smuggled small quantities of food into the city. Evading the Guardia Civil's checkpoints became a crucial concern for a great many ordinary people.

There is no question that among consumers, market vendors, and small shopkeepers, the *estraperlo* trade was crucial to survival. Families resorted to it as a strategy to make up some portion of the caloric deficiencies they faced. Vendors and shopkeepers traded food through extralegal channels in order to compensate for profits lost as a consequence of shortages, price controls, and rationing. Joaquim Esteba Esteve, a l'Abaceria Central fruit and vegetable vendor, asserted that although there was much scarcity after the war, retailers who were quick-witted could do well. The black market saved a lot of people, he said. Because not much was coming into El Born, vendors had to look elsewhere for supplies and sometimes sell things door-to-door without being noticed by authorities. Joaquim's father was too afraid to engage in the practice, so he carried out such activities on behalf of his family's business on a secret basis and was able as a consequence to bring extra money home.[20] Black marketing after the war, as had been the case during the conflict, intensified social relations between food retailers and consumers. Based upon clandestinity and dependent upon familiarity and trust, vendors extended the scope of their commercial activities from the legally sanctioned spaces in market halls to the apartment houses of their neighbors and their clientele. Though inflated prices were part and parcel of the practice, food vendors tended to describe their black-market activities as rational, necessary, and even beneficial to the community, given the circumstances. While black marketing certainly reflected the endurance of subversive individualism, vendors held that they were only acting to facilitate the distribution of food in a period of disruption and shortage. Such interpretations fly in the face of broader public views that linked black marketing with increasingly pejorative attitudes toward shopkeepers, traders, intermediaries, monopolies, wholesalers, and traffickers across Spain in the second half of the twentieth century.[21] Irrespective of more generalized public derision, black marketing was often a daring and desperate act carried out on a mass basis by individuals coping with the regime's untenable postwar food policies.

## Changes and Continuities in the Political Economy of Food Retailing

Structural problems in the city's provisioning system that caused shortages and encouraged black market trade notwithstanding, there were both changes and continuities in the political economy of food retailing in Barcelona during the first decades of Franco's rule. The Nationalists' military victory in 1939 was followed by attempts to erase Spain's Republican past through sweeping purges, tens of thousands of executions, and some 40,000 military tribunals by 1950.[22] After being captured by the Gestapo in France, Catalan Generalitat President Lluís Companys was brought back to Spain and tortured before being shot by a firing squad at Montjuïc Castle on October 15, 1940. All the political institutions established by the 1932 Catalan statute of autonomy having been suspended, the Nationalist victors moved to reconstruct the Catalan polity according to a new set of parameters. Franco's program of de-Catalanization involved outlawing the teaching of Catalan language, literature, and history, and banning the use of the language in public life. Among the first orders of business was the appointment of a mayor loyal to the new regime, Miquel Mateu i Pla, who would answer to the captain general and the civil governor of the province of Barcelona. Part of the purge involved the dismissal of all municipal market personnel hired after the July 1936 uprising.[23] There was also an immediate transfer of the food reserves held by the Junta Comarcal del Barcelonés to the municipal quartermaster.[24] The functionaries working at the Junta Comarcal del Barcelonés food depot quickly turned over 21,902 kilos of rice, 19,759 kilos of lentils, 4,870 kilos of garbanzos, and 13,427 kilos of salt cod, along with other food reserves whose value totaled more than 122,000 pesetas. As a gesture of "gratification," the municipal commission awarded five hundred pesetas each to the twenty-four men and women who had worked at the food depot so that they could "reorient" their lives after having lost their jobs.[25] There were clearly some who evaded the purge through collaboration with the new authorities and were rewarded for doing so.

The imposition of the Franco regime brought about fundamental changes in the relationship of market vendors and shopkeepers to the state. With the implementation of restrictions upon the right of free assembly, the associational networks that food retailers had worked to develop all suffered interruption, just as they had under the Primo de Rivera dictatorship. Shopkeepers, vendors, and municipal administrators were compelled to enroll in the national vertical syndicates, which viewed workers' and managers' interests as one and the same, and thus effectively silenced the efforts of its constituents to represent class-based interests. There was also a purge of food retailers, though not a sweeping or thorough one. With the Nationalist victory, shopkeepers selling food, drink, and domestic fuel had to register with the mayor's office and supply a certificate from neighborhood municipal authorities that testified to their adherence to the *Glorioso Movimiento Nacional*, along with proof of having been in business before the Civil War began. All those who had joined the food-retailing sector during the war were, at least in theory, closed down.[26]

Market vendors in general seem to have escaped the fate of shopkeepers. There is no evidence in the registries of a purge of stall-keepers or of a disruption in the chains of fixed-title ownership. In fact, the Franco-era municipal authorities in Barcelona moved to reaffirm pre-existing retail provisioning policies. We can see this at various levels. First of all, the 1942 market code, apart from reinstituting the power of lieutenant mayors and stripping city councilmen of their authority, was virtually identical to the 1928 code it supplanted and thus differed very little from the 1898 ordinances governing market trade in food. The newly appointed market directors and inspectors, selected for their loyalty to the single Movimiento Party state, moved quickly to embrace the long-established precepts about the limitation of unfair competition in the sector. Secondly, within the constructs of the vertical syndicalist system itself, the new regime authorized the revival of some of the retailing associations that had earlier functioned to defend members' interests. Though there was no tolerance for market-based vendor associationalism, some trade-specific associations were deemed acceptable. The butchers moved quickly to take advantage of the opportunity to regroup themselves.[27]

When Nationalist forces entered the city on January 26, 1939, they issued a decree ordering the dissolution of all civil, cultural, and commercial centers, associations, and guilds. The Asociació de Carnissers de Barcelona thus ceased to exist in a legal sense. Still, following the orders of General Juan Yagüe, speaking by radio address to the city in the name of Franco himself, the associations' general secretary, Venancio Sans y Prats, reported to work the morning after the occupation as if he faced no danger. Though he had taken the position as general secretary on an interim basis in 1937, there was nothing ostensibly revolutionary about Sans y Prats or the Associació de Carnissers' wartime activities; they were staunch defenders of private property even though they were not advocates of laissez-faire commerce on the retail level. Clearly, the new regime needed the butchers' knowledge, expertise, and collaboration to attempt to restore a sense of normalcy to the city. After helping to conduct a commercial census of butchers in shops and markets in the city on behalf of the provincial Comisión Oficial de Incorporación Industrial y Mercantil, the association was absorbed into the Falange's Sindicato Provincial de Ganadería (Provincial Livestock Syndicate) by November 1940. In the meanwhile, and for reasons that remain unclear, Venancio Sans y Prats was detained by the military authorities for a period of ten months but was then released and allowed to return to his work with the city's butchers, participating in the management and operation of a new Centro Técnico Administrativo, with offices at 14 Trafalgar Street.

A few years later, Sans y Prats was approached by a group of men seeking to create a new butchers' guild that sought official approval to operate from within the vertical syndicate in which they were inscribed. The proposal was approved by the authorities in 1944, and the butchers held an assembly to elect a new board on November 9, with Salvador Cararach assuming the presidency of what was to be the Gremio de Carniceros de Barcelona. This was the same Salvador Cararach who had arranged to purchase the gown that Santa Caterina's 1930 Market Queen wore in the grand cavalcade and ball, who had been a signatory to the ardently Catalanist expression of food-retail associational support for Francesc Macià's leadership in November 1931, and who had served as president of the forerunner butchers' association in the city from 1932 to 1934. How he survived the purge is unclear. But the fact is that he did and that there was a carryover in leadership and organization among the city's butchers from the Republic to the Franco regime. The circumstances of the bargain that must have been involved are not reflected in official records or accounts.[28]

Tolerance for the revival of some of the trade-specific food-retailing associations was in keeping with the general pattern of continuity in city's provisioning strategies. There is no convincing evidence that the Franco regime's municipal governments in Barcelona envisioned, expected, or encouraged the growth of food-retailing enterprises that went beyond the model represented by public market halls and private neighborhood shops before the late 1950s. Soon after the war's end, efforts began to expand the public market-hall system. The first of a new generation of food market halls was inaugurated on December 16, 1944. Located in a newer part of the Eixample near the construction site upon which the first façade of Gaudí's mammoth expiatory temple stood, the Sagrada Família market hall was built to accommodate vendors who had long sold from stalls in the open air along Sicília Street. Endorsing the longstanding goal of providing each new neighborhood with its own market, the state, here under a new ideological guise, used market-hall construction as symbolic capital in an effort to legitimize its rule on a neighborhood level. The opening ceremonies held for the new Sagrada Família Market harnessed all the usual rhetorical components to assert the municipality's devotion to the well-being of the urban populace.[29] When the *Vanguardia Española* published an end-of-the-year account detailing the "magnitude" of municipal projects undertaken in 1944, it highlighted the completion of the Sagrada Família Market as proof of the regime's concern for the citizenry.[30] The fact that the stall auctions generated more than seven million pesetas for municipal coffers could hardly have served as a disincentive for further such undertakings.[31]

## Coping with Corruption and Oppression

On the flip side, many vendors readily described the corruption that characterized much of the early Franco era's administration of public markets in the city. In addition to the problems related to food scarcity, spiraling inflation, and the black market, vendors faced new challenges associated with appeasing graft-inclined directors. Francesc Colominas Aznar, a La Llibertat Market vendor who sold salt cod alongside his wife in the 1940s, asserts that the directors during the immediate postwar period took advantage of those who struggled to operate their stalls during the food crisis. He described the dramatic increase in the number of inspectors during those years as figures who were especially feared. The government-imposed price controls were unreasonable and the inspectors knew it, Francesc asserted. Profit margins were too narrow, and vendors were left with little choice but to sell at higher prices in order to survive. The inspectors roamed the markets seizing stocks and closing stalls. To get by, vendors had to remain in the good graces of the director, the inspectors, and municipal veterinarians. There were well-known cases of graft. One involved a market director who ran a *pension* on the side and provisioned it completely on the basis of what he extorted from market vendors. The director in question would one day ask a fruit vendor for two kilos of oranges. On another day, he would demand an eye of round roast from a butcher, and on another day, seafood from a fishmonger. At

Christmastime, directors and inspectors would often take note of which vendors had, and which vendors had not, contributed money toward their holiday "gifts." Those who had not done so were forced to turn over food during the rest of the year as punishment. This was a new practice that had not taken place systematically before the war. Francesc had first-hand knowledge of such systemic corruption at La Llibertat and Sants markets, though he maintained that it occurred more widely throughout the period.[32] His half-brother, Semi Colominas, describes similar practices at Santa Caterina Market. There, desperate vendors sold items for which they were not licensed at prices above the government-set margins and were forced to pay food bribes to inspectors and directors as a result. Semi recalls that among the fishmongers at Santa Caterina, some collected monies to pay off the inspectors. He himself admitted to having been responsible for providing a salt cod every week to the director and arranging among his fellow vendors to split the cost of this extra expense.[33]

Coping with corruption involved considerable acumen and took various forms. Joaquim Esteba began working at the age of fourteen in his parents' L'Abaceria Central fruit and vegetable stall when the war broke out. At the conflict's end, he hoped to learn a trade at the Escola Industrial but quickly abandoned that illusion when he discovered that students there were required to wear uniforms, raise their arms up to the Fascists, and join the Movimiento's Frente de Joventudes. Joaquim claims not to have feared the inspectors, though on one occasion he was sanctioned for selling tomatoes above the set profit margin and had to arrange a bribe through a lawyer in the amount of fifteen or twenty thousand pesetas in order to keep his stall open. All the early Franco-era market directors were *enxufats*, he asserted, using a term that refers to appointments acquired through political influence. Recalling the situation at L'Abaceria Central in particular, he described being enlisted in the late 1940s to collaborate in a scheme to provide the director with food "gifts." The arrangement involved the director's sister, who would come by once a week to pick up two or three things without ever paying. Numerous vendors participated. But it really was not all that abusive a practice, he maintained, because under that director's reign, Joaquim noted, the market was clean and well run, and they only gave over enough food to feed his family. Others directors were much worse, he said.[34]

Significantly, men were much more willing than women to openly discuss market graft and corruption. Not particularly known for their reticence, female market vendors may have been less directly involved in systematic arrangements to bribe officials, a task that might have been perceived as an extension of the earlier male-dominated retail associations wherein men formed networks designed to directly engage with the state in defense of their commercial interests. It may well have been the case that women working in the markets made their own arrangements with the male officials who governed over them, perhaps on a more discreet basis through the functionaries' wives or other female relatives who could pass unnoticed in the market as consumers. Some female vendors simply refused to be subjected to systematic extortion. Such was the case with Carme Valls Roig, who told the director of La Concepció that if he needed something he could ask for it but that she was not in a position to make a regular commitment.[35]

The heavy-handedness of the early Franco-era administration of Barcelona's public markets, like vendors' responses, took various forms. Maria Cararach recalled that the first years after the war were especially hard. Among the forms of repression she remembered most vividly was that which involved municipal authorities in the market attempting to stamp out the use of Catalan. As had been the case during the Primo de Rivera dictatorship of the 1920s, the language of municipal administration in the city abruptly shifted to Spanish (that is, Castilian) at the end of the war. Cararach remembers that upon hearing vendors speaking Catalan at Santa Caterina in the early 1940s, the authorities would angrily accuse them of sounding "like dogs."[36] "Hablar cristiano!" they ordered. There is no question but that vendors took en masse to addressing municipal employees in Castilian, but their linguistic practices with customers showed more durability. A few clients did not speak Catalan, Cararach explained, and as a courtesy vendors spoke Catilian to them, but generally Catalan had always dominated at Santa Caterina up to that point. Here we see the limits of early Franco-era totalitarian cultural policies. Castilian was mandated as the official language by the regime; its use in education, in law, and in public life was made mandatory. Publication in Catalan was severely limited in the first two decades of the regime, and even many Catalan place names in Barcelona were replaced by Castilian ones. As such, Catalan was legally relegated to informal use among family and friends. But markets and shops constituted intermediate spaces linking public and private realms. The exchanges taking place in them must be understood on the basis of their intersectionality, and as illustrative of the analytical folly inherent in any attempt to draw firm boundaries between the public and the private as a useful framework for understanding how people experienced and understood their lives. Despite concerted efforts to wipe out Catalan nationalist sentiments, and even though Castilian was imposed in municipal administration and other official realms, the use of the Catalan language was never eradicated in small-scale food commerce under the Franco dictatorship.

My two Catalan aunts have both testified to and exemplified this reality. Rosa Maria Martí, my mother's older sister, remembers the neighborhood surrounding La Concepció Market during her youth in the 1940s and 1950s as an area where Catalan predominated in virtually all of the shops, and certainly in the market. Her sister-in-law Maria Ramón, whose parents were Aragonese, grew up nearby and quickly mastered Catalan in order to better communicate with her peers in the neighborhood. Shopping at La Concepció Market daily from the late 1940s until her health no longer permitted her to do so just a few years ago, my Tieta Maria always shifted easily between Catalan and Castilian, depending on the linguistic preferences of the vendors and shop owners whom she patronized so faithfully over time. But she also communicated in both languages with the women she talked to in the market, whether neighbors or fellow parishioners standing in line at her favorite stalls. She bought food from both Catalan- and Castilian-speaking vendors and never made a distinction. I did not realize until I was an adult that Catalan was not her native language.

Indeed, the languages used in food commerce more generally varied from neighborhood to neighborhood, depending on the degree to which retailers and their clientele were comprised of immigrants from regions beyond Catalonia. Even where vendors and shopkeepers were mostly Catalan, it was bilingualism in commerce that predominated through all the years of the dictatorship. Language choice was a pragmatic matter. Vendors used Catalan with Catalan-speaking customers but switched to Castilian if their clients did not understand or were not fluent. To do otherwise might risk the sale. Likewise, native Castilian-speaking vendors, whose numbers grew over time, often inserted Catalan words and phrases in dealing with Catalan-speaking customers as a way to establish intimacy and to assert themselves as legitimate participants in the market communities through which they sought to earn a living.

### Female Market Vendors as Exceptions to the Regime's Rhetoric and Policy toward Women

The widespread and ongoing use of the Catalan language was just one of the ways in which public markets and private neighborhood shops remained largely immune to the regime's cultural rhetoric. The continued presence of women as market vendors was another. The long-established gender-based divisions of labor and family strategies established in Barcelona's food-retailing sector persisted through the first decades of the Franco regime and beyond. Markets were the most visible examples, where women continued to constitute a majority among those who actually waited on the consuming public, whether as title-holders of individual stalls, as vendors working in family-economy arrangements, or as apprentices or clerks.

Municipal registries show that the pattern of independent female entrepreneurship in fixed-stall title acquisition persisted after the war. Between 1937 and 1949, during the height of the food crisis, 58.41 percent of all fixed-stall permits were issued to women; between 1950 and 1960, at a time when the regime's rhetoric stressing the importance of female devotion to domesticity was most intense, 57.42 percent of fixed-stall permits in the city were acquired by women.[37] There is no evidence that the Franco regime sought to exclude women from market-based retailing. In outlining the new procedures for stall auctions in the 1942 code, women's right to contract without the permission of their husbands was re-asserted.[38] Yet in many other areas of the Spanish economy in that period, married women faced new legal and cultural impediments to working outside the home. In the early 1940s, the Franco regime instituted policies that were meant to act as financial incentives for women to confine their activities to the domestic realm and to raise large families according to a model that Aurora G. Morcillo terms "true Catholic womanhood."[39] A reversal of Second Republic–era efforts to legislate equal rights for women in the workplace, in politics, and in the home, Franco's pronatalist policies were patterned after those of other fascist states and included marriage loans and subsidies that increased with the birth of each child. Additional legislation prohibited women's access to many professions, restricted married women's participation in the workforce, and legalized gender-based pay.[40] The regime's rhetoric glorified the role of full-time mothers as central to the organic well-being of the National-Catholic state.[41] Even after the 1961 passage of a new labor law prohibiting workplace discrimination on the basis of sex, married women in Spain were still required to have their husbands' permission in order to work outside the home. While it was not until the 1960s and early 1970s that the feminist movement in Spain began to regain strength and momentum to counter cultural and legal barriers to economic equality, historians have yet to explore the degree to which women in various regions of the country or different strata of society were impacted by the regime's rhetoric, policy, and ideology. What is certain is that female market vendors in Barcelona did not need the Franco regime to tell them that the family unit was the foundation of an orderly and prosperous society. Nor did they heed the regime's call in the 1940s and 1950s to devote their activities strictly to the domestic sphere.

Through the entire course of the dictatorship, women continued to work in the city's markets, acquiring stall titles in their own name more often than men. The regime's shift in policy toward women had virtually no impact on the way that market vendors organized their lives, their families, or their understanding of the boundaries supposedly demarcating public from private concerns. The children of market vendors continued to grow up in and around the markets where their parents worked, often beginning to help out in the stalls at a young age. Men and women continued meeting and marrying within markets, joining together to operate their food-retailing enterprises, and women continued to work full-time even after their children were born. The tradition of passing stall licenses on to children or other family members persisted as well. The vast and complicated familial networks that had come to characterize Barcelona's markets through the first decades of the century survived the disruption of the war and the postwar years and continued to flourish through the return of prosperity and the reinvigoration of consumer culture in the 1960s and beyond. An abundance of personal testimony attests to such continuities.

## Work, Family, and Community Ties in the Franco-Era Markets

Market work represented an appealing option for women who could not depend upon a husband's income for support. Antonia Peña Martín, who had worked as a clerk selling poultry and eggs in both Santa Caterina and La Boqueria markets prior to the war, gave birth to her only daughter, Lluïsa, in 1940. Widowed early on, she moved into a small apartment in Gràcia and took a job in a fruit and vegetable shop near L'Abaceria Central Market. Doing so allowed her to become familiar with the market and with the opportunities available therein. Lluïsa was just nine years old when Antonia secured a job for her at a L'Abaceria Central vegetable stall. After a short time, the vendor for whom Lluïsa worked became ill and was forced to retire. For a time, Lluïsa worked the stall on her own, though her mother took care of wholesale purchasing and stocking. Ultimately, mother and daughter went into business together in the market when Antonia was able to acquire the legal permits for a pair of adjacent stalls. Antonia, Lluïsa, and later Lluïsa's husband and then her daughter, worked the stalls through the second half of the twentieth century.[42] Her story illustrates how clerks could become fixed-title holders and how family-economy arrangements could serve as the basis for successful stall businesses.

The vast majority of vendors appear in this period to have relied upon some form of family-economy arrangement in working their stalls. Francesc Colominas began to work in his parents' Sants Market salt cod stalls when he was fifteen. The war had just ended, and his family lacked the resources to keep him in school. In 1952, at the age of twenty-eight, he became engaged to marry Joana Calvet Terrado, who was a third-generation Sants fishmonger. Together, the couple moved quickly to find a stall of their own to operate. Francesc recalls that salt cod vendors so often followed in their parents' footsteps that those stalls were hard to acquire. In his family alone, four of the five children had taken up the trade. In time, Francesc and Joana identified a single woman with a salt cod permit at La Llibertat Market who was looking to retire. But not surprisingly, four or five other salt cod vendors had their eyes on the stall for their own children, and a bidding war for the permit ensued. With financial help from his parents, Francesc was able to acquire the stall and get an apartment within view of La Lliberat. Francesc and Joana operated their market stall together until retirement. Through the birth of two sons, one in 1956 and the other in 1965, Joana continued to work alongside Francesc. The couple asserted that they loved their work, one another, and the market from which they plied their trade.[43] In addition to offering another example of marriage in the market and residential choices that valued proximity to place of work, their story illustrates the role played by tradition, especially within the salt cod specialization, in underpinning the ongoing reliance upon family-economy arrangements through the second half of the twentieth century.

While children were ubiquitous in the markets in these decades, the family-economy arrangements stemming from marriage in the market took many forms. Marriage did not always imply the immediate consolidation of stall businesses. Maria Teresa Fernández Mitjans began work in her father's fresh fish stall at Santa Caterina Market in 1956 when she was just eleven years old. She recalled that in the 1950s, the market was full of children working in their parents' stalls; these youthful market vendors did not typically ask for wages from their parents, though they did expect the occasional new pair of shoes or money to go to the movies. At the age of twenty-two, Maria Teresa married a young man she had met in the market whose family also sold fish. Thereafter, she continued to work in her father's stall while her husband worked with his mother from the stall directly in front of hers. The process of consolidating their respective family business only took place later on, when their parents retired from market work. Maria Teresa, like most market women, worked through her pregnancies. Her customers, she explained, saw her grow up, marry, and raise her children.[44] She described her "parishioners" affectionately as a rewarding and important part of her life. Her account also offers evidence of the persistent sense of community at Santa Caterina that linked vendors in bonds of sociability to the neighborhood consumers they served.

The fact that so many vendors were related to one another and that so many stalls were operated as family enterprises did not always preclude newcomers from entering the sector. Asunción Conejero Moreno was born in 1931, and though her parents were never involved in food retailing, she was attracted to market work. Asunción began working in Santa Caterina Market in the postwar period at the age of fourteen. Beginning as a clerk in a fruit and vegetable stall, she soon moved to take a job with a fresh fish vendor, and by seventeen, she had acquired her own fixed permit. Asunción asserted that her story was not an uncommon one because so little capital was needed to enter into market trade in the late 1940s. Asunción's sister came to help her in the stall, and as a consequence of spending time in the market, she met and married one of the other fishmongers. In time, Asunción also married a Santa Caterina fishmonger with whom she entered into a family-economy arrangement. The vendors welcomed her, she recalled. When Asunción gave birth to a daughter, her mother-in-law, who had earlier operated a stall at La Barceloneta's open-air wholesale fish market known as La Platxeta, provided child care so that her daughter-in-law could continue to work the stall. Living near the market made it possible for Asunción to have her baby brought down for feedings and for her to combine the domestic obligations of motherhood with her life's work selling fish. When Asunción's daughter reached the age of fourteen, she joined her mother in the market. Eventually, Asunción acquired another license and gave over her original stall to her daughter, who, she claimed, loved the trade and enjoyed the art and science of selling fresh fish as much as she did. Like so many others, Asunción described the fishmongers at Santa Caterina as a family.[45] The attitudes she expressed suggest how markets functioned at the intersection of family life and commerce and thus casts women's work in them as an extension of their roles as caretakers.

Characteristic of a range of specializations, endogamous marriages were particularly prevalent among fishmongers in the decades after the war. Pere Malla Vila's family history attests to the long-term endurance of such practices. Pere's maternal grandmother began selling fish in Gràcia as an ambulatory vendor before she was even ten years old. When L'Abaceria Central opened, her parents acquired a fixed-stall title for her and set her up to work from the new market. In due course, Pere's grandmother married the son of fishmonger in the market and immediately made plans to acquire a second permit so that she and her new husband could work together. While eager to get ahead, the couple found that they could not expand their operations within L'Abaceria Central because four or five families dominated the fresh fish business there and so were able to snatch up any stall that became available. Pere explained that market vendor families were often closed circuits; the children of vendors typically married within their own specializations. Unable to expand their business at L'Abaceria Central, Pere's maternal grandparents turned instead to La Llibertat Market, where an aunt and a cousin had a larger fresh fish stall. The aunt had died young, and the cousin had no experience in buying stock, so Pere's grandfather acquired their stall titles and began the work of expanding the family's fish enterprise from within the La Llibertat market-hall structure.[46]

Like his maternal grandfather before him, Pere Malla's father was working as a clerk in a fresh fish stall at L'Abaceria Central when he met and married his wife. Though his mother's parents had moved over to La Llibertat Market, they had never given up the L'Abaceria Central stall. Pere's uncle, in fact, operated that stall through the course of the Franco regime before selling it in the late 1970s. When Pere's parents married, his maternal grandparents set the young couple up in La Llibertat Market, where they had acquired additional stall permits and expanded their operations. Pere himself began working in his parents' La Llibertat Market stalls in 1958 at the age of twelve. He says that he had looked forward to being able to do so and had always aspired to take up his family's trade.

As a third-generation vendor with a heightened sense of historical consciousness, Pere Malla was well positioned to testify to the nature of the family economy within Barcelona's fresh fish specialization both before and after the Spanish Civil War. He observed, for example, that fish retailing in the city's markets was frequently undertaken by a husband and wife team, but that just as often women carried out such enterprises entirely on their own. As was the case in many fishmonger families, Pere's mother sold directly to the public while his father took responsibility for going to the wholesale fish market in the wee hours of the morning to acquire the stock they would retail from both their La Llibertat and L'Abaceria Central stalls. Such arrangements made sense, Pere explained, because stocking the market involved heavy lifting and thus considerable physical strength. Selling directly to the public, the women who worked fresh fish stalls faced different physical challenges; they had to stand in cramped spaces for long hours and often suffered from ailments related to circulation as a consequence. The perceived ad-vantages of having women attend to market customers stemmed from their pos-session of much more knowledge about how to best prepare the fish they offered for sale. Pere noted that because men in his day knew little about cooking, it was only logical that women should more often take responsibility for the actual sales. In so doing, they could use their culinary knowledge to encourage consumers to buy particular types of fish and try new recipes. From the time he began to work at the age of twelve until he went away to fulfill his military service at eighteen, Pere accompanied his father to buy stock. When he returned home at age twenty, he took over that responsibility from his father. He recalled that in his youth, there were approximately forty women and five men selling fish directly to the public at La Llibertat Market, yet only about half the women were working the stalls entirely on their own. The rest had husbands who bought wholesale, delivered the fish to the market, and helped their wives set up the stalls before the doors were opened to the public in the morning. Among the women who operated their fish stalls on an individual basis, about half were widows; the rest had husbands who worked in other occupations. His account thus offers a particularly crisp snapshot of the gender balance among fresh fish vendors during the Franco era.

Not surprisingly, Pere Malla also married within his family's retail specializa-tion. He met his wife-to-be in 1959 when he was thirteen and she was fourteen. The attraction began when he helped her carry some crates into the market, after which they went to have coffee together. It was a cold winter day, he remembered, and from then on they continued to see one another on a regular basis. The young couple had friends in common from the neighborhood; most were the children of La Llibertat Market fishmongers. Their courtship lasted ten years. Malla notes that six or seven married couples, all children of fishmongers, emerged from that adolescent cohort. In his matrimony, we see once more a union based on affec-tion, tradition, and pragmatism. He wed into a larger fishmonger family than his own. Thus united, Pere explained, he could boast of having relatives of one sort or another selling fish in all but one of the city's markets. Pere's wife shared many of his earliest experiences working in her family's stalls. She was well prepared to embark on a lifetime of market trade, and thus marriage to the son of a fishmon-ger represented a clear advantage.

Though marriages among the children of fishmongers were widespread, so too was the ongoing incidence in the postwar period of male market vendors, in a range of specialties, marrying their female clerks. Market work, even in the absence of a family tradition, remained a viable option for women needing to earn wages. Many women found work assisting in market-based food-retailing enterprises where no family members were available to help out. Carmen Gonzáles Morales was thirteen years old when she began working as a clerk at Santa Caterina Market in 1956.[47] She recounted that she had a number of female friends who worked as butchers' assistants and that they would get together after hours to socialize. Carmen was courted by a butcher but claims that in those days she had little interest in men. She ultimately succeeded in getting her own stall, and after meeting and marrying a man she had met outside the market, she and her husband opened and operated a small supermarket in the adjacent town of Badalona. After becoming widowed at a young age and being left with children to support, she sold the supermarket, took an apartment near Santa Caterina, and returned to selling beef from a market stall located therein. By then, three of her old friends who had worked as clerks had married the title-holding vendors who employed them. Such marriage strategies had long been common before and continued to occur on a frequent basis for decades after the war. Marriages between male stall-title holders and female clerks took place in all the food-retailing specializations and in all the markets of the city. The endurance of the practice attests to the fact that market work in Barcelona involved complex and enduring social relations. Among vendors, intermarriage and reliance on family-economy strategies reinforced the creation of complicated retailing networks. Markets were public spaces where food was bought and sold but also where both love and friendship could be cultivated.

Though the war and the postwar period involved profound disruptions in food supply and thus introduced new challenges for those who operated small-scale retailing firms, there was much continuity in the social and cultural dimensions of market-based commerce. Vendors' personal testimonies attest to the endurance of consumer loyalty to specific stalls as well as to the value placed on humor, theatrics, and personal affection in food sales. Isabel Colera Magrans was born in 1934 and worked her entire life as a poulterer in L'Abaceria Central Market. Isabel's grandmother, Quimeta, had been an ambulatory vendor in Sant Andreu until she married and set up a poultry shop with her husband in Gràcia. With the opening of L'Abaceria Central, Isabel's grandparents lost a portion of their clientele to the new market; in hopes of rebuilding their customer base, they acquired two fixed-stall permits in L'Abaceria Central and began selling from there. Isabel's mother began working at a young age in the market and eventually passed the family's stalls on to her. Isabel never married, and her mother continued coming to the market to help her until she died in 1990 at the age of eighty-four. Isabel explained that the vendors at L'Abaceria Central thought of themselves as a family. She said that she knew everyone in the market and always had her own loyal clientele. A "client" was something more than a customer, according to Isabel.[48] "Clients" were those women with whom vendors conversed about family matters, cooking, trips to the dentist or the doctor, dietary restrictions, and where to find the best handymen for household repairs. Clients could also, she said, count on the extension of informal credit and even on home deliveries of the chicken to make their midday escudella. She described the market as part of the social life of Gràcia in the years following the war, recalling live music on holidays and dancing in the aisles after the doors closed on Christmas Eve.

Other vendors offered similar accounts of the social atmosphere at Gràcia's markets in the period. Joana Calvet was born in 1933 and started working alongside her mother in Sants Market in the mid-1940s when she was still an adolescent. It was there that she met her husband, Francesc Colominas, who worked in his family's salt cod stalls. Francesc claims that he watched her work for about a year before deciding that she was the one he should marry. Joana had little interest in school; early on in her youth she determined that she wanted to sell fish because, she said, she was carrying the skills inside her that were necessary to succeed. She asserted that she liked the atmosphere of the market and has never regretted becoming a vendor. Joana was twenty when she and her husband acquired their salt cod stalls at La Llibertat Market in 1953. Francesc claims that she had the innate skills needed to attract and maintain a faithful pool of clients. She, in turn, said that she knew her parishioners' lives from top to bottom and her friendships were based on them more so than on relations with other vendors or neighbors. Joana was known for sharing recipes with her clients, and not just those that involved cod, but also for a wide range of other dishes and desserts. She says that she would counsel young wives who suspected that their husbands were cheating on them. Joana would tell them that husbands had to be won over and that the best route was through their stomachs. The couple consciously put on a show every day in the market. Joana would complain humorously to her clients about Francesc, usually making up improbable infractions that he had committed. Buying salt cod from Joana was such an entertaining proposition that her clients' husbands would later ask what had gone on that day in the market.[49]

Clearly some market specializations were especially known for their theatrics. In Joaquim Esteba's estimation, the fishmongers at L'Abaceria Central were the most inclined to combine commerce with humor and practical jokes. Joaquim was a second-generation fruit and vegetable vendor whose father's illness obligated him to join the family business at the age of fourteen in 1936. Working at L'Abacera Central throughout his life, he had many friends among the vendors. His vivid memories of the market in the 1940s and 1950s included a great deal of spontaneity surrounding the celebration of Carnival. He recalled that one year a fishmonger, who was a very large man, dressed up as a baby, put a pacifier in his mouth and a traditional infant's straw cap on his head and had himself pushed around the market in an oversized stroller. The effect was hilarious, meeting with uproarious laughter on the part of vendors and customers alike. Another year, a fishmonger couple, Joaquim recalled, dressed up as Tarzan and Jane for Carnival and were hauled down to the police station for indecency as a result. The man was wearing an animal skin, the woman a dress made from newspapers, and neither of them had anything else on. Yet another fishmonger brought a toy gun into the market and pretended that he was executing the annoying and ubiquitous market cats. He was so convincing that animal rights advocates paid the market director a visit to protest the presumed abuse. He also remembered pie-throwing and whipped-cream battles during Carnival as part of the rollicking antics. Throughout the year, he said, fishmongers engaged in fake fights to amuse the market customers.[50] Humor and theatrics in the marketplaces of the city were clearly a way for vendors to alleviate stress, but such high jinks certainly added to the fun that consumers could sometimes derive from food shopping, even in difficult times.

Although La Llibertat vendors showed less inclination to celebrate Carnival in the market than those working from L'Abaceria Central, they certainly understood the importance of sociability in building bonds of loyalty with consumers. Pere Malla explains some of the complexities involved in the process. Vendors had to know how to size up their customers on the basis of their way of talking and dressing. Some liked to buy small amounts of pricier food; others tended to buy larger amounts of cheaper goods. Successful vendors would never cheat their "clients," but they had to know how to make them buy what they wanted them to on any given day. Throughout his life, he says, about 70 percent of the shoppers at La Llibertat have been "clients," while the rest have shown no loyalty to any particular stall. If their regular clients were facing problems in their lives, they often told vendors about them. Vendors took messages for their clients and transmitted bits of neighborhood news. The best vendors, according to Malla, were those whose main characteristic was an open and spontaneous way of dealing with people.[51]

Most of the holiday festivities at La Llibertat were associated with Christmas and with Gràcia's unique celebration of Sant Medir. At Christmastime, vendors decorated their stalls, connected a record-player to the public-address system, and dedicated songs to each other, to family members, and to their favorite clients. Though Sant Medir was organized from outside the market, numerous vendors participated in neighborhood *colles* that distributed candy and flowers and undertook the pilgrimage to the shrine outside the city where the festivities culminated. At La Llibertat, as at L'Abaceria Central and other markets in the city, food shopping involved much more than a simple exchange of money for alimentary goods during the years of the Franco regime. Going to the market could be stressful when shortages or strained budgets were involved, but the process of food shopping also involved an element of entertainment and often even the satisfaction that comes from enduring friendship, among vendors and consumers alike.

The personal testimonies that vendors offered about their lives, their work, and their communities have broader historical significance. They provide evidence for the fact that in market-based food retailing in Barcelona, women very often worked openly and visibly from a young age, after marriage, and throughout their lifecycles. The supposed U-shaped curve interpretation of women's work, asserting high levels of paid labor in the earliest phases of industrialization followed by a dramatic retreat to domestic and reproductive specialization until the second half of the twentieth century when women again re-entered the workforce in large numbers, does not hold up in this context.[52] In fact, a growing and significant body of scholarship suggests that the U-shaped-curve interpretation is not supported by the weight of evidence documenting women's work patterns in much of Spain.[53] Enriqueta Camps, Pilar Pérez-Fuentes, Cristina Borderías, Rubén Pallol, and others have shown tremendous heterogeneity in married women's work patterns, structured by a range of circumstances, contexts, and opportunities.[54] Women's contributions to the family economy appear to have been much more widespread than indicated in either national or municipal census data. The case of Barcelona's food vendors clearly shows that women's work was vital to family well-being during the first decades of Franco's dictatorship, that the state actually endorsed it through its regulatory structures, and that individual families pursued a range of strategies, including living near the market and relying on extended households for child care, in order to facilitate wives' ability to continue working in the markets throughout their lives. The social bonds that linked men and women together and that so often led to marriage in the market and to reliance upon family-economy arrangements were crucial to the ability of vendor households to generate the income upon which they depended to survive.

## Economic Recovery

The immediate postwar policies of economic autarky proved a failure. Spain could not prosper outside the international economic order. Increasingly pressured by labor unrest and domestic financial and industrial interests, the Franco regime in the 1950s moved to liberalize the economy. In 1951, the ministries of commerce and agriculture loosened controls over the economy, and thereafter, with newly acquired credits from the United States, Spain imported industrial machinery, vehicles, and food. Exports to Europe of oranges, olive oil, and minerals resumed, and the state moved toward reviving the tourist industry as a source of revenue.[55] Along with the dramatic influx of emigrant remittances, all of these factors contributed to an important increase in standards of living, which finally climbed in 1954 to pre–Civil War levels.[56] Economic recovery intensified between 1955 and 1960 and was particularly strong in Barcelona. In the province of Barcelona, per-capita income grew by 99 percent, while in Spain as a whole the increase was 61 percent.[57] After a decade and a half of economic disruption and stagnancy, growing levels of demand for consumer products in Barcelona were also spurred by the expansion in the industrial sector and by unprecedented immigration from the Catalan and Spanish countryside. Shantytowns and then cheaply constructed worker high-rises mushroomed along a ring surrounding the metropolis.

The revival of consumerism in Barcelona by the early 1960s was most visibly evidenced by the sea of SEAT-600 cars that had overtaken virtually every corner of the city. But the acquisition of *electrodomèstics,* such as refrigerators and televisions, and the myriad of new products for sale in department stores also transformed the material realities of life during those years of recovery. Food retailing was one of the economic sectors first benefitting from the new levels of prosperity. After years of rationing, shortages, and inflation, consumers were able to begin enjoying foods that they had otherwise limited to holidays and special occasions. Shoppers could increasingly afford to spend more and buy better-quality food in the markets and shops of the city, eat more often in restaurants, and conspicuously display their newfound affluence in the choices they made in order to feed their families.

Economic recovery and the revival and broadening of consumerism had a significant impact upon the operation of small-scale food retailing in Barcelona's public market halls. As both per-capita income and food imports rose, the level of sales in the city's markets increased, and stall businesses became more profitable enterprises. Some portion of the vendor population experienced upward social mobility, and the black market, along with the emotional stress involved in engaging in illegal forms of trade, largely disappeared. Though mid-twentieth-century consumerist culture is often too narrowly viewed as being exclusively focused on the act of shopping for clothes, appliances, and furnishings in large-scale enterprises, in Barcelona it was also intimately connected with such institutions as public markets, where older forms of small-scale commerce in food flourished. Most women continued to shop on a daily basis in their neighborhood markets, where they purchased their family's food but also went in pursuit of varied forms of sociability and emotional gratification associated with the act of consumption. Press accounts stress the degree to which markets became increasingly crowded and women shoppers began socializing more frequently in market bars and cafés.[58] The intensification of consumerism and its widespread expression through food shopping acted to strengthen the degree to which public market halls operated as social and commercial nuclei within the neighborhoods where they were situated.

Yet the reinvigoration of older expressions of consumerism in food retailing was only one part of the story. Structural changes afoot both expanded and challenged the hegemony of the city's public market-hall system as the primary vehicle for the retailing of food. Once the economy began to recover, Franco-era municipal regimes in Barcelona undertook a prolific program of market-hall building. As of 1850, the city had constructed two public market halls; between 1850 and 1898, it constructed seven more. By 1934, the number of publicly operated retail food market halls had grown to a total of sixteen. One new market, Sagrada Família, was inaugurated in 1944. Then between 1950 and 1975, the city built twenty-one new market halls, thus opening the way for dramatic expansion of stall operations by existing food-retailing families and new groups immigrating to the city.

In addition to addressing the complex challenges associated with housing shortages and the lack of basic infrastructural services such as water, electricity, and public transport, Franco-era municipal authorities in Barcelona expanded the existing polynuclear market-hall system. Municipal defense of the approach was unequivocal.[59] New market halls continued to be held up by municipal officials and the press alike as key components in the network of public services and as proof of the regime's commitment to the well-being of the citizenry. A press report in 1950 about the inauguration of the new Mare de Déu del Carme market hall on the edge of the Raval asserted that "few times does the opportunity arise to invest capital at good interest while making, at the same time, a contribution to the ask of collective exaltation."[60] Thereafter, all the other new public market halls in Barcelona were built in peripheral and largely immigrant areas of the city.

These markets were smaller than those constructed prior to the war; most could accommodate only between 160 and 200 stalls. Still, like their predecessors, these new structures quickly became central points for local food shopping and as such helped to consolidate social ties among the immigrant residents of newly emerging neighborhoods.

The Mare de Déu de L'Estrella market hall, located in an area just beyond Gràcia known as La Salut, stands as a case in point. Inaugurated in 1957, it actually had its origins as a private initiative undertaken by La Salut resident Eusebio Santos, who was disturbed by the fact that the fifty thousand persons living in the new apartment blocks of the neighborhood, his wife among them, were forced to travel a significant distance across the city in order to buy food.[61] Santos financed the construction of the market, issued stall licenses to would-be vendors, but then, like other entrepreneurs before him, was unable to secure municipal authorization to open and operate the structure. While the completed market stood empty for eight months, newly established neighborhood groups petitioned the city to authorize its opening.[62] Ultimately, Santos sold the structure to the stall-titleholders, who conveyed their interests to the city, and the market was authorized and put into operation under municipal control. So even before L'Estrella market hall became the nucleus of food retailing within La Salut, it had helped to foment consciousness of collective neighborhood interests among residents. Other studies confirm this. Pamela Beth Radcliff finds that the demand for markets in underserved areas of Madrid and Barcelona was taken up by some of the new neighborhood associations that formed after 1964.[63]

Franco-era market inaugurations closely resembled those of the past. The rituals marking the opening of markets always included religious officials, vendors, consumers, and municipal authorities, and were usually presided over by the mayor.[64] At the 1957 opening of L'Estrella market hall, Barcelona mayor Josep Maria Porcioles[65] declared that "the opening of this structure serves as more proof of the city government's preoccupation with the problems that are related to the daily lives of the citizenry. It is an event that very directly affects human existence, especially in reference to our housewives . . . This market is therefore an act of love, and I hope that you will know how to use it with the civil comportment that is characteristic of our beloved Barcelona."[66] Hints of distrust in the working classes and the hope that market-based food retailing would forestall discontent are revealed in such rhetoric.

Franco-era municipal authorities also moved after 1950 to renovate twenty-two of the city's oldest market halls. In addition to repairing leaky roofs and fixing shoddy pavements, the city invested in upgraded refrigeration facilities in both wholesale and retail market halls.[67] These measures, according to the deputy mayor in charge of provisioning, Manuel Borrás París, formed part of the municipality's efforts to take markets beyond their historic roles and adapt them to the needs of the city's new conditions and circumstances.[68] Borrás called for the imposition of new standards of aesthetic uniformity in the city's market stalls and better standards of hygiene, "so that the markets may reach the maximum plentitude that is currently obligatory in the nutritional sector."[69]

Such improvements contributed to the mid-twentieth century flourishing of public market hall-based food retailing. At La Boqueria alone in 1954, more than four thousand people worked in food retailing, with only a fourth of them actually holding fixed-stall permits. The rest were clerks and assistants, who were often but not always related to the stallholders. Descriptions in the press of La Boqueria Market in 1954 emphasized the visible affluence of vendors there, who were catering to as many as fifteen to twenty thousand customers a day.[70] Noting that female butchers were increasingly wearing gold and diamond jewelry to work, one press report asserted that if vegetarianism were to spread, the city's jewelers would lose an "important and growing clientele."[71] At another market in 1957, a reporter noticed a shiny new black car parked outside the structure. "Is there an official visit today?" he inquired. "No," he was told, "the vehicle belongs to one of our butchers."[72] Small-scale food retailing was clearly booming. Everywhere, the popular perceptions were that market vendors in general, and butchers in particular, were faring well in their businesses.

## New Forms of Competition

Economic recovery and demographic expansion caused demand for food to soar in Barcelona during the 1950s. Though in the late nineteenth century, the city had been vested with one market for every 37,500 persons, by the mid-1950s the ratio had risen to one market for every 59,000 residents.[73] Barcelona's population had grown by more than 70 percent since 1930; by 1955 it reached 1.74 million. Municipal investment in new market construction could not keep up with demand. Without abandoning its commitment to public market-hall administration, municipal authorities as of 1956 began to pursue new strategies for expanding the food-retailing infrastructure. Citing the ideal situation as one in which there would be one market for every 25,000 residents, the city moved toward authorizing the opening of smaller indoor markets to be developed by private investors and termed *galerías comerciales*.[74] By then, some investors had already completed the construction phase of their development, though like L'Abaceria Central and L'Estrella markets before them, these commercial spaces sat unused for a time, awaiting municipal authorization to open.

Though the authorization of the new galerías comerciales represented a step toward food-policy liberalization, these privately operated markets were subjected to high levels of municipal control.[75] The city reserved the right to revoke stall licenses and mandated that such retail centers have entrances from two public streets and include modern refrigeration facilities. Gradually, galerías comerciales opened across Barcelona, especially where the regular municipal markets were located farthest from new residential areas. Different both in terms of scale and morphology, galerías comerciales were almost always carved out of the ground floors of existing apartment buildings rather than consisting of free-standing structures, and they only rarely included more a couple of dozen stalls. As such, they represented change while still incorporating notable continuities.

Indeed, the construction of small private markets brought greater competition but also acted to further decentralize food retailing. While galerías comerciales robbed older markets of some of their clientele, they also emerged as even more localized centers of neighborhood-based social and commercial exchange. The relationships of familiarity and loyalty underlying the daily transactions between vendors in the galerías comerciales and their customers, in my observations, replicated long-established patterns in the city's larger municipal market halls. More significantly, it was the introduction of supermarkets in the late 1950s, along with the vast expansion in automobile and electrical refrigeration ownership, that signaled the coming of real change in Barcelona's provisioning system and marked the beginnings of a profound shift in consumer habits. Despite increases in the supply of food resulting from the opening of new markets, prices continued to rise. Between August 1956 and July 1958, for example, the cost of living in Barcelona increased by 27.85 percent.[76] Such conditions encouraged provisioning authorities to license food-retailing firms that could offer much greater economies of scale.

After opening their doors in Madrid, San Sebastian, Bilbao, Gijón, and A Coruña, the first supermarkets appeared in Barcelona in 1958.[77] By 1960, there were seven operating in the city. Ironically, the inaugural events held to mark their opening were remarkably similar to those scripted for public market halls. They were attended by municipal and religious figures, along with crowds of shoppers, and they were touted by those presiding over the ceremonies as improvements in the city's system of public services.[78] In keeping with past practices, the inauguration ceremonies were sometimes set to coordinate with municipal and religious celebrations, such as those held for the city's patron saint, La Mercè.[79] Such was the case with the opening of the Autoservicio Granvia, for example, in 1959. Franco-era municipal authorities hailed supermarkets as a sign of the return of prosperity and of the regime's willingness, under technocratic influence, to embrace new economic forms.

Supermarkets were the newest consumerist institutions in their day, much like department stores had been earlier. Huge displays and an expansive selection of pre-packaged and uniform goods sold themselves without the intervention of individual vendors or shopkeepers. The elements of social exchange and personal loyalty, so central to retail exchange in market halls and shops, all but ceased to exist in these new self-service institutions. Indeed, the coming of supermarkets introduced new, much higher levels of anonymity in the economic exchange of money for food. Averaging about four hundred square meters and usually equipped with between four and seven check-out lines, these stores allowed customers to wander the aisles, touch merchandise, examine the range of competing brand names, enter and leave, without necessarily having spoken more than a few words to the cashier or any other employee. In supermarkets, customers could shop without experiencing the pressures that came along with entering one of the city's markets where vendors expected loyalty from their clients to be expressed in daily purchases or called out to them as they passed through the aisles as an enticement to buy.[80] Similar pressures and expectations involved entering neighborhood shops, where owners and clerks expected their customers not to leave without making a purchase.

In economic terms, the experience of shopping in supermarkets also differed in significant ways from shopping in the city's market halls and neighborhood shops. The new supermarkets were time-savers because consumers could typically get in and out of them more quickly than they could the traditional markets. The wide variety of goods available in one place alleviated the need to stand in line many times over in order to acquire the provisions necessary to feed a family. But because there were so many fewer supermarkets than market halls or neighborhood shops, they typically involved consumers traveling longer distances to the point of retail sale. Riding the bus to shop for food became a more common practice in the 1960s, though it became less so as supermarkets increasingly mined the city's landscape by the end of the twentieth century. Consumers also encountered lower prices in supermarkets resulting from economies of scale in purchasing and from backwards vertical integration in processing and production. In 1958, 330 grams of ground beef, which sold for 28 pesetas at regular butcher shops and stalls, sold for 12 pesetas in the city's supermarkets.[81] The move to import larger quantities of meat from other European countries such as Denmark enhanced the ability of supermarkets to offer beef at lower prices. Different from the markets in terms of competitive pricing, time efficiency, and anonymity, supermarkets played in their own ways to the sensuality long characteristic of food shopping in Barcelona. Enticing displays of novel prepackaged and processed foods, opportunities to freely touch and examine products without the obligation to purchase them, and more frequent sampling of new brands constituted a different kind of consumerist experience.[82] Supermarket shopping facilitated the expression of individual preferences for specific branded convenience foods and was less communally oriented than market-hall shopping.

It was not until the mid-1960s that supermarkets began to put a serious dent in market-hall and neighborhood shop sales. Initially, there was enough demand to sustain public and private markets, shops, and new supermarkets without affecting the rising prosperity of those engaged in small-scale food retailing. In fact, some vendors and shopkeepers were able to profit from the introduction of this new self-service model for the sale of food. The most direct beneficiaries came from among the ranks of the city's roughly five thousand grocers who mostly operated small neighborhood shops, but who also held stalls in the city's markets.

The reaction of neighborhood grocers to the competitive threat posed by the opening of supermarkets in Barcelona speaks volumes about the commercial networks that retailers were able to maintain over the long term, despite changes in political regime. Paralleling the interruption posed by the Primo de Rivera dictatorship, after which the Cercle d'Ultramarins emerged stronger than ever, there was a similar lull in effective commercial associationalism among grocers in Barcelona during the first decades of the Franco regime. Thereafter, the grocers regrouped within the legal vertical syndicate system and re-emerged to advocate for their commercial interests under the banner of the Gremio de Detallistas de Ultramarinos.[83] On March 12, 1959, the Gremio met at the Fomento del Trabajo Nacional building on the Via Laietana in Barcelona. The discussion at the meeting surrounded the supermarket question and the fear that they "could result in the total disappearance of the small establishments" in the city.[84] Members debated whether they should oppose plans to build fifteen new supermarkets in Barcelona or join together to invest in them. Representatives of the Madrid grocers' guild attended and urged their counterparts in Barcelona to adapt rather than fight the new retail model. After extended discussion, the Gremio voted to move into the supermarket business as aggressively as possible. They agreed to petition the city for low-interest loans for grocers anxious to invest in supermarket ventures. Their platform called for tight municipal control over supermarket placement; new ones should only be located where they would pose the least competition to existing grocers. They called also for limitations upon the right to invest in supermarkets with non-guild members restricted to 25 percent of the shares. Through such proposals, grocers attempted to meet head on the challenge posed by supermarkets. Incapable of halting the introduction and spread of these new retailing entities, the grocers reverted to asserting their traditional rights to secure municipal protection from free-market competition. This strategy proved successful for some shopkeepers and market vendors, who were able to establish independent supermarkets that proved able to compete with chains over the long run.

One important example is that of Tomasa Totoliu, who became a Concepció Market fixed-permit vendor in 1911 and worked a set of poultry stalls as a family business with her children through the course of the war and postwar food crises. While creating and maintaining a profitable network of stall businesses that extended into La Boqueria and other markets, Tomasa's children and grandchildren expanded their family's operations dramatically. In 1967 they opened what would prove to be a very viable small supermarket, called Superestalvi, directly across València Street from La Concepció Market. From that base, they moved to create a local chain of supermarkets and shops selling frozen foods, rotisserie chicken, and prepared dishes. The original Superestalvi supermarket, in the hands of Tomasa's son Blai Capdevila Totoliu, became a limited public corporation under the name of Establiments d'Alimentació, S.A., in 1985.[85] A grandson, Salvador Capdevila i Nogué, established a food retailing, processing, and distribution operation called Avinova, with stalls in La Boqueria and a shop located nearby. Avinova's business plan involved the transformation of the family's La Boqueria stalls to specialize in a wide range of poultry, eggs, exotic game, prepared foods, and some thirty varieties of high-end goose-liver products.[86] Avinova, which has won various awards, caters to the most discerning home cooks as well as to many of Barcelona's finest restaurants and food service companies. The respect that Salvador Capdevila commands in the market and in the city was reflected in his election to the presidency of the Associació de Comerciants del Mercat de la Boqueria in 2011, upon the untimely death of its longtime president and global market ambassador, Manel Ripoll.

There were several other significant cases of successful backwards and forwards horizontal and vertical integration from among the ranks of Barcelona's food-vendor population in response to the introduction of supermarkets in the late 1950s, though few such initiatives went big while still holding onto their original family stalls. Despite new forms of competition, it is significant that markets remained so viable through the 1970s. None of the public market halls went out of business, new construction to serve burgeoning peripheral neighborhoods was ongoing, and overall there was more continuity than change in the polynuclear system.

The remarkable twentieth century resilience of food market halls in Barcelona can in part be explained by the fact that they were not institutions that were hostile to the growth of consumerism. Rather, they were arenas in which the resurgence of consumerism in food was expressed through purchasing on the basis of desire as well as need. There was gratification and assertion of social standing in the special purchases that women made for weekend meals, for example, and such choices went beyond calculations of simple nutritional necessity. In fact, it is reasonable to postulate that while the Spanish economy was in shambles during the 1940s and early 1950s and few durable and semidurable goods were available for purchase, the widest-spread expressions of consumerism among women remained attached to food shopping. In such dire material circumstances, the most frequently enjoyed creature comforts were alimentary. Consumption of anything that was expensive carried a heavy load of meaning and implied, at least in a transitory sense, a modicum of social success. The ability of consumers to negotiate the black market and to, for example, arrange for higher-than-average levels of white bread consumption for their families might also be viewed as expressions of consumerist desire. Out of the lean years of the twentieth-century food crisis, through the gradual recovery of the 1950s, through the superfluity in food that characterized the late 1960s and 1970s, consumerist attitudes toward food reached new levels of fervor. Where and what one ate, how carefully food was prepared, and how exclusively it was purchased became crucial markers of social standing, cultural acumen, and refined taste—values embraced by the working and middle classes alike.

Markets also continued to prosper through the first decades of supermarket growth because women rarely chose one type of retailing enterprise over another; rather, they typically shopped in both. As remains the case today, some supermarkets, especially those located nearest to market halls, did not sell fresh meat or fish and offered only limited selections of fruits and vegetables. As such, supermarkets initially carved out their niche in canned goods, dairy products, and pre-packaged foods such as flour, rice, pasta, sugar, cookies, puddings, plus cleaning fluids, paper goods, soft drinks, beer, wine, and liquor. It was more often the larger hypermarkets, which did not appear until the 1970s, that offered a full range of goods, including those that typically were offered for sale in the public market halls. Located on the periphery of the city, hypermarkets remained destinations for automobile-owning families who mostly shopped in them on weekends. The main pattern from the mid-1960s onward involved consumers purchasing some items in supermarkets, other items in their neighborhood markets, and still others in nearby shops.

Just as department stores and supermarkets lured customers with attractive displays and offered buyers a form of recreation as they shopped, so too did the city's market halls. One particular change in policy enhanced the ability of markets to cash in on growing levels of consumerist demand. In 1949, the municipality began to convey a new category of stall permit along the outside perimeter of the market halls to individuals selling kitchenware, costume jewelry, clothing, and other semidurable goods. Such stalls thereafter became ubiquitous and colorful components of quite a number of the city's market halls. Moreover, Sant Antoni Market had long had its auxiliary *encants* flea market, which by 1954 comprised 630 separate stalls selling nonalimentary goods around the exterior of the market and along adjacent streets on Mondays, Wednesdays, Fridays, and Saturdays. La Boqueria likewise had its administratively conjoined flower, bird, and newsstand markets stretching up Las Ramblas to the Plaça de Catalunya. The iconic flower stalls in particular, which date back to before the relocation of the main food market in the space that had once been the Convent of Sant Josep, testify to the endurance of consumerist desire associated with market shopping over the long run.

Yet there were significant changes in the later twentieth century. Between 1964 and 1976, while the population of the city continued to grow, the total number of food-retailing enterprises dropped by approximately two thousand.[87] After that, the trend reversed itself; economic downturn and slightly more liberalized commercial regulations brought new actors into the sector.[88] Both displaced rural agricultural and unemployed industrial workers moved into food retailing in significant numbers. By the early 1990s, the city had a higher ratio of food-retailing enterprises per capita than did the rest of Spain, with one firm for every 114 inhabitants versus a national figure of one for every 164.[89] There were comparative differences in scale as well. While only 10 percent of Barcelona's food-retailing establishments measured more than sixty square meters, 28 percent were larger than that in Spain more generally.[90] In the last decades of the twentieth century, policy-makers and economic analysts alike began to speak of the problem of food-retailing *minifundismo* in Barcelona.[91] The markedly higher number of individual enterprises than in other cities in Spain—and in comparison to Northern

Europe—became associated in the technical literature with backwardness, inefficiency, high prices, and poor hygienic conditions.

Still, the concept of *minifundismo* can be misleading. While small businesses showed much continuing vigor, medium-sized self-service stores and supermarkets were capturing a greater share of consumer expenditures in certain types of groceries.[92] Pre-packaged and especially processed foods were increasingly being purchased by consumers from points of retail sale that measured over sixty square meters.[93] Nonetheless, one form—the small-scale market stall or neighborhood shop versus the larger-scale self-service store—had not actually prevailed over the other. Barcelona's food-retailing system had not followed a direct course moving from open-air markets, to enclosed market halls, to shops and stores, and then to super- or hypermarket preeminence. The food-retailing firms that supplied Barcelona's population varied widely in size and form through the last quarter of the twentieth century.

One important explanation for the persistence of small-scale retailing in Barcelona's food sector lies in the strength, endurance, and expansion of the polynuclear municipal market system. Market vendors faced stiff regulatory limitations on the physical expansion of their operations. The consolidation of individual stall licenses for enterprises that often measured less than five square meters into larger-scale businesses was a long and laborious process that was well underway in the 1920s but not yet complete in any sense by the end of the century. Moreover, in Barcelona, the municipal government continued to build, upgrade, and operate public market halls until much later than was the case in most other Spanish and European cities. Municipal governments under the authority of the constitutional monarchy of the Restoration, the Primo de Rivera dictatorship, the Second Republic, and the Franco regime never abandoned their commitment to organizing food distribution around neighborhood market halls. Even the authorization of the smaller, privately run galerías comerciales reflected this commitment. Through the last decade of the twentieth century, forty-one municipally operated market halls—one for every 44,000 urban residents—remained as viable anchors and commercial central places in neighborhoods across the city.[94] There were actually more market halls per capita in 1988 than in 1940, and more market halls per capita at the end of the century in Barcelona than in any other European city.[95] Surrounding each of these retail institutions were clusters of food shops whose location in relation to the market hall and to one another remained closely regulated by municipal authorities. Public market halls in 1992 commanded a 60.8 percent share of the fresh food sales in the city, and traditional neighborhood shops accounted for another 16.3 percent. The smaller galerías comerciales accounted for another 6.8 percent.[96] Public market halls dominated in sales of fresh vegetables, fruit, fish, meat, and poultry. Food-shopping patterns that involved a trip to the neighborhood market and a series of commercial transactions and social exchanges with small-scale retailers remained one of the most prevalent everyday experiences for urban residents.

## Food and Catalan Identity in the Franco Era

By the early 1960s, food and Catalan identity had become more firmly and definitively linked. Several factors help to explain this. Memories of food scarcity imbued eating with a greater sense of solemnity. The generation of Civil War survivors, much like those who had lived through the Great Depression of the 1930s and other subsistence crises elsewhere, tended to treat food as a sacred commodity that above all else should never be wasted or taken for granted. Once the food crisis had passed, those attitudes persisted, alongside growing appetites for foods that for so long had been scarce or dear. The connection between food and identity, as we know, is a powerful one. Foods evoke childhood memories, connote individual and class status, and serve as markers that help to define culture and community. This has been the case everywhere, though in Spain it has been manifested in a particular set of ways that are tied to the larger political history of the state.

In many respects, Spain has followed a tortured path to national unity, an elusive goal that remains contested to this day. The power of local bonds—that is, allegiance to what is called *la patria chica*—has been an enduring characteristic. Because so much of Spain's urban population in the twentieth century was comprised of immigrants from the countryside, ties to the village or town of origin, or to those of parents or grandparents, remained deeply meaningful. With the dramatic growth of automobile ownership from the late 1950s onward, the weekend excursion to the countryside became a mass ritual that produced increasingly intense traffic jams out of major cities on Friday nights and back into them on Sunday evenings. Where villages of origin were too distant from the cities in which people lived and worked during the week, the purchase of a country house with a garden, what is known in Catalan as *la caseta i l'hortet*, became a key consumerist aspiration that spread to the working-class population in the second half of the twentieth century. The pattern of urban exodus on weekends, holidays, and during the month-long summer vacation that virtually all salaried workers were granted by law under the Franco regime, provided respite from the intensity of city life, an opportunity to socialize with relatives and friends, and the chance to eat local foods. Whether it was artisanal sausages and cured meats, particular varieties of cheese, wild mushrooms, small-batch-production olive oils and wines, or whatever the local agricultural complex produced, the revival of consumerism and the return of prosperity generated a frenzied commitment to enjoying foods that expressed what the French call *terroir*.[97] Spaniards from every region increasingly valued eating foods that were supposed to embody the land, the geography, the climate, and the essential spirit of a particular locality.

For the most part, the new pursuit of *terroir* had benign implications for Spanish nationalism. Stunted in terms of its nineteenth-century development, the fundamental symbols, definitions, and terms of Spanishness were left for twentieth-century intellectuals, artists, and political regimes to work out.[98] Growing Catalan and Basque nationalist movements, even those that were primarily federalist and nonseparatist, became viewed as dangerous threats to the integrity and well-being of the Spanish state. The Franco regime took extreme measures to address the problem, revoking Catalan political bodies and driving cultural institutions either underground or out of business altogether. The use of the Catalan language in politics, law, and education was forbidden. Symbols of Catalan nationalism, such as the flag, were outlawed, and at least initially, publication in Catalan was prohibited. When publishing in Catalan began again, it was censored, persecuted, and subjected to unprosecuted terrorist attacks. A great many Catalans took this hard, which led to the reaffirmation of a distinct identity and a deepened commitment to the defense of Catalan culture and language under siege.[99] One of the key sites for the zymotic growth of Catalan identity under Franco was the family dining room, where Catalan could be spoken freely, the regime could be openly challenged without fear, and women served food that they had purchased in public arenas where the use of the Catalan language could not be effectively prohibited.

Market vendors tended to be apolitical in word, though their promotion of particular foods that carried *terroir* meanings and of specific preparations cast as "traditional" and "typical" certainly carried nationalist connotations. Coinciding with a revival of interest in Catalan folklore in the 1960s, a new generation of cookbooks and food-related treatises began to appear that asserted Catalan culinary traditions in ways that were much more explicit than had been the case in the nineteenth and early twentieth centuries.[100] All these books emphasized Catalonia's difference and distinction from Spain while asserting a certain Euro-cosmopolitan aesthetic. As such, they reflected some loosening of the Franco regime's grip on expressions of Catalanism while also signaling the central place of food in the renewal and revival of consumer culture that coincided with economic recovery. The new discourses on what Catalan culinary traditions entailed meant that food consumption choices could be read by some as an expression of a specific Catalan identity. Choosing to shop in markets from familiar vendors who doled out culinary advice became viewed as more authentic than patronizing the newer self-service outlets where processed foods dominated the merchandise line and anonymity rather than community defined social relations between consumers and retailers. Arguably then, since the strength of consumer demand ultimately determines the success of any retail enterprise, the ability of Barcelona's market vendors to survive in the face of new forms of more highly capitalized competition in the sector must be attributed in part to the renewed enthusiasm for capturing the essence of Catalan culinary traditions at the dinner table.

Tourism played a major role in the recovery of the national economy but also in the mid-twentieth-century Catalan culinary renaissance. There are press accounts from the 1950s that report growing numbers of tourists visiting La Boqueria Market to gawk at the sights and sounds and to touch base with the popular culture that was so intensely on display therein.[101] The interest of at least some of these tourists in visiting La Boqueria was underpinned by the increasing attention paid to food and travel in United States magazines. Between 1951 and 1965, the editors of *House Beautiful* published a series of articles on the cuisine of the Western world. Compiled in a large-format and heavily illustrated cookbook with an abundance of color photos, *Cuisines of the Western World* appeared in 1965.[102] The chapter on Spain was entitled "Paella, Gazpacho and Spanish Omelets," with the subheading, "In the food of Spain, the two Indies meet for a culinary adventure."[103] Curiously, the recipe for Andalusian gazpacho called for the use of V-8 vegetable juice as a base, and the recipe for paella recommended Uncle Ben's converted long-grain rice. With no real attention to authenticity, readers were encouraged to re-invent Spanish food using ingredients that could be found in U.S. supermarkets. Other English-language books focusing specifically on Spain's culinary culture had already begun to appear. Elizabeth Cass's *Spanish Cooking* was published in London in 1957, and Betty Wason's *The Art of Spanish Cooking* came out in the U.S. in 1963.[104] Both authors cautioned against viewing Spain as one country in terms of its culinary traditions. Wason counted between six and eight culinary "countries" within Spain; Cass argued for thirteen distinct regional traditions.[105]

Attention to the particularities of a definable Catalan cuisine also appeared in

Time-Life's 1969 *The Cooking of Spain and Portugal,* written by Peter S. Feibleman as part of the Foods of the World series.[106] The chapter "Catalonia: All Things in Season" included a stunning two-page color photograph of a fruit stall in La Boqueria Market showing women vendors and customers going about their daily routines. In describing Catalonia, Feibleman wrote, "The Catalan tongue is not simply a dialect but a language in its own right, with its own grammar and syntax and its own literature—including, incidentally, the oldest printed cookbook in Spain and one of the oldest in the western world."[107] His description of the culinary tradition of Catalonia was cast in romantic essentialist terms that warmed the hearts of those living in the Franco-era Catalan diaspora. In Feibleman's estimation, "Perhaps the salient feature of the Catalonian character is a thrifty, piercing business sense, which has affected the region's modern kitchens as much as it once did her castles and palaces. Nothing is misused and nothing misplaced in a land where independence is all, wealth is independence, and plentiful good food symbolizes wealth."[108] Through these sorts of publications, well-informed tourists were guided into thinking of Spain's culinary tradition in *patria chica* terms. With respect to Catalonia, the link between food and aspirations for political independence could not have been more explicitly drawn.

Initially though, it was not Barcelona to which tourists flocked in the 1950s and 1960s. Rather, the most appealing Catalan destination for tourists pouring in from Europe and elsewhere was the Costa Brava, which extends from the town of Blanes sixty miles northeast of Barcelona to the French border. Alongside massive hotel-construction projects that increased the number of available rooms between 1961 and 1970 from 35,023 to 129,081, there was an explosion in the restaurant business catering to both tourists and residents of Catalonia.[109] New eateries opened in converted rural country houses and all along the coast in hotels and specialized restaurants alike. It was from within this burgeoning new industry that what Colman Andrews calls the "revivification of Catalan cuisine" took place beginning in the 1960s.[110] Andrews emphasizes the role played by innovative chefs catering to motorists and other tourists in the Empordà in creating a syncretic blend between "traditional Catalan country cooking, bourgeois Barcelona home cooking, . . . the imagination of the region's younger chefs," and "France's nouvelle cuisine, which crossed international borders in the 1970s faster that a jet-set smuggler."[111] This was the fertile ground upon which Ferran Adrià would make his mark at the acclaimed El Bulli, and from which the craze for so-called "molecular gastronomy" took root and radiated outward to reshape global tastes and culinary practices at the end of the twentieth century.[112]

Back in Barcelona, a new form of food pornography emerged in the early 1960s that was directly linked to the tourist trade but also to Catalan nationalism and to enduring connections with family members living abroad. The Barcelona firm Soberanas began to produce a new line of postcards that featured *platos típicos* (typical dishes). The color postcards came in standard four-by-six-inch size and in an enlarged 21.5-by-15-centimeter format. In addition to serving as ways for tourists to show friends and family back home what they were eating while vacationing in Spain, they were also designed for a domestic audience as a collectible series that numbered into the thousands. As such, they constitute an intriguing body of evidence documenting popular conceptions of taste at the time. The *platos típicos* line was part of Soberanas's larger Escudo de Oro (gold shield) brand of postcards. Many of the earlier postcards carried an embossed gold shield in the upper left-hand corner that innocuously featured a chef's toque situated above a crossed fork and spoon. Number 17 in an initial series of twenty-five depicted a simple salt cod dish with potatoes and boiled eggs in a terracotta cazuela, atop which sat a wooden fork meant to drive home the claim of authenticity. Pictured next to the dish is a glass of wine, a hunk of bread, an olive oil cruet, salt, a tomato, and some cloves of garlic that represent a monographic expression of the fusion of Columbian Exchange foods with older ingredients. On the reverse, the text, written in Spanish, read "Bacalao con Patatas a La Catalana," followed by a recipe that was clearly aimed at a domestic audience.

By 1964, the *platos típicos* postcards of Catalan foods had begun to feature a gold-embossed shield in the upper left-hand corner within which the Catalan flag appeared along with the Catalan spelling of *Catalunya* in place of the Spanish *Cataluña*. Number 653, for example, showed a plate of wild mushrooms, a sausage, a *porró* glass vessel filled with red wine, and the obligatory wooden fork and piece of round peasant bread. On the reverse, it simply read, now in Catalan rather than Spanish, "Rovellons a la brasa amb botifarra." These kinds of postcards were wildly popular among Spaniards more broadly. Some were distributed by Iberia Airlines in the early 1970s in a version that carried recipes in both Spanish and English. One of the Iberian Airlines *platos típicos* postcards that featured "Pig's Feet with Peas" had an embossed gold shield that said "España" and contained an image of the Spanish flag. It was sent by Carmen Casares to the younger of her two daughters, Manena Fayos, from Barajas Airport in Madrid as Carmen was preparing to board a flight to the United States so she could meet her new grandson, who had been born in West Virginia. Carmen wrote, "This postcard is just for you, with peas and all . . . be good, don't skip school, and do your homework." Another

Iberian Airlines *platos típicos* postcard carried the Catalan flag and offered a recipe for "Rabbit with 'Romesco' Sauce," which signaled official Spanish tolerance of the effort to assert Catalan particularity through culinary practice.

The two-volume *platos típicos* collection that I inherited from my father contains fifty-one Soberanas postcards, along with several dozen more produced by other firms. The most significant of all of these is Number G-45, a large-format card carrying the Catalan flag in a gold shield and showing a plate of *Seques amb butifarra,* the bean-and-sausage dish about which Josep Pla wrote in his magisterial 1971 *El Que Hem Menjat.* This card was sent from Barcelona by my grandfather, P. Martí Roig, to my family in West Virginia in the summer of 1964. Its Catalan nationalist harnessing of food as metaphor could not be clearer in that the image and the poem he wrote to us on the reverse built upon the discourse on Catalan cooking that was articulated by Josep Cunill de Bosch in 1923 and discussed above in chapter 1. My translation of the missive is as follows:

> This dish of dried beans and sausage
> Is a typical dish of the Catalans
> Covering the *porró* is a freedom cap
> That all men wore before
> The well-imbibed and fed Catalan
> Is a defender of Liberty
> The wine tends not to injure
> The pour from the Spout is thin
> To enable one to savor
> And, gulp . . . satisfied.
> *Visca* . . . . . . the . . . Liberty . . .
> Of the Catalans,
> And the wine of the Priorat
> All while dancing a Sardana

I was not old enough to read any language when this postcard arrived in our mail, and I did not discover it until I recently began to analyze my father's collection. But the message was one that was certainly impressed upon me—an Appalachian-Catalan hybrid growing up in the United States—from a young age. Hybridity has its advantages and its burdens. The stress of attempting to integrate oneself into two cultures has meant for many of us that we never feel fully legitimate in either. Great efforts were made on the part of my Catalan family to make sure that I turned out to be Catalan. Lesson number one was that being Catalan meant eating like a Catalan as much as speaking Catalan itself. This was a curriculum that I embraced with enthusiasm as a child, and though its constructed historical significance eventually became clear to me, it also helps to explain why I have dedicated myself to writing this book.

More significantly, then, the twentieth-century history of markets and food vendors in Barcelona illustrates how crises driven by war, revolution, dictatorship, and economic collapse ultimately reinforced consumerist attitudes toward food and food purchasing, transforming tastes in the long run through unanticipated manifestations. The ways in which women in Barcelona provisioned their households in the tumultuous first decades of the twentieth century, during the Spanish Civil War, and through the lean years of the 1940s remained closely tied to specific long-established rules operating in the marketplace for food. Women's acumen as food purchasers became all the more urgent within the context of rising prices, hoarding, shortages, and black market trade. Over the course of the longer food crises, women's skillful negotiation of the marketplace continued to be laden with symbolic cultural meanings that translated into personal assignations of status, power, and honor within extended families and neighborhood communities. With economic recovery in the late 1950s, food reemerged at the center of consumer culture and became an ever-more-important element of individual, family, and collective identity. These political dramas of the twentieth century did more to reenforce than to undermine the ongoing important role that market halls and market vendors played in urban life.

Memories of food scarcity for the vast majority of people made food shopping and consumption all the more solemn and celebratory acts in the 1960s and 1970s when the supply chains feeding the city's markets restored abundance. The wedding of Catalan nationalist identities with foodways and taste, hinted at since the 1830s, was consummated in reaction to the Franco regime's program of cultural repression. Shopping in Barcelona's markets, which were public spaces in which the use of Catalan was never effectively prohibited under Franco's rule, was easily in keeping with this new discourse in which food was increasingly politicized as part of the identity politics of opposition to the dictatorship.

The new chefs and food writers who rose to prominence in the 1970s had helped to impute meaning to the taste for Catalan foods such as *pa amb toma-quet* (bread rubbed with tomato) and *mongetes amb butifarra* (white beans with sausage), but they were not inventing a tradition from whole cloth. The foods to which they assigned Catalanist meaning had been prepared by both urban and rural women over the course of the twentieth-century food crisis and before. Though there were significant changes in diet—and even food-shopping habits with the proliferation of self-service shops and grocery stores in Barcelona after 1959—food had long formed part of collective memory. The new vogue for "typical" and "authentic" foods reinforced the value of shopping in the city's food markets, where the exchange of recipes between female vendors and consumers was both a long-established perk and a deeply embedded social habit.

So the revolution in Catalan taste did not begin with the wild experimentation of Ferran Adrià and the success of El Bulli, hailed by some during its lifetime as the best restaurant in the world. Nor was it a strictly top-down process imposed on the public by writers in search of folk traditions that might underpin political and cultural programs of opposition to the Franco regime. Some time ago, Lluís Casassas i Simó described "the weight of psychological factors", which continued to draw people to Catalan markets in the 1970s not just for economic reasons but also "to maintain social relations."[113] I am contending here that a key element of those relations was the informal discourse among women about cooking, which helped to define a new Catalan cuisine of plenty and sophistication in the second half of the twentieth century. In Barcelona's markets, older tastes were reinforced through long-standing bonds between vendors and their loyal clienteles, while newer food habits were promoted by the availability of a wider selection of ingredients, a great many of which involved claims of authenticity as part of a much more complicated understanding of what constituted Catalan *terroir*. In a culture under siege, a new enthusiasm for eating that accompanied economic recovery opened the way for redefinitions of the traditional. These shifts laid the groundwork for dramatic culinary innovation by the star chefs that paralleled the earlier achievements of Catalan artists such as Miró and Dalí. They also set the stage for the explosion in international attention and taste for Catalan cuisine at the turn of the twenty-first century.

## Conclusion

Barcelona distinguished itself from most other cities in Western Europe by up-
holding its commitment to a municipally owned and operated polynuclear system
of market halls over the full course of the twentieth century. When most urban
authorities definitively abandoned the market-hall paradigm of food retailing
after World War II, Barcelona doubled the number of such structures serving
its population. With the transition to democracy that followed Franco's death in
1975, municipal authorities recommitted themselves to the market-hall system
in Barcelona and began a thoroughgoing program of renovation. Thus the city's
markets remained vibrant institutions in the early twenty-first century despite
many of them undergoing dramatic physical and commercial reconfiguration.
Vendors, particularly through their market-based associations, came to exercise
greater agency than ever before in terms of management, but they also shared a
greater portion of the cost of operation. In recent years, the markets of Barcelona,
and particularly La Boqueria, have become the objects of tremendous laudatory
international attention. Still, all those involved in making the system work face
serious challenges related to intensifying competition, ongoing changes in food
purchasing and eating habits, and shifts in the structure of demand.

The survival of Barcelona's twentieth-century markets has been due to a series of factors. Municipal strategies to standardize and rationalize provisioning
provided stability and enhanced perceptions of fairness in the system for vendors
and consumers alike. The 1898 municipal market code served as a platform from
which the terms of trade in the city's markets could be renegotiated in subsequent
decades to the advantage of the municipal corporation but also sometimes in the
interests of vendors and their customers. Markets in Barcelona have survived in
part because their political utility as symbolic capital (supposedly confirming the
commitment of public authorities to the well-being of the urban population) has

been fodder too tempting for any twentieth-century municipal regime—irrespective of ideological orientation—to pass up. Ongoing municipal investment in the
physical infrastructure of the market halls during the 1960s and 1970s also prevented them from ever falling into a state of advanced disrepair that would have
predicated abandonment of the system.[1] That ownership and control of market
halls also served as a vital source of revenue from stall rents and from fines imposed
on vendors further enhanced the markets' appeal for municipal authorities. The
survival of the market hall-based system in Barcelona was underpinned as well by
the mutual dependency that developed between vendors and the regulating authorities who protected them from unbridled competition in the food-retailing sector.

But ultimately the success of Barcelona's markets has in very large part been
due to the tenacity of the vendor population itself, which individually and collectively exercised tremendous agency in the consolidation and profitability of their
small-scale firms. Vendors lobbied effectively for greater commercial rights in the
first decades of the twentieth century, and they assumed the cost of crucial stall
upgrades that improved both hygiene and aesthetics. In so doing, they responded
to the changing nature of demand for food that was shaped by consumerist, medical, and even political discourses. As a whole, vendors exhibited tremendous capacity and inclination for adaptation. Before and after the food crisis that gripped
Spain from 1936 to 1955, market stalls were dissemination points for new tastes,
new recipes, and new values, particularly those that went beyond satisfying the demands of the stomach and sought to please those of the palate as well. That market
shopping became increasingly associated with longings for what was "authentic"
and "typical" in the Catalan culinary repertoire at a time when the culture was
under siege and American-style supermarkets were encroaching only enhanced
their appeal for a large segment of the consuming public aligning itself against
Franco's rule. Commercial studies that characterized late-twentieth-century
market vendors as disinclined to embrace change run counter to the longer-term
evidence demonstrating their ongoing adaptation to shifting political, cultural,
technological, and commercial circumstances.[2]

Barcelona's polynuclear market-hall system structured the rhythms of everyday life in the twentieth-century city, particularly for women. Markets were key
places where neighbors met and talked and thus operated as ebullient centers
of neighborhood sociability that reduced levels of anonymity in the industrial
metropolis. Because markets were located in high-density residential districts according to the logic of food-shopping proximity, they drew mainly on foot traffic.
Even after electrical refrigerators and automobiles became objects of mass con-

sumption, the generation of women who had come of age in the dire conditions of the post–Civil War period continued its habit of shopping six days a week in their neighborhood markets, in part because of the social contact, consumerist satisfaction, and entertainment that were involved. The persistence of consumer demand thus constitutes another key factor in helping to explain the durability of Barcelona's markets as retail institutions.

Market halls operated as both commercial and social hubs in each of the neighborhoods they served. They were residential poles that attracted vendors seeking to live as close as possible to their places of work, and they functioned in symbiotic relationship to shops with horizontal integration and cooperation between them. Locating food shops in the environs of markets even supposed certain advantages for competitors seeking to siphon off clientele. Indeed, Barcelona's market halls acted as physical points of intersection for a series of formal and informal networks of varying character and dimension. They were spaces within which vendors formed bonds among themselves and from which endogamous marriage patterns and family-economy arrangements persisted. They were platforms from which associational networks emanated that conjoined vendor and shopkeeper interests in the mixed economy of food commerce. And they were axes around which municipal, provincial, and national food policies took shape.

The history of Barcelona's food markets speaks to larger issues. It illustrates surprising continuities in twentieth-century Spain that are otherwise obscured by the weight of dramatic regime change. The new political economy of food retailing codified in 1898 was a mixed economy that rejected mid-nineteenth-century liberalism and reestablished longer-term patterns of tight municipal control in the provisioning sector alongside privately operated for-profit enterprises. The Franco regime brought Spain's Republican and democratic experiment to an end, imposing in its place a single-party state that has been defined variously as totalitarian, authoritarian, as an expression of National-Catholicism, and by a range of other labels. Most histories of twentieth-century Spain have thus understandably emphasized rupture. The scholarship on the Franco dictatorship itself often focuses on ways in which the regime recast itself over time, marginalizing the fascist Falange Party and embracing technocratic central planning as of 1959. Some scholars, however, are now calling for greater attention to twentieth-century continuities. Pamela Beth Radcliff, for example, has cast the neighborhood and family associations flourishing in the last fifteen years of the Franco dictatorship as a sort of revival of the rich republicanist civil society that had characterized urban Spain in the first decades of the century.[3] This book offers a similar vision. While the changes brought on by the triumph of the Nationalists in 1939 were profound and devastating in many regards, we can see through the administration of Barcelona's public food-market system some highly significant institutional and policy continuities that involved less disruption than might otherwise be supposed. Recognizing the anomalous circumstances surrounding the extended economic crisis of the war and postwar periods, it remains evident that for most ordinary people, there were also tremendously important social and cultural continuities that the Franco regime either endorsed or was unable to eradicate. Female entrepreneurship in the markets, widespread reliance on family-economy arrangements, and the use of market space for neighborhood-based sociability were not disrupted by the imposition of the dictatorship. And with respect to Catalan identities, the regime's attempts at repression ultimately backfired. With the return of prosperity in the 1960s, the connection between "Catalanism" and ways of eating became all the more tightly drawn than they had been prior to the Civil War. For these and many other reasons, historians of Spain must reconsider how we slice up the chronological periods that comprised the twentieth century and re-envision where some heretofore unrecognized stretches of continuity might be located.

The history of Barcelona's market vendors also offers some further insight about Western Europe's social structure. Market vendors in Barcelona experienced upward social mobility in the early twentieth century and became part of the city's new lower middle class, which tended to own limited capital and employ little labor outside the family or household unit. The activities of market vendors' associations in the first decades of the century testify to the emergence of collective identities and to the pursuit of policies and regulations that would protect them from unbridled competition in the food-retailing sector. Like food shopkeepers, market vendors aligned themselves with the forces of order and at least tacitly endorsed the legitimacy of all the regimes under which they operated. They did not join broader working-class movements in the decades leading up to the war for the simple reason that they were vested in the concept of private property, albeit on a small scale, as well as in the pursuit of profit through commerce. Market-vendor associations' most enthusiastic political allegiances were left republican and Catalanist, though some individual vendors ultimately choose to support the Nationalists during the Civil War, usually as an expression of their support for the Church. Generally speaking, Barcelona's vendors stayed clear of antimodernist movements, most likely because they adapted both on their own and through associational pressure to the changing circumstances of the early-twentieth-century economic landscape. But under Franco's rule, they adjusted their strategies, in some instances incorporating key figures from earlier days into positions of influence within the vertical syndicalist system and advocating for a continuation of policies that limited the competition they faced. In this way, the political inclinations of the market vendors of Barcelona illustrate some of the key points made by Jonathan Morris about shopkeepers in late-nineteenth- and early-twentieth-century Milan. Morris asserts that Western Europe's lower middle class cannot be defined by one particular set of political identities, by a singular movement toward the right, or by any collective trajectory other than a response to local circumstances.[4]

Indeed, what we can discern about Barcelona's market vendors is that they lived and worked within a variegated and fluid social order that defies strict theoretical pigeon-holing. Without discounting the tremendous social polarization that pitted exploited workers against the owners of the means of production in the city, a significant portion of the population fell in between. Various occupational groups were neither proletarian nor properly bourgeois. Complicating matters further is the fact that the new lower middle class itself was far from homogeneous. Comprised initially of shopkeepers and artisans, it came to include telephone operators, department store clerks, minor bureaucrats, and technical personnel. Sharing an eagerness to define themselves as belonging to a place in the social order above that of the proletariat, the lower middle class had its own internal hierarchies and rankings. Market vendors, for example, could be looked down upon by artisans with small shops, even though they often had much in common in terms of the limits of their acquisitive powers.

Status insecurity does appear to have been endemic among Western Europe's lower-middle-class groups, and certainly the ways in which Barcelona's market women were cast in early-twentieth-century popular theater reflects such perceptions. Here, class and gender intersect once more. In magazines such as *La Dona Catalana*, we can see the unease with which men reacted to women in the labor force and a palpable eagerness to enforce prescriptive ideals mandating female specialization in the domestic arts.[5] Some lower-middle-class groups were not characterized by significant levels of married women's employment in the formal economy. But because the market vendor population included so many married women working outside their homes in spaces where they had direct contact with both the consuming public and municipal authorities, they were more apt to be stereotyped as picturesque aberrations, however sympathetically. Market women's own personal testimonies sometimes belie a subtext of concern with establishing and maintaining personal honor within their neighborhood communities and among their body of "parishioners" as an antidote to a sense of contested social and cultural identity.

This book has emphasized continuities in female entrepreneurship and family-economy arrangements in the markets of Barcelona. The evidence of widespread and ongoing female market-stall license acquisition serves as further proof that industrialization did not bring an end to women's work in the formal economy and that domestic ideologies—even under Franco-era National Catholicism—were prescriptive frameworks rather than rigid determinants of actual behavior or strategy. Women's work in the markets contributed to family well-being over the long run and to the viability of small-scale commerce in food even after the appearance of supermarkets and other more highly capitalized competitors in the sector. As such, gender patterns of work are inextricably linked to the vibrancy of market trade more generally, and to the upward social mobility of vendors more specifically. In the much more socially fluid and less class-conscious city that Barcelona has become today, operating a successful stall in any one of the markets is widely viewed as an indicator of commercial success and a privileged platform from which innovative vendors can tap into the profits of the food craze, tourist-based or otherwise, that defines the broader culinary culture of our times.

Comparing Barcelona's contemporary market system with that which took shape a century ago reveals a series of notable continuities. The municipal regimes that have ruled Barcelona since the establishment of Spain's constitutional democracy in 1978 have shown unwavering support for the polynuclear market-hall model of food retailing. The city's markets remain pivotal commercial anchors but also act as platforms from which the municipality has staged an unending series of promotional campaigns. Though in 1989 the municipal administration of Pasqual Maragall undertook an anti-*minifundista* campaign with the goal of modernizing Barcelona's food-retailing infrastructure, the city's rhetorical commitment to the markets remained deep and its use of gendered imagery in association with provisioning was as evocative as it had been in the Market Queen Cavalcade of 1930. Not only did authorities in 1989 host a highly publicized visit by the reigning Miss World—Linda Petursdottir of Iceland—to three of the city's market halls to promote the increased consumption of salt cod, the city also crowned, with much fanfare, a new Queen of the Markets. Rather than a virginal young woman dressed in white, this time it was the aging character actress Mari Santpere, who received the honor and a host of ceremonial duties along with it. Known for her comedic talents and her charisma, Mari Santpere's image was linked to the reputed flamboyance of the mature and successful market woman and to the theatrics that were associated with market trade. Her reign was commemorated by the baptism of a new fiberglass and polyester *geganta*[6] in her image, measuring 2.6 meters in height. Though Santpere died just three years later, her likeness lived on as a symbol of the female food vendor and of the consolidation of her social and economic position within the urban polity. The markets of Barcelona survived over the course of the twentieth century. So too did the civic pageantry that publicly projected the internal structuring role of women within the markets' social world of food retailing.[7]

But there were also very significant changes. The first and most obvious of these has to do with the role of Mercabarna, which is the limited liability corporation that administers the food unit of Barcelona's Zona Franca wholesale district. Between 1971 and 1984, Mercabarna helped to engineer the relocation of Barcelona's wholesale markets and its Escorxador slaughterhouse. El Born, the Central Fish Market, and the Central Flower Market all moved out of the center of the city to the Zona Franca in the last third of the twentieth century. Thereafter, Mercabarna expanded dramatically to encompass ninety square hectares of wholesale and warehousing space, which currently serve as the source of fresh foodstuffs for some ten million consumers in northeastern Spain, southern France, northern Italy, and the Balearic Islands. Employing 25,000 people and serving as a distribution point for over eight hundred food companies, Mercabarna's location near the port and south of the Mountain of Montjuïc facilitates transport connections by air, road, rail, and sea while also introducing new logistical challenges to individual market vendors. Mercabarna's very existence has altered the nature of retail vendors' social relations with suppliers. Travel to and from Mercabarna involves greater time and expense than did daily trips to El Born and other wholesale centers inside the city. As a consequence, Barcelona's late-twentieth- and early-twenty-first-century market vendors have seen increased costs associated with stocking their stalls, or have relied more extensively on intermediaries to deliver supplies. While there is no question that Mercabarna is a model of industrial efficiency and corporate social responsibility, its development and operation has lengthened rather than shortened the food chain "from farm gate to table" in many if not most instances. Producer-vendors, though highly sought after by the most select consumers and chefs, are very much an exception in Barcelona's early-twenty-first-century markets.

The second fundamental change in Barcelona's contemporary market system in comparison with that of a century ago is in levels of capitalization for retail vendors. In the early 1980s, various interest groups within the newly restored democratic municipal government undertook the development of a comprehensive plan to revitalize the city's market halls in the wake of the prolonged economic crisis of the 1970s and the inherited deficits from the Franco era.[8] The endeavor was spurred by the proliferation of galerías comerciales and the growing incidence of private real-estate speculation channeling through their construction in places that drew customers away from fully functioning public market halls located nearby. When in 1985 the City of Barcelona's Special Plan for Commercial Alimentary Facilities was promulgated (known by its Catalan acronym PECAB), it took dead aim at retail minifundismo. The "problems" of too many firms per head and the remarkably small average surface area per firm in the food-retailing sector were identified as the supposed obstacles to curbing inflation and modernizing what authorities cast as a provisioning system lagging behind cities such as Paris in the march toward modernity.[9] A key part of the proposed solution was to dramatically thin out the population of market vendors by cajoling, convincing, or otherwise compelling a large proportion of the smallest vendors to give up their stalls.

In 1992, Barcelona's city council created the IMMB (Institut Municipal de Mercats de Barcelona) as a new autonomous municipal body to administer the market halls. Since then, the IMMB has implemented policies designed to carry out the fundamental visions of the PECAB. They have renovated markets, dramatically reducing the number of stalls but increasing their physical dimensions and the level of investment in them, and thus reversed the old policies of keeping market-stall businesses small. Article 32 of Barcelona's current market code holds that no individual can hold title to more than half of the stalls in a given market. The previous ordinances had strictly limited the number of stall permits that individuals could hold to two, though there were, as we have seen, ways to work around this rule that involved marriage and kinship. Still, firm concentration, which had long been legally blocked, has become a measure of market success, even a necessity, given the elevated costs that vendors now have to incur. Article 41 of the current code stipulates that when markets are renovated, vendors have the right to occupy a stall in the transformed structure but only after paying a proportional share of the construction costs. Article 42 requires that all vendors belong to market-based associations that exercise a significant voice in management and administration but are also held responsible for contributing economically to cover all their market's expenses, including the routine cleaning and security costs of the structures in which they work. In other words, Barcelona's markets are no longer viable venues for marginal small-family firms. Those that have survived are more heavily capitalized and embrace modern business principles and accounting practices.

The renovated market halls of the city, which include La Concepció, Santa Caterina, La Barceloneta, and La Llibertat, involve dramatic commercial and aesthetic reconfiguration. Public parking, loading and unloading facilities, and garbage collection are built beneath the markets' main floors. In addition to extending hours of operation, the IMMB has established a newly calculated commercial mix of stall specializations in each renovated structure and allocated at least some portion of the space for in-house supermarkets operated by Caprabo, Mercadona, Carrefour, and other large-scale, heavily capitalized chains. In some instances, the inclusion of supermarkets has aroused vendors' ire. Initially, the supermarkets were limited to selling pre-packaged and dry goods, beverages, and cleaning fluids so that their product lines would not replicate what the vendors had for sale. More recently, arrangements have broadened what the "supermarkets in the market halls" have on offer. Where preserving the architectural heritage embodied in the market hall has been possible, the structures have been gutted to their bones and rebuilt according to the relevant codes. In other cases, artists and architects of great renown have been commissioned to reconceptualize market design and create a new generation of food-retailing monuments, as in the case of Enric Miralles's and Benedetta Tagliabue's collaboration with Toni Comella in the redesign of Santa Caterina, or MiAS Arquitectes' reconceptualization of the Barceloneta structure. The endeavors of the IMMB have produced spectacular results, though they have not achieved the PECAB's aim of reducing the price of food. Nostalgic yearnings for the less-upscale markets of the past also remain a common current among some portion of the neighborhoods' clientele.

Even though change has been a significant current, the PECAB and the IMMB both embraced tradition in certain respects. The market halls continue to be envisioned as anchors within a clustering of neighborhood-based food-retailing firms in keeping with the polynuclear model. Certain underserved areas, such as Fort Pienc, have been designated for the construction of new markets or for the development of other food-retailing outlets. When the Fort Pienc market hall opened its doors in 2003, it featured fourteen stalls and an in-house Mercadona supermarket for greater ease of consumer "one-stop shopping." The Fort Pienc market complex also included a 150-bed retirement home, a 200-bed student residence hall, a day-care facility, and a neighborhood civic center. Here we see a clear case in which the IMMB's innovations pay homage to the past not only in adhering to the logic of food-shopping proximity but also in valuing the social importance of markets as justification for investment in urban renovation and development. Perhaps most obviously, there are conclusions that can be drawn from this book that have contemporary significance in the quest to build a more livable city. Public markets, where effectively managed and appropriately located in high-density residential areas, can contribute to public well-being and operate, as Cerdà long ago envisioned, as anchors in a larger system of urban social services.

According to the IMMB, Barcelona's markets are currently visited by 65 million people each year and have an annual economic impact of between 950 million and 1.1 billion euros. The fact that there is much at stake in Barcelona's markets should elude no one. While their impact is greatest in terms of the everyday lives of their regular shoppers, they have become intimately enmeshed with the city's international fame as a destination for foodies. In the last decades of the twentieth century, Barcelona became a culinary mecca, and the city's gastronomy began to rival its architectural patrimony for the attention of tourists and permanent residents alike. Yet the renowned Ferran Adrià and his Michelin star-wielding chef counterparts represented only one element of a phenomenon that extended beyond the emergence of wildly innovative preparations based on what many refer to as the new "molecular gastronomy." The haute-cuisine food craze gripping Catalonia also had its defenders of "authenticity," most notably in the person of the late chef Santi Santamaria, who famously accused Adrià of failing to value what was "traditional" and purportedly more healthful in the Catalan culinary repertoire.[10] Erupting as front-page news in the summer of 2008, the dispute between Adrià and Santamaria lasted for months and was dubbed a "gastromedia soap opera."[11] Ultimately, even Spanish prime minister José Luis Zapatero "had to intervene in the ongoing debate."[12] One thing united both camps, however, and that was that food provenance mattered vitally. Even more broadly across the social spectrum, it was understood that skill in finding the highest-quality foods constituted a key marker not just of social status, but of personal integrity and competence as well. In early-twenty-first-century Barcelona, sybarites and ordinary consumers alike agree that the public market halls remain the best source of the freshest and most exquisite ingredients to be had in the city. While there were chefs and restaurateurs who championed the merits of a variety of markets, none bore as close a relationship to the city's culinary fortunes as La Boqueria.

A must-see along Las Ramblas, La Boqueria is Barcelona's most famous and most lauded market.[13] It features over 250 stalls that attract customers, chefs, and gourmands from around the globe. Tens of thousands of tourists visit La Boqueria each day to photograph its colorful displays, to sample exotic fruits, and to try to get a seat at one of its sublime eateries. The best-known of them all is the Bar Pinotxo, where the brother and sister duo of Joan and Maria Bayen built a small family firm with a global reputation and a customer base attracted as much by the siblings' theatrics as by the delectable dishes whose preparation for years was under the charge of Maria's late son, chef Albert Asín. Another market bar that has achieved international acclaim for its haute cuisine is El Quim de la Boqueria, where eggs accompanied by a range of exquisite components such as baby squid or carmelized foie gras are among the signature dishes. Listed in *Where Chefs Eat*, Quim Márquez opened a branch of his eatery called Quemo in Hong Kong in 2013.[14] In fact, La Boqueria has long operated as a platform from which Catalan culinary innovation has been launched. From the early 1960s and until his suicide in the market in 1987, La Boqueria was the home away from home and daily haunt of the "dandy" chef, the "poet of the ovens," Ramon Cabau Gausch.[15] Though Cabau's formal training was in pharmacy and law, he married a restaurateur's daughter and devoted his professional life to elaborating on "traditional" Catalan cuisine at his famous eatery, the Agut d'Avignon. His success can be measured in the fact that he is considered to have laid the groundwork on which Ferran Adrià established the new Catalan cuisine. Recently, the president of La Boqueria's vendor association, Salvador Capdevila i Nogué, who might be termed a King of the Market in his own right, spoke to me about Cabau. He told me that he was a beloved figure at La Boqueria and is credited with encouraging vendors to offer exotic varieties of foods and to maintain the highest standards of quality and freshness. "The new cooking started with Ramon Cabau," President Capdevila explained. Why Cabau chose to kill himself remains a mystery, at least to the public. Where and how he chose to die seems easier to comprehend. On the morning of March 31, 1987, he made his usual rounds through La Boqueria, passed out flowers to his favorite vendors, stopped by the Bar Pinotxo for a last coffee, and then, in the rear of the market, he downed a cup of water laced with cyanide before falling to the ground. A quarter-century later, the pathos cast by Cabau's suicide can still be palpably felt in the cavernous space that is La Boqueria, and the impact that he had in propelling the market's transformation into a cathedral of gastronomy remains vividly on display.

La Boqueria is a market unlike any other in the city, perhaps the world. As such, it generates all manner of debate. On most days, about half of those entering the market are tourists, many of whom only purchase a fruit-juice drink, if anything at all. On Saturdays, the bulk of La Boqueria's customers are residents of Barcelona in search of all manner of food. La Boqueria has not been reconfigured to include a supermarket, though subterranean work has expanded parking and modernized other infrastructural elements. Most notably, its administrative offices have been remodeled to include significant space for its powerful vendor association (officially known as the Associació de Comerciants de la Boqueria) and a separate floor with a culinary classroom wherein the curriculum features "simple or sophisticated" foods based on "culinary tradition and innovation." In a nutshell, these words sum up what not only La Boqueria but the rest of Barcelona's markets have to offer. Whether one appreciates or takes issue with the dramatic remodelizations that have been completed or are in progress, whether the tourists that clog the aisles of La Boqueria are cast as an annoyance or as a commercial boon, Barcelona's markets and the population of vendors working in them must be recognized as remarkably adaptable to changes in the nature and structure of demand. The current efforts to lure in a younger customer base, to offer more prepared foods for take-home customers, and to cater to the sophisticated tastes of the early-twenty-first-century consumer are expressions of a much longer tradition of adjustment to changing economic, political, social, and cultural contexts.

# Notes

*Abbreviations used in notes:*

| | |
|---|---|
| ACA | Arxiu de la Corona d'Aragó, Secció Hisenda |
| AGCB | Arxiu del Gremi d'Empresaris Carnissers i Xarcuters de Barcelona i Provincía |
| AHCB | Arxiu Històric de la Ciutat de Barcelona |
| AHCOCINB | Arxiu Històric Cambra Oficial de Comerç, Indústria i Navegació de Barcelona |
| AMAB | Arxiu Municipal Administratiu de Barcelona |
| ARSAM | Administrative Records Sant Antoni Market, Barcelona |
| BC | Biblioteca de Catalunya |
| CDMAE | Institut del Teatre, Centre de Documentació i Museu de les Arts Escèniques |
| DPAMAB | Deposit Pre-artxivatge del Arxiu Municipal Administratiu de Barcelona |
| IMMB | Institut Municipal de Mercats de Barcelona |

## PREFACE

1. "Més mercats que a cap ciutat europea," *Diario de Barcelona*, Fascicle 28, October 16, 1988. Still, as Manuel Guàrdia and José Luis Oyón point out, Barcelona fell short of long-established ideals in terms of the optimal number of food markets. The *Enciclopedia Espasa* in the 1920s adverted that there should be one market hall for every 20,000 to 30,000 urban inhabitants and that as cities grew, new markets should be added. See "Introducció: Els mercats com a creadors de ciutat," in Manuel Guàrdia and José Luis Oyón, eds., *Fer ciutat a través dels mercats: Europa, segles XIX i XX* (Barcelona: Museu d'Història de Barcelona, 2010), 54.

2. Antonio Jimenéz-Landi, *A First Look at a City in Spain* (New York: Franklin Watts, 1961), 13.

3. The Institución Libre de Enseñanza, which had a profound impact over the long run on Spanish intellectual life, was established in Madrid in 1876 by Francisco Giner de los Rios and others, as a pedagogical experiment that built upon the philosophical premises of Christian Friedrich Krause.

4. Joan Busquets, *Barcelona: The Urban Evolution of a Compact City* (Rovereto: Nicoldi and Presidents and Fellows of Harvard College, 2005).

5. Guàrdia and Oyón, "Introducció," 54.

6. José Luis Oyón, *La quiebra de la ciudad popular: Espacio urbano, inmigración y anarquismo en la Barcelona de entreguerras, 1914–1936* (Barcelona: Edicions del Serbal, 2008), 329.

CHAPTER 1. THERE WERE ROYALS AMONG THEM: A 1930 MARKET QUEEN VIGNETTE

1. Oral history interview with Francesca Orriols Palmada and Lluís Casals, conducted by the author, May 18, 1992.

2. All of the fifteen municipally owned and operated retail market halls elected Queens in 1930, but so too did three open-air markets (Porvenir—popularly known as El Ninot—whose market hall was not inaugurated until 1933; Horta, whose hall was inaugurated in 1951; and Sagrera, whose hall was inaugurated in 1955). Two wholesale markets (the Central Fish Market and El Born Central Fruit and Vegetable Market) also elected Queens that year, as did the Encants Market, which sold used nonalimentary goods.

3. Oral history interview with Maria Cararach Vernet, conducted by the author, May 5, 1992.

4. There had, in fact, been periodic Market Queen elections before and after 1930, but none with the same significance over the long term to the memories of vendors at Santa Caterina. It should be noted that there are wider idiomatic meanings to the term "la reina del mercat" that include references to the dominant entity in a commercial market and to the alpha female in a given context.

5. Barcelona was not alone in establishing such celebrations. Valencia, Seville, and other Spanish cities also held Market Queen pageants in the early twentieth century. Cádiz celebrated a Fiesta de Los Mercados in 1961 with the election of "Miss Mercados." See *ABC Edición de Andalucía,* November 1, 1961, 32. The practice extended as well to some cities in Latin America. The popularity of Market Queen pageants is also evidenced through the theater. Guillerm Perin and Miguel de Palacio's 1909 *La Reina de los Mercados* was staged in Madrid but set in Paris in 1797. The play tells the story of Sucette, who is crowned queen of the markets of that city. She rides in an elaborate cavalcade that culminates in a grand banquet and ball at the Hotel de Ville, but she anguishes over the expectation that she will marry for money and influence rather than love. CDMAE, registre 13.678.

6. ARSAM, documents dated 6 April 1895, 12 June 1895, 28 March 1896, 24 March 1902, 1 April 1902, 21 March 1904, 10 March 1905, 2 April 1906, 13 December 1906, 20 December 1911, 19 December 1913, and 27 May 1929.

7. See *Diario de Barcelona,* June 21, 1905, 7021, for scheduled military band performances in both Santa Caterina and La Concepció markets.

8. ARSAM, document dated 21 April 1910.

9. ARSAM, document dated 13 October 1910. The Treasury Commission demanded an accounting of expenditures from these two market directors as a consequence of the vendor petitions.

10. The film is also referenced in some sources as *Cabalgata de los Mercados en Barcelona.*

11. Testimony of Llúcia Pi Gelabert and Paquita Pi Gelabert from *El Meu Avi: Fructuós Gelabert. El Somni d'un Pioner* (Barcelona: TVC, 2003). Online video accessed December 9, 2013, http://www.tv3.cat/elmeuavi/2003/gelabert/capitulo.htm.

12. ARSAM, documents dated 29 November 1923, 3 July 1926, 11 October 1926, 3 May 1927, 25 May 1927, and 27 December 1927.

13. ARSAM, document dated 20 February 1930.

14. This is an example of the "double patriotism" that Michonneau discusses in regard to certain monuments in Barcelona. Stéphane Michonneau, *Barcelona: Memòria i Identitat: Monuments, Commemoracions i Mites,* trans. Rosa Martínez (Vic: Eumo, 2001).

15. The term *dictablanda* is a play on words: in contrast to *dictadura* (dictatorship), which literally means "hard rule," *dictablanda* literally means "soft rule."

16. Javier Tusell and Genoveva Queipo de Llano, "The Dictatorship of Primo de Rivera, 1923–1931," in José Alvarez Junco and Adrian Shubert, eds., *Spanish History since 1808* (London: Arnold, 2000), 218.

17. See Javier Tusell and Genoveva G. Quiepo de Llano, "La Invención de un Estilo: El Rey Viajero," in *Alfonso XIII: El Rey Polémico* (Madrid: Taurus, 2001), 137.

18. Joan Antoni de Güell i López, born in 1874, trained in law, served as mayor of Barcelona from 1930–31, went into exile during the Spanish Civil War, and died in Mallorca in 1958. *Diccionari Barcanova d'Història de Catalunya*, ed. Ramon Sòria i Ràfols (Barcelona: Barcanova, 1989).

19. *Anuario Estadístico de la Ciudad de Barcelona* (Barcelona: Henrich y Compañia, 1903–1921), *Año IV para 1905*, 305–19, and *Año IX para 1910*, 574–75. See also *Diario de Barcelona*, 1–6 June 1930, 21 May 1945, 4; and AHCB, "Festejos y Bailes: Las Reinas del Mercado," in *Barcelona Antigua y Moderna: El Mercado de La Boquería, 1840–1944. Recuerdos, Evocaciones, Perspectivas* (Barcelona: Publicidad Gabernet, 1944), 12–14.

20. Neither Kaplan nor Michonneau take up these rituals, though their frameworks for interpretation apply here easily. Temma Kaplan, *Red City Blue Period: Social Movements in Picasso's Barcelona* (Berkeley: University of California Press, 1992); and Michonneau, *Barcelona: Memòria i Identitat*.

21. *Barcelona Antigua y Moderna*, 12–14.

22. *Diario de Barcelona*, 1 June 1930, 55; 3 June 1930, 16.

23. Ibid., 1 June 1930, 55.

24. Ibid., 3 June 1930, 16.

25. *Barcelona Antigua y Moderna*, 13.

26. *Diario de Barcelona*, 3 June 1930, 16.

27. Francesca Orriols Palmada and Lluís Casals, interview, May 18, 1992.

28. *Diario de Barcelona*, 3 June 1930, 15.

29. Oral history interview with Semi Colominas Aluja, conducted by the author, May 11, 1992.

30. *Diario de Barcelona*, 1 June 1930, 5.

31. Roser Nicolau-Nos and Josep Pujol-Andreu, "Urbanization and Dietary Change in Mediterranean Europe: Barcelona, 1870–1935," in Peter J. Atkins, Peter Lummel, and Derek J. Oddy, eds., *Food and the City in Europe since 1800* (Aldershot, Eng.: Ashgate, 2007), 44.

32. It should be noted that as the second Count of Güell and son of the most important patron of Catalan modernist architecture, the mayor's support of the monarchy and its dictatorship positioned him awkwardly in relation to the growing Catalanist movement that increasingly cut across class divisions in the 1920s. Kaplan, *Red City, Blue Period*, 159–63.

33. Nicolau-Nos and Pujol-Andreu, "Urbanization and Dietary Change," 44. Long a staple of the diet, dried and salted fish were increasingly replaced by the consumption of fresh fish in the 1920s and 1930s. Changes in supply, technology, and taste between 1870 and 1935 redefined salt cod as the food of the poor. Municipal statistics show that Barcelona's salt cod prices per kilogram were approximately half those of pork, veal, and fresh fish in the summer of 1915. *Gaceta Municipal de Barcelona*, Año II 1915, No. 29, 21 July 1915, 18.

34. Pamela Beth Radcliff, "The Emerging Challenge of Mass Politics," in Alvarez Junco and Shubert, eds., *Spanish History since 1808*, 152.

35. Galvany and Sant Gervasi's joint market float was based on the Catalan playwright Angel Guimerà's iconic character "Manelic" as an allegory to the essentialist image of peasant dignity and loving Catalan husbandhood. La Llibertat Market's float, entitled "Fivaller Ante Fernando de Antequerra

Exigendose el Pago del Vertigal de Carne," evoked a symbol of Barcelona's defiance as a civic polity to feudal privilege. Sant Antoni Market's float was a tribute to the "Tambor del Bruch," the humble hero of Catalan resistance to Napoleon's forces of occupation. And La Concepció Market, most blatantly, constructed its float as a tribute to Wilfred the Hairy, legendary founder of the independent Catalan polity in the ninth century.

36. Felipe Fernández-Armesto holds that the revolution is an ongoing one, with modern trends as "legatees of a long tradition." *Near a Thousand Tables: A History of Food* (New York: Free Press, 2002), xiii, 54.

37. Nicolau-Nos and Pujol-Andreu characterize the 1870 to 1935 period in Barcelona as one in which "the consumption of animal protein was closely related in the public mind with health and bodily strength." "Urbanization and Dietary Change," 39.

38. Jordi-Joan Alsina i Canudas, *Gastronomia, Festes i Tradicions a Catalunya* (Barcelona: Morales i Torres Editores, 2007), 21–29.

39. Radcliff notes that the female consumer protests set off by turn-of-the-century bad harvests had "offered a specific gendered reading of the crisis, employing the powerful metaphor of the (male) government as failed breadwinner. Through this discourse, they exposed the shame of a government incapable of providing for its 'weaker' members and thereby questioned its masculine legitimacy to rule on its own paternalistic terms." "The Emerging Challenge of Mass Politics," 153.

40. Jordi Maluquer de Motes, "Consumo y Precios," in *Estadísticas Históricas de España*, ed. Albert Carreras and Xavier Tafunell (2nd ed., rev.; Bilbao: Fundaciòn BBVA, 2005), 2:1257. The figures for Spain as a whole that Maluquer de Motes offers show that in 1830 69.4 percent of family income was devoted to food, with a gradual decline to 65.7 percent in 1900 and 60.1 percent in 1939. Nicolau-Nos and Pujol-Andreu, in treating Barcelona specifically, cite a 1933 study by the Institut d'Investigacions Econòmiques that considered "families with incomes of less than 500 *pesetes* a month, the largest group in the city," for whom 65 percent of income still went to food. See "Urbanization and Dietary Change," 42.

41. Carlos Barciela, Jesús Giráldez, Grupo de Estudios de Historia Rural, and Inmaculada López, in "Sector Agrario y Pesca," in *Estadísticas Históricas de España*, 1: 260–62, note that the growth of larger concerns in the fishing sector accompanied the decline of traditional fishing operations from the late nineteenth century onward.

42. La Barceloneta Market's entry was entitled "Una Barca"; Sagrera-Horta's was simply "Barca"; and the Mercado Central de Pescado offered up its elaborate and multifaceted procession described above, "Barca Catalana." *Diario de Barcelona*, 3 June 1930.

43. Generally speaking, female market vendors had long been the subject of some greater or lesser degree of cultural derision. We can see this in Quevado's novel *La Vida del Buscón*, in which female market vendors are cast as feisty and shameless in their battle with the rooster-king whose horse has stolen a cabbage. The vendors retaliated, and Quevado wrote that the market women "are always shameless" (*siempre son desvergonzadas*). Francisco Quevado, *La Vida del Buscón Llamado don Pablos*, ed. Carolyn Nadeau (Newark, Del.: European Masterpieces, 2007), 8. The stereotype of the unseemly female market vendor has persisted through time and cut across cultural and national boundaries. Victoria E. Thompson argues that the new market halls of mid-nineteenth-century Paris were partly designed to better control/contain the sexuality of female vendors. *The Virtuous Marketplace: Women and Men, Money and Politics in Paris, 1830–1870* (Baltimore: Johns Hopkins University Press, 2000),

and "Urban Renovation, Moral Regeneration: Domesticating the *Halles* in Second-Empire Paris," *French Historical Studies* 20, no. 1 (Winter 1997): 87–109. See also Linda J. Seligmann, who notes that in Peru "market women have the reputation of being sexually promiscuous, aggressive, and a social irritant," even though "they sometimes deliberately represent themselves as defying appropriate comportment." *Peruvian Street Lives: Culture, Power, and Economy among Market Women of Cuzco* (Urbana: University of Illinois Press, 2004), 15.

44. Jacqueline Lindenfeld, *Speech and Sociability in French Urban Marketplaces* (Amsterdam and Philadelphia: J. Benjamins Publishing Co., 1990).

45. Alfons Roure, *La Reina del Mercat: Sainet en tres actes* (Barcelona: La Escena Catalana, no. 220, Archivo Teatral Moderno, n.d.).

46. The model of identity that emphasizes contestation is well established in the literature on women's history in Spain and beyond. See Victoria Loreé Enders and Pamela Beth Radcliff, "General Introduction: Contesting Identities/Contesting Categories," in Victoria Loreé Enders and Pamela Beth Radcliff, eds., *Constructing Spanish Womanhood: Female Identity in Modern Spain* (Albany: State University of New York Press, 1999), 1.

47. Nash discusses the impact of biological essentialism in the discourse on women in the early twentieth century, noting that one significant long-term impact was legitimization of "a negative attitude towards women's right to employment in the labor market, even among the working classes." Mary Nash, "Un/Contested Identities: Motherhood, Sex Reform and the Modernization of Gender Identity in Early Twentieth-Century Spain," in Enders and Radcliff, eds., *Constructing Spanish Womanhood*, 28. See also Mary Nash, "Identidad de género, discurso de la domesticidad y la definición del trabajo de las mujeres de España del siglo XIX," in Georges Duby and Michelle Perrot, dirs., *Historia de las Mujueres en el Occidente* (Madrid: Taurus, 1993), vol. 4.

48. Ildefons Cerdà divided the working class (*la clase obrera*) into four categories: *oficiales, aprendices, peones,* and *ayudantes.* He placed all the market vendors in the city into the *peones* category. Ildefons Cerdá, *Teoría General de la Urbanización, Reforma y Ensanche de Barcelona*, vol. 2, *La Urbanización Considerada como un Hecho Concreto: Estadística Urbana de Barcelona* (1867; repr., Madrid: Instituto de Estudios Fiscales, 1968), 645.

49. It is not entirely clear whom he was counting in the ranks of the market vendors and whether he included the large numbers of peasant women selling food from ambulatory or fixed positions. He noted as well that many women, especially vegetable vendors, operated more than one stall, so the numbers appear inflated as a consequence. This comment suggests that he was counting licenses rather than individuals. Ibid., 627.

50. Àngels Solà, "Las Mujeres como productoras autónomas en el medio urbano (siglos XIV–XIX)," in Cristina Borderías, ed., *La Historia de las Mujeres: Perspectivas Actuales* (Barcelona: Asociación de Investigación en Historia de las Mujeres and Icaria Editorial, 2009), 251. See also Àngels Solà, "Las Mujeres y sus negocios en el medio urbano," in Isabel Morant, M. Ortega, A. Lavrin, and P. Pérez Cantó, eds., *Historia de las Mujeres en España y América Latina*, vol. 3, *Del Siglo XIX a los umbrales del XX* (Madrid: Ediciones Cátedra, 2006), 381–403.

51. There is considerable work on medieval widows running commercial establishments. See, for example, Pierre Bonnassie, *La Organización del Trabajo en Barcelona a Finales del Siglo XV* (Barcelona: CSIC, 1975); and Carme Batlle i Gallart, "Noticias Sobre la Mujer Catalana en el Mundo de los Negocios, s. XIII," in Ángela Muñoz Fernández and Cristina Segura, eds., *El Trabajo de las Mujeres*

*en la Edad Media Hispana* (Madrid: Asociación Cultural Al-Mudayna, 1988), 201–21. For the early modern period, see Marta Vicente i Valentín, "El Treball de la Dona dins els Gremis a la Barcelona del segle XVIII (una aproximació)," *Pedralbes: Revista d'Història Moderna* 8, no. 1 (1988): 267–76; Marta Vicente, "El Treball de les Dones en els Gremis de la Barcelona Moderna," *L'Avenç* 142 (1990): 36-40; and Marta Vicente, "Mujeres Artesanas en la Barcelona Moderna," in Isabel Pérez Molina et al., eds., *Las Mujeres en el Antiguo Régimen: Imagen y Realidad (S. XVI-XVIII)* (Barcelona: Icaria Editorial, 1994), 59–90. With respect to the nineteenth century, Juanjo Romero finds that women's independent ownership of commercial establishments was mainly as widows, though his work does not explicitly consider the food-retailing sector. Juanjo Romero Marín, "La Maestría Silenciosa: Maestras Artesanas en la Barcelona de la Primera Mitad del siglo XIX," *Arenal: Revista de Historia de las Mujeres* 4, no. 2 (1997): 275–94; Juanjo Romero Marín, "La Força d'una Cadena Descansa Sobre l'Anella més Dèbil: Mestresses Artesanes Barcelonines al segle XIX," in Ramon Grau, coord., *Barcelona Quaderns d'Història*, vol. 11, *La Ciutat i les Revolucions, 1808–1868. II. El Procés d'Industrialització* (Barcelona: Ajuntament de Barcelona, 2006), 93–100; and Juanjo Romero-Marín, "Artisan Women and Management in Nineteenth-Century Barcelona," in Robert Beachy, Béatrice Craig, and Alastair Owens, eds., *Women, Business and Finance in Nineteenth-Century Europe: Rethinking Separate Spheres* (Oxford: Berg, 2006), 81–95.

52. There is a growing body of scholarship on female entreprenurship, often related to the history of the family firm. See Barbara Curli, "Women Entrepreneurs and Italian Industrialization: Conjectures and Avenues for Research," *Enterprise and Society* 3, no. 4 (December 2002): 634–56; Lina Gálvez Muñoz and Paloma Fernández Pérez, "Female Entrepreneurship in Spain during the Nineteenth and Twentieth Centuries," *Business History Review* 81, no. 3 (2007): 495–515; Katrina Honeyman, "Doing Business with Gender: Service Industries in British Business History," *Business History Review* 81, no. 3 (2007): 471–93; Àngels Solà, "Las Mujeres y Sus Negocios"; Danielle van dern Heuvel, *Women and Entrepreneurship: Female Traders in the Northern Netherlands, c. 1580–1815* (Amsterdam: Aksant, 2007); Alison C. Kay, *The Foundations of Female Entrepreurship: Enterprise, Home and Household in London, c. 1800–1870* (New York: Routledge, 2009); Jill Christine Jepson, *Women's Concerns: Twelve Women Entrepreneurs of the Eighteenth and Nineteenth Centuries* (New York: Peter Lang, 2009); Galina Ulianova, *Female Entrepreneurs in Nineteenth-Century Russia* (London: Pickering & Chatto, 2009); Melanie Buddle, *The Business of Women: Marriage, Family, and Entrepreneurship in British Columbia, 1901–51* (Vancouver: University of British Columbia Press, 2010); Juliet E. K. Walker, *The History of Black Business in America: Capitalism, Race, Entrepreneurship* (Chapel Hill: University of North Carolina Press, 2011).

53. According to Béatrice Craig, women retailers in France had more generally tended to operate short-lived enterprises in the nineteenth century. See Béatrice Craig, "Petites Bourgeoises and Penny Capitalists: Women in Retail in the Lille Area during the Nineteenth Century," *Enterprise and Society* 2, no. 2 (2001): 198–224.

54. Àngels Solà argues for the urgency of studying autonomous female business ownership among married women in the nineteenth and twentieth century, a subject about which very little is known. "Las Mujeres como productoras autonomas," 254.

55. The king had survived multiple attempted regicides before the imposition of the dictatorship. The two most serious were in Paris in 1905 and in Madrid on his wedding day in 1906. Other less significant attacks took place in 1902, 1903, 1908, and 1913. Tusell and Queipo de Llano, *Alfonso XIII,*

158–60; Charles Petrie, *King Alfonso and His Age* (London: Chapman and Hall, 1963), 104.

56. *Diario de Barcelona*, 1 June 1930, 3.

57. Tusell and Queipo de Llano note that while the king's travels through Spain familarized him with regional and local authorities, they also afforded him some contact with the public. Tusell and Queipo de Llano, *Alfonso XIII*, 137.

58. National Archives and Records Administration, RG59 LM/3, Laughlin to State Department 7 June 1930, cited by Mercedes Cabrera, "El Rey Constitucional," in *Alfonso XIII: Un Político en el Trono*, ed. Javier Moreno Luzón (Madrid: Marcial Pons Historia, 2003), 83–110.

59. See especially Michonneau, *Barcelona: Memòria i identitat*.

60. Manuel Guàrdia and Albert García Espuche, "1888 y 1929: Dos Exposiciones, Una Sola Ambición," in Alejandro Sánchez, dir., *Barcelona, 1888–1929: Modernidad, Ambición y Conflictos de Una Ciudad Soñada* (Madrid: Alianza Editorial, 1992), 30.

61. Montserrat Miller, "Mercats noucentististes de Barcelona: Una interpretació dels seus orígens i significant cultural," *Revista de l'Alguer: Anuari Acadèmic de Cultura Catalana* 4 (December 1993): 93–106; Montserrat Miller, "Les Reines dels Mercats: Cultura municipal i gènere en el sector del comerç al detall d'aliments de Barcelona," in Guàrdia and Oyón, eds., *Fer ciutat a través dels mercats*, 299-328. See also in that volume, Estaban Castañer, "La difusió dels mercats de ferro a Espanya (1868–1936)," 233–62. Castañer shows how the monumentalization of markets was a broader pattern in Spain during this period.

62. Kaplan, *Red City, Blue Period*, 20.

63. Helen Tangires, *Public Markets and Civic Culture in Nineteenth-Century America* (Baltimore: Johns Hopkins University Press, 2003); Helen Tangires, "Lliçons d'Europa: La reforma del mercat public als Estats Units derant el Període Progressista, 1894–1922," in Guàrdia and Oyón, eds., *Fer ciutat a través dels mercats*. Tangires sees market halls in the United States, specifically in early-nineteenth-century Philadelphia and New York, as sites for political assertions about commitment to the "common good" and the "moral economy." For an exploration of the importance of the concept of the "common good" in sixteenth- and seventeenth-century Barcelona, see Luis Cortegeura's *For the Common Good: Popular Politics in Barcelona, 1580–1640* (Ithaca: Cornell University Press, 2002).

64. Michonneau argues that the incorporation of popular culture into civic rituals was a more common practice in the 1920s, though not one that effectively bound the subaltern classes of the city with the middle classes under the Primo de Rivera dictatorship. Michonneau, *Barcelona: Memòria i identitat*, 429.

65. Michonneau writes that Barcelona's municipal government acted as "a veritable memory parliament" and that it used the city's streets and public places after 1860 as a prescriptive text "to disseminate a new moral and political order." Ibid., 17–20.

66. *Diario de Barcelona*, 3 June 1930, 16.

67. Guàrdia and García Espuche, "1888 y 1929," 26.

68. See Michonneau's interpretation of the Poble Espanyol in *Barcelona: Memòria i identitat*, 286-90.

69. Temma Kaplan notes with respect to Barcelona in this period that "[w]hatever meaning church or civic authorities imputed to them, the ceremonies and procession could in fact mean anything and everything the audience desired." Kaplan, *Red City, Blue Period*, 9. I would submit that the same applies to the participants in these market rituals.

70. U.S. Department of Commerce and Labor, *Municipal Markets and Slaughterhouses in Europe*, Special Consular Reports, vol. 42, part 3 (Washington: Government Printing Office, 1910), 36.

71. Ibid., 36.

72. Ibid., 41.

73. Ibid., 65.

74. James Schmiechen and Kenneth Carls, *The British Market Hall: A Social and Architectural History* (New Haven: Yale University Press, 1999), 187.

75. Peter Atkins and Derek Oddy, "Food and the City," in Adkins, Lummel, and Oddy, eds., *Food and the City*, 3.

76. Paul M. Hohenberg and Lynn Hollen Lees, *The Making of Urban Europe, 1000–1994* (Rev. ed.; Cambridge: Harvard University Press, 1995), 227; Carreras and Tafunell, dirs., *Estadísticas Históricas*, vol. 1, Cuadro 6.5, 488.

77. Atkins and Oddy, "Food and the City," 1.

78. Josep Termes, *De la Revolució de Setembre a la fi de la Guerra Civil (1868–1939)*, vol. 6 of *Història de Catalunya*, dir. Pierre Vilar (Barcelona: Edicions 62, 1987), 97–98, 283.

79. Guàrdia and Oyón, eds., *Fer ciutat a través dels mercats*.

80. Colman Andrews, *Catalan Cuisine: Europe's Last Great Culinary Secret* (New York: Atheneum, 1988), 4.

81. Josep-Maria Garcia-Fuentes, Manel Guàrdia Bassals, and José Luis Oyón Bañales, "Reinventing Edible Identities: Catalan Cuisine and Barcelona's Market Halls," in Ronda L. Brulotte and Michael A. Di Giovine, eds., *Edible Identities: Food as Cultural Heritage* (Burlington, VT: Ashgate, 2014).

82. Anton Pujol, "Cosmopolitan Taste: The Morphing of the New Catalan Cuisine," *Food, Culture, & Society* 12, no. 4 (2009): 438.

83. Rudolf Grewe, Amadeu-J. Soberanas, and Joan Santanach i Suñol, *Llibre de Sent Soví. Llibre de totes maneres de potatges de menjar. Llibre de totes maneres de confits* (Barcelona: Barcino, 2004), 18. For an English-language treatment, see Joan Santanach i Suñol and Robin M. Vogelzang, *The Book of Sent Soví: Medieval Recipes from Catalonia* (Woodbridge, Suffolk: Tamesis; Barcelona: Barcino, 2008). An important interpretation of the recipes contained in the *Llibre de Sent Soví* and other medieval Catalan cookbooks can be found in Josep Lladonosa i Giró, *La Cuina Catalana: Més Antiga* (Barcelona: Editorial Empúries, 1998).

84. The *sofregit* in question here was one to which the tomatoes and peppers from the Columbian Exchange had not yet been added. Rather, it involved the sautéing of onions and various other ingredients in small amounts of oil or lard as the basis of a range of dishes. The *picada* involved the use of a mortar and pestle to combine elements that could thicken a subsequent preparation, most typically toasted bread, almonds, and/or cooked egg yolks, along with ingredients that imparted flavor, such as parsley, spices, or liver. The *picada* served the same purpose in Catalan cuisine as did the *roux* in French and other culinary traditions. Sent Sovi contained no recipes that included *roux*. Grewe et al., *Llibre de Sent Soví*, 24–26.

85. Mestre Robert, *Libre del Coch: Tractat de cuina medieval*, ed. Veronika Leimgruber (Barcelona: Curial Edicions Catalanes, 1996).

86. Ibid., 13.

87. Bruno Laurioux, "Les livres de cuisine italiens à la fin du XVe et au début du XVIe siècle: Expressions d'un syncrétisme culinaire méditerranéen," 73–88, in *La Mediterrània: Àrea de convergència*

*de sistemas alimentaris, segles V–XVIII* (Palma de Mallorca: Institut d'Estudis Baleàrics, 1996). On the Mediterranean diet, see Garcia-Fuentes et al., "Reinventing Edible Identities."

88. See Antoni Riera i Melis, *Senyors, Monjos i Pagesos: Alimentació i Identitat Social als segles XII i XIII* (Barcelona: Institut d'Estudis Catalans, 1997); Isidra Maranges, *La Cuina Catalana Medieval: Un Festí per als Sentits* (Barcelona: Rafael Dalmau Editor, 2006); Ramon Agustí Banegas López, "El consumo de la carne y las mentalidades en el mundo urbano de la baja edad media: Barcelona durante los siglos XIV y XV," *Ex novo: Revista d'Història i Humanitats* 5 (2008): 81–96. Available online at: http://www.raco.cat/index.php/ExNovo/article/viewArticle/144784/0, accessed 19 December 2013; *Actes. Col·loqui d'Història de l'Alimentació a la Corona d'Aragó*, vols. 1 and 2(1995). Available online at: http://dialnet.unirioja.es/servlet/libro?codigo=12528, accessed 19 December 2013.

89. María de los Ángeles Pérez Samper, "La alimentación catalana en el paso de la edad media a la edad moderna: La mesa capitular de Santa Ana de Barcelona," *Pedralbes* 17 (1997): 79–120.

90. Ibid., 87.

91. Ibid., 83.

92. Sydney Wilfred Mintz, *Sweetness and Power: The Place of Sugar in Modern History* (New York: Penguin Books, 1986); Elizabeth Abbott, *Sugar: A Bittersweet History* (London: Duckworth Overlook, 2009); Jack Turner, *Spice: The History of a Temptation* (New York: Knopf, 2004).

93. M. Mercè Gras Casanovas and M. Angels Pérez Samper, "Alimentació i Societat a la Catalunya Moderna," *Pedralbes* 31 (1991): 36–37.

94. María de los Ángeles Pérez Samper, "El pan nuestro de cada día en la Barcelona Moderna" *Pedralbes* 22 (2002), 29–72.

95. Andrews, *Catalan Cuisine*, 29.

96. *Allioli*, made originally without egg yolks, dates to the classical period, with forms appearing in a variety of Mediterranean cuisines. It was used as an accompaniment to grilled meat and fish, rice, vegetables, and sometimes used as a thickening agent in soups. See note 84 for a description of *picada*.

97. See Rafael d'Amat i de Cortada i de Santjust, Barò de Maldà, and Ramon Boixareu, *Calaix de Sastre*. 11 vols. (Barcelona: Curial Edicions Catalanes and Institut Municipal d'Història, 1987).

98. Joan de Déu Domènech, *Xocolata cada dia: A taule amb el baró de Maldà. Un estil de vida el segle XVIII* (Barcelona: Edicions la Magrana, 2004), 96.

99. Ibid., 220.

100. Benedict Anderson, *Imagined Communities: Reflections on the Origins and Spread of Nationalism* (2nd ed.; London: Verso, 2006).

101. Josep Cunill de Bosch, *La Cuina Catalana: Aplec de fórmules per a preparer tota mena de plats amb economia i facilitat, propi per a server a guia a les mestresses de casa i a totes les cuineres en general* (1923; repr., Barcelona: Parsifal Edicions, 1996), 9.

102. Ibid., 10.

103. John Brewer and Roy Porter, eds., *Consumption and the World of Goods* (New York: Routledge, 1993); Carole Shammas, *The Pre-Industrial Consumer in England and America* (Oxford: Oxford University Press, 1990); Peter N. Stearns, "Stages of Consumerism: Recent Work on the Issues of Periodization," *Journal of Modern History* 69, no. 1 (March 1997): 102–17.

104. Stearns, "Stages of Consumerism," 102. See also Simon Schama, *The Embarrassment of Riches: An Interpretation of Dutch Culture in the Golden Age* (New York: Vintage Books, 1987); Maxine

Berg and Helen Clifford, eds., *Consumers and Luxury: Consumer Culture in Europe, 1650–1850* (Manchester, Eng.: Manchester University Press, 1999); Daniel Roche, *A History of Everyday Things: The Birth of Consumption in France, 1600–1800* (Cambridge: Cambridge University Press, 2000); and Maxine Berg and Elizabeth Eger, *Luxury in the Eighteenth Century* (Basingstoke: Palgrave, 2002).

105. Gabriel Tortella, *The Development of Modern Spain: An Economic History of the Nineteenth and Twentieth Centuries* (Cambridge: Harvard University Press), 75.

106. Lídia Torra Fernández, "Las 'botigues de teles' de Barcelona: Aportación al estudio de la oferta de tejidos y el crédito al consumo (1650–1800)," *Revista de Historia Económica* (2nd Ser.), 21 (2003): 89–105; Lídia Torra Fernández, "Les xarxes de crèdit en el desevolupament comercial tèxtil a la Barcelona del set-cents," in Ramon Grau, coord., *El segle de l'absolutisme, 1714–1808* (Barcelona: Ajuntament de Barcelona, 2002), 221–34. See also Jaume Torras, Montserrat Duran, and Lídia Torra, "El Ajuar de la Novia: El Consumo de Tejidos en los Contratos Matrimoniales de una Localidad Catalana, 1600–1800," in *Consumo, Condiciones de Vida y Comercialización: Cataluña y Castilla, siglos XVII-XIX*, dir. J. Torras and B. Yun (Valladolid: Junta de Castilla y León, 1999), 61–70; and Lídia Torra Fernández, "Pautas del Consumo Textil en la Cataluña del Siglo XVIII: Una Visión a Partir de los Inventarios *Post-Mortem*," ibid., 89–106. Consumerism was not just taking shape in Catalonia and Castile. Recent studies document early modern shifts in attitudes toward material goods in Valencia, Seville, Murcia, León, and in other regions of Spain. See Daniel Muñoz Navarro, ed., *Comprar, Vender y Consumir: Nuevas aportaciones a la historia del consumo en la España moderna* (València: Publicaciones de la Universitat de València, 2011).

107. Marta V. Vicente, *Clothing the Spanish Empire: Families and the Calico Trade in the Early Modern Atlantic World* (New York: Palgrave Macmillan, 2006), 9–15.

108. Albert Garcia Espuche, "Introducció," 15, and "Una ciutat d'adroguers," 29, in Albert Garcia Espuche, Maria dels Àngels Pérez Samper, Sergio Solbes Ferri, Julia Beltrán de Heredia Bercero, and Núria Miró i Alaix, *Drogues, dolços i tabac: Barcelona 1700* (Barcelona: Ajuntament de Barcelona, Institut de Cultura, 2010); Antoni Riera i Melis, "Documentació notarial i història de l'alimentació," *Estudis d'Història Agrària* 13 (1999): 41–42; Gras Casanovas and Pérez Samper, "Alimentació i Societat a la Catalunya Moderna," 36–37.

109. Gras Casanovas and Pérez Samper, "Alimentació i Societat a la Catalunya Moderna," 37.

110. John Benson, *The Rise of Consumer Society in Britain, 1880–1980* (London: Longman, 1994), 4.

CHAPTER 2. CITY OF MARKETS: THE PRE-INDUSTRIAL BACKDROP

1. José Ramón Lasuén and Ezequiel Baró, "Sectors Quinaris: Motor de Desenvolupament de l'Àrea Metropolitana de Barcelona," in *Pla Estratègic Metropolità de Barcelona*. Available online at: http://www.bcn.es/plaestrategicdecultura/pdf/Sectors_Quinaris.pdf, accessed 20 December 2013. Lasuén's interpretation represents one of many critiques of the "Pirenne Thesis," which privileged network functions—that is, economic ties among cities—over central-place functions linking urban towns to their hinterlands (though Pirenne did not use network and central-place theory models or language in his work). See Henri Pirenne, *Medieval Cities: The Origins and Revival of Trade* (Princeton: Princeton University Press, 1980); and Hohenberg and Lees, *The Making of Urban Europe*. Lasuén's view draws on the work of Guy Bois, *The Transformation of the Year One Thousand: The Village of Lournand from Antiquity to Feudalism* (New York: St. Martin's Press, 1992), and others. This interpretation

of "common consumption" as the basis of urban growth has been recently emphasized by Manuel Guàrdia, José Luis Oyón, and Nadia Fava in their work on Barcelona's markets. See Manuel Guàrdia and José Lluis Oyón, "Los Mercados Públicos en la Ciudad Contempránea: El Caso de Barcelona," *Revista Bibliográfica de Geografía y Ciencias Sociales* 12, no. 744 (August 2007), available online at: http://www.ub.edu/geocrit/b3w-744.htm, accessed 20 December 2013; and Guàrdia and Oyón, eds., *Fer ciutat a través dels mercats,* 14.

2. Jaume Sobrequés Callicó, *Barcelona: Aproximació a Vint Segles d'Història* (Barcelona: La Busca, 1999), 15.

3. As quoted ibid., 18.

4. Ibid., 19; Guàrdia and Oyón, "Los Mercados Públicos en la Ciudad Contempránea."

5. Busquets, *Barcelona,* 23.

6. Sobrequés, *Barcelona,* 19.

7. Felipe Fernández-Armesto, *Barcelona: A Thousand Years of the City's Past* (Oxford: Oxford University Press, 1992), 5.

8. Ibid., 5.

9. Guàrdia and Oyón, "Los Mercados Públicos en la Ciudad Contemporánea." See also Fernand Braudel, *Civilization and Capitalism, 15th–18th Centuries,* trans. and revised by Siân Reynolds, 3 vols. (New York: Harper and Row, 1982).

10. Pere Ortí Gost, "Protegir i controlar el mercat alimentari: De la fiscalitat reial a la municipal (segles XII–XIV)," in Museu d'Història de Barcelona, Institut de Cultura, *Alimentar la ciutat: El proveïment de Barcelona del segle XIII al segle XX,* MUHBA Llibrets de Sala, 12 (Barcelona: Ajuntament de Barcelona, Institut Municipal de Mercats, Museu d'Història de Barcelona, Institut de Cultura, 2013), 12.

11. Pere Benito i Monclús, "Crisis de subsistènci i polítiques frumentàries," ibid., *10–11.*

12. "Each year, of the 100 jurors, five were elected to govern the city with the help of a standing council of thirty members, known as the *Trenenari.*" Of equal institutional importance was the founding of the Corts Catalanes in 1283, one of the earliest medieval parliaments in Europe, and the establishment of the Generalitat in 1287. Initially charged with collecting taxes, the Generalitat became the highest Catalan governmental body after 1640 and is the basis of Catalan autonomous rule today. Busquets, *Barcelona,* 40.

13. Ibid., 40.

14. Ortí Gost, "Protegir i controlar el mercat alimentari," 12.

15. Busquets, *Barcelona,* 63.

16. Ramon Grau, "Gènesi del mercat actual," in Xavier Olivé and Llorenç Torrado, eds., *Boqueria: 150 Aniversari* (Barcelona: Ajuntament de Barcelona, 1986), 5; Danielle Provansal and Melba Levick, *Els Mercats de Barcelona* (Barcelona: Ajuntament de Barcelona, 1992), 215.

17. Josep R. Llobera, *Foundations of National Identity: From Catalonia to Europe* (New York: Berghahn Books, 2004), 68.

18. James S. Amelang, *Honored Citizens of Barcelona: Patrician Culture and Class Relations, 1490–1714* (Princeton: Princeton University Press, 1986), 8–9.

19. William H. Robinson and Carmen Belen Lord, "Introduction," in William H. Robinson, Jordi Falgàs, and Carmen Belen Lord, eds., *Barcelona and Modernity: Picasso, Gaudí, Miró, Dalí* (New Haven: Cleveland Museum of Art in association with Yale University Press, 2006), 5.

20. Peter Spufford, *Power and Profit: The Merchant in Medieval Europe* (New York: Thames & Hudson, 2002), 380–85.

21. Juanjo Cáceres Nevot, "El proveïment de cereals," in Museu d'Història de Barcelona, *Alimentar la ciutat*, 18.

22. Llobera, *Foundations of National Identity,* 77; Busquets, *Barcelona,* 57–59.

23. Albert Garcia Espuche and Manuel Guàrdia i Bassols, *Espai i Societat a la Barcelona Pre-Industrial* (Barcelona: Edicions la Magrana and Institut Municipal d'Història, 1985), 21, 47.

24. James S. Amelang, trans. and ed., *A Journal of the Plague Year: The Diary of the Barcelona Tanner Miquel Parets, 1651* (New York: Oxford University Press, 1991), 31.

25. Ibid.

26. Amelang, *Honored Citizens,* passim.

27. E. P. Thompson, "The Moral Economy of the English Crowd in the Eighteenth Century," *Past and Present* 50 (February 1971): 76–136; Corteguera, *For the Common Good.*

28. J. H. Elliot, *The Revolt of the Catalans* (Cambridge: Cambridge University Press, 1963).

29. Amelang, ed., *Journal of the Plague Year,* 36.

30. Amelang, "People of the Ribera: Popular Politics and Neighborhood Identity in Early Modern Barcelona," in Barbara B. Diefindorf and Carla Hesse, eds., *Culture and Identity in Early Modern Europe (1500–1800): Essays in Honor of Natalie Zemon Davis* (Ann Arbor: University of Michigan Press, 1993), 127.

31. Amelang, ed., *Journal of the Plague Year,* 37.

32. Ibid., 126.

33. Ibid., 46–47.

34. Ibid., 18.

35. Luis R. Corteguera, "Pa i política a la Barcelona dels segles XVI i XVII," in Museu d'Història de Barcelona, *Alimentar la ciutat,* 16.

36. Pol Serrahima Balius, "Les interferències de la Catedral en el proveïment del pa," ibid., 22–23.

37. The term "neo-foral" in Spanish history refers to the legal accomodation between the Castilian Crown and specific historic kingdoms with longstanding charters and legal traditions, known as *fueros.* A number of regions, including the Basque Country, Catalonia, Aragon, and Valencia, were able to successfully insist upon the inviolability of their fundamental laws while recognizing the sovereignty of the Castilian monarch. The period of neo-foralism came to an abrupt end with the Bourbon accession to the throne.

38. "Centralising forces led to the suppression of teaching in Catalan in 1760." Busquets, *Barcelona,* 80.

39. Albert Cubeles i Bonet and Ferran Puig i Verdaguer, "Les Fortificacions de Barcelona," in Oriol Bohigas, Museu d'Història de la Ciutat de Barcelona, et al., *Abajo Las Muralles!!! 150 Anys de l'Enderroc de les Muralles de Barcelona* (Barcelona: Institut de Cultura, Museu d'Història de la Ciutat, 2004), 61.

40. Pierre Vilar, *Catalunya dins l'Espanya Moderna: Recerques sobre els fonaments econòmics de les estructures nacionals,* 4 vols. (Barcelona: Edicions 62, 1964–68).

41. Salvador Giner, *The Social Structure of Catalonia* (Sheffield: Anglo-Catalan Society Occasional Publications, 1984).

42. J. K. J. Thomson, *A Distinctive Industrialization: Cotton in Barcelona, 1728–1832* (Cambridge: Cambridge University Press, 1992).

43. Raymond Carr, *Spain 1808–1975*, 2nd ed. (Oxford: Clarendon Press, 1982), 35.

44. Ibid., 36.

45. Busquets, *Barcelona*, 83. These figures from the 1717 *cadastre* ordered by the Marquis de Campoflorida suggest a somewhat larger population than is otherwise estimated by some scholars, typically in the lower thirty thousands. See, for example, Ramon Grau i Fernández, "La Metamorfosi de la ciutat enmurallada: Barcelona, de Felip V a Ildefons Cerdà," in *Evolució Urbana de Catalunya*, ed. Miquel Tarradell et al. (Barcelona: Edicions de la Magrana, Institut Municipal de Barcelona, 1983), 67.

46. Busquets, *Barcelona*, 83.

47. Sobrequés, *Barcelona*, 61. Pierre Vilar, in *Catalunya dins l'Espanya Moderna*, gives slightly different figures, along with a discussion of competing sources. Gary Wray McDonogh, in *Good Families of Barcelona: A Social History of Power in the Industrial Era* (Princeton: Princeton University Press, 1986), follows Vilar's calculations, citing a figure of 34,005 in 1717 and 111,410 in 1787.

48. Martin Wynn, ed., *Planning and Urban Growth in Southern Europe* (London: Mansell Publishing Limited), 113.

49. Tortella, *The Development of Modern Spain*, 26.

50. The three main types of bread produced in the municipal bread ovens were *blanc, mitjà*, and *moré*. Irene Castells, "Els Rebomboris del Pa de 1789 a Barcelona," *Recerques: Història, Economia, Cultura* 1 (1970): 51–81, 54. See also Jaume Carrera Pujal, *Historia Política y Económica de Cataluña, Siglos XVI a XVIII*, 3 vols. (Barcelona: Bosch, 1946–47), 3:363; and Pérez Samper, "El Pan Nuestro de Cada Día," 29–72.

51. There were at least two municipal bread ovens operating in the city. The older facilities in the Customs House were supplemented by the *pastim* ovens located on Tallers Street in the Raval. The Tallers Street *pastim* was operated by municipal functionaries who alternated public with private production in response to periods of crises and plenty. E. Moreu-Rey, *Revolució a Barcelona el 1789* (Barcelona: Institut d'Estudis Catalans, 1967), 23.

52. Castells, "Els Rebomboris," 69.

53. Moreu-Rey, *Revolució a Barcelona*.

54. Castells, "Els Rebomboris," 69–70.

55. See Mercè Renom, *Conflictes socials i revolució: Sabadell, 1718–1823* (Vic: Eumo Editorial, 2009).

56. Castells, "Els Rebomboris," 71.

57. See Pierre Vilar, *La Catalogne dans l'Espagne Moderne: Recherches sur les Fondements Économiques des Structures Nationales* (Paris: S.E.V.P.E.N., 1962), 2:391.

58. Castells, "Els Rebomboris," 68. The literature on pre-industrial food rioting is extensive, and the potential for food riots to set off much larger uprisings is unquestionable. See E. P. Thompson, "The Moral Economy of the English Crowd in the Eighteenth Century," *Past and Present* 50 (February 1971): 76–136; E. P. Thompson, "The Moral Economy Reviewed," 259–351; Temma Kaplan, "Social Movements of Women and the Public Good," in Cristina Borderías and Mercè Renom, eds., *Dones en Moviment(s), segles XVIII–XXI* (Barcelona: Icaria Editorial, 2008), 19–47; and Mercè Renom, "Les Dones en els Moviments, Socials Urbans Preindustrials: Catalunya en el Context Europeu," ibid., 49–75.

59. E. J. Hobsbawm, *Primitive Rebels: Studies in Archaic Forms of Social Movement in the 19th and 20th Centuries* (New York: W. W. Norton, 1965).

60. Castells, "Els Rebomboris," 72.

61. Kaplan, "Social Movements of Women," 28–29.

62. Renom, "Les Dones en els Moviments," 66. Renom cites d'Amat i Cortada, *Calaix de Sastre*, 1:214.

63. Ibid., 56, 63.

64. As cited in Moreu-Rey, *Revolució a Barcelona*, 63.

65. Renom, "Les Dones en els Moviments," 67.

66. Ibid., 69.

67. Mercè Renom, "Les formes i el lèxic de la protesta a la fi de l'Antic Règim," *Recerques* 55 (2007): 5–33.

68. Renom, "Les Dones en els Moviments," 62.

69. Castells, "Els Rebomboris," 55.

70. Ibid., 75–76.

71. Marina López Guallar, "L'administració municipal del proveïment del pa (1714–1799)," in Museu d'Història de Barcelona, *Alimentar la ciutat*, 24-25.

72. Maria Rosa Bulto Blajot, "Dificultades para la abactecimiento de pan en el siglo XVIII," in Pedro Voltes Bou, ed., *Divulgación histórica de Barcelona*, vol. 12, *Los Abastecimientos de la ciudad: Oficios y Técnicas, Índice Analítico de los Tomos I-XII textos del Boletín Semanal radiado desde la emisora "Radio Barcelona" por el Instituto Municipal de Historia de la Ciudad*, 12 (Barcelona: Ayuntamiento de Barcelona, Instituto Municipal de Historia, 1965).

73. Braudel, *Civilization and Capitalism*. For Catalonia, see Carme Batlle i Gallart, *Fires i Mercats: Factors de Dinamisme Econòmic i Centres de Sociabilitat, segles XI a XV* (Barcelona: Rafael Dalmau, 2004); Lluís Casassas i Simó, *Fires i Mercats a Catalunya* (Barcelona: Edicions 62, 1978); and Albert Carreras and Lídia Torra Fernández, *Història Econòmica de les Fires a Catalunya* (Barcelona: Generalitat de Catalunya, Departament de Comerç, Turisme i Consum, 2004).

74. Jaime Sobrequés i Callicó, "El Precio y la Reglamentación de la Venta de Carne," in Voltes Bou, ed., *Divulgación histórica de Barcelona*, 12:31–33.

75. Ramon A. Banegas López, "Abastar de carn la ciutat," in Museu d'Història de Barcelona, *Alimentar la ciutat*, 30-31.

76. Provansal and Levick, *Els Mercats de Barcelona*, 215.

77. Amelang, "People of the Ribera," 126.

78. Banegas López, "Abastar de carn la ciutat," 30–31; Manuel Sánchez Martínez, "Vi i tavernes a la Barcelona medieval," in Museu d'Història de Barcelona, *Alimentar la ciutat*, 28-29.

79. Pere Verdés-Pijuan, "Fiscalitat i proveïment: Dues cares de la mateixa moneda?" ibid., 14-15.

80. Gaspar Feliu, "El pa de Barcelona al segle XVIII: Continuïtats i canvis," ibid., 26-27.

81. Ibid.

82. AGCB, *Ordenanzas de el Marqués de las Amarillas*, 30 June 1752. See articles 5, 14, 16, 17, 18, 22, 29, 32, 35, 36, and others.

83. There were numerous slaughterhouses inside the eighteenth-century walls. Nestor Luján, "Pequeña historia de los mercados barceloneses," *Especial para La Vanguardia*, 26 October 1983, 5.

84. Amelang, *Honored Citizens*, 7.

85. Grau, "Gènesi del mercat actual," 5; Provansal and Levick, *Els Mercats de Barcelona*, 215.

86. Wynn, ed., *Planning and Urban Growth*, 113; Amelang, in *Honored Citizens*, 11, notes that the city had earlier included "two separate guilds of *hortalans*, or urban gardeners."

87. Montserrat Rumbau, *La Barcelona de Principis del Segle XIX* (Barcelona: Tibidabo Edicions, 1993), 24.

88. "El Mercado de San Jose(1)," *Diario de Barcelona*, 9 December 1972, 21.

89. Provansal and Levick, *Els Mercats de Barcelona*, 215; Centre d'Estudis i Documentació Arxiu Històric del Raval, *El Mercat de la Boqueria* (Barcelona: Associació de Treballadors Autònoms de la Boqueria, 1982), 2.

90. López Guallar, "L'administració municipal del proveïment de pa," 24–25.

91. Busquets, *Barcelona*, 60.

92. Amelang, *Honored Citizens*, 6.

93. Amelang, "People of the Ribera," 130.

94. Busquets, *Barcelona*, 69. Busquets reminds us that Josep Lluís Sert referred to Las Ramblas as "the heart of the city" in his book *Can Our Cities Survive? An ABC of Urban Problems, Their Analysis, Their Solutions* (Cambridge: Harvard University Press, 1942).

95. Amelang, *Honored Citizens*, 195–210.

96. Ibid., 190–91; Elliot, *Revolt*, 322.

97. Amelang, *Honored Citizens*, 194.

98. As in Joan Fernández de Heredia's "La Vesita," as cited ibid., 195.

99. Joan Amades, *Històries i Llegendes de Barcelona: Passejada pels Carrers de la Ciutat Vella*, Vol. 1 (Barcelona: Edicions 62, 1984), 830.

100. "Curiosidades Históricas: Reglamento de la Pescadería, en el siglo XIV 'Die Jouis prima die Ffebruarii anno predicto [1375],'" reprinted in *Gaceta Municipal de Barcelona* 1 (1914): 12.

101. ACA, *Manual de la Taxa del Comercio*, 1717. Secció Hisenda, Sèrie Inv. 1, Sig. 3457.

102. Vicente, "Mujeres Artesanas en la Barcelona Moderna," 74–80.

103. AGCB, *Ordenanzas del Marqués de las Amarillas*. See articles 80, 83, and 85.

104. Ibid., article 28.

105. Vicente, "El Treball de la Dona," 267–76.

106. We know that women had long worked as *revendedoras* in Barcelona. In the 1717 *Manual de la Taxa de Comercio*, no fewer than 24 of the 221 members of the Confraternity of *Revendedors* were women. ACA, *Manual de la Taxa del Comercio*, 1717. Secció. Hisenda, Sèrie Inv. 1, Sig. 3457.

107. James Casey, *Early Modern Spain: A Social History* (New York: Routledge, 1999), 204–205.

CHAPTER 3. MIRRORS OF URBAN GROWTH: MARKET BUILDING
THROUGH THE LONG NINETEENTH CENTURY

1. Busquets, *Barcelona*, 88.

2. One of the grooms would become Fernando VII (r. 1813–1833), known as "El Deseado" during his captivity in France by Napoleon's forces, and infamous for restoring absolutism in Spain when he returned to take the throne.

3. Grau, "Gènesi del mercat actual," 23.

4. Provansal and Levick, *Els Mercats de Barcelona*, 41.

5. M. García Verano, *Historia del nacionalismo catalán* (Madrid: Editora Nacional, 1970), Appendix, as cited in Fernández-Armesto, *Barcelona*, 166.

6. For an account of this period, see Isabel Burdiel, "The Liberal Revolution, 1808–1843," in Alvarez Junco and Shubert, eds., *Spanish History since 1808*, 18–32.

7. *Pronunciamentos* became regular vehicles for Spanish nineteenth-century regime change. They were declarations made by military officers, usually from provincial garrisons, that when followed

more broadly resulted in the creation of a new government. For an insightful analysis, see Carolyn P. Boyd, "The Military and Politics, 1808–1874," ibid., 64–79.

8. Tortella, *The Development of Modern Spain*, 91.

9. Busquets, *Barcelona*, 101.

10. Busquets, *Barcelona*, 101. Busquets cites Richard Ford's *A Hand-book for Travellers in Spain* (London: John Murray, 1845). As David S. Landes notes, "Italy moved ahead faster" than Spain in terms of industrialization, though "a few centers of exceptional (if modest) adaptability escaped the general fate. In Spain, Catalonia diverged from the rest and as early as the eighteenth century began mechanizing textile manufacture." *The Wealth and Poverty of Nations: Why Some Are So Rich and Some So Poor* (New York: W. W. Norton, 1999), 250. See also Thomson, *A Distinctive Industrialization*.

11. Rosa M. Garcia i Domènech, "Mercats a Barcelona a la primera meitat del segle XIX," in *Actes del II Congrés d'Història del Pla de Barcelona*, vol. 1, *Història Urbana del Pla de Barcelona* (Barcelona: Ajuntament de Barcelona, 1985), 191.

12. Ibid., 191.

13. *Gaceta Municipal de Barcelona*, 26 April 1948, 253.

14. Maria Rosa Bultó Blajot, "El Consumo de la Carne en Barcelona," in Voltes Bou, ed., *Divulgación histórica de Barcelona*, 12:37.

15. "Nuestros Centros de Abastos: El Mercado del Borne," *Gaceta Municipal de Barcelona*, 14 November 1949, 1281; Garcia i Domènech, "Mercats a Barcelona," 192.

16. *Diario de Barcelona*, 5 October 1826.

17. Ibid., 10 October 1835.

18. Ibid., 10 October 1835.

19. Garcia i Domènech, "Mercats a Barcelona," 192.

20. *Gaceta Municipal de Barcelona*, 26 April 1948, 253.

21. Carr, *Spain 1808–1839*, 165; Grau, "Gènesi del mercat actual," 23–24. Grau asserts that the attack on Sant Josep had more to do with the popular desire to see a market project driven forward than it did with explicit anticlericalist sentiment.

22. Luján, "Pequeña historia de los mercados," 7. Vapor Bonaplata, the first steam-powered textile factory in Spain, was also the first target of Luddism.

23. Carr, *Spain, 1808–1975*, 166; Fernández-Armesto, *Barcelona*, 143.

24. Garcia i Domènech, "Mercats a Barcelona," 192.

25. Ibid., 195.

26. Grau, "Genesi del Mercat actual," 24. The market was named for and ultimately dedicated to San José, but the name never caught on in popular usage.

27. See William J. Callahan, "Church and State, 1808–1874," in Alvarez Junco and Shubert, eds., *Spanish History since 1808*, 49–63.

28. Garcia i Domènech, "Mercats a Barcelona," 191.

29. Grau, "Genesi del mercat actual," 24; Garcia i Domènech, "Mercats a Barcelona," 191. Among the architects for La Boqueria were José Massanés, Josep Mas i Vila, Josep Oriol Mestres, and Miquel Berge.

30. Garcia i Domènech, "Mercats a Barcelona," 196.

31. Ibid., 196.

32. José Artís Balaguer, "El Primitivo Mercado de Santa Catalina," in Voltes Bou, ed., *Divulgación histórica de* Barcelona, 12:84.

33. Garcia i Domènech, "Mercats a Barcelona," 197.

34. Ibid., 197.

35. Ibid., 198. On August 14, 1846, Sant Martí de Provençals producer-vendors petitioned to have the order rescinded mandating that they sell their produce at Santa Caterina Market, presumably because of the low level of trade taking place there. On June 23, 1848, Santa Caterina's own retail vendors complained to the city about the lack of fish stalls in the market. Later that summer, the municipality forced vendors at El Born and La Boqueria to draw lots to determine who would move to Santa Caterina: 50 vegetable and 30 fruit vendors from La Boqueria and 30 vegetable and 10 fruit vendors from El Born were moved to the new market. Then, on November 27 of that year, the fish deposit was moved from El Born into Santa Caterina as well. Thus we can see that Santa Caterina took some time to build its clientele. For 1865 figures, see Guàrdia, Oyón, and Fava, "El sistema de mercats de Barcelona," 265, in *Fer ciutat a través dels mercats: Europa, segles XIX i XX*, edited by Manuel Guàrdia and José Luis Oyón (Barcelona: Museu d'Història de la Ciutat de Barcelona, 2010).

36. Busquets, *Barcelona*, 108.

37. Guàrdia and Oyón, "Introducció," 24; Schmiechen and Carls, *The British Market Hall*, 146.

38. Schmiechen and Carls, *The British Market Hall*, 146.

39. Guàrdia and Oyón, "Introducció," 25, 27.

40. Garcia i Domènech, "Mercats a Barcelona," 194.

41. Ibid., 196; Guàrdia and Oyón, "Introducció," 27.

42. Garcia i Domènech, "Mercats a Barcelona," 196.

43. Guàrdia, Oyón, and Fava, "El sistema de mercats," 264.

44. Pierre Bourdieu, *Outline of a Theory of Practice*, trans. Richard Nice (Cambridge: Cambridge University Press, 1977).

45. "Nuestros Centros de Abastos: El Mercado de San José," *Gaceta Municipal de Barcelona*, 17 October 1949, 1218.

46. AHCB, *Barcelona Antigua y Moderna: El Mercado de la Boqueria, 1840–1944*; "Nuestros Centros de Abastos."

47. Carr, *Spain, 1808–1975*, 133, 229, 236, 247. Consumos were abolished in 1820 but reimposed with the restoration of absolutism in 1823. They were opposed by consumers and by municipal authorities, who viewed them as symbols of abusive centralized control by the state.

48. See Demetrio Castro, "The Left: From Liberalism to Democracy," in Alvarez Junco and Shubert, eds., *Spanish History since 1808*, 80–92.

49. Fernández-Armesto, *Barcelona*, 168.

50. Ibid., 168.

51. Gabriel Cardona, *A Golpes de Sable: Los Grandes Militares que Han Marcado la Historia de España* (Barcelona: Editorial Ariel, 2008), 160.

52. Francesc Curet, *La Jamància: Las Bullangues de 1842 i 1843* (Barcelona: Rafel Dalmau, 1990).

53. See Jesús Cruz, "The Moderate Ascendency, 1843–1868," in Alvarez Junco and Shubert, eds., *Spanish History since 1808*, 33–48.

54. *Revolución de Barcelona, Proclamando la Junta Central: Diario de los Acontecimientos de que ha sido teatro esta ciudad durante los meses Setiembre, Octubre, y Noviembre de 1843. Redactado por un testigo de vista* (Barcelona: Imprenta D. Manuel Saurí, 1844), 153. This source offers the verse in its orginal Catalan as follows: "A Cristina y Narvaez / y á tots los moderats / dintre de una paella / los freixirem plegats."

55. As cited in Josep Termes, *Anarquismo y Sindicalismo en España, 1864–1881* (Barcelona: Editorial Crítica, 2000), 392.

56. Guillem Martínez, *Barcelona Rebelde: Guía Historica de una Ciudad* (Barcelona: Debate Editorial and Random House Mondadori, 2009), 189.

57. Ibid.

58. Ibid.

59. Fernández-Armesto, *Barcelona*, 169.

60. The name never caught on in common usage and was officially changed after the 1868 Revolution that drove Isabel II into exile.

61. Artis Balaguer, "El Primitivo Mercado de Santa Catalina," 12:85.

62. "Mercado de Santa Caterina: Breve historial con motivo de la celebración de su primer centenario," *Gaceta Municipal de Barcelona*, 26 April 1948, 256.

63. Busquets, *Barcelona*, 117.

64. London's population density in 1858 was 86 persons per hectare; the population density of Paris in 1859 was 356; the population density of Madrid in 1857 was 384. Albert Serratosa et al., *Semiòtica de l'Eixample Cerdà* (Barcelona: Edicions Proa, 1995), 133.

65. Karl Marx and Friedrich Engels, *Collected Works*, vol. 23 (New York: International Publishers, 1988), 586.

66. Guàrdia, Oyón, and Fava, "El sistema de mercats," 265. See "Mercats, productes alimentaris, i venedors, 1856," table on that page. The authors draw their statistics from Ildefons Cerdá, *Monografia estadística de la clase obrera en Barcelona en 1856, edición en facsímil en Teoría general de la urbanización*, vol. 2 (Madrid: IEAL, 1968), 61.

67. Guàrdia, Oyón, and Fava, "El sistema de mercats," 264.

68. The classic account of this episode is Victor Gordan Kiernan, *The Revolution of 1854 in Spanish History* (Oxford: Clarendon Press, 1966).

69. Adrian Shubert, *A Social History of Modern Spain* (London: Unwin Hyman, 1990), 170–71.

70. Antoni Nicolau i Martí and Albert Cubeles i Bonet, "El 150è aniversari de l'enderrocament de les muralles: Repensant la ciutat contemporània," in Bohigas et al., *Abajo las Murallas!!* 31.

71. Ibid., 32–33.

72. Ibid., 31.

73. Ibid., 33.

74. Among the sources on Cerdà's plan are Busquets, *Barcelona*; Marina López Guallar, ed., *Cerdà and the First Barcelona Metropolis, 1853–1897* (Barcelona: Museu d'Història de Barcelona, 2010); Michonneau, *Barcelona: Memòria i identitat*; Arturo Soria Puig and Ildefonso Cerdá, *Cerdá: The Five Bases of the Theory of Urbanization* (Madrid: Electa, 1999); Fabián Estapé, *Vida y Obra de Ildefonso Cerdá* (Barcelona: Ediciones Península, 2001); Brad Epps, "Modern Spaces: Building Barcelona," in Joan Ramon Resina, ed., *Iberian Cities* (New York: Routledge, 2001); Serratosa et al., *Semiòtica de l'Eixample Cerdà*; Carles Sudrià, "La modernidad de la capital industrial de España," in Sánchez, dir., *Barcelona 1888–1929*, 44–56; Wynn, ed., *Planning and Urban Growth*.

75. Busquets, *Barcelona*, 121–22.

76. Ibid., 122–23. See also Chantal Béret, Chrystèle Burgard, and Musée de Valence, eds., *Nouvelles de nulle part: Utopies Urbaines, 1789–2000* (Valence: Réunion des Musées Nationaux, 2001).

77. See also Marius de Geus, *Ecological Utopias: Envisioning the Sustainable Society* (Utrecht: International Books, 1999).

78. Busquets, *Barcelona*, 122–29.

79. Ibid., 15.

80. Ibid.

81. AHCB. This was Point 15 of the city council's 1855 "Memoria que la Comisión elegida . . . ha presentado proponiendo las buenas bases generales que en su concepto debieran adoptarse para el ensanche de esta ciudad." As cited in Manel Guàrdia and José Luis Oyón (with Xavier Creus), "La formació del modern sistema de mercats de Barcelona," *X Congrés d'Història de Barcelona-Dilemes de la fi de segle, 1874–1901*.

82. McDonogh, *Good Families of Barcelona*, 21. McDonogh uses Joan Rebagliato's "L'evolució demogràfica i dinámica social al segle XIX," in J. Salrach, ed., *Història Salvat de Catalunya* (Barcelona: Salvat, 1978), 5:3–17, for a figure of 188,787 inhabitants in Barcelona in 1856–57 and 533,000 inhabitants as of 1900. McDonogh notes that the latter "represents the population after consolidation with smaller surrounding cities."

83. Wynn, ed., *Planning and Urban Growth*, 118.

84. Kaplan, *Red City, Blue Period*, 5.

85. Castañer, "La difusió dels mercats de ferro," 234–35.

86. Guàrdia and Oyón, "Introducció," 36.

87. Ibid., 36, 38.

88. Guàrdia and Oyón, "La formació del modern sistema de mercats," 4–5.

89. Ibid., 6; Guàrdia, Oyón, and Fava, "El sistema de mercats," 268.

90. Guàrdia and Oyón, "Introducció," 34, 54, 34.

91. Ibid., 38.

92. David Álavarez Márquez and Olga García González, "El mercat de Born de Barcelona vist des de les certificacions de la Maquinista," 2010 Universitat Politécnica de Catalunya Treball final de carrera dels estudis de d'Arquitectura Tècnica, accessed 27 December 2013, http://upcommons.upc.edu/pfc/handle/2099.1/12027.

93. Castañer, "La difusió dels mercats de ferro," 235; Álavarez Márquez and García González, "El mercat de Born," 27–28.

94. Josep Durany i Sastre, *Mercat de Sant Antoni (1882–1982)*, Breu Història Biogràfica (Barcelona: n.p., 1982), 7.

95. Guàrdia and Oyón, "La formació del modern sistema de mercats," 7.

96. Pere Joan Ravetllat i Mira and Carme Ribas, "El mercat de Sant Antoni: Quatre nous espais," *D'UR* (October 2010), 01/2010: 86–93, accessed 27 December 2013, (http://hdl.handle.net/2099/10222,

97. "El Mercat de la Concepció," *L'Opinio*, 5 December 1931.

98. La Llibertat opened in 1875.

99. Opened in 1892, L'Abaceria Central was initially a privately owned structure and was not purchased by Barcelona's council until 1912.

100. Both El Clot and Unió markets were inaugurated in 1889.

101. Founded in 1855, La Maquinista Terrestre i Marítima was deeply involved in the shipbuilding, railroad, and machine-tool industries.

102. Castañer, "La difusió dels merkats de ferro," 236–39.

103. This was not the only time that Alfonso XII was linked to civic rituals commemorating a

market. The year before, the king had attended the inauguration of Madrid's La Cebada Market. Ibid., 239.

104. *Diario de Barcelona*, 29 November 1876.

105. Ibid.

106. Tortella, *The Development of Modern Spain*; David Ringrose, *Spain, Europe, and "The Spanish Miracle," 1700-1900* (New York: Cambridge University Press, 1996).

107. *Diario de Barcelona*, 26 September 1882. Retail sales did not actually begin until a few days later.

108. Michonneau, *Barcelona: Memòria i identitat*. See especially "Colom, la Torre Eiffel de Barcelona," 123–42.

109. Provensal and Levick, *Els Mercats de Barcelona*, 40–41.

110. N. Fava and M. Guàrdia Bassols, "The Sense of Insecurity: Integrated Solutions. The Case of Barcelona's Covered Market Systems," accessed 29 December 2013, http://www.researchgate.net/publication/239927130_THE_SENSE_OF_INSECURITY_INTEGRATED_SOLUTIONS_THE_CASE_OF_BARCELONA'S_COVERED_MARKETS_SYSTEMS.

111. Michel Foucault, *Discipline and Punish: The Birth of the Prison* (New York: Pantheon Books, 1977).

112. Jeremy Bentham, *The Panopticon Writings*, ed. Miran Bozovic (London: Verson, 1995).

113. Thompson, *The Virtuous Marketplace*, and Thompson, "Urban Renovation, Moral Regeneration."

114. Thompson, *The Virtuous Marketplace*, 108–109.

115. AHCB, *Reglamento para el régimen de los mercados de esta ciudad*. Aprobado por el Exmo. Ayuntamiento en consistorio de 13 de Abril de 1898. Entit. 1-25, caixa 2,1.

116. The 1833 *Cyclopedia of Anecdotes* attributes the term to Samuel Johnson.

117. Guàrdia, Oyón, and Fava, "El sistema de mercats," 264–65.

118. Ibid., 265–66.

119. Salomé Rekas i Mussoms and Ramon Arús i Masramon, "El Bornet, de la realidad a la tela," *Informe 8 B.MM* 66, October 2005, accessed 2 January 2014, *http://www.bcn.cat/publicacions/b_mm/ebmm66/08-17.pdf*. In addition to Martí i Alsina, other nineteenth-century artists who chose the old Born as subject included Arcadi Mas i Fondevila, Lluís Rigalt, Santiago Rusiñol, and Dionís Baixeras.

CHAPTER 4. FOR THE LOVE OF FOOD: CONSUMER
CULTURE IN THE CITY AND ITS MARKETS

1. Michael B. Miller, *The Bon Marché: Bourgeois Culture and the Department Store, 1869–1920* (Princeton: Princeton University Press, 1981); Susan Porter Benson, *Counter Cultures: Saleswomen, Managers, and Customers in American Department Stores, 1890–1940* (Urbana: University of Illinois Press, 1986); Geoffrey Crossick and Serge Jaumain, eds., *Cathedrals of Consumption: The European Department Store, 1850–1939* (Aldershot, Eng.: Ashgate, 1999); Jan Whitaker, *The Department Store: History, Design, Display* (London: Thames and Hudson, 2011).

2. Though a few shopping arcades along the lines of the Parisian *passages* began to appear in Madrid and Barcelona in the 1840s, the first department store in Spain was opened in Barcelona in 1881. It was Almacenes El Siglo, located along Las Ramblas, featuring nineteen sections on two floors.

The establishment of department stores in Spain lagged behind that of England and France but ran ahead of Italy, Denmark, Austria, and Russia. For an account of the nineteenth-century development of modern retailing forms in Spain, see Jésus Cruz, *The Rise of Middle-Class Culture in Nineteenth-Century Spain* (Baton Rouge: Louisiana State University Press, 2011), 125–29. See also Pilar Toboso Sánchez, *Pepín Fernández, 1891–1982: Galerías Preciados, el pionero de los grandes almacenes* (Madrid: LID Editorial Empresarial, 2001). Though there are no scholarly histories of restaurants in Spain, evidence clearly shows that they were late-eighteenth-century innovations there as elsewhere. The literature on restaurant history includes Pierre Andrieu, *Fine Bouche: A History of the Restaurant in France*, trans. Arthur L. Hayward (London: Cassell, 1956); Rebecca L. Spang, *The Invention of the Restaurant: Paris and Modern Gastronomic Culture* (Cambridge: Harvard University Press, 2000); Elliott Shore, "Dining Out: The Development of the Restaurant," in Paul Freedman, ed., *Food: The History of Taste* (Berkeley: University of California Press, 2007).

3. Michael J. Winstanley, *The Shopkeeper's World, 1830–1914* (Manchester, Eng.: Manchester University Press, 1983); Geoffrey Crossick and Heinz-Gerhard Haupt, *The Petite Bourgeoisie in Europe, 1780–1914: Enterprise, Family and Independence* (London: Routledge, 1995).

4. John Benson and Laura Ugolini, "Historians and the Nation of Shopkeepers," in John Benson and Laura Ugolini, eds., *A Nation of Shopkeepers: Five Centuries of British Retailing* (London: I. B. Taurus, 2003), 2.

5. Benson and Ugolini note that "no matter how one accounts for the resilience of such 'traditional' forms of distribution, it should be remembered that as of 1980–81, small independent stores still accounted for more than 30 per cent of all British retail trade." "Historians and the Nation of Shopkeepers," 5. See also Jonathan Morris, *The Political Economy of Shopkeeping in Milan, 1886–1922* (Cambridge: Cambridge University Press, 1988).

6. Castañer, "La difusió dels merkats de ferro," 237.

7. Ibid.

8. Guàrdia and García Espuche, "1888 y 1929," 26, 34.

9. Guàrdia, Oyón, and Fava, "El sistema de mercats," 270. The authors note that Ramon Grau has stressed the shared parentage of the iron markets and the exhibition palace built by Fontserè for the Ciutadella fairgrounds.

10. Ibid., 270. The authors cite Actes Municipals, 28/6/1881, núm. 63, fol. 419, held in the AMAB.

11. Ibid., 279.

12. Guàrdia and Oyón, "Introducció," 36. According to Baron Haussmann, Napoleon III had been amused by train stations, which he called "vast umbrellas," and called for the Halles pavillions to be designed in their image. The authors cite Bertrand Lemoine, *L'architecture du fer: France XIXe siècle* (Seyssel: Champ Vallon, 1986), 166. See also Walter Benjamin, *The Arcades Project*, trans. Howard Eiland and Kevin McLaughlin (Cambridge: Belknap Press, 1999).

13. The Catalan Renaixença was a nineteenth-century movement that sought, among other goals, to revive the use of the Catalan language in literary and artistic circles and in high culture more broadly. It is generally dated to the 1833 publication of Bonaventura Carles Aribau's poem "La Pàtria" in *El Vapor* magazine. Apolitical in its orientation until the early 1890s, the Renaixença served as an underpinning for more explicit forms of Catalan nationalism thereafter. See Jordi Falgàs, "Greeting the Dawn: The Impact of the Renaixença in Periodicals and Architecture," in Robinson, Falgàs, and Lord, eds., *Barcelona and Modernity*, 27–31.

14. Michonneau, *Barcelona, memòria i identitat*, 62–67, 123–42.

15. See ibid., passim; Richard Frederick Maddox, *The Best of All Possible Islands: Seville's Universal Exposition, the New Spain, and the New Europe* (Albany: State University of New York Press, 2004); David Hill Gelernter, *1939: The Lost World of the Fair* (New York: Free Press, 1999); Jill Jonnes, *Eiffel's Tower and the World's Fair Where Buffalo Bill Beguiled Paris, the Artists Quarreled, and Thomas Edison Became a Count* (New York: Viking, 2009).

16. Rossend Casanova, *El Castell dels Tres Dragons* (Barcelona: Museu de Ciències Naturals de Barcelona, 2009), 28.

17. While Lluís Domènech i Montaner (1849–1923) is best known as the architect of some of Barcelona's most significant modernist complexes, including the Palau de la Música Catalana and the Hospital de la Santa Creu i Sant Pau, the Cafè-Restaurant is an example of *protomodernisme*, a style that presaged the more famous turn-of-the-century architectural movement. In the Cafè-Restaurant (which, it should be noted, was not fully completed until after the Exposición ended), we see the fusing of Catalan neogothic elements with forms drawn from Toledo's Synagogue of Santa María and the Mesquita de Córdoba. Casanova, *El Castell dels Tres Dragons*, 16, 30.

18. Ibid., 16.

19. Ibid., 25.

20. Ibid., 25.

21. Cánovas del Castillo served six terms as prime minister of Spain before he was killed by the Italian anarchist assassin, Michele Angiolillo, in 1897.

22. Casanova, *El Castell dels Tres Dragons*, 25.

23. Ibid., 18.

24. Ibid., 25. With the closing of the fair, the Castle of the Three Dragons ceased operation as a cafè-restaurant and was used for a variety of other purposes.

25. Nestor Luján, *Veinte Siglos de Cocina en Barcelona: De las Ostras de Barcino a los Restaurantes de Hoy*, trans. Sofia de Ruy-Wamba Guixeres (Barcelona: Ediciones Folio, 1993), 90.

26. Ibid., 90–91.

27. Juan Artigas y Feiner, *Guía Itineraria y Descriptiva de Barcelona: De Sus Alrededores y de la Exposición Universal* (Barcelona: Librería y Tipografía Católica, 1888), 247, 265.

28. Luján, *Veinte Siglos de Cocina*, 91.

29. Ibid., 91. Ultimately a piece of ephemera, the hotel was torn down soon after the Exposición ended. Ironically, the demolition took sixty days, seven more than its construction.

30. For an account of the historiography treating the relationship between food and social status, see Paul Freedman, "Introducción: Una nueva historia de la cocina," in Paul Freedman, ed., *Gastonomía: Historia del paladar* (València: Publicaciones Universitat de València, 2009).

31. Luis Almerich, *El Hostal, La Fonda, La Taberna y El Café en la Vida Barcelonesa* (Barcelona: Ediciones Libreria Millà, 1945), 76.

32. Thorstein Veblen, *The Theory of the Leisure Class: An Economic Study of Institutions* (New York: Macmillan, 1899).

33. Karl Baedeker's 1913 *Spain and Portugal: Handbook for Travellers* (Leipsic: Karl Baedeker, 1913), xxviii.

34. Mrs. Villiers-Wardell, *Spain of the Spanish* (New York: Charles Scribner's Sons, 1915), 252.

35. Luján, *Veinte Siglos de Cocina*, 117.

36. H. O'Shea, *A Guide to Spain* (London: Longmans, Green and Co., 1865) 40, 52; Almerich, *El Hostal, La Fonda, La Taberna y El Café*, 79.

37. Luján, *Veinte Siglos de Cocina*, 117–20.

38. Teresa-M. Sala, in *La vida cotidiana en la Barcelona de 1900* (Madrid: Silex, 2005), offers a vivid account of Las Ramblas and especially of the space immediately in front of La Boqueria Market that is drawn from the accounts of women writers such as Dolors Monserdà, Teresa Claramunt, and Caterina Albert (writing under the pen name of Victor Català), as well as from the renderings of Dionís Baixeras, whose drawings of four women whose dress represented the changing character of the area according to time of day: morning, noon, afternoon, and festive evening. See pages 24–28.

39. A popular Valencian drink made from tigernuts and sugar.

40. Amades, *Històries i Llegendes*, 1:189–90.

41. This figure comes from Viñas y Campi, *El Indicador de España y de Sus Posesiones Ultramarinas: Inscripción General de todas las clases comprendidas en el Subsidio Industrial y de Comercio, las de la Magistratura y Administración y las casas estranjeras que faciliten antecedentes al efecto. Año económica 1864 á 1865* (Barcelona: Imprenta de Narciso Ramírez, 1865). ACA Secció Hisenda, Sèrie Inv. 1, Sig. 4889.

42. Viñas y Campi, ibid., lists three beer factories in the city in 1864–65. These were Miret y Tersa, Luis Moritz, and Jaime Rovira. ACA, Secció Hisenda, Sèrie Inv. 1, Sig. 4889. By 1896, the *Anuario-Riera* lists seven beer factories in the city, under the names of Baldomero Claramunt, Enrique Comas y Comp., José Damm, R. Fernández Bicet, Luis Moritz, Juan Petit, and Laureano Sirerou. AHCB, *Anuario-Riera: Guía General de Cataluña: Comercio, Industria, Profesiones, Artes y Oficios, Propiedad Urbana, Rústica y Pecuniaria, Datos Estadísticos, Geográficos y Descriptivos y Sección de Propaganda* (Barcelona: Eduardo Riera Solanich, Centro de Propaganda Mercantil, 1896).

43. AHCB, *Anuario-Riera: Guía General de Cataluña*, 1896.

44. Ibid. *Tavernas, bodegas,* and *bodegones* were all establishments where men congregated to drink and, in the case of the latter two categories, where alcohol could also be purchased for home consumption.

45. Josep Pla, *Llagosta i pollastre: Sobre la cuina catalana* (Barcelona: Editorial Selecta, 1952); Josep Pla and Francesc Català-Roca, *El que hem menjat* (Barcelona: Ediciones Destino, 1972). See also Jaume Fàbrega, *La cuina de Josep Pla: A taula amb l'autor de "El que hem menjat"* (Barcelona: Edicions La Magrana, 1997).

46. Pla, *El que hem menjat*, 260. Pla also praised the *mortadella* sandwich, a cheaper alternative.

47. The term *sandwich* entered the lexicon as a consequence of John Montagu's (1718–92) proclivity for eating meat between two slices of bread as a convenience food. Montagu, the fourth Earl of Sandwich, served as special ambassador of the English monarch to Madrid, where it was common to serve travelers cured ham between two slices of bread. More commonly, eighteenth-century Spaniards ate omelet slices on bread as a kind of forerunner to today's open-faced *montadito* sandwiches, which are a popular variety of *tapa*. While the term *sandwich* can be attributed to those imitating John Montagu's tastes, the use of bread as a carrier or enveloper of other foods has a much broader and older history traceable to all the Mediterranean and European regions where leavened bread held a privileged place within culinary traditions and cultures. See de Déu Domènech, *Xocolata cada dia*, 141.

48. Cruz, *The Rise of Middle-Class Culture*, 133.

49. Ibid., 83. Cruz borrows Lorna Weatherhills's distinction between the emergence of "front stage" and "back stage" areas of the bourgeois household as set forth in her *Consumer Behavior and Material Culture in Britain, 1660–1760* (London: Routledge, 1996).

50. Josep Pla, *Un Señor de Barcelona* (Barcelona: Destino, 1945); Martha E. Altisent, "Images of Barcelona," in Martha E. Altisent, ed., *A Companion to the Twentieth-Century Spanish Novel* (Suffolk: Tamesis, 2008), 138.

51. This process is traced by Castañer in "La difusió dels mercats de ferro," 233–62.

52. Fernández-Armesto, *Barcelona,* 172.

53. Pascual Madoz Ibáñez, *Articles Sobre el Principat de Catalunya, Andorra i Zona de Parla Catalana del Regne d'Aragó al "Diccionario geográfico-estadístico de España y sus Posesiones de Ultramar"* (Barcelona: Curial Edicions Catalanes, 1985), 205; Montserrat Rumbau, *La Barcelona de fa 200 anys* (Barcelona: Tibidabo Edicions, 1990), 235.

54. Cerdá, *Monografía estadística de la clase obrera*; Fernández-Armesto, *Barcelona,* 173.

55. Fernández-Armesto, *Barcelona,* 173.

56. M. Pérez Samper, "Cullera de fusta, forquilla de plata," in *Catálogo de la Exposición Seure a Taula? Una història del menjar a la Mediterrània* (Andorra and Barcelona: Govern d'Andorra, Disputació de Barcelona, Museu d'Arqueologia de Catalunya, Ajuntament de Gavà, Museu de Gavà, 1996), 35.

57. Ibid. 35.

58. Joaquim Villar i Ferran, *Topografía mèdica de la villa de Viella y general del Valle de Arán,* 92, cited in Llorenç Prats, *La Catalunya Rància: Les condicions de vida materials de les classes populars a la Catalunya de la Restauració segons les topografies mèdiques* (Barcelona: Editorial Alta Fulla, 1996), 116.

59. Bonfili Garriga i Puig, *Topografía médica de S. Cugat del Vallés,* cited in Prats, *La Catalunya Rància,* 114.

60. Prats, *La Catalunya Rància,* 117.

61. Ibid., 118.

62. Tortella, *The Development of Modern Spain,* 65–93.

63. Braudel discusses the general European decrease in meat supply that followed the "waning" of the Middle Ages, which, he says, became "progressively worse, lasting well into the nineteenth century." He notes that the reduction in meat consumption was more pronounced in Mediterranean regions than in the North. *Civilization and Capitalism,* vol. 1, *The Structures of Everyday Life: The Limits of the Possible,* 193–97.

64. Nicolau-Nos and Pujol-Andreu, "Urbanization and Dietary Change," 40.

65. Ibid., 41.

66. Ibid., 42.

67. Ibid., 44.

68. Ibid., 39.

69. Joan Ràfols Casamada, "La innovación tecnológica como factor de reubicación de la producción láctea," *Scripta Nova: Revista Electrónica de Geografía y Ciencias Sociales* 69 (1 August 2000), accessed 2 January 2014, http://www.ub.edu/geocrit/sn-69-14.htm.

70. D. Díez i Quijano, "Horta," in M. Cahner, coord., *Gran Geografia Comarcal de Catalunya,* vol. 8, *Barcelonés: Baix Llobregat* (Barcelona: Enciclopèdia Catalana, S.A., 1982), 265, as quoted in Ràfols Casamada, "La innovación tecnológica."

71. Departament d'Estadística, Ajuntament de Barcelona, *100 Anys d'Estadística Municipal* (Barcelona: Ajuntament de Barcelona, 2000), 112.

72. Ibid., 112.

73. Ràfols Casamada, "La innovación tecnológica." Ràfols Casamada reports a stunning 2,800-percent increase in milk consumption in Spain from 1857 to 1997.

74. Anna Raurell i Torrent, "Avaluació de la incidència de diversos productes làctics en la variació de les característsques organolèptiques i reològiques de la xocolata" (PhD diss., Universitat de Vic, 1999), cited in Maria Antònia Martí Escayol, *El Plaer de la xocolata: La història i la cultura de la xocolata a Catalunya* (Valls: Cossetània Edicions, 2004), 151.

75. Martí Escayol, *El Plaer de la xocolata*, 151.

76. Pla, *El que hem menjat*, 325.

77. Ibid., 268–71, 312–14. Pla asserts that Spain, at the time of his writing in 1972, had not developed broadly appreciated cheese varieties beyond *manchego* (made from sheep's milk) and *mahón* (made from cow's milk). Spanish cheeses were mainly consumed on a local basis and produced especially in mountainous areas of the North, where sheep farming was most common. *Mató* (elsewhere known as *recuit*) was produced in a number of Catalan areas, including the environs of Barcelona, and was typically eaten as a dessert food drizzled with honey or sugar and nuts.

78. Salvador Llobet, "L'explotació del camp," in L. Solé Sabarís, *Geografia de Catalunya* (Barcelona: Editorial Aedos, 1958), 466, cited in Ràfols Casamada, "La innovación tecnológica."

79. Gemma Tribó, "La ramaderia a les portes de Barcelona: el cas del Baix Llobregat (1850–1930)," *Estudis d'Història Agrària* 13 (2000): 107–26.

80. Ràfols Casamada, "La innovación tecnológica."

81. Ibid.

82. Martí Escayol, *El Plaer de la xocolata*, 155.

83. Eliseu Trenc and Pilar Vélez, *Alexandre de Riquer: Obra gràfica* (Barcelona: Caixaterrasa, Marc Martí, 2006), 18–19.

84. Ibid., 18.

85. Eliseu Trenc, "Modernista Illustrated Magazines," in Robinson et al., eds. *Barcelona and Modernity,* 61.

86. Marc Martí Ramon, "Ramon Casas i l'Anís del Mono," 83, in Marc Martí Ramon, coord., *Ramon Casas i el Cartell* (València: Museu Valencià de la Il·lustració i de la Modernitat, Diputació de València Àrea de Cultura, Caja de Ahores del Mediteráneo Obras Sociales, 2005).

87. Ibid.

88. Trenc and Vélez, *Alexandre de Riquer,* 18–19, 26. Two artistic traditions emerged to define Catalan and Valencian commercial art in the decades that followed. A modern and synthetic style inspired by Steinlen and Toulouse-Latrec was practiced most notably by Ramon Casas and Antoni Utrillo. The other was specifically art-nouveau and dominated by Alexandre de Riquer.

89. Hans J. Teuteberg, "El Nacimiento de la Era del Consumidor," in Freedman, ed., *Gastronomía,* 239.

90. Amades, *Històries i Llegendes,* 1:75–76.

91. Ibid., 1:75.

92. "Consumo Medio por habitante de los principales articulos alimenticios," *Anuario Estadístico de la Ciudad de Barcelona, Año V para 1906,* 502.

93. Joan Amades, *L'Escudella* (Tarragona: Edicions El Mèdol, 2002), 119, 112, 113.

94. For the definitive study of the formulation of Barcelona's late-nineteenth-century elite, see McDonogh, *Good Families of Barcelona.*

95. Gras Casanovas and Pérez Samper, "Alimentació i Societat a la Catalunya Moderna," 33–34.

96. María de los Ángeles Pérez Samper "Los Recetarios de Mujeres y para Mujeres: Sobre la conservación y transmisión de los saberes domésticos en la época moderna," *Cuadernos de Historia Moderna* 19 (1997): 123.

97. *La Cuynera Catalana: Reglas útils, fácils, seguras y económicas per a cuynar bé* (1851; repr., 3rd ed., Barcelona: Alta Fulla, 1996), 8; Pérez Samper, "Los Recetarios de Mujeres," 153.

98. Jésus Cruz, *The Rise of Middle-Class Culture,* 35.

99. Pérez Samper, "Los Recetarios de Mujeres," 121. See, for example, the popular eighteenth-century treatises of Eliza Smith, *The Compleat Housewife: Accomplish'd Gentlewoman's Companion* (London: J. Pemberton, 1727); Hannah Glasse, *The Art of Cookery Made Plain and Easy* (London: n.p., 1747); and Maria Eliza Ketelby Rundell, *A New System of Domestic Cookery: Formed upon Principles of Economy, and adapted to the use of Private Families* (London: John Murray, 1808). For France, see Louise Béate Utrecht-Friedel, *Le Petit Cuisinier habile, ou l'art d'apprêter les Alimens avec délicatese et économie: Suivi d'un petit Traité sur la conservation des Fruits et Légumes les plus estimés. Par Madame Fr. Nouvelle edition corrigée et augmentée* (Paris: l'auteur, 1814).

100. Pérez Samper, "Los Recetarios de Mujeres," 133.

101. Clifford Geertz, "The Bazaar Economy: Information and Search in Peasant Marketing," *American Economic Review* 68, no. 2 (May 1978): 28–32.

102. ARSAM, document dated 28 August 1914.

103. ARSAM, document dated 20 November 1897.

104. ARSAM, document dated 27 October 1911.

105. ARSAM, documents dated 4 October 1906, 15 November 1906, 13 December 1906, 5 January 1907, 27 July 1911, 15 February 1912, 29 July 1914, 20 October 1923.

106. ARSAM, document dated 9 October 1918.

107. See, for example, the 20 November 1931 issue of *La Publicitat.*

108. *La Publicitat,* 20 November 1931.

109. *L'Opinió,* 15 April 1933.

110. *L'Opinió,* 5 December 1931.

111. ARSAM documents dated 13 March 1928, 21 August 1933, 4 February 1935, 11 June 1935, 9 November 1935, 24 January 1936, 30 January 1936, and 12 February 1936.

112. Eladia M. Vda. De Carpinell, *Carmencita o la Buena Cocinera.* Reprinted over the course of the twentieth century, the oldest version of this text is in the Biblioteca Nacional de España and dates to 1899. The newest version dates to 2011, published in Valladolid by Editorial Maxtor.

113. Oral history interview with Antonia Peña Martín, conducted by the author, 21 May 1992.

114. Carpinell, *Carmencita,* author's prologue.

115. Isabel Segura i Marta Selva, *Revistes de Dones, 1846–1935* (Barcelona: Edhasa, 1984), 289–90.

116. Núria Pi i Vendrell, *Bibliografia de la Novel·la Sentimental Publicada en Català entre 1924 i 1938* (Barcelona: Diputació de Barcelona, 1986), 106.

117. Assumpta Sopeña i Nualart, "La publicitat com a font documental per la història contemporànea: *El Hogar y La Moda* (1913–1931)," *Gazeta: Actes de les Primeres Jornades d'Història de la Premsa* 1 (1994): 367.

118. Cristina Dupláa, *La Voz Testimonial de Montserrat Roig* (Barcelona: Icaria, 1996), 113; Adolfo Perinat and María Isabel Marrades, *Mujer, Prensa y Sociedad en España* (Madrid: Centro de Investigaciones Sociológicas, 1980), 275.

119. See, for example, Guillem D'Oloro's "Antifeminisme" on page 7 in the 30 October 1925 issue of *La Dona Catalana: Revista de Modes i de la Llar*. AHCB R. 1925 Fol.

120. See *La Dona Catalana*, 9 October 1925–19 November 1926.

121. J. Rondissoni, *Rondissoni Culinaria: El Recitario de un gran maestro* (6th ed.; Barcelona: Bon Ton, 1999), 3–5.

122. Ruth Schwartz Cowan, *More Work for Mother: The Ironies of Household Technology from the Open Hearth to the Microwave* (New York: Basic Books, 1983).

123. *La Dona Catalana*, 9 April 1926, 4.

124. Santi Santamaria, in throwing down the gauntlet against Ferran Adria's cuisine in the so-called 2008 "Stoves War," was echoing Antonieta's sentiments from a distance of more than seven decades' time. For an account of the 2008 "Stoves War," see Pujol, "Cosmopolitan Taste."

125. José Rondissoni, *Culinaria: Nuevo Tratado de Cocina. Mil Recetas de Cocina, Pastelería, i Repostería* (Barcelona: Bosch, ca. 1946).

126. José Rondissoni, *Culinaria Exprés: Selección de Recetes para preparer con la Olla a Presión* (Barcelona: Bosch, 1960), and *Recetario para la parrilla eléctrica Setur* (publisher unknown, no date, but there is an extant copy available in the Biblioteca Nacional de España).

127. Vásquez Montalbán, introduction, Rondissoni, *Rondissoni Culinaria*, 4.

128. Pla, *El que hem menjat*, 260–63. The white beans that Pla deemed best were of the *ganxet* variety.

129. Ibid., 263.

130. Ibid., 12.

131. Claude Lévi-Strauss, *The Raw and the Cooked* (New York: Harper and Row, 1969); Pierre Bourdieu, *Distinction: A Social Critique of the Judgement of Taste*, trans. Richard Nice (Cambridge: Cambridge University Press, 1985); Roland Barthes, "Toward a Psychosociology of Contemporary Food Consumption," in Carole Counihan and Penny Van Esterik, eds., *Food and Culture: A Reader* (New York: Routledge, 1997), 22; Michel de Certeau, Luce Giard, and Pierre Mayol, *The Practice of Everyday Life*, vol. 2, *Living and Cooking*, trans. Timothy J. Tomasick (Minneapolis: University of Minnesota Press, 1998); and Massimo Montanari, *Food Is Culture* (New York: Columbia University Press, 2006). On the limits of the structuralist approach, see Stephen Mennell, *All Manners of Food: Eating and Taste in England and France from the Middle Ages to the Present* (Oxford: Blackwell, 1985).

CHAPTER 5. NEW POLITICAL ECONOMIES: MUNICIPAL CONTROL AND ASSOCIATIONALISM IN THE MARKETS BEFORE THE CIVIL WAR

1. See table 1 from Gary McDonough, *Good Families of Barcelona*, 21, for sources on Barcelona's population from 1370 to the annexation of the village of Horta in 1904, the Zona Franca in 1920, Sarrià in 1921, and the portion of Sant Adrià to the south of the Besòs River in 1929.

2. Sobrequés Callicó, *Barcelona*, 145.

3. AMAB, "Presupuestos Ordinarios de Gastos," *Gazeta Municipal de Barcelona* (Barcelona, 1931), 27–134.

4. See Juan Piqueras Haba, "La filoxera en España y su difusión espacial, 1878–1926," *Cuadernos de Geografía* 77 (2005): 101–36.

5. Joan Connelly Ullman, *The Tragic Week: A Study of Anticlericalism in Spain, 1875–1912* (Cambridge: Harvard University Press, 1968), 105; McDonogh, *Good Families of Barcelona*, 26.

6. José Alvarez-Junco, *The Emergence of Mass Politics in Spain: Populist Demagoguery and Republican Culture, 1890–1910* (Sussex: Sussex Academic Press, 2002), 122–42.

7. Ullman, *The Tragic Week*, is the classic study of this episode. See also Kaplan, *Red City, Blue Period*, 93–103, for an explicit analysis of women's participation in the "Tragic Week."

8. Carr, *Spain, 1808–1975*, 446.

9. Temma Kaplan, "Female Consciousness and Collective Action: The Case of Barcelona, 1910–1918," *Signs* 7, no. 3 (Spring 1982): 545–66; Radcliff, "The Emerging Challenge of Mass Politics," 138–54.

10. On *pistolerismo*, see Antoni Jutglar, *Historia Crítica de la Burguesía en Cataluña* (Barcelona: Anthropos Editorial, 1984), 424–25; and Paul Heywood, *Marxism and the Failure of Organized Socialism in Spain, 1879–1936* (Cambridge: Cambridge University Press, 2003), 74.

11. Kaplan, *Red City, Blue Period*, 152.

12. Andrew Hamilton Lee, "Mothers without Fathers or Nothing More Than a Woman: Gender and Anarchism in the Work of Federica Montseny, 1923–1929" (PhD diss., New York University, 2012), 75.

13. E. J. Hobsbawm, *Revolutionaries: Contemporary Essays* (New York: Pantheon Books, 1973), 84; Jordi Borja, *Luces y Sombras del Urbanismo en Barcelona* (Barcelona: Editorial UOC, 2009), 237–38.

14. Fava and Guàrdia Bassols, "The Sense of Insecurity."

15. Ibid.

16. Borja, *Luces y Sombras*, 238.

17. Crucial among these was the "lexical and grammatical standardization of the [Catalan] language, successfully realized by Pompeu Fabra in 1913–18." Enric Ucelay da Cal, "The Restoration: Regeneration and the Clash of Nationalisms, 1875–1914," in Alvarez Junco and Shubert, eds., *Spanish History since 1808*, 133-34.

18. Barcelona's Restoration-era mayors were appointed by royal decree until 1917, and then again, under the Primo de Rivera dictatorship, from 1923 to 1931.

19. Ucelay da Cal, in "The Restoration," 131, speaks to this urban rivalry, describing it as a "a zero-sum game for Spain, whereby Barcelona's claims would be recognized at the expense of Madrid's pretensions."

20. Irene Fattacciu, "Gremios y evolución de las pautas de consumo en el siglo XVIII: La industria artesanal de chocolate," in Muñoz Navarro, ed., *Comprar, Vender y Consumir*, 159-62.

21. Pere Molas Ribalta, *Los Gremios Barceloneses del siglo XVIII: La estructura corporativa ante el comienzo de la revolución industrial* (Madrid: Confederación Española de Cajas de Ahorros, 1970).

22. Guàrdia and Oyón, "Introducció," 44.

23. AHCB, *Almanaque del Diario de Barcelona para el año 1859*, 154.

24. Javier Casares Ripol and Alfonso Rebollo Arévalo, *Distribución commercial* (2nd ed.; Madrid: Civitas, 2000), 232.

25. The city was also operating two open-air markets at that time. Sagrera had seventy-seven stalls and Horta had seventy-two. Both were enclosed in modern market-hall structures in the early 1950s.

26. AGCB, Ayuntamiento de Barcelona, *Reglamento u Ordenanza de Carnicerías: Aprobado por la Junta Provincial de Abastos en sesiones de 11 de abril y 6 de julio, 1927*, 13–14.

27. AHCB, *Reglamento para el régimen de los mercados, 1898*.

28. Joaquim M. Puigvert i Solà, "De manescals a veterinaris: Notes per a una sociologia històrica de la professió veterinària a Catalunya," *Estudis d'Història Agrària* 17 (2004): 729–50.

29. ARSAM, document dated 1 December 1911.

30. In some markets, such as Santa Caterina, rural producer-vendors held on to space inside the structure in areas designated for them in the rear or along one side of the building.

31. AHCB, *Reglamento para el régimen de los mercados, 1898*.

32. ARSAM, document dated 2 February 1905.

33. ARSAM, document dated 4 February 1915.

34. The fact that the documents relating to the *legalización* of stall titles at Sant Antoni are addressed to all the market directors in the city indicates that the increasing sedentariness of vendors was a broader phenomenon.

35. ARSAM, *Mercado de San Antonio: Tarifas para los presupuestos del Año 1919*. A separate category of fresh fish vendors paid daily rents through the period, but they represented a small percentage of the overall number of vendors at each market and were extremely stable and sedentary as well.

36. ARSAM, documents dated 5 January 1895, 23 November 1899, and 30 December 1902. Article 22 of the 1898 code explicitly obligated vendors to familiarize themselves with all its elements and made cheap copies of the code available for purchase.

37. AMAB, *Suplemento a la Gaceta Municipal de Barcelona*, Año II, 20 January 1915, xv, and 10 February 1915, lii.

38. AHCB, *Reglamento para el régimen de los mercados*, 1898, articles 1, 29, 30, 48, 49, and 50.

39. Ibid., articles 37, 39, and 40.

40. Ibid., article 23.

41. Guàrdia, Oyón, and Fava, "El sistema de mercats," 271.

42. AGCB, "L'Escorxador: Resum de dades biogràfiques," *La Veu dels Carnissers: Butlletí de la Associació de Carnissers de Barcelona,* May 1936, 12.

43. AGCB, Feliciano Serra y Vidal, *Memoria y Estadística de los Mataderos Municipales de Barcelona* (Barcelona, 1903), 45.

44. ARSAM, documents dated 28 May 1898 and 23 August 1902.

45. AMAB, *Suplemento a la Gaceta Municipal de Barcelona*, Año II, 20 January 1915, xv, and 10 February 1915, lii.

46. AGCB, "L'Escorxador: Resum de dades biogràfiques," 12.

47. AGCB, *La Veu dels Carnissers*, May 1936, 12–13.

48. AHCB, "Memoria Social," n.d., Entid. 1–25, caixa 2, 10.

49. AMAB, Actes Municipals, 31 January 1906, índex, caixa 138, vol. 1, fol. 250, as cited in Guàrdia, Oyón, and Fava, "El sistema de mercats," 280.

50. J. M. Pujades, "Un Mercado central de frutas y verduras," *Revista del Instituto Agrícola Catalán de Sant Isidre*, 20 December 1913, year LXII, quad. 24, 371, as cited in Guàrdia, Oyón, and Fava, "El sistema de mercats," 280.

51. "Las subsistencias y el mercado de Barcelona," *Revista del Instituto Agrícola Catalán de Sant Isidre*, 5 February 1916, year LXV, quad. 3, 33, as cited ibid., 281.

52. AMAB, Actes Municipals, 9 November 1916, index, núm. 217, VI, fol. 48 v., as cited ibid., 281.

53. Guàrdia, Oyón, and Fava, "El sistema de mercats," 283.

54. AHCB, "Memoria Social," n.d., Entid. 1–25, caixa 2, 10.

55. Guàrdia, Oyón, and Fava, "El sistema de mercats," 282–85.

56. Ibid., 285.

57. In some cases, stall permits were issued to individuals who claimed indigency. While seemingly rare, the practice shows that municipal authorities understood that the market hall-based system of food retailing served multiple purposes, including social welfare.

58. AHCB, *Reglamento para el régimen de los mercados,* 1898, Article 17.

59. ARSAM, document dated 18 November 1921.

60. ARSAM, documents dated 6 February 1908, 17 May 1910, 4 October 1911, 25 May 1912, and 22 May 1917.

61. DPAMAB, R-100, caixa 22 #10879, documents dated 6 April 1923 and 7 August 1923.

62. DPAMAB, R-100, caixa 13, #10062, document dated 16 January 1919.

63. ARSAM, document dated 4 March 1925.

64. ARSAM, document dated 1 July 1914.

65. ARSAM, document dated 8 October 1914.

66. DPAMAB, R-100, caixa 29 #11619, document dated 12 September 1930.

67. *Anuario Estadístico de la Ciudad de Barcelona, Año I para 1902.* All tabulations, unless otherwise specified, are by the author.

68. Ibid.

69. AHGC, *Reglamento u Ordenza de Carnicerías,* 1927, article 5.

70. AHCOCINB, Ayuntamiento de Barcelona, Comisión de Abastos, *Reglamento para la venta, en tiendas de pescado fresco y mariscos: Aprobado pro la Exma. Comisión Municipal Permanente en session de 30 julio de 1929,* article 2, caixa 792.3.

71. Guàrdia, Oyón, and Fava, "El sistema de mercats," 288.

72. Ibid., 286.

73. AHCB, *Reglamentos para el régimen de los mercados,* 1898, article 19, and Ayuntamiento de Barcelona, *Reglamentos de los Mercados en General y de los especiales de Pescado y Frutas y Verduras al Por Mayor: Aprobado por la Excma. Comisión Municipal Permanente en sesión de 31 enero de 1928,* article 9. Entid. 1-25, caixa 2.1.

74. The family firm was established in 1830. Alicia Sánchez and María Pomés, *Historia de Barcelona: De los Orígenes a la Actualidad* (Barcelona: Editorial Optima, 2000), 195.

75. AHCB, *Anuario General de España Bailly-Baillière-Riera: Comercio, Industria, Agricultura, Ganadería, Minería, Propiedad, Profesiones y Elemento Oficial,* vol. 1 (Barcelona: Sociedad Anónima Anuarios Bailly-Ballière-Riera Reunidos, 1915).

76. AHCB, *Anuario-Riera: General y Exclusivo de España por orden Alfabético de Provincias, de Partidas Judiciales y de Ayuntamientos con todos los pueblos agregados y los mismos,* vol. 1, 1904, Año 9 de la publicación (Barcelona: Centro de Propaganda Mercantil, 1904); Anuario General de España Bailly-Baillière-Riera 1915 and 1929.

77. See Teresa Solà Parera and Àngels Solà Parera, "El creixament urbà de Gràcia en les dècades de 1820 i 1830: Anàlisi de la urbanització Trilla," in *El Pla de Barcelona i la Seva Història: Actes del 1er Congrés d'història del Pla de Barcelona, celebrat a l'Institut Municipal d'Història el dies 12 i 13 de novembre del 1982* (Barcelona: Edicions La Magrana, Institut Municipal d'Història de l'Ajuntament de Barcelona, 1984), 389–410.

78. AHCB, "Nuestros Centros de Abastos: La Abacería Central," *Gaceta Municipal de Barcelona,* 17 July 1950, 741.

79. Ibid., 742.

80. Ibid., 742.

81. *Diario de Barcelona,* 13 December 1892.

82. "El Mercat 'Abaceria Central' de Gràcia," *L'Opinió,* 31 December 1939.

83. AHCB, "Nuestros Centros de Abastos: La Abacería Central," 744.

84. *Diario de Barcelona,* 21 December 1892.

85. AHCB, "Nuestros Centros de Abastos: La Abacería Central," 745.

86. "El Mercat 'Abaceria Central' de Gràcia," *L'Opinió,* 31 December 1939; AHCB, "Nuestros Centros de Abastos: La Abacería Central," 745.

87. AHCB, *Reglamentos para el régimen de los mercados, 1898.*

88. Different markets were authorized to issue licenses to peasant vendors from different areas of the surrounding hinterland.

89. Oral history interview with Maria Marqués Ruiz, conducted by the author, 19 May 1992. Marqués Ruiz explained that in the past the social nature of the market clientele varied over the course of the day, with ladies shopping with their servants later in the morning than working women did. Evidence of this pattern also comes from a 2 September 1911 petition by Josefa Aguilar y Monfull, Ramon Manero, and Antonio Plana requesting permission to operate two fish shops on Sicília Street in what was then a peripheral part of the Eixample known as "Poblet." In asserting the merits of their case, the petitioners stated that because nearby residents were almost all working class they "did not always dispose of the sufficient time to go the most proximate market and invest two hours in shopping." The Treasury Commission accepted their petition of September 6. DPAMAB, R-100, caixa 17, #10637, documents dated 2 September 1911 and 6 September 1911.

90. *Diario de Barcelona,* 27 July 1898.

91. Ibid., 28 July 1898.

92. Ibid.

93. DPAMAB, R-110, caixa 44, #30074, two documents dated 24 February 1921 (hereinafter a and b); and caixa 24, #11299, document dated 30 April 1926. This latter document is a petition signed by thirteen La Boqueria fixed-license stall vendors, eight of whom were male and five of them female. The lieutenant mayor charged with overseeing provisioning ordered that the peasant vendors be moved back to their previous location two weeks later, on May 5.

94. DPAMAB, R-100, caixa 17, #10637, document dated 13 February 1904.

95. Ibid.

96. Ibid.

97. The evidence for the existence of these organizations is scattered through various archives and in the press. The administrative record of Sant Antoni Market includes documents attesting to the active role of the Asociación de Vendedores del Mercado de Sant Antonio as of October 1911. Other references appear in the DPAMAB and in the AHCOCINB.

98. With respect to El Born, see DPAMAB, R-100, caixa 17, #10637, document dated 13 February 1904; with respect to Sant Antoni, the record begins in October 1911 and continues until November 1924 when, under the dictatorship, all vendors were absorbed into the Comisión Mixta del Trabajo en el Comercio al Detall. With respect to La Concepció, see "El Mercat de la Concepció," in *L'Opinió,*

5 December 1931; with respect to Sants and Hostafrancs, see ARSAM document dated 24 February 1921; with respect to El Clot, see DPAMAB, R-100, caixa 44, #30074, document dated 1 February 1920; with respect El Ninot, see "Avui Serà Inaugurat el Nou Mercat del Ninot," *L'Opinió*, 15 April 1933.

99. ARSAM, document dated 9 October 1919.

100. DPAMAB, R-100, caixa 44, #30074, documents dated 1 February 1920 and 24 May 1921.

101. "El Mercat de la Boqueria i el seu aspecte social," *La Publicitat*, 20 November 1931.

102. AHCOCINB, 12, 2-23-B, 794–3, Venta al Por Menor de narangas en el Puerto. Petición de la Ca. de Vendedores para que se prohiba. 11 March 1914.

103. ARSAM, document dated 22 December 1919.

104. DPAMAB, R-100, caixa 19, #10680, document dated 2 July 1921.

105. ARSAM, document dated 28 July 1910.

106. ARSAM, document dated 20 December 1911.

107. ARSAM document dated 4 October 1911.

108. DPAMAB, R-100, caixa 44, #30074, document (a) dated 24 February 1921.

109. Ibid.

110. Ibid. This speaks to Michael Seidman's discussion about the various forms of individualism whose prevalence he has written about during the Civil War. Among the varieties of individualism he explores, this form of consumer fraud in salt cod weights, documented as taking place in 1921, most approximates what Seidman labels as subversive "acquisitive individualism." Michael Seidman, *Republic of Egos: A Social History of the Spanish Civil War* (Madison: University of Wisconsin Press, 2002), 7.

111. ARSAM, document dated 17 June 1921.

112. DPAMAB, R-100, caixa 44, #30074, document (b) dated 24 February 1921.

113. ARSAM, document dated 17 June 1921.

114. Centre Gremial dels Carnissers, Cámara de Vendedores en los Mercados, the Gremio de Pescado Salada, the Associació dels Carnissers, and the Associación de Hortelanos del Llobregat.

115. DPAMAB, R-100, caixa 17, # 10615, documents dated 23 July 1921, 21 October 1921,

116. DPAMAB, R-100, caixa 19, #10680, document dated 20 July 1921.

117. Ibid.

118. Ibid.

119. DPAMAB, R-100, caixa 17, #10637, document dated 20 July 1921.

120. DPAMAB, R-100, caixa 19, #10680, document dated 20 July 1921.

121. DPAMAB, R-100, caixa 17, #10637, document dated 20 July 1921.

122. DPAMAB, R-100, caixa 17, #10634, document dated 13 August 1921.

123. DPAMAB, R-100, caixa 17, #10634, document dated 6 October 1921.

124. AHCOCINB, Don Josep Castany i Gelats, *Homenatge a Don Manuel Sorigué i Casas* (Barcelona: Cercle d'Ultramarins, Queviures i Similars, 1925), 9, BI/321-610. 1/4064230. See also BC, *Estatutos de la Unión Gremial de Barcelona* (Barcelona, 1905), Monografies 2004–12, C. 5/4.

125. DPAMAB, R-100, caixa 44, #30074, document (a) dated 24 February 1924.

126. DPAMAB, R-100, caixa 21, #10853, document dated 30 November 1923.

127. AHCB, see extant copies of its monthly, *La Unión: Órgano de la Unión de Vendedores de Pescado de Barcelona y su Provincia*, January 1930-April 1931.

128. ARSAM, document dated 25 November 192; *La Vanguardia,* 9 September 1924. See also Maria Jesús Espuny i Tomàs, "La Comisión Mixta del Trabajo en el Comercio de Barcelona," 165–70, in José María Ortiz de Orruño Legarda and Santiago Castillo, coord., *Estado, protesta y movimientos sociales: Actas del III Congreso de Historia Social en España. Vitoria-Gasteiz, julio de 1997* (Bilbao: Universidad del País Vasco, 1998).

129. AHCB, *Llibre d'Or del Cercle d'Ultramarins, Queviures i Similars, 1883–1933* (Barcelona, 1933), B, 1933-fol. (1), 664–331.882.

130. AHCB, *Llibre d'Or,* 6.

131. AHCOCINB, Castany i Gelats, *Homenatge a Don Manuel Sorigué i Casas,* 7.

132. AHCB, *Llibre d'Or,* 43.

133. Ibid., 8.

134. *Anuario Estadístico de la Ciudad de Barcelona, Año I para 1902.*

135. AHCOCINB, Castany i Gelats, *Homenatge a Don Manuel Sorigué i Casas,* 15.

136. Ibid., 21.

137. AGCB, *Gremis de Proveïments de Barcelona, Els Gremis i el Moment d'Ara* (Barcelona: Gràf. Esmandia, 1931.

138. AGCB, Venancio Sans y Prats, *Libro Diario de la 'Asociación de Carniceros de Barcelona' y del 'Gremio Sindical de Carniceros de Barcelona,' 1912–1963* (Barcelona, 1967).

139. *Anuario Estadístico de la Ciudad de Barcelona, Año I para 1902.*

140. Guàrdia, Oyón, and Fava, "El sistema de mercats," 288.

141. AGCB, Sans y Prats, *Libro Diario.*

142. Jeffrey M. Pilcher, *The Sausage Rebellion: Public Health, Private Enterprise, and Meat in Mexico City, 1890–1917* (Albuquerque: University of New Mexico Press, 2006), 5.

143. AGCB, Sans y Prats, *Libro Diario.*

144. AGCB, Ayuntamiento de Barcelona, *Reglamento u Ordenanza de Carnicerías,* 1927.

145. AGCB, "Retem tribut a la Justícia," *La Veu dels Carnissers,* May 1936, 1–4.

146. "Carniceras y Carniceros Rebeldes," *Diario de Barcelona,* 29 March 1936.

147. *La Vanguardia,* 24 March 1936, 8.

148. AGCB, Sans y Prats, *Libro Diario;* "Un Desgravi" and "Agraïment," *La Veu dels Carnissers,* April 1936, 12 and 16; "Tal com s'havia anunciat . . . ," ibid., June 1936, 5; "Retem tribut a la Justícia," ibid., May 1936, 4.

149. AGCB, Sans y Prats, *Libro Diario.*

150. Slaughterhouse data from Barcelona and Madrid clearly demonstrate the growing demand for meat from younger beasts in the former and the taste for beef in the latter. In 1935, Barcelona's Escorxador processed just over 3.5 million kilos of beef, as compared to the nearly 19.3 million kilos of beef processed in Madrid's slaughterhouses; likewise, Barcelona's Escorxador processed just over 12 million kilos of veal, while the figures for Madrid was just under 1.4 million. AGCB, "L'Escorxador: Cotització oficial," *La Veu dels Carnissers,* April 1936, 13.

151. Nicolau-Nos and Pujol-Andreu, "Urbanization and Dietary Change," 41.

152. Ibid., 46.

153. Ibid., 40.

154. Per-capita consumption of eggs in Barcelona increased from 98.7 in 1900 to 135.1 in 1914. Per capita consumption of milk in Barcelona increased from 13 liters in 1900 to 60.9 in 1914. Ibid., 40.

288 NOTES TO PAGES 141–145

155. Per-capita consumption of poultry and rabbit in Barcelona increased from 4.9 kilos in 1914 to 6 kilos in 1933. Per-capita consumption of fish in Barcelona increased from 19.1 kilos in 1914 to 29.4 kilos in 1933. Ibid., 47.

156. J. Raventós, *L'Alimentació Humana* (Barcelona: n.p., 1923), 31, as cited ibid., 47.

157. AGCB, *La Veu dels Carnissers,* "Fent Balanç" and "L'Escorxardor: Cotització oficial," April 1936, 10–13.

158. They also pointed to the problem of bread prices in Paris that had resulted from an excessive number of bakeries and which Parisian authorities had moved to resolve through policies that strictly limited the establishment of new outlets. AGCB, "Fent Balanç," *La Veu dels Carnissers,* April 1936, 10–11.

159. Guàrdia, Oyón, and Fava have calculated this on the basis of 1932 tax roles. "El Sistema de Mercats," 288.

160. La Revolució's *Libro de Registro,* which lists stall licenses issued for that market from 1892 to 1912, is one of the few extant documents that include the addresses of vendors. According to my calculations, 48.83 percent of the market licenses recorded in that source were issued to persons who listed the name and number of their street followed by the word *tienda* (shop). I was able to work with this registry in between interviewing vendors at L'Abaceria Central in 1991–92, and I owe a debt of gratitude to the market director at that time, Xavier Trull, for kindly granting me access to this crucial historical document held as part of the administrative records there.

161. "Asamblea de los Vendedores de Mercado," *Diario de Barcelona,* 3 September 1930.

162. Ibid.

163. Ibid.

164. AHCB, "Los Vendedores de los Mercados: Manifestación de Protesta," *La Unión: Órgano de la Unión de Vendedores de Pescado de Barcelona y su Provincia,* July 1930, 7–8.

165. AHCB, "Nuestra Adhesión," *La Unión,* April 1931, 1.

166. The so-called *descans dominical* (Sunday rest) was established for wage workers in most of the economy in September 1904. But Sundays were traditionally an important shopping day in Barcelona, so markets and shops did brisk business. Sunday closing involved a disruption, but it also afforded market vendors one day of rest in what was otherwise a very demanding work regime. On the history of the CADCI, see Manuel Lladonosa i Vall·llebrera, *Catalanisme i Moviment Obrer: El CADCI entre 1903 i 1923* (Barcelona: Publicacions de l'Abadia de Montserrat, 1988); Departament de Cultura, Junta Directiva del Centre Autonomista de Dependents del Comerç i de la Indústria, *Centre Autonomista de Dependents del Comerç i de la Indústria (CADCI) 1903–1939: Cataluyna avant!* (Barcelona: Department of Culture, 1992); Ma. Jesús Espuny Tomás, Guillermo García González, and Olga Paz Torres, *Los Obreros del Comercio: Un Análisis histórico-jurídico de la dependencia mercantil catalana* (Madrid: Dykinson, 2011).

167. AHCB, *Llibre d'Or,* 63–70. I am indebted to the insight on the matter of Sunday closing of the markets provided to me by Francesc Puigdomènech.

168. AHCOCINB, L'obertura dels establiments de peix el diumenge. Federación Española de Armadores de Buques de Pesca, 795–39. 12-C, 8-K-1, 1935.

169. AHCB, Gremis de Proveïments de Barcelona, *Els Gremis i el Moment d'Ara.*

170. A "junta directiva" comprised of eleven men drew up the statement. Among them were Enric Sánchez on behalf of the Unió General de Vendedors de Mercats de Barcelona; Lluís Vall on

behalf of the Associació de Vendedors del Mercat de Sant Antoni; Salvador Cararach on behalf of the Associació dels Carnissers; and Antoni Torrent on behalf of the Gremi de Pesca Salada. The interests of market-based trade in food were clearly represented among those who drafted the statement.

171. AHCB, Gremis de Proveïments de Barcelona, *Els Gremis i el Moment d'Ara*.

172. Ibid.

173. "La reglamentación de establecimientos de ultramarinos," *La Vanguardia,* 14 December 1932.

174. AHCB, *Llibre d'Or,* 74.

175. Nigel Townson, "The Second Republic, 1931–1936: Sectarianism, Schisms, and Strife," in Alvarez Junco and Shubert, eds., *Spanish History since 1808,* 228.

176. Termes, *De la Revolució de Setembre,* 377.

177. Ibid., 379.

178. Ibid., 380.

179. Ibid., 380.

180. AGCB, *La Veu dels Carnissers,* "Bases per a la Reglamentació del comerç al detall d'articles de menjar, beure i cremar d'us domèstic, en la ciutat de Barcelona," February 1936, 19-20. The specializations were as follows: Ultramarins i Queviures (colonial foodstuffs and provisions—i.e., grocers); Cafès, bars i tavernes; Confiteries i pastisseries (confectioners and pastry shops); Fruiteries (fruit shops); Carnisseries i cansaladeries (general butchers and pork butchers); Peixeteries (fresh fish); Pesca salada (salted fish); Vaqueries i lleteries (cowsheds and milk shops); Granaries en general i llegums cuits (granaries in general and cooked legumes); Ous, aviram i caça (eggs, poultry, and game); Carboneries (cooking coal shops); Fleques (bakeries); Restaurants; and Tendes especialitzades, no definides (specialized shops, not defined).

181. Ibid. The minimum distances between shops and market halls were as follows:

| Shop Specialization | Minimum Distance from Each Other in the Casc Antic and the Eixample | Minimum Distance from Each Other in Annexed Areas | Minimum Distance from Market Halls |
|---|---|---|---|
| Carnisseries i cansaladeries | 200 m | 250 m | 700 m |
| Peixeteries | 300 m | 400 m | 800 m |
| Vaqueries i lleteries | 100 m | 150 m | — |
| Fleques | 250 m | 300 m | 300 m |
| Restaurants | 50 m | 100 m | — |
| All others | 100 m | 150 m | 150 m |

*Source: La Veu dels Carnissers,* "Bases per a la Reglamentació del comerç al detall d'articles de menjar, beure i cremar d'us domestic, en la ciutat de Barcelona," February 1936, 19–20. Table by the author.

182. AHCOCINB, Obertura de nous establiments del ram de l'alimentació, caixa 795-38, 12-C, 12-2.

183. AHCOCINB, Comunicación de Cardús sobre la venta ambulante, caixa 796-27, 12, 12-B.

184. AGCB, *La Veu dels Carnissers,* "Extracte de la reunió general extraordinària celebrada el dia 26 del mes de març," April 1936, 16.

185. *La Vanguardia,* 31 March 1936.

186. Ibid.

187. Ibid.

188. José María García Madaria, *Estructura de la Administración Central, 1808–1931* (Madrid: Instituto Nacional de Administración Pública, 1982), 214.

189. AHCOCINB, *Reglamento para la venta, en tiendas, de pescado fresco y mariscos, 1929.*

190. Ibid.

191. AHCOCINB, *Disposicions de la Generalitat sobre els inspectors de proveïments, 1934,* caixa 792-24, 2-12-A.

CHAPTER 6. LAYERED NETWORKS: QUOTIDIAN LIFE IN THE MARKETS
BEFORE AND DURING THE CIVIL WAR

1. The "champagne" in question was most often locally produced *mèthode champenoise* wine refermented in bottles, or what we know today as "cava." It came mainly from the Alt Penedès and especially the town of Sant Sadurní d'Anoia, and was made using Parellada, Xarel·lo, and Macabeu grapes. The industry had its origins in the 1870s with the experimentation of Manuel Raventós i Domènech and Josep Raventós i Fatjó, which was based on the French methods set forth by Dom Pérignon. Lluís Bettonica and Lluís Bosch, *Els Caves de Catalunya* (Barcelona: Trebol, 1983), 39.

2. Charles Augustus Stoddard, *Spanish Cities* (New York: Charles Scribner's Sons, 1892), 12–13.

3. Ibid., 15.

4. As we have seen, per-capita fresh meat consumption in Barcelona fell 28.8 percent from 1914 to 1933. It is interesting, though, that the opposite was true of cured meats, which were highly valued in a period when the *sandvitx* had become all the rage. Per-capita cured meat consumption in the city rose 73.7 percent from 1914 to 1933. Nicolau-Nos and Pujol-Andreu, "Urbanization and Dietary Change," 46.

5. One of the best recent studies is José Luis Oyón's *La Quiebra de la Ciudad Popular.* See also Paul Heywood, *Marxism and the Failure of Organised Socialism in Spain*; and Chris Ealham, *Class, Culture, and Conflict in Barcelona, 1898–1937* (London: Routledge/Cañada Blanch Studies on Contemporary Spain, 2005).

6. Borja de Riquer i Permanyer, *Lliga Regionalista* (Barcelona: Edicions 62, 1976); Termes, *De la Revolució de Setembre*; Charles Edward Ehrlich, *Lliga Regionalista: Lliga Catalana, 1901–1936* (Barcelona: Editorial Alpha, 2004).

7. Historians focusing on Northern Europe have suggested that lower-middle-class groups had the potential to play key intermediary roles among urban social classes in the late nineteenth and early twentieth centuries. See Geoffrey Crossick and Heinz-Gerhard Haupt, eds., *Shopkeepers and Master Artisans in Nineteenth-Century Europe* (London: Methuen and Co., 1984), 18.

8. Sarah Hughes and Brady Hughes, *Women in Ancient Civilizations* (Washington: American Historical Association, 1988), 10.

9. See, for example, Niara Sudarkasa, *Where Women Work: A Study of Yoruba Women in the Marketplace and in the Home* (Ann Arbor: University of Michigan Press, 1973); Gracia Clark, *African Market Women: Seven Life Stories from Ghana* (Bloomington: University of Indiana Press, 2010); Jennifer Alexander, *Trade, Traders, and Trading in Rural Java* (Singapore and New York: Oxford University Press, 1987); Seung-mo Chung, *Markets: Traditional Korean Society,* translated by Yoon-jung Cho and

Eun-young Min (Seoul: Ewha Womans University Press, 2006); Seligmann, *Peruvian Street Lives*; Ina Dinerman, "Economic Alliances in a Regional Mexican Economy," *Ethnology* 17, no. 1 (1978): 53–64; Florence E. Babb, *Between Field and Cooking Pot: The Political Economy of Marketwomen in Peru* (Austin: University of Texas Press, 1989); Francesca Miller, "Women in the Social, Political, and Economic Transformation of Latin America and the Caribbean," in Richard L. Harris and Jorge Nef, eds., *Capital, Power, and Inequality in Latin America and the Caribbean* (Lanham: Rowan & Littlefield, 2008), 174–95; Lindenfeld, *Speech and Sociability in French Urban Marketplaces*; Thompson, *The Virtuous Marketplace* and "Urban Renovation, Moral Regeneration."

10. Historians of Spain and of Europe more generally agree that the formation of the guild system had a prejudicial impact on women's ability to participate on an independent basis in the formal economy. Yet there were exceptions and loopholes. In Genoa, there was considerable parity between husbands and wives engaged in artisanal work, and in Venice, where guilds had less political power, women's work was defended by urban authorities. Likewise in Spain, Paulino Iradiel has shown that Valencian female artisans had greater economic independence than their noble counterparts and could in some instances ply their trades irrespective of whether they were married or not. With respect to Barcelona, Teresa Vinyoles has recently shown that in the late Middle Ages there were women who owned their own businesses and contracted apprentices in certain areas of textile production. Teresa Maria Vinyoles i Vidal, "La mujer bajomedieval a través de las ordenanzas municipales de Barcelona," in Seminario de Estudios de la Mujer de la Universidad Autonoma de Madrid, ed., *Las mujeres medievales y su ámbito jurídico: Actas de la II Jornadas de Investigación Interdisciplinaria* (Madrid: Universidad Autónoma, 1983), 137–54. See also Solà "Las Mujeres como productoras autónomas"; Batlle, "Noticias sobre la mujer catalana," 201–21; Ricardo Córdoba de la Llave, "El papel de la mujer en la actividad artesanal cordobesa a fines del sigle XV," in Muñoz Fernández and Segura, eds., *El Trabajo de las mujeres en al Edad Media Hispana*, 99–112; Coral Cuadrada Majó, "Les dones en el treball urbá (segles XIV–XV)," *Anuario de Estudios Medievales* 29 (1999): 219–34; Natalie Zemon Davis "Women in the Crafts in Sixteenth-Century Lyon," *Feminist Studies* 8, no. 1 (1982): 46–80; Roberto Greci, "Donne e corporazioni: La fluidità di un rapport," in Angela Groppi, ed., *Il lavoro delle donne* (Roma: Laterza, 1996), 71–91; Bonassie, *La organización del trabajo en Barcelona*; Paulino Iradiel, "Familia y function de la mujer en actividades no agrarias," in Yves-René Fonquerne, Alfonso Estaban, Casa de Velásquez, eds., *La condición de la mujer en la Edad Media: Actas del Coloquio celebrado en la Casa de Velázquez del 5–7 de noviembre de 1984* (Madrid: Universidad Complutense-Casa de Velázquez, 1984), 223–60.

11. ACA, *Manual de la Taxa del Comercio, 1717*. Secció Hisenda, Sèrie Inv. 1, Sig. 3457. For recent approaches to the study of women's work in the family economy, see Cristina Borderías and Pilar Pérez-Fuentes, "Mujeres, trabajos, y economías familiars en España (siglos XIX y XX)," in Borderías, ed., *La Historia de las Mujeres*, 269–308.

12. ACA, *Manual de la Taxa del Comercio, 1717*. Sección Hisenda, Sèrie Inv. 1, Sig. 3457. The largest number of women in any of the guild organizations associated with food sales were in the Confraria de Revendedors (Confraternity of Resellers), where at least 24 of the 221 members listed were female.

13. Marta Vicente, "'Comerciar en Femení': La identitat de les empresàries ala Barcelona del segle XVIII," *Recerques: Història/Economia/Cultura* 56 (2008): 48. See also Marta Vicente, "Textual Uncertainties: The Written Legacy of Women Entrepreneurs in Eighteenth-Century Barcelona," in Marta Vicente and Luis Corteguera, eds., *Women, Texts and Authority in the Early Modern Spanish*

*World* (Aldershot, Eng.: Ashgate, 2003), 183–95; and Gayle K. Brunelle, "Policing the Monopolizing Women of Early Modern Nantes," *Journal of Women's History* 19, no. 2 (Summer 2007): 10–35.

14. Leonore Davidoff and Catherine Hall, *Family Fortunes: Men and Women of the English Middle Class, 1780–1850* (2nd ed.; London: Routledge, 2003).

15. Robert Beachy, Béatrice Craig, and Alastair Owens, eds., *Women, Business and Finance;* Sara Horrell and Jane Humphries, "Women's Labour Work Participation and the Transition to the Male Breadwinner Family, 1790-1865," *Economic History Review* 48 (1995): 89–117.

16. Gálvez Muñoz and Fernández Pérez, "Female Entreprenuership in Spain"; Àngels Solà, "Negocis i identitat laboral de les dones," *Recerques: Història/Economia/Cultura* 56 (2008): 5–18; Àngels Solà, "Impressores i llibreteres a la Barcelona dels segles XVIII i XIX," *Recerques: Història/Economia/Cultura* 56 (2008): 91–129; Juanjo Romero Marín, "Presència femenina a la gestió dels negocis artesans barcelonins: 1823–1860," *Recerques: Història/Economia/Cultura* 56 (2008): 165–80; Cristina Borderías, "La historia de las mujeres a las puertas del nuevo milenio: Balance y perspectivas," in Borderías, ed., *La Historia de las Mujeres,* 5–27; Cristina Borderías, "La transición de la actividad femenina en el mercado de trabajo Barcelonés (1856–1930): Teoría social y realidad histórica en el sistema estadístico moderno," in Carmen Sarasúa and Lina Gálvez-Muñoz, eds., *Mujeres y Hombres en los mercados de trabajo: ¿Privilegios o eficiencia?* (San Vicente de Raspeig: Publicaciones de la Universidad de Alicante, 2003), 241–76.

17. ACA, *Contribución Industrial de Barcelona: Matricula—Todas las Tarifas* 1848 Secció Hisenda, Sèrie Inv. 1, Sig.12545.

18. Ibid. Using Manuel Saurí's and José Matas' *Guía General de Barcelona* (Barcelona: Imprenta de Manuel Saurí, 1849), Àngels Solà has calculated similar figures for independent female entrepreneurship in the food retailing sector. She finds that 22 percent of the butcher shops in the city were owned by women in 1849, as well as 10.4 percent of the pork, ham, and sausage shops, 6.5 percent of the cafés, 14.7 percent of the taverns and bodegas. For market stalls, she finds that 96.42 percent of the egg stalls, 90 percent of vegetable stalls, and 72.8 percent of the fresh and dried fruit stalls were in the hands of women. She does not include those listed as widows in these calculations. "Las mujeres y sus negocios," 389.

19. All of the market-stall categories in the 1848 tax rolls were listed as paying half the *cuotas* as shops.

20. ACA, Viñas y Campi, *El Indicador de España y Sus Posesiones Ultramarinas,* Secció Hisenda, Sèrie Inv. 1, Sig. 4889. Though clearly not offering a full picture of the retail economy in food, *El Indicador* does offer some further hints of the advance of female entrepreneurship in shopkeeping. Of the 309 *tiendas de comestibles y ultramarinos* in Barcelona, 32 (10.35 percent) are listed in the names of women; only two of these women are indicated as being widows.

21. Cerdá, *Estadística Urbana de Barcelona,* 622–27.

22. ACA, *Contribuciones Industriales y del Comercio,* 1873. Secció Hisenda. Sèrie Inv. 1, Sig. 12687.

23. Arts. 6 and 8, 1885 *Código Comercial de España.*

24. Lucy A. Sponsler, "The Status of Married Women under the Legal System of Spain," *Journal of Legal History* 3 (1982): 125–82; Mary Nash, *Mujer, Familia y Trabajo en España, 1875–1936* (Barcelona: Anthropos, 1983), 20, 371–73.

25. Sponsler, "The Status of Married Women," 125.

26. AHCB, *Reglamento para el régimen de los Mercados, 1898.*

27. AHCB, *Reglamentos de los Mercados en General, 1928.*

28. Stephen Jacobson, "Law and Nationalism in Nineteenth-Century Europe: The Case of Catalonia in Comparative Perspective," *Law and History Review* 20, no. 2 (June 2002): 320.

29. Ibid., 315.

30. Termes, *De la Revolució de Setembre,* 83–86.

31. Dolors Comas d'Argemir, "Household, Family, and Social Stratification: Inheritance and Labor Strategies in a Catalan Village (Nineteenth and Twentieth Centuries)," *Journal of Family History* 13, no. 1 (1988); Abraham Isaevich, "Corporate Household and Ecocentric Kinship Group in Catalonia," *Ethnology* 20 (1981): 227–90.

32. AMAB, *Gazeta Municipal de Barcelona: Presupeusto Ordinario de Gastos Interior y Especial de la Zona de Ensanche para 1931.*

33. Administrative Records Boqueria Market, *Mercado de San José, Relación de Vendedores con Puesto Fijo Existente en este Mercado.* Data tabulated by the author based on 613 records of stall acquisition from June 1920 through May 1925.

34. *L'Opinió,* 15 April 1933; "L'Obra constructive de l'Ajuntament: El Nou Mercat del Ninot," *Gaseta Municipal de Barcelona,* 2 October 1933, 1007–15.

35. The 1898 code did not include such a provision. The recognition of family-economy arrangements appears in the 1928 code as Article 18. AHCB, *Reglamentos de los Mercados en General,* 1928.

36. AHCB, Article 42, *Reglamentos de los Mercados en General, 1928.*

37. Here, *crac* means "ace" or "crackerjack."

38. See, for example, ARSAM documents dated 16 October 1913, 15 August 1917, 27 May 1918.

39. *La Publicidad,* 7 August 1918.

40. Rekas i Mussoms and Arús i Masranom, "El Bornet."

41. Francesca Orriols Palmada, interview, 20 March 1992.

42. MAE, Josep Maria de Sagarra, *Obres Completes: Prosa,* vol. 2 (Barcelona: Editorial Selecta, 1967). The play opened at the Teatre Poliorama on 21 March 1935, starring Mercè Nicolau in the role of Antònia.

43. Roure, *La Reina del Mercat,* 3. In the original, the line reads: "Doncs que s'interessi pel de casa seva, que prou feina hi té, que la seva senyora, segons diuen, és una mena de balancí que tothom s'hi gronxa!"

44. Ibid., 3.

45. AHCB, Ramon Juncosa, *Mercat del Guinardo,* in *Almanac de la Cooperació* (1938), 170–95.

46. AHCB, Juncosa, *Mercat del Guinardó,* 179.

47. MAE, Sagarra, *La Rambla de les Floristes,* 1613–14.

48. Ibid., 1614–16.

49. *La Reina del Mercat* opened in the Teatre Espanyol on 8 January 1927; *El Casori de la Tresina* opened in the same theater on 12 June that same year.

50. Roure, *La Reina del Mercat,* 28.

51. MAE, Alfons Roure, *El Casori de la Tresina.*

52. MAE, Josep Burgas, *A la Remei l'han fet Reina o el Premi d'esser Bonica,* 46. The play opened at the Teatre Novetats on 2 October 1917.

53. Jose Olives Puig, "Deterioración Urbana e Inmigración en un Barrio de Casco Antiguo de Barcelona: Sant Cugat del Rec," *Revista de Geografía* 3 (1969): 40-72; Lluís Casassas i Simó and Pau

Vila, *Barcelona i la Seva Rodalia al llarg del Temps* (Barcelona: Editorial Aedos, 1974); Oriol Bohigas, Manuel Guàrdia, Joan Fuster, Antoni Nicolau, Xavier Peiró, Rafel Torrella, Daniel Venteo, et al., *La Construcció de la gran Barcelona: L'Obertura de la Via Laietana, 1908–1958* (Barcelona: Museu d'Història de la Ciutat, 2001).

54. AHCB, José Artís Balaguer, "El Primitivo Mercado de Santa Catalina," 86.

55. Oral history interview with Carme Giner Folch, conducted by the author, 10 May 1992.

56. DPAMAB, R-100 series, caixa 17, # 10637, documents dated May 1921 and 29 July 1921.

57. Ibid.

58. Maria Cararach Vernet, interview, 5 May 1992.

59. Oral history interview with Joan Mani Burgada, conducted by the author, 8 April 1992.

60. Dolors Monserdà de Macià, *La Fabricanta: Novel·la de costums barcelonins, 1860–1875* (Barcelona: Edicions l'Eixample, 1992).

61. Gary W. McDonogh, "Monserdà's Barcelona: Women and the City at the Turn of the Century," *Ideas '92* 7 (Fall 1990): 59–60.

62. Jaume Fabre and Josep Maria Huertas Claveria, *Tots els Barris de Barcelona*, vol. 2, *Els barris que foren independents* (Barcelona: Edicions 62, 1976), 11; Solà Parera and Solà Parera, "El creixament urbà de Gràcia," 389–410.

63. Fabre and Huertas, *Tots els Barris*, 2:20.

64. Ibid., 2:22.

65. Mercè Rodoreda, *La Plaça del Diamant* (Barcelona: Club Editor, 2004). The English-language version is Mercè Rodoreda, *The Time of the Doves*, trans. David H. Rosenthal (New York: Taplinger Publishing, 1980).

66. Oral history interview with Joana Grillé Fornell, conducted by the author, 1 June 1992.

67. Oral history interview with Josefa Noguerolas Casas and Tomàs Sancho Roman, conducted by the author, 19 May 1992.

68. Administrative Records of Boqueria Market, Barcelona, *Mercado de San José: Relacion de Vendedores con puesto fijo existente en enste Mercado, 1920*.

69. Oral history interview with Núria Manadé Ginestà, conducted by the author, 20 March 1992.

70. Oral history interview with Rafel Martí Fiol, conducted by the author, 11 May 1992.

71. Oral history interview with Mercè Miró García, conducted by the author, 13 March 1992.

72. ARSAM documents dated 28 March 1908, 29 December 1915, 20 January 1916, 28 January 1916, 18 April 1916, 22 May 1916, and 2 June 1916.

73. ARSAM, with respect to violations of food packaging regulations, see documents dated 5 April 1904, 15 June 1905, 4 August 1905, 12 July 1906, 14 July 1908, 21 June 1909, 13 June 1914, 28 August 1916, 6 September 1916, 9 June 1917, 27 May 1918, and 1 June 1918; with respect to the use of illegal meat preservatives (*nievelina, valhol,* and *ozono*), see documents dated 30 August 1902, 18 August 1905, 7 June 1906, 7 November 1906, 17 August 1906, 9 October 1912, a, b, and c, 10 June 1913, 24 August 1916, 2 September 1916, 9 June 1917, 20 June 1917, 27 May 1918, and 18 June 1921.

74. Radcliff, "The Emerging Challenge of Mass Politics," 152.

75. María Luz Arriero, "Los motines de subsistencias en España, 1895–1905," *Estudios de Historia Social* 30 (1984): 193–250.

76. Pamela Beth Radcliff, "Women's Politics: Consumer Riots in Twentieth-Century Spain," in Enders and Radcliff, eds., *Constructing Spanish Womanhood*, 323.

77. *La Vanguardia de Barcelona*, 11 January 1918.

78. Ibid.

79. Ibid.

80. Ibid., 23 January 1918.

81. I am indebted to Juanjo Romero Marín for sharing his insights and some of his research on the 1918 consumer uprising.

82. Lester Golden, "The Women in Command: The Barcelona Consumer War of 1918," *UCLA Historical Journal* 6 (1985): 5–32; Lester Golden, "Les dones com avantguarda: El Rebombori del pa de gener de 1918," *L'Avenç* 44 (December 1981): 45-50.

83. AHCB, *Llibre d'Or del Cercle d'Ultramarins, Queviures i Similars*, 25.

84. *La Vanguardia de Barcelona*, 23 January 1918.

85. Golden, "The Women in Command," 13.

86. Ibid., 20.

87. *La Vanguardia de Barcelona*, 16 January 1918.

88. Ibid., 23 January 1918.

89. Radcliff, "Women's Politics," 303.

90. Joan Manent i Peses, *Records d'un sindicalista libertari* (Paris, 1977), 29, quoted in Golden, "The Women in Command," 20.

91. Ealham, *Class, Culture and Conflict*, 102–18.

92. Michael Seidman, "Women's Subversive Individualism in Barcelona during the 1930s," *International Review of Social History* 48 (1992): 172.

93. In addition to those sources already cited, see Lynne Taylor, "Food Riots Revisited," *Journal of Social History* 30, no. 2 (Winter 1996): 483–96.

94. Kaplan, "Female Consciousness and Collective Action," 545–66.

95. Kaplan, *Red City, Blue Period*, 119; Temma Kaplan, "Women and Communal Strikes in the Crisis of 1917–1922," in *Becoming Visible: Women in European History*, ed. Renate Bridenthal, Claudia Koontz, and Susan Mosher Stuart (2nd ed.; Boston: Houghton Mifflin, 1987), 429–49.

96. Joan B. Culla Clarà, *El republicanisme lerrouxista a Catalunya, 1901–1923* (Barcelona: Curial, 1986).

97. Albert Pérez Baró, *Història de les Cooperatives a Catalunya* (Barcelona: Editorial Crítica, 1989).

98. Townson, "The Second Republic, 1931–1936," 233.

99. Ibid., 234.

100. Ibid., 234.

101. Seidman, *Republic of Egos*.

102. Ibid., 45.

103. *Solidaridad Obrero*, 4 October 1936.

104. Ibid.

105. ARSAM, documents dated 22 October 1936, 30 November 1936a, and 30 November 1936b.

106. ARSAM, 2 November 1937.

107. ARSAM, 19 November 1937.

108. ARSAM, 26 November 1937.

109. *Estadística: Resumenes demográficos de la Ciudad de Barcelona. El Periodo 1936 a 1938 y de 1939*, 22, cited in Seidman, "Women's Subversive Individualism," 172.

110. Seidman, *Republic of Egos*, 102.

111. Oral history interview with Isabel Colera Magrans, conducted by the author, 1 June 1992.

112. Josefa Nogueroles Casas and Tomás Sancho Roman, interview, 19 May 1992.

113. Mayor Joan Pich i Pon (1878–1937) was forced to resign because of his involvement in the scandal.

114. Antonia Peña Martín, interview, 8 May 1992.

115. Joan i Jacint Reventós, *Dos Infants i la Guerra: Records de 1936–39* (2nd ed.; Barcelona: Club Editor, 1978), 101.

116. Ibid., 102.

117. Mercè Miró García, interview, 13 March 1992.

118. Maria Cararach Vernet, interview, 5 May 1992.

119. Carme Giner Folch, interview, 10 May 1992.

120. Oral history interview with Antoni Jover Barceló, conducted by the author, 3 June 1992.

121. Maria Teresa Miller, "Un Grapat d'Anècdotes Autobiogràfiques, 1930–1945," unpublished manuscript in the author's possession, 2007.

CHAPTER 7. AND TIME GOES ON: MARKET VENDOR LIFE AND WORK UNDER FRANCO

1. Oral history interview with Semi Colominas Aluja, conducted by author, 11 May 1992.

2. Oral history interview with Rosa Sanaluja Cot, conducted by author, 14 May 1992.

3. Carme Molinero and Pere Ysàs, *Patria, Justicia y Pan: Nivell de Vida i Condicions de Treball a Catalunya, 1939-1951* (Barcelona: La Magrana, 1985), 176 and Appendix 9.

4. Ibid., Appendix 9, 178.

5. Oral history interview with Francesc Barceló Duran, conducted by author, 25 May 1992.

6. Molinero and Ysàs, *Patria, Justica y Pan*, 178.

7. Amando de Miguel, *La Vida Cotidiana de los Españoles en el Siglo XX* (Barcelona: Planeta, 2001), 95; Antonio Cazorla Sánchez, *Fear and Progress: Ordinary Lives in Franco's Spain, 1939–1975* (Oxford: Wiley-Blackwell, 2009).

8. Molinero and Ysàs, *Patria, Justica y Pan*, 190.

9. Ibid., 198–202.

10. Seidman, *Republic of Egos*, 239, 235.

11. Ibid., 239.

12. Manel Risques, Angel Duarte, Borja de Riquer, and Josep M. Roig Rosich, *Història de la Catalunya Contemporània* (Barcelona: Pòrtic, Biblioteca Universitària, 1999), 351.

13. Borja de Riquer and Joan B. Culla, *El Franquisme i la Transició Democràtica (1939–1988)*, Vol. 7 of *Història de Catalunya*, dir. Pierre Vilar, 125.

14. Ibid., 126.

15. Ibid., 127.

16. Molinero and Ysàs, *Patria, Justica y Pan*, 183.

17. Riquer and Culla, *El Franquisme i la Transició Democràtica*, 129.

18. Ibid., 128.

19. Ibid.

20. Oral history interview with Joaquim Esteba Esteve, conducted by author, 13 May 1992.

21. de Miguel, *La Vida Cotidiana,* 94.

22. Francesc Cabana, *37 anys de Franquisme a Catalunya: Una visió econòmica* (2nd ed.; Barcelona: Pòrtic, 2001), 20; Helen Graham, *The Spanish Civil War: A Very Short Introduction* (Oxford: Oxford University Press, 2005), 129.

23. ARSAM, backdated document dated 31 January 1936.

24. Miquel Mateu i Pla (1898–1972) served as mayor of Barcelona from 27 January 1939 to 17 April 1945. The Junta Comarcal del Barcelonés was created by decree of the Generalitat on 23 September 1937 as the organism through which food was distributed to hospitals, clinics, nurseries, and social-aid establishments of various kinds.

25. DPAMAB, R-100 series, caia 40, #15022, documents dated 22 March 1939 and 1 April 1939.

26. DPAMAB, R-100 series, #32019–32032, document dated 20 July 1939.

27. AGCB. The narrative that follows is drawn from Sans y Prats, *Libro Diario.*

28. Other trade-specific associations appear to have followed the same course of action. By 1945, the fresh fish retailers in the city were back in open operation with Santiago Caba Almirall serving as president of a new Gremio de Detallistas de Pescado Fresco. DPAMAB, R-100 Series, caixa 42, #16288, document dated 31 January 1945.

29. *Diario de Barcelona,* 12 January 1944.

30. *La Vanguardia Española,* 31 December 1944.

31. AHCB, *Gaceta Municipal de Barcelona,* "La obra constructiva del Ayuntamiento: El Mercado de la Sagrada Familía," 12 April 1948, 211.

32. Oral history interview with Francesc Colominas Aznar and Joana Calvet Carrado, conducted by author, 22 May 1992.

33. Semi Colominas Aluja, interview, 11 May 1992.

34. Joaquim Esteba Esteve, interview, 13 May 1992.

35. Oral history interviews with Carmen Valls Roig, conducted by the author, 18 July 1990 and 19 June 1992.

36. Maria Cararach Vernet, interview, 5 May 1992.

37. Administrative Records Area de Proveïments i Consum (now Institut Municipal de Mercats de Barcelona), *Llibres de Registre,* and Administrative Records Santa Caterina, l'Abaceria Central, and Sant Antoni markets. Data collected and tabulated by the author. La Boqueria is not included in these calculations.

38. AHCB, Ayuntamiento de Barcelona, *Reglamentos de los Mercados en General y de los especiales del de pescado, y de frutas y verduras, al por mayor, y de los encantes,* 1942, article 9, section E. Entit. 1-25, caixa 2, 1.

39. See Aurora G. Morcillo, *True Catholic Womanhood: Gender Ideology in Franco's Spain* (Dekalb: Northern Illinois University Press, 2000); Aurora Morcillo Gómez, "Shaping True Catholic Womanhood: Francoist Educational Discourse on Women," in Enders and Radcliff, eds., *Constructing Spanish Womanhood,* 51–69.

40. See Gálvez Muñoz and Fernández Pérez, "Female Entreprenuership in Spain," 503–505, for a discussion of new legal impediments to women's entrance into business concerns in the post–Civil War era.

41. See Mary Nash, "Towards a New Moral Order: National Catholicism, Culture and Gender," in Alvarez Junco and Shubert, eds., *Spanish History since 1808,* 289–302.

42. Antonia Peña Martín, interview, 21 May 1992.

43. Francesc Colominas Aznar and Joana Calvet Terrado, interview, 22 May 1992.

44. Oral history interview with Maria Teresa Fernández Mitjans, conducted by the author, 27 March 1992.

45. Oral history interview with Asunción Conejero Moreno, conducted by the author, 27 March 1992.

46. Oral history interview with Pere Malla Vila, conducted by the author, 25 May 1992.

47. Oral history interview with Carmen González Morales, conducted by the author, 11 May 1992.

48. Oral history interview with Isabel Colera Magrans, conducted by the author, 1 June 1992.

49. Oral history interview with Francesc Colominas Aznar and Joana Calvet Terrado, conducted by the author, 22 May 1992.

50. Oral history interview with Joaquim Esteba Esteve, conducted by the author, 13 May 1992.

51. Oral history interview with Pere Malla Vila, conducted by the author, 25 May 1992.

52. Claudia Goldin, "The U-Shaped Female Labor Force Function in Economic Development and Economic History," in T. Paul Schultz, ed., *Investment in Women's Human Capital and Economic Development* (Chicago: University of Chicago Press, 1995), 61–90.

53. Borderías and Pérez-Fuentes, "Mujeres, trabajos y economías familiars," 296.

54. Enriqueta Camps, *La formación del mercado de trabajo industrial en Cataluña del S. XIX* (Madrid: Ministerio de Trabajo y Seguridad Social, 1995); Enriqueta Camps, "Las tranformaciones del Mercado de trabajo en Cataluña (1850–1925): Migraciones, ciclos de vida y economías familiars," *Revista de Historia Industrial* 11 (1997): 45–53; Pilar Pérez-Fuentes, *Vivir y morir en las minas: Estrategias familiars y relaciones de género en la primera industrialización vizcaína: 1877–1913* (Bilbao: Servicio Editorial Universidad del País Vasco, 1993); Pilar Pérez-Fuentes, "El trabajo de las mujeres en la España del los siglos XIX y XX: Consideraciones metodológicas," *Arenal: Revista de Historia de las Mujeres* 2, no. 2 (1995): 219–45; Pilar Pérez-Fuentes, *Ganadores de pan y amas de casa: Otra mirada sobre la industrialización vasca* (Bilbao: Servicio Editorial Universidad del País Vasco, 2004); Cristina Borderías, *Entre Líneas: Trabajo e identidad femenina en la España Contemporánea. La Compañia Telefónica Nacional de España* (Barcelona: Icaria Editorial, 1993); Cristina Borderías, "El Trabajo de las mujeres en la Cataluña contemporánea desde la perspectiva de los hogares: Balance y perspectivas," *Arenal: Revista de historia de las mujeres* 9, no. 2 (2002) 269–300; Cristina Borderías, "Women Workers in the Barcelona Labour Market, 1856–1936," in Angel Smith, ed., *Red Barcelona: Social Protest and Labour Mobilization in the Twentieth Century* (London: Routledge, 2002), 142–67; Borderías, "La Transición de la actividad femenina," 241–276; Cristina Borderías, "A Gendered View of Family Budgets in Mid-nineteenth Century Barcelona," *Histoire et Mésure* 18, nos. 1/2 (2003): 113–47; Rubén Pallol, "Mujer, familia y trabajo en el Madrid de la segunda mitad del XIX," paper presented at the XIII Coloquio Internacional de la Asociación Española de Investigación de Historia de las Mujeres, Barcelona, 19–21 October 2006, CD-Rom edition; Arantza Pareja, "Pequeños negocios femeninos, grandes aportaciones para la familia: Las mujeres bilbaínas a principios del S. XX," paper presented at the XIII Coloquio Internacional de la Asociación Española de Investigación de Historia de las Mujeres, Barcelona, 19–21 October 2006, CD-Rom edition.

55. For an account of the economic take-off, see Sebastian Balfour, "The *Desarollo* Years, 1955–1975," in Alvarez Junco and Shubert, eds., *Spanish History since 1808,* 277–88.

56. de Riquer and Culla, *El Franquisme i la Transicio Democratica*, 189.

57. Ibid., 186.

58. *Diario de Barcelona*, "De mercado en mercado: Ayer en la de la Boquería," 10 March 1964.

59. *Solidaridad Nacional*, 28 May 1950 and 14 June 1956; *La Prensa*, 17 March 1950; *La Vanguardia Española*, 31 May 1958.

60. *La Prensa*, 17 March 1950.

61. *Diario de Barcelona*, 1 September 1957.

62. *El Destino*, 29 October 1955; *La Vanguardia Española*, 31 August 1957.

63. Pamela Beth Radcliff, *Making Democratic Citizens in Spain: Civil Society and the Popular Origins of the Transition, 1960–1978* (Basingstoke and New York: Palgrave Macmillan, 2011), 9, 33–34, 77. A number of the neighborhood associations also took the initiative to monitor market-based trade in defense of consumer interests.

64. *El Correo Catalan*, 10 June 1950; *La Vanguardia Española*, 31 March 1958.

65. Josep Maria Porcioles i Colomer served as mayor of Barcelona from 1957 to 1973.

66. *Diario de Barcelona*, 31 May 1957.

67. *La Prensa*, 17 March 1950; *El Destino*, 21 January 1956; *Diario de Barcelona*, 11 March 1959.

68. *Solidaridad Nacional*, 14 June 1956.

69. *El Destino*, 21 January 1956.

70. Ibid., 12 December 1954.

71. Ibid. 75.

72. *Diario de Barcelona*, 1 September 1957.

73. *Barcelona Revista* 4, (1955).

74. *Solidaridad Nacional*, 14 June 1956.

75. *La Prensa*, 1 August 1958.

76. *Diario de Barcelona*, 15 July 1958.

77. *La Vanguardia Española*, 23 December 1958.

78. *Diario de Barcelona*, 15 July 1958; *El Noticiero Universal*, 13 March 1959; *Solidaridad Nacional*, 20 December 1959.

79. *El Correo Catalan*, 24 September 1959.

80. The ongoing use of vendor calls in the markets of the city in the early 1960s is documented in a series of newspaper columns entitled "De Mercado en Mercado," in which a journalist using the pseudonym "Poker" went from one market to another, recording anecdotes. See *Diario de Barcelona*, 10 March 1964, on La Boqueria, 14 March 1964 on Hostafrancs, 17 March 1964 on Sants, and 21 March 1964 on El Clot.

81. *Diario de Barcelona*, 24 September 1958.

82. See Sibylle Braendi, "Women and the New Self-Service Stores in the Food and Beverage Sector, 1948–1970," paper presented at the History of Consumption as Social History Conference, Freie Universität, Berlin, 2 June 1994.

83. The organization included those licensed to retail foods included in the *ultramarinos, conservas,* and *comestibles* categories.

84. *El Noticiero Universal*, 13 March 1959.

85. For information on Establiments d'Alimentació, S.A, see http://www.superestalvi.com/inici/, accessed 6 January 2014.

86. Jordi Mas and Òscar Ubide, *Boqueria Gourmand* (Barcelona: Viena Edicions, 2010), 32–33.

87. BC Ayuntamiento de Barcelona, *Estudio Sobre el Comercio Minorista de Alimentación: Análisis de una Encuesta* (Barcelona: Ayuntamiento de Barcelona, Gabinete Tecníco de Programación, 1976), 68.

88. Marçal Tarragó i Balagué, dir., *PECAB: Pla especial de l'equipament comercial alimentari de la ciutat de Barcelona* (Barcelona: Ajuntament de Barcelona, Àrea de Proveïments i Consum, 1990), 13. Figures provided in the PECAB may be misleading, though, because they lump wholesaling and retailing firms together. The increases are nonetheless significant. There was a 25-percent increase in general grocery firms, a 78-percent increase in green-grocery firms, and a 38-percent increase in butchers.

89. Ibid., 10–12. The contrast with France, where there were 200 inhabitants per food-retailing establishment, was even starker, as is comparison with the greater Parisian metropolitan area, where the ratio was one food retailer for every 204 inhabitants.

90. Ibid., 11–12. Forty percent were larger than that in France.

91. The terms *latifundismo* and *minifundismo* have most often been used to describe land-tenure systems featuring either a small number of individuals owning huge tracts of land or a large number of individuals owning very small tracts. Here, obviously, the term *minifundismo* is used in reference to a commercial system in which large numbers of small enterprises predominate in a specific sector of the economy and in a particular urban context.

92. BC Ayuntamiento de Barcelona, *Estudio Sobre el Comercio Minorista de Alimentación*, 85–86. This study shows that in Barcelona by 1976, 10.3 percent of alimentary expenditures were taking place in self-service or supermarket enterprises. The figure for Madrid is here given as 8.8 percent.

93. No author given, "Les mestreses de casa continuen preferint el mercat," *El Taulell* 1, Federació de Gremis de Detallistes de Productes Alimenticis i Associacions de Concessionaris de Mercats de Catalunya (hereinafter FEGRAM), (1992): 8. The article gives a figure of 60.1 percent of pre-packaged foods sold in supermarkets and 9.4 percent in hypermarkets.

94. *Diario de Barcelona*, "Barcelona 1888–1988," Fascicle 28, "Més mercats que a cap ciutat europea," 16 October 1988, 191–92.

95. Ibid., 188. In 1940, the figure was one for every 58,000 inhabitants.

96. "Les mestresses de casa continuen preferint el mercat," 8. The data presented in this article for pre-packaged goods offers an inverted picture from that of fresh food. In pre-packaged goods, public market halls had only an 8.6 percent share of the market, traditional neighborhood shops a 13.3-percent share, and galeries comercials a 5.9-percent share. The article also offers crucial age-based analysis for female food-shopping patterns in relation to neighborhood residence in 1992. These variations will be discussed in more detail in the epilogue.

97. See Koleen M. Guy, *When Champagne Became French: Wine and the Making of a National Identity* (Baltimore: Johns Hopkins University Press, 2007); Amy B. Trubek, *The Taste of Place: A Cultural Journey into Terroir* (Berkeley: University of California Press, 2008).

98. On late-nineteenth and early-twentieth-century Spanish, Catalan, and Basque nationalism, see Ucelay Da Cal, "The Restoration," 121–54. On the left Republican-Socialist coalitions' efforts in addressing stunted Spanish nationalism, see Sandie Holguin, *Creating Spaniards: Culture and National Identity in Republican Spain* (Madison: University of Wisconsin Press, 2002).

99. See Hank Johnston, *Tales of Nationalism: Catalonia, 1939–1975* (New Brunswick: Rutgers

University Press, 1991); Daniele Conversi, *The Basques, the Catalans, and Spain: Alternative Routes to Nationalist Mobilisation* (Reno: University of Nevada Press, 1997); John Hargreaves, *Freedom for Catalonia? Catalan Nationalism, Spanish Identity and the Barcelona Olympic Games* (Cambridge: Cambridge University Press, 2000).

100. Among these were Vincenç Serrano, *Manuel del boletaire català* (Barcelona: Editorial Barcino, 1959); Josep Iglesies, *El llibre de cuina de Scala Dei* (Barcelona: Fundació Francesc Blasi Vallespinosa, 1963); the anonymously authored *Catalunya llaminera: Descripció de les postre típiques Catalanes* (Barcelona: Editorial Millà, 1968); Antoni R. Dalmau's *200 plats casolans de cuina catalana: Recull de receptes populars* (Barcelona: Editorial Millà, 1969).

101. "El Mercado de la Boquería: Ese Gigantesco Bodegon," *El Destino*, 12 December 1954; "El Mercado de San José, o de la Boquería, cumplió años ayer," *Diario de Barcelona*, 20 March 1958.

102. Elizabeth Gordon, *Cuisines of the Western World* (New York: Golden Press, 1965).

103. Ibid., 47–51.

104. Elizabeth Cass, *Spanish Cooking* (London: A. Deutsch, 1957); Betty Wason, *The Art of Spanish Cooking* (Garden City, N.Y.: Doubleday, 1963).

105. Gordon, *Cuisines of the Western World*, 47.

106. Peter S. Feibleman, *The Cooking of Spain and Portugal* (New York: Time-Life Books, 1969).

107. Ibid., 85.

108. Ibid.

109. Table 1, in Jordi Maluquer de Motes, "El Turismo, motor fundamental de la economic de Cataluña," Unitat d'Història Econòmic (UHE) Working Paper 2011_12, Universitat Autònoma de Barcelona, 29 March 2011, accessed 15 July 2012, http://www.h-economica.uab.es/wps/2011_12.pdf.

110. Andrews, *Catalan Cuisine*, 24.

111. Ibid., 25.

112. Colman Andrews, *Ferran: The Inside Story of El Bulli and the Man Who Reinvented Food* (New York: Gotham Books, 2011).

113. Casassas i Simó, *Fires i Mercats a Catalunya*, 257.

## CONCLUSION

1. There were twenty-five market modernization projects undertaken in Barcelona between 1944 and 1971.

2. PECAB, 11.

3. Radcliff, *Making Democratic Citizens*, 3.

4. Morris, *The Political Economy of Shopkeeping in Milan*, 289.

5. Arnau González i Vilalta, ed., *La irrupció de la dona en el Catalanisme, 1931–1936* (Barcelona: Publicacions Abadia de Montserrat, 2006), 36.

6. *Gegants* are large puppets built on frames that are carried on the shoulders of robust individuals during religious and civic processions. Most sizable Catalan towns have sets of *gegants* (usually a male and female) that depict cultural types in caricature (aristocrats, merchants, wealthy peasants, Moors, Indianos, etc). For discussion of the historical significance of *gegants* in Barcelona's civic culture, see Kaplan, *Red City, Blue Period*.

7. Guàrdia and Oyón, "Introducció," 57.

8. Garcia-Fuentes and Oyón, "Reinventing Edible Identities."

9. PECAB, 11–12.

10. Santiago Santamaria i Puig (1957–2011) was the first Catalan chef to earn three Michelin stars for his El Racó de Can Fabes restaurant in Sant Celoni. In 2008, Santamaria published *La cocina al desnudo: Una vision renovadora del mundo de la gastronomía* (Madrid: Temass de Hoy, 2008), in which he explicitly questioned the safety of some of the chemicals and processes that are fundamental to the so-called "molecular gastronomy" as practiced by Ferran Adrià and marketed through the Texturas Albert y Ferran Adrià brand of commercial food additives.

11. Term coined by José Carlos Capel and referenced in Anton Pujol's "Cosmopolitan Taste," 438.

12. Ibid.

13. La Boqueria was named best market in the world by the Project for Public Spaces in 2005 at its Great Markets/Great Cities conference in Washington, D.C. More recently, it was listed first in CNN's July 2012 best ten markets of the world report. The number of food magazines including articles referencing or highlighting La Boqueria is tremendous.

14. Joe Warwick, *Where Chefs Eat: A Guide to Chefs' Favourite Restaurants* (London: Phaidon, 2013).

15. Colman Andrews, "Ramon Cabau Gausch: A 'Poet of the Ovens,'" *Los Angeles Times,* 28 June 1987.

# Bibliography

## ARCHIVAL COLLECTIONS

Administrative Records Sant Antoni Market, Barcelona

Arxiu de la Corona d'Arago

Arxiu del Gremi d'Empresaris Carnissers i Xarcuters de Barcelona i Província

Arxiu Històric Cambra Oficial de Comerç i Navegació de Barcelona

Arxiu Històric de la Ciutat de Barcelona

Arxiu Municipal Administratiu de Barcelona

Biblioteca de Catalunya

Deposit Pre-artxivatge del Arxiu Municipal Administratiu de Barcelona

Institut Municipal de Mercats de Barcelona

Institut del Teatre, Centre de Documentació i Museu de les Arts Escèniques

## IMMB MARKET REGISTRIES, AJUNTAMENT DE BARCELONA

Plaza Mercado San José-Libro Registro de los puestos fijos de este Mercado con expression de sus concesionarios y de los demas datos referentes al asunto-Principiado en el 1 de Diciembre de 1891.

Mercado de San José-Relacion de Vendedores con puesto fijo existente en este Mercado, 1920.

Plaza Mercado Santa Catalina-Libro Registro, ca. 1863–1927.

Plaza Mercado Santa Catalina-Libro Registro, ca. 1927–1942.

Plaza Mercado Santa Catalina-Libro Registro, ca. 1942ff.

Plaza Mercado Santa Catalina-Indice de Concesionarios, ca. 1958–968.

Mercado de Sant Antonio-Libro Registro, ca. 1882ff.

Mercado de San Antonio-Relacion de los concesionarios de puestos fijos en este Mercado, 1913–15.

Mercado de San Antoni-Tarifas para el año 1948.

Mercado de la Abacería Central-Libro Registro, ca. 1898–1960.

Mercado de la Abacería Central-Libro Registro, ca. 1949–1971.

Mercado de la Abacería Central-Libro Registro (Especiales-No Comestibles), ca. 1948–1972.

Mercado de la Barceloneta-Libro Registro, ca. 1884ff.

Mercado de Clot-Libro Registro, ca. 1889ff.

Mercado de la Concepción-Libro Registro, ca. 1888ff.

Mercado de Galvany-Libro Registro, ca. 1927ff.

Mercado de la Hostafrancs-Libro Registro, ca. 1888ff.

Mercado de Libertad-Libro Registro, ca. 1875ff.

Mercado del Ninot-Libro Registro, ca. 1933ff.

Mercado de la Revolución-Libro Registro, ca. 1882–1913.

Mercado de San Andres-Libro Registro, ca. 1900ff.

Mercado de Sant Gervasio-Libro Registro, ca. 1912ff.

Mercado de Sants-Libro Registro, ca. 1913ff.

Mercado de Sarrià-Libro Registro, ca. 1911ff.

Mercado de la Union-Libro Registro, ca. 1889ff.

## BOOKS AND ARTICLES

Abbott, Elizabeth. *Sugar: A Bittersweet History.* London: Duckworth Overlook, 2009.

Ajuntament de Barcelona, Departament d'Estadística. *100 Anys d'Estadística Municipal.* Barcelona: Ajuntament de Barcelona, 2002.

Álavarez Márquez, David, and Olga García González. "El mercat de Born de Barcelona vist des de les certificacions de la Maquinista." 2010 Universitat Politécnica de Catalunya Treball final de carrera dels estudis de d'Arquitectura Tècnica. Accessed 27 December 2013. http://upcommons.upc.edu/pfc/handle/2099.1/12027.

Alexander, Andrew, Dawn Nell, Adrian R. Bailey, and Gareth Shaw. "The Co-Creation of a Retail Innovation: Shoppers and the Early Supermarket in Britain." *Enterprise and Society* 10, no. 3 (2009): 529–58.

Alexander, Jennifer. *Trade, Traders, and Trading in Rural Java.* Singapore and New York: Oxford University Press, 1987.

Alexander, N., and G. Akehurst, eds. *The Emergence of Modern Retailing, 1750–1950.* London: Frank Cass, 1999.

Almerich, Luis. *El Hostal, La Fonda, La Taberna y El Café en la Vida Barcelonesa.* Barcelona: Ediciones Libreria Millà, 1945.

Alsina i Canudas, Jordi-Joan. *Gastronomia, Festes i Tradicions a Catalunya.* Barcelona: Morales i Torres Editores, 2007.

Altisent, Martha E., ed. *A Companion to the Twentieth-Century Spanish Novel.* Suffolk: Tamesis, 2008.

Álvarez Junco, José. *The Emergence of Mass Politics in Spain: Populist Demagoguery and Republican Culture, 1890–1910.* Sussex: Sussex Academic Press, 2002.

———. *La Ideología Política del Anarquismo Español, 1868–1910.* 2nd ed. Madrid: Siglo Veintiuno de España Editores, 1991.

Álvarez Junco, José, and Adrian Shubert, eds. *Spanish History since 1808.* London: Arnold, 2000.

Amades, Joan. *Històries i Llegendes de Barcelona: Passejada pels Carrers de la Ciutat Vella,* vol. 1. Barcelona: Edicions 62, 1984.

———. *L'Escudella.* Tarragona: Edicions El Mèdol, 2002.

———. *Les Diades Populars Catalanes.* 2 vols. Barcelona: Editorial Barcino, 1932, 1935.

Amelang, James. *"Gent de la Ribera" i Altres Assaigs sobre la Barcelona Moderna.* Vic: Eumo, Universitat de Vic, 2008.

———. *Honored Citizens of Barcelona: Patrician Culture and Class Relations, 1490–1714.* Princeton: Princeton University Press, 1986.

———, trans. and ed. *A Journal of the Plague Year: The Diary of the Barcelona Tanner Miquel Parets, 1651.* New York: Oxford University Press, 1991.

———. "People of the Ribera: Popular Politics and Neighborhood Identity in Early Modern Barcelona." In *Culture and Identity in Early Modern Europe (1500–1800): Essays in Honor of Natalie Zemon Davis,* edited by Barbara B. Diefindorf and Carla Hesse. Ann Arbor: University of Michigan Press, 1993.

Anderson, Benedict. *Imagined Communities: Reflections on the Origins and Spread of Nationalism.* 2nd ed. London: Verso, 2006.

Andrews, Colman. *Catalan Cuisine: Europe's Last Great Culinary Secret.* New York: Atheneum, 1988.

———. *Catalan Cuisine: Vivid Flavors from Spain's Mediterranean Coast.* Boston: Harvard Common Press, 1999.

———. *Ferran: The Inside Story of El Bulli and the Man Who Reinvented Food.* New York: Gotham Books, 2011.

Andrieu, Pierre. *Fine Bouche: A History of the Restaurant in France.* Translated by Arthur L. Hayward. London: Cassell, 1956.

*Anuario Estadístico de la Ciudad de Barcelona.* Barcelona: Henrich y Compañia, 1903-1921.

Arranz, Manuel. *La Rambla de Barcelona: Estudi d'Història Urbana.* Barcelona: Rafael Dalmau, 2003.

Arriero, María Luz. "Los motines de subsitencias en España, 1895–1905." *Estudios de Historia Social* 30 (1984): 193–249.

Artigas y Feiner, Juan. *Guía Itineraria y Descriptiva de Barcelona: De Sus Alrededores y de la Exposición Universal.* Barcelona: Librería y Tipografía Católica, 1888.

Artís Balaguer, José. "El Primitivo Mercado de Santa Catalina." In *Divulgación histórica de Barcelona,* edited by Pedro Voltes Bou. Vol. 12, *Los Abactecimientos de la ciudad, Oficios y Técnicas, Índice Analítico de los Tomos I-XII, Textos del Boletín Semenal radiado desde la emisora "Radio Barcelona" por el Instituto Municipal de Historia de la Ciudad.* Barcelona: Ayuntamiento de Barcelona, Instituto Municipal de la Historia, 1965.

Atkins, Peter J., Peter Lummel, and Derek J. Oddy, eds. *Food and the City in Europe since 1800.* Aldershot, Eng.: Ashgate, 2007.

Ayuntamiento de Barcelona. *El Consumo y la Distribución de Alimentos en Barcelona*. Barcelona: Ayuntamiento de Barcelona, Gabinete Tecníco de Programación, 1967.

———. *Estudio Sobre el Comercio Minorista de Alimentación: Análisis de una Encuesta*. Barcelona: Ayuntamiento de Barcelona, Gabinete Tecníco de Programación, 1976.

Babb, Florence E. *Between Field and Cooking Pot: The Political Economy of Marketwomen in Peru*. Austin: University of Texas Press, 1989.

Baedeker, Karl. *Spain and Portugal: Handbook for Travellers*. Leipsic: Karl Baedeker, 1913.

Baics, Gergely. "Feeding Gotham: A Social History of Urban Provisioning, 1780–1860." PhD diss., Northwestern University, 2009.

Balfour, Sebastian. "The *Desarollo* Years, 1955–1975." In *Spanish History since 1808*, edited by José Alvarez Junco and Adrian Shubert. London: Arnold, 2000.

———. *Dictatorship, Workers, and the City: Labour in Greater Barcelona since 1939*. Oxford: Clarendon Press, 1989.

Banegas López, Ramon Agustí. "Abastar de carn la ciutat." In Museu d'Història de Barcelona, Institut de Cultura, *Alimentar la ciutat: El proveïment de Barcelona del segle XIII al segle XX*. MUHBA Llibret de Sala, 12. Barcelona: Ajuntament de Barcelona, Institut Municipal de Mercats, Museu d'Història de Barcelona, Institut de Cultura, 2013.

———. "El Consumo de carne y las mentalidades en el mundo urbano de la baja edad media: Barcelona durante los siglos xiv y xv." *Ex Novo: Revista d'Història i Humanitats* 5 (2008): 81–96. Accessed 19 December 2013.

Barber, E. J. W. *Women's Work: The First 20,000 Years. Women, Cloth, and Society in Early Times*. New York: W. W. Norton, 1994.

*Barcelona Antigua y Moderna: El Mercado de La Boquería, 1840–1944: Recuerdos, Evocaciones, Perspectivas*. Barcelona: Publicidad Gabernet, 1944. In AHCB, B 1944 8 op. 1.

Barciela, Carlos, Jesús Giráldez, Grupo de Estudios de Historia Rural, Inmaculada López. "Sector Agrario y Pesca." In *Estadistícas Históricas de España, Siglos XIX-XX*, edited by Albert Carreras and Xavier Tafunell. Vols. 1-3. 2nd ed. Bilbao: Fundación BBVA, 2005.

Barrenechea Vinatea, Ramón. *Crónicas sabrosas de la vieja Lima*, vol. 2. Lima: Ediciones Peisa, 1970.

Barthes, Roland. "Toward a Psychosociology of Contemporary Food Consumption." In *Food and Culture: A Reader*, edited by Carole Counihan and Penny Van Esterik. New York: Routledge, 1997.

Barton, Simon. *A History of Spain*. New York: Palgrave Macmillan, 2009.

Batlle i Gallart, Carme. *Fires i Mercats: Factors de Dinamisme Econòmic i Centres de Sociabilitat, segles XI a XV*. Barcelona: Rafael Dalmau, 2004.

———. "Noticias Sobre la Mujer Catalana en el Mundo de los Negocios, s. XIII." In *El Trabajo de las Mujeres en la Edad Media Hispana*, edited by A. Muñoz and C. Segura. Madrid: Al-Mudaya, 1988.

Beachy, Robert, Béatrice Craig, and Alastair Owens, eds. *Women, Business and Finance in Nineteenth-Century Europe: Rethinking Separate Spheres*. Oxford: Berg, 2006.

Behar, Ruth, and Deborah A. Gordon, eds. *Women Writing Culture*. Berkeley: University of California Press, 1995.

Belasco, Warren, and Roger Horowitz, eds. *Food Chains: From Farmyard to Shopping Cart*. Philadelphia: University of Pennsylvania Press, 2009.

Belasco, Warren, and Philip Scranton, eds. *Food Nations: Selling Taste in Consumer Societies*. New York: Routledge, 2002.

Bell, David, and Gill Valentine. *Consuming Geographies: We Are Where We Eat*. London: Routledge, 1997.

Beltrán Cortés, Fernando. *Apuntes para una Historia del Frío en España*. Madrid: Consejo Superior de Investigaciones Científicas, 1983.

Benito i Monclús, Pere. "Crisis de subsistènci i polítiques frumentàries." In Museu d'Història de Barcelona, Institut de Cultura, *Alimentar la Ciutat: El proveïment de Barcelona del segle XIII al segle XX*. MUHBA Llibret de Sala, 12. Barcelona: Ajuntament de Barcelona, Institut Municipal de Mercats, Museu d'Història de Barcelona, Institut de Cultura, 2013.

Benjamin, Walter. *The Arcades Project*. Translated by Howard Eiland and Kevin McLaughlin. Cambridge: Belknap Press, 1999.

Benson, John. *The Rise of Consumer Society in Britain, 1880–1980*. London: Longman, 1994.

Benson, John, and Gareth Shaw, eds. *The Evolution of Retail Systems, c. 1800–1914*. Leicester: Leicester University Press, 1992.

Benson, John, and Laura Ugolini, eds. *A Nation of Shopkeepers: Five Centuries of British Retailing*. London: I. B. Taurus, 2003.

Benson, Susan Porter. *Counter Cultures: Saleswomen, Managers, and Customers in American Department Stores, 1890–1940*. Urbana: University of Illinois Press, 1986.

Bentham, Jeremy. *The Panopticon Writings*. Edited by Miran Bozovic. London: Verso, 1995.

Béret, Chantal, Chrystèle Burgard, and Musée de Valence, eds. *Nouvelles de nulle part: Utopies Urbaines, 1789-2000*. Valence: Réunion des Musées Nationaux, 2001.

Berg, Maxine, and Elizabeth Eger. *Luxury in the Eighteenth Century*. Basingstoke: Palgrave, 2002.

Berg, Maxine, and Helen Clifford, eds. *Consumers and Luxury: Consumer Culture in Europe, 1650–1850*. Manchester, Eng.: Manchester University Press, 1999.

Bettonica, Lluís, and Lluís Bosch. *Els Caves de Catalunya*. Barcelona: Trebol, 1983.

Biosca, Genoma, and Joan Sanromà. *Cooperativa Obrera La Lealtad: 1892–1992*. Barcelona: Vila de Gràcia, Barcelona Cooperativa La Lealtad, 1992.

Bohigas, Oriol, Manuel Guàrdia, Joan Fuster, Antoni Nicolau, Xavier Peiró, Rafel Torrella, and Daniel Venteo. *La Construcció de la gran Barcelona: L'obertura de la Via Laietana, 1908–1958*. Barcelona: Museu d'Història de la Ciutat, 2001.

Bohigas, Oriol, Museu d'Història de la Ciutat de Barcelona, et al. *Abajo Las Muralles!!! 150 Anys de l'Enderroc de les Muralles de Barcelona*. Barcelona: Institut de Cultura, Museu d'Història de la Ciutat, 2004.

Bohstedt, John. *The Politics of Provisions: Food Riots, Moral Economy, and Market Transition in England, c. 1550–1850*. London: Ashgate, 2010.

Bois, Guy. *The Transformation of the Year One Thousand: The Village of Lournand from Antiquity to Feudalism.* New York: St. Martin's Press, 1992.

Bonnassie, P. *La Organización del Trabajo en Barcelona a Finales del Siglo XV.* Barcelona: CSIC, 1975.

Borderías, Cristina. "El Trabajo de las mujeres en la Cataluña contemporánea desde la perspectiva de los hogares: Balance y perspectivas." *Arenal: Revista de historia de las mujeres* 9, no. 2 (2002): 269–300.

———. *Entre Líneas: Trabajo e identidad femenina en la España Contemporánea. La Compañia Telefónica Nacional de España.* Barcelona: Icaria Editorial, 1993.

———. "A Gendered View of Family Budgets in Mid-nineteenth Century Barcelona." *Histoire et mésure* 18, nos. 1/2 (2003): 113–47.

———, ed. *Joan Scott y las Políticas de la Historia.* Barcelona: Asociación Española de Investigación de Historia de las Mujeres and Icaria Editorial, 2006.

———. "La Feminización de los estudios sobre el trabajo de las mujeres: España en el contexto internacional (1969–2002)." *Sociología del Trabajo* 48 (2003): 57–124.

———, ed. *La Historia de las Mujeres: Perspectivas Actuales.* Barcelona: Asociación Española de Investigación de Historia de las Mujere and Icaria Editorial, 2009.

———. "La transición de la actividad femenina en el mercado de trabajo Barcelonés (1856–1930): Teoría social y realidad histórica en el sistema estadístico moderno." In *Mujeres y Hombres en los mercados de trabajo: ¿Privilegios o eficiencia?,* edited by Carmen Sarasúa and Lina Gálvez Muños. San Vicente de Raspeig: Publicaciones de la Universidad de Alicante, 2003.

———. "Women Workers in the Barcelona Labour Market, 1856–1936." In *Red Barcelona: Social Protest and Labour Mobilization in the Twentieth Century,* edited by Angel Smith. London: Routledge, 2002.

Borderías, Cristina, and Mercè Renom, eds. *Dones en Moviment(s), segles XVIII–XVI.* Barcelona: Icaria Editorial, 2008.

Borderías, Cristina, and Pilar Pérez-Fuentes. "Mujeres, trabajos, y economías familiares en España (siglos XIX y XX)." In *La Historia de las Mujeres: Perspectivas Actuales,* edited by Cristina Borderías. Barcelona: Asociación Española de Investigación de Historia de las Mujeres and Icaria Editorial, 2009.

Borja, Jordi. *Luces y Sombras del Urbanismo en Barcelona.* Barcelona: Editorial UOC, 2009.

Bourdieu, Pierre. *Distinction: A Social Critique of the Judgement of Taste.* Translated by Richard Nice. Cambridge: Harvard University Press, 1985.

———. *Outline of a Theory of Practice.* Translated by Richard Nice. Cambridge: Cambridge University Press, 1977.

Bouton, Cynthia. *The Flour War: Gender, Class, and Community in the Late Ancien Régime French Society.* University Park: Pennsylvania State University Press, 1993.

Bowlby, Rachel. *Carried Away: The Invention of Modern Shopping.* New York: Columbia University Press, 2001.

Boyd, Carolyn P. "The Military and Politics, 1808–1874." In *Spanish History since 1808*, edited José Alvarez Junco and Adrian Shubert, 64–79. London: Arnold, 2000.

Braendi, Sibylle. "Women and the New Self-Service Stores in the Food and Beverage Sector, 1948–1970." Paper presented at the History of Consumption as Social History Conference, Freie Universität, Berlin, 2 June 1994.

Braudel, Fernand. *Civilization and Capitalism, 15th-18th Centuries*, vols. 1–3. Translated and revised by Siân Reynolds. New York: Harper and Row, 1982.

Brenan, Gerald. *The Spanish Labyrinth: An Account of the Social and Political Background of the Civil War*. 2nd ed. Cambridge: Cambridge University Press, 1974.

Brewer, John, and Roy Porter, eds. *Consumption and the World of Goods*. New York: Routledge, 1993.

Bridenthal, Renate, Claudia Koontz, and Susan Mosher Stuart. *Becoming Visible: Women in European History*. 2nd ed. Boston: Houghton Mifflin, 1987.

Brulotte, Ronda, and Michael A. Di Giovine, eds. *Edible Identities: Food as Cultural Heritage*. Burlington, VT: Ashgate, 2014.

Brunelle, Gayle K. "Policing the Monopolizing Women of Early Modern Nantes." *Journal of Women's History* 19, no. 2 (Summer 2007): 10–35.

Buddle, Melanie. *The Business of Women: Marriage, Family, and Entrepreneurship in British Columbia, 1901–51*. Vancouver: University of British Columbia Press, 2010.

Bull, Anna Cento, and Paul Corner. *From Peasant to Entrepreneur: The Survival of the Family Economy in Italy*. Oxford: Berg, 1993.

Bulto Blajot, Maria Rosa. "Dificultades para la abactecimiento de pan en el siglo XVIII." In *Divulgación histórica de Barcelona*, edited by Pedro Voltes Bou. Vol. 12, *Los Abactecimientos de la ciudad: Oficios y Técnicas, Índice Analítico de los Tomos I-XII, Textos del Boletín Semenal radiado desde la emisora "Radio Barcelona" por el Instituto Municipal de Historia de la Ciudad*. Barcelona: Ayuntamiento de Barcelona, Instituto Municipal de la Historia, 1965.

———. "El Consumo de la Carne en Barcelona." In *Divulgación histórica de Barcelona*, edited by Pedro Voltes Bou. Vol. 12, *Los Abactecimientos de la ciudad: Oficios y Técnicas, Índice Analítico de los Tomos I-XII, Textos del Boletín Semenal radiado desde la emisora "Radio Barcelona" por el Instituto Municipal de Historia de la Ciudad*. Barcelona: Ayuntamiento de Barcelona, Instituto Municipal de la Historia, 1965.

Burdiel, Isabel. "The Liberal Revolution, 1808–1843." In *Spanish History since 1808*, edited by José Alvarez Junco and Adrian Shubert, 18–32. London: Arnold, 2000.

Busquets, Joan. "Barcelona: Rethinking Urbanistic Projects." In *Shaping the City: Studies in History, Theory and Urban Design*, edited by Edward Robbins and Rodolphe El-Koury. New York: Routledge, 2004.

———. *Barcelona: The Urban Evolution of a Compact City*. Rovereto: Nicoldi and Presidents and Fellows of Harvard College, 2005.

Cabana, Francesc. *37 anys de Franquisme a Catalunya: Una visió econòmica*. 2nd ed. Barcelona: Pòrtic, 2001.

Cabrera, Mercedes. "El Rey Constitucional." In *Alfonso XIII: Un Político en el Trono*, edited by Javier Moreno Luzón. Madrid: Marcial Pons Historia, 2003.

Cáceres Nevot, Juanjo. "El proveïment de cereals." In Museu d'Història de Barcelona, Institut de Cultura, *Alimentar la ciutat: El proveïment de Barcelona del segle XIII al segle XX*. MUHBA Llibret de Sala, 12. Barcelona: Ajuntament de Barcelona, Institut Municipal de Mercats, Museu d'Història de Barcelona, Institut de Cultura, 2013.

Cahner, M., coord. *Gran Geografia Comarcal de Catalunya*. Vol. 8, *Barcelonés: Baix Llobregat*. Barcelona: Enciclopèdia Catalana, 1982.

Callahan, William J. "Church and State, 1808–1874." In *Spanish History since 1808*, edited by José Alvarez Junco and Adrian Shubert, 49–63. London: Arnold, 2000.

Camps, Enriqueta. *La formación del mercado de trabajo industrial en Cataluña del S. XIX*. Madrid: Ministerio de Trabajo y Seguridad Social, 1995.

———. "Las Tranformaciones del Mercado de trabajo en Cataluña (1850–1925): Migraciones, ciclos de vida y economías familiars." *Revista de Historia Industrial* 11 (1997): 45–53.

Canut, Enric, and Francesc Navarro i Ferré. *Els formatges a Catalunya*. Barcelona: Alta Fulla, 1980.

Capel, Horacio. *El Modelo Barcelona: Un Examen Crítico*. Barcelona: Edicions del Serbal, 2005.

Cardona, Gabriel. *A Golpes de Sable: Los Grandes Militares que han Marcado la Historia de España*. Barcelona: Editorial Ariel, 2008.

Carpinell, Eladia M. Vda. de. *Carmencita o la Buena Cocinera*. Valladolid: Editorial Maxtor, 2011.

Carr, Raymond. *Spain, 1808–1975*. 2nd ed. Oxford: Clarendon Press, 1982.

———, ed. *Spain: A History*. Oxford: Oxford University Press, 2000.

Carrera Pujal, Jaume. *Historia Política y Económica de Cataluña, Siglos XVI a XVIII*. Vol. 3. Barcelona: Bosch, 1946–47.

Carreras, Albert, and Lídia Torra Fernández. *Història Econòmica de les Fires a Catalunya*. Barcelona: Generalitat de Catalunya, Departament de Comerç, Turisme i Consum, 2004.

Carreras, Albert, and Xavier Tafunell, dirs. *Estadísticas Históricas de España, Siglos XIX-XX*. 2nd ed. Bilbao: Fundación BBVA, 2005.

Casanova, Rossend. *El Castell dels Tres Dragons*. Barcelona: Museu de Ciències Naturals de Barcelona, 2009.

Casares Ripol, Javier, and Alfonso Rebollo Arévalo. *Distribución commercial*. 2nd ed. Madrid: Civitas, 2000.

Casassas i Simó, Lluís. *Fires i Mercats a Catalunya*. Barcelona: Edicions 62, 1978.

Casassas i Simó, Lluís, and Pau Vila. *Barcelona i la Seva Rodalia al llarg del Temps*. Barcelona: Editorial Aedos, 1974.

Caselles, Antònia. "Barcelona's Urban Landscape: The Historical Making of a Tourist Product." *Journal of Urban History* 35 (2009): 815–32.

Casey, James. *Early Modern Spain: A Social History.* London: Routledge, 1999.

Cass, Elizabeth. *Spanish Cooking.* London: A. Deutsch, 1957.

Castañer, Esteban. "La difusió dels mercats de ferro a Espanya (1868–1936)." In *Fer ciutat a través dels mercats: Europa, segles XIX i XX,* edited by Manuel Guàrdia and José Luis Oyón. Barcelona: Museu d'Història de Barcelona, 2010.

Castañer Muñoz, Esteban. *L'Architecture métalique en Espagne: Les Halles au XIXe siècle.* Perpignan: Presses Universitaires, 2004.

Castañer i Muñoz, Esteve. "Elements Tradicionals i Renovadors en els Primers Projectes de Mercats de Ferro a Barcelona (1848–1973)." *Miscellània: Butlletí del Museu Nacional d'Art de Catalunya* 2 (1994): 201-14.

Castell, Jaume. *El Menjar en la Història: Des d'Allò que Menjava Carlemany fins a Considerar que L'Ossada és Bella.* Barcelona: Cossetània Edicions, 2004.

Castells, Irene. "Els Rebomboris del Pa de 1789 a Barcelona." *Recerques: Història, Economia, Cultura* 1 (1970): 51–81.

Castells Durán, Antoni. *Les Collectivizacions a Barcelona: 1936–1939.* Barcelona: Editorial Hacer, 1993.

Castro, Demetrio. "The Left: From Liberalism to Democracy." In *Spanish History since 1808,* edited by José Alvarez Junco and Adrian Shubert. London: Arnold, 2000.

*Catalunya llaminera: Descripció de les postre típiques Catalanes.* Barcelona: Editorial Millà, 1968.

Cazorla, Antonio. "Early Francoism, 1939–1957." In *Spanish History since 1808,* edited by José Alvarez Junco and Adrian Shubert, 260–76. London: Arnold, 2000.

Cazorla Sánchez, Antonio. *Fear and Progress: Ordinary Lives in Franco's Spain, 1939–1975.* Oxford: Wiley-Blackwell, 2009.

Centre d'Estudis i Documentació Arxiu Històric del Raval. *El Mercat de la Boqueria.* Barcelona: Associació de Treballadors Autònoms de la Boqueria, 1982.

Cerdá, Ildefons. *Monografía estadística de la clase obrera en Barcelona en 1856.* Facsimile edition, *Teoría general de la urbanización.* Vol. 2. Madrid: IEAL, 1968.

———. *Teoría General de la Urbanización, Reforma y Ensanche de Barcelona.* Vol. 2, *La Urbanización Considerada como un Hecho Concreto: Estadística Urbana de Barcelona.* 1867. Reprint, Madrid: Instituto de Estudios Fiscales, 1968.

Charnon-Deutsch, Lou, and Jo Labanyi, eds. *Culture and Gender in Nineteenth-Century Spain.* Oxford: Oxford University Press, 1995.

Charvat, Frank J. *Supermarketing.* New York: Macmillan, 1961.

Chung, Seung-mo. *Markets: Traditional Korean Society.* Translated by Yoon-jung Cho and Eun-young Min. Seoul: Ewha Woman's University Press, 2006.

Clark, Gracia. *African Market Women: Seven Life Stories from Ghana.* Bloomington: University of Indiana Press, 2010.

Clarke, Roger, Stephen Davies, Paul Dobson, and Michael Waterson. *Buyer Power and Competition in European Food Retailing.* Cheltenham: Edward Elgar Publishing, 2002.

Comas d'Argemir, Dolors. "Household, Family, and Social Stratification: Inheritance and

Labor Strategies in a Catalan Village (Nineteenth and Twentieth Centuries)." *Journal of Family History* 13, no. 1 (1988): 143-63.

Conversi, Daniele. *The Basques, the Catalans, and Spain: Alternative Routes to Nationalist Mobilisation.* Reno and Las Vegas: University of Nevada Press, 1997.

Corbín Ferrer, Juan-Luis. *El Mercado de Valencia: Mil Años de Historia.* 2nd ed. Valencia: Federico Domenech, 1900.

Córdoba de la Llave, Ricardo. "El papel de la mujer en la actividad artesanal cordobesa a fines del sigle XV." In *El trabajo de las mujeres en al Edad Media Hispana,* edited by Ángela Muñoz Fernández and Cristina Segura, 99–112. Madrid: Asociación Cultural Al-Mudayna, Instituto de la Mujer, Ministerio de Cultura, 1988.

Corteguera, Luis. *For the Common Good: Popular Politics in Barcelona, 1580–1640.* Ithaca: Cornell University Press, 2002.

Corteguera, Luis R. "Pa i política a la Barcelona dels segles XVI i XVII." In Museu d'Història de Barcelona, Institut de Cultura, *Alimentar la ciutat: El proveïment de Barcelona del segle XIII al segle XX.* MUHBA Llibret de Sala, 12. Barcelona: Ajuntament de Barcelona, Institut Municipal de Mercats, Museu d'Història de Barcelona, Institut de Cultura, 2013.

Counihan, Carole, and Penny Van Esterik, eds. *Food and Culture: A Reader.* New York: Routledge, 1997.

Cowan, Brian William. *The Social Life of Coffee: The Emergence of the British Coffeehouse.* New Haven: Yale University Press, 2005.

Cowan, Ruth Schwartz. *More Work for Mother: The Ironies of Household Technology from the Open Hearth to the Microwave.* New York: Basic Books, 1983.

Cox, Nancy, and Karin Dannehl. *Perceptions of Retailing in Early Modern England.* London: Ashgate, 2007.

Craig, Béatrice. "Petites Bourgeoises and Penny Capitalists: Women in Retail in the Lille Area during the Nineteenth Century." *Enterprise and Society* 2, no. 2 (2001): 198–224.

Cronin, Anne M., and Kevin Hetherington, eds. *Consuming the Entrepreneurial City: Image, Memory, Spectacle.* New York: Routledge, 2008.

Crossick, Geoffrey, and Heinz-Gerhard Haupt. *The Petite Bourgeoisie in Europe, 1780–1914: Enterprise, Family and Independence.* London: Routledge, 1995.

———, eds. *Shopkeepers and Master Artisans in Nineteenth-Century Europe.* London: Methuen and Co., 1984.

Crossick, Geoffrey, and Serge Jaumain, eds. *Cathedrals of Consumption: The European Department Store, 1850–1939.* Aldershot, Eng.: Ashgate, 1999.

Cruz, Jésus. "The Moderate Ascendency, 1843–1868." In *Spanish History since 1808,* edited by José Alvarez Junco and Adrian Shubert, 33–48. London: Arnold, 2000.

———. *The Rise of Middle-Class Culture in Nineteenth-Century Spain.* Baton Rouge: Louisiana State University Press, 2011.

Cuadrada Majó, Coral. "Les dones en el treball urbá (segles XIV–XV)." *Anuario de Estudios Medievales* 29 (1999): 219–34.

Cubeles i Bonet, Albert, and Ferran Puig i Verdaguer. "Les Fortificacions de Barcelona." In Oriol Bohigas, Museu d'Història de la Ciutat de Barcelona, et al., *Abajo Las Muralles!!! 150 Anys de l'Enderroc de les Muralles de Barcelona*. Barcelona: Museu d'Història de la Ciutat, 2004.

Culla Clarà, Joan B. *El republicanisme lerrouxista a Catalunya, 1901–1923*. Barcelona: Curial, 1986.

Cunill de Bosch, Josep. *La Cuina Catalana: Aplec de fórmules per a preparer tota mena de plats amb economia i facilitat, propi per a server a guia a les mestresses de casa i a totes les cuineres en general*. 1923. Reprint, Barcelona: Parsifal Edicions, 1996.

Curet, Francesc. *La Jamància: Las Bullangues de 1842 i 1843*. Barcelona: Rafel Dalmau, 1990.

Curli, Barbara. "Women Entrepreneurs and Italian Industrialization: Conjectures and Avenues for Research." *Enterprise and Society* 3, no. 4 (December 2002): 634–56.

Dalmau, Antoni R. *200 plats casolans de cuina catalana: Recull de receptes populars*. Barcelona: Editorial Millà, 1969.

———. *Siete días de furia*. Barcelona: Edicions Destino, 2009.

d'Amat i de Cortada i de Santjust, Rafael, Baró de Maldà, and Ramon Boixareu. *Calaix de Sastre*. 11 vols. Barcelona: Curial Edicions Catalanes and Institut Municipal d'Història, 1987.

Davidoff, Leonore, and Catherine Hall. *Family Fortunes: Men and Women of the English Middle Class, 1780–1850*. 2nd ed. London: Routledge, 2003.

Davis, Dorothy. *Fairs, Shops, and Supermarkets: A History of English Shopkeeping*. Toronto: University of Toronto Press, 1996.

Davis, Natalie Zemon. "Women in the Crafts in Sixteenth-Century Lyon." *Feminist Studies* 8, no. 1 (1982): 46–80.

Davidson, Alan. *Food History Comes of Age: A Study in How Things Happen, with Special Attention to a Sine Qua Non—The Ripeness of the Time, the Need for Accidental Catalysts, the Importance of a Nucleus, the Impact of Coincidence*. Amsterdam: Praemium Erasmianum Foundation, 2003.

Davidson, Robert. *Jazz Age Barcelona*. Toronto: University of Toronto Press, 2009.

de Certeau, Michel Luce Giard, and Pierre Mayol. *The Practice of Everyday Life*. Vol. 2, *Living and Cooking*. Translated by Timothy J. Tomasick. Minneapolis: University of Minnesota Press, 1998.

de Déu Domènech, Joan. *Xocolata cada dia: A taule amb el baró de Maldà. Un estil de vida el segle XVIII*. Barcelona: Edicions la Magrana, 2004.

Degen, Monica, "Fighting for the Global Catwalk: Formalizing Public Life in Castlefield (Manchester) and Diluting Public Life in el Raval (Barcelona)." *International Journal of Urban and Regional Planning* 27 (2003): 867–80.

de Geus, Marius. *Ecological Utopias: Envisioning the Sustainable Society*. Utrecht: International Books, 1999.

De Grazia, Victoria. *American Supermarkets Versus European Small Shops: Or, How Transnational Capitalism Crossed Paths with the Moral Economy in Italy during the 1960s.* Trondheim: Norwegian University of Science and Technology, 2002.

———. *Irresistable Empire: America's Advance through Twentieth Century Europe.* Cambridge: Belknap, 2005.

De Grazia, Victoria, and Ellen Furlough, eds. *The Sex of Things: Gender and Consumption.* Berkeley: University of California Press, 1996.

del Castillo y Mayone, Joaquin, and Anna Maria Garcia Rovira. *Las Bullangas de Barcelona ó Sacudimientos de un Pueblo Oprimido por el Despotismo Ilustrado.* Vic: Eumo and Institut Universitari d'Història Jaume Vicens i Vives, 1994.

Delgado, Manuel. *Elogi del Vianant: Del "Model Barcelona" a la Barcelona Real.* Barcelona: Edicions de 1984, 2004.

de Miguel, Amando. *La Vida Cotidiana de los Españoles en el Siglo XX.* Barcelona: Planeta, 2001.

Departament de Cultura, Junta Directiva del Centre Autonomista de Dependents del Comerç i de la Indústria. *Centre Autonomista de Dependents del Comerç i de la Indústria (CADCI) 1903–1939: Cataluyna avant!* Barcelona: Department of Culture, 1992.

Departament d'Estadística, Ajuntament de Barcelona. *100 Anys d'Estadística Municipal.* Barcelona: Ajuntament de Barcelona, 2000.

de Riquer, Borja, and Joan B. Culla. *El Franquisme i la Transició Democràtica (1939–1988).* Vol. 7, *Història de Catalunya*, directed by Pierre Vilar. Barcelona: Edicions 62, 1994.

de Riquer i Permanyer, Borja. *Lliga Regionalista.* Barcelona: Edicions 62, 1976.

de Sagarra, Josep Maria. *Obres Completes: Prosa*, vol. 2. Barcelona: Editorial Selecta, 1967.

Deutsch, Tracey. "Putting Commerce in Its Place: Public Markets in U.S. History." *American Quarterly* 56, no. 2 (2005): 481-88.

Dewer, David, and Vanessa Watson. *Urban Markets: Developing Informal Retailing.* London: Routledge, 1990.

Diefindorf, Barbara B., and Carla Hesse, eds. *Culture and Identity in Early Modern Europe (1500–1800): Essays in Honor of Natalie Zemon Davis.* Ann Arbor: University of Michigan Press, 1993.

Dinerman, Ina. "Economic Alliances in a Regional Mexican Economy." *Ethnology* 17, no. 1 (1978): 53–64.

Dobson, Paul W., Michael Waterson, and Stephen Davies. "The Patterns and Implications of Increasing Concentration in European Food Retailing." *Journal of Agricultural Economics* 54, no. 1 (March 2003): 111–25.

Dupláa, Cristina. *La Voz Testimonial de Montserrat Roig.* Barcelona: Icaria, 1996.

Duby, Georges, and Michelle Perrot. *Historia de las Mujueres en Occidente*, vol. 4. Madrid: Taurus, 1993.

Durany i Sastre, Josep. *Mercat de Sant Antoni (1882-1982): Breu Història Biogràfica.* Barcelona: n.p., 1982.

Ealham, Chris. *Class, Culture, and Conflict in Barcelona, 1898–1937.* London: Routledge/ Cañada Blanch Studies on Contemporary Spain, 2005.

Ehrlich, Charles Edward. *Lliga Regionalista: Lliga Catalana, 1901–1936.* Barcelona: Editorial Alpha, 2004.

Einhorn, Barbara. *Cinderella Goes to Market: Citizenship, Gender and Women's Movements in East Central Europe.* New York: Verso, 1993.

Elliot, J. H. *The Revolt of the Catalans.* Cambridge: Cambridge University Press, 1963.

Enders, Victoria Loreé, and Pamela Beth Radcliff, eds. *Constructing Spanish Womanhood: Female Identity in Modern Spain.* Albany: State University of New York Press, 1999.

Epps, Brad. "Modern Spaces: Building Barcelona." In *Iberian Cities,* edited by Joan Ramon Resina. New York: Routledge, 2001.

———. "Space in Motion: Barcelona and the Stages of (In)visibility." *Arizona Journal of Hispanic Cultural Studies* 6 (2002):193–204.

Esenwein, George R. *Anarchist Ideology and the Working-Class Movement in Spain, 1868– 1898.* Berkeley: University of California Press, 1989.

Espuny i Tomás, María Jesús. "La Comisión Mixta del Trabajo en el Comercio de Barcelona." In *Estado, protesta y movimientos sociales: Actas del III Congreso de Historia Social en España: Vitoria-Gasteiz, julio de 1997,* coordinated by José María Ortiz de Orruño Legarda and Santiago Castillo, 165–170. Bilbao: Universidad del País Vasco, 1998.

Espuny Tomás, Ma. Jesús, Guillermo García González, and Olga Paz Torres. *Los Obreros del Comercio: Un Análisis histórico-juridico de la dependencia mercantile catalana.* Madrid: Dykinson, 2011.

Estapé, Fabián. *Vida y Obra de Ildefonso Cerdá.* Barcelona: Ediciones Península, 2001.

Everly, Kathryn. *Catalan Women Writers and Artists: Revisionist Views from Feminist Space.* Lewisburg: Bucknell University Press, 2003.

Fabre, Jaume. "L'Exposició que no va Salvar una Dictadura ara fa Cinquanta Anys." *L'Avenç* 16 (Abril 1979): 63–69.

Fabre, Jaume, and Josep Maria Huertas Claveria. *La Barcelona del Segle XX: Burgesa i Revolucionària.* Barcelona: Flor de Vent Edicions, 2000.

———. *Tots els Barris de Barcelona.* Vol. 2, *Els barris que foren independents.* Barcelona: Edicions 62, 1976.

Fàbrega, Jaume. *Catalunya per sucar-hi pa: Guia comarcal d'atractius turístics, productes, plats, vins i festes gastronòmiques del Països Catalans.* Barcelona: Duxelm, 2007.

———. *El Convit de Tirant: Cuina i Comensalitat de la Edat Mitgana a Ferran Adrià.* Collecció d'assaig Argent Viu. Lleida: Pagès Editors, 2007.

———. *El Gust d'un Poble: Els Plats Més Famosos de la Cuina Catalana: De Verdaguer a Guadi: El Naixament d'una Cuina.* Tarragona: Cossetània Edicions, 2002.

———. *La cuina de Josep Pla: A taula amb l'autor de "El que hem menjat."* Barcelona: Edicions La Magrana, 1997.

———. *Totes les Sopes: Brous, Escudelles i Sopes d'Arreu.* Valls: Cossetània, 2008.

———. *Traditional Catalan Cooking.* Translated by Paul Martin. Barcelona: La Magrana, 1997.

Fàbrega, Jaume, and Josep-Maria Terricabras. *La Cultural del Gust al Països Catalans: Espais Geogràfics, Socials i Històrics del Patrimoni Culinari Català.* Tarragona: Edicions El Mèdol, 2000.

Falgás, Jordi. "Greeting the Dawn: The Impact of the Renaixença in Periodicals and Architecture." In *Barcelona and Modernity: Picasso, Gaudí, Miró, Dalí,* edited by William H. Robinson, Jordi Falgàs, and Carmen Belen Lord, 27–31. New Haven and London: Cleveland Museum of Art in association with Yale University Press, 2006.

Farr, James R. *Artisans in Europe, 1300–1914.* Cambridge: Cambridge University Press, 2000.

Fattacciu, Irene. "Gremios y evolución de las pautas de consumo en el siglo XVIII: La industria artesenal del chocolate." In *Comprar, Vender y Consumir: Nuevas aportaciones a la historia del consumo en la España moderna,* edited by Daniel Muñoz Navarro. València: Publicaciones de la Universitat de València, 2011.

Fava, N., and M. Guàrdia Bassols. "The Sense of Insecurity: Integrated Solutions: The Case of Barcelona's Covered Markets." Accessed 29 December 2013. http://www.cityfutures2009.com/PDF/26_N_Fava_M_Gurdia_Bassols.pdf.

Feibleman, Peter S. *The Cooking of Spain and Portugal.* New York: Time-Life Books, 1969.

Feliu, Gaspar. "El pa de Barcelona al segle XVIII: Continuïtats i canvis." In Museu d'Història de Barcelona, Institut de Cultura, *Alimentar la ciutat: El proveïment de Barcelona del segle XIII al segle XX.* MUHBA Llibret de Sala, 12. Barcelona: Ajuntament de Barcelona, Institut Municipal de Mercats, Museu d'Història de Barcelona, Institut de Cultura, 2013.

Fernández-Armesto, Felipe. *Barcelona: A Thousand Years of the City's Past.* Oxford: Oxford University Press, 1992.

———. *Near a Thousand Tables: A History of Food.* New York: Free Press, 2002.

Fisher, M. F. K. *The Art of Eating.* New York: Collier Books, 1990.

Fischler, Claude, and Estelle Mason. *Manger: Français, Européans face à l'alimentation.* Paris: Editions Odile Jacob, 2008.

Flandrin, Jean Louis, Massimo Montanari, Albert Sonnenfeld, et al. *Food: A Culinary History from Antiquity to the Present.* New York: Columbia University Press, 1999.

Fonquerne, Yves-René, Alfonso Estaban, and Casa de Velásquez, eds. *La condición de la mujer en la Edad Media: Actas del Coloquio celebrado en la Casa de Velázquez del 5–7 de noviembre de 1984.* Madrid: Universidad Complutense-Casa de Velázquez, 1984.

Ford, Richard. *A Hand-book for Travellers in Spain.* London, 1845.

Foucault, Michel. *Discipline and Punish: The Birth of the Prison.* New York: Pantheon Books, 1977.

Fradera, Josep Maria. *Indústria i Mercat: Les Bases Comercials de la Indústria Catalana Moderna.* Barcelona: Editorial Crítica, 1987.

Freedman, Paul H., ed. *Food: A History of Taste.* Berkeley: University of California Press, 2007.

———, ed. *Gastonomía: Historia del paladar.* València: Publicaciones Universitat de València, 2009.

Freidberg, Susanne. *Fresh: A Perishable History.* Cambridge: Belknap Press of Harvard
University Press, 2009.

Gálvez Muñoz, Lina, and Paloma Fernández Pérez. "Female Entrepreneurship in Spain
during the Nineteenth and Twentieth Centuries." *Business History Review* 81, no. 3
(2007): 495–515.

Gambler, Wendy. "Gendered Concerns: Thoughts on the History of Business and the History of Women." *Business and Economic History* 23 (1994): 129–40.

García i Espuche, A., M. Guardia, F. J. Monclús, and J. L. Oyón. "Modernization and Urban
Beautification: The 1888 Barcelona World's Fair." *Planning Perspectives* 6, no. 2 (May
1991): 139–59.

Garcia Espuche, Albert, Maria dels Àngels Pérez Samper, Sergio Solbes Ferri, Julia Beltrán
de Heredia Bercero, and Núria Miró i Alaix, *Drogues, dolços i tabac: Barcelona 1700.*
Barcelona: Ajuntament de Barcelona, Institut de Cultura, 2010.

Garcia Espuche, Albert, and Manuel Guàrdia i Bassols. *Espai i Societat a la Barcelona Pre-
Industrial.* Barcelona: Edicions la Magrana and Institut Municipal d'Història, 1985.

Garcia-Fuentes, Josep-Maria, Manel Guàrdia Bassals, and José Luis Oyón Bañales. "Re-
inventing Edible Identities: Catalan Cuisine and Barcelona's Market Halls." In *Edible
Identities: Food as Cultural Heritage,* edited by Ronda L. Brulotte and Michael A. Di
Giovine. Burlington, VT: Ashgate, 2014.

Garcia i Domènech, Rosa M. "Mercats a Barcelona a la primera meitat del segle XIX."
In *Història Urbana del Pla de Barcelona.* Vol. 1, *Actes del II Congrés d'Història del Pla de
Barcelona.* Barcelona: Ajuntament de Barcelona, 1985.

García Madaria, José María. *Estructura de la Administración Central, 1808–1931.* Madrid:
Instituto Nacional de Administración Pública, 1982.

García Queipo de Llano, Genoveva. "La Crisis de la Monarquía Constitucional: Alfonso
XIII en su Tiempo." In *La Corona en la Historia de España,* edited by Javier Tusell,
Ángeles Lario, and Florentino Portero. Madrid: Biblioteca Nueva, 2003.

García Verano, M. *Historia del nacionalismo catalán.* Madrid: Editora Nacional, 1970.

Geertz, Clifford. "The Bazaar Economy: Information and Search in Peasant Marketing."
*American Economic Review* 68, no. 2 (May 1978): 28–32.

Gelernter, David Hill. *1939: The Lost World of the Fair.* New York: Free Press, 1999.

Giner, Salvador. *The Social Structure of Catalonia.* Sheffield: Anglo-Catalan Society Occasional Publications, 1984.

Giralt Casadesús, R. *Mercados: Teoría y Práctica de su Construción y Funcionamiento.* Barcelona: Cuerpo de Arquitectos Municipales de España, 1937.

Glasse, Hannah. *The Art of Cookery Made Plain and Easy.* London, n.p., 1747.

Golden, Lester. "Les dones com avantguarda: El Rebombori del pa de gener de 1918."
*L'Avenç* 44 (December 1981): 45-50.

———. "The Women in Command: The Barcelona Consumer War of 1918." *UCLA Historical Journal* 6 (1985): 5–32.

Goldin, Claudia. "The U-Shaped Female Labor Force Function in Economic Development and Economic History." In *Investment in Women's Human Capital and Economic Development*, edited by T. Paul Schultz, 61–90. Chicago: University of Chicago Press, 1995.

González i Vilalta, Arnau, ed. *La irrupció de la dona en el Catalanisme, 1931–1936*. Barcelona: Publicacions Abadia de Montserrat, 2006.

Gordon, Elizabeth. *Cuisines of the Western World*. New York: Golden Press, 1965.

Graham, Helen. *The Spanish Civil War: A Very Short Introduction*. Oxford: Oxford University Press, 2005.

Graham, Helen, and Jo Labanyi, eds. *Spanish Cultural Studies: An Introduction. The Struggle for Modernity*. New York: Oxford University Press, 1995.

Gras Casanovas, M. Mercè, and M. Ángels Pérez Samper. "Alimentació i Societat a la Catalunya Moderna." *Pedralbes* 31 (1991): 36–37.

Grau, Ramon. *Barcelona Quaderns d'Història*, vol. 11, *La Ciutat i les Revolucions, 1808–1868. II. El Procés d'Industrialització*. Barcelona: Ajuntament de Barcelona, 2006.

———, coord. *El Segle de l'absolutisme, 1714–1808*. Barcelona: Ajuntament de Barcelona, 2002.

———. "Gènesi del mercat actual." In Xavier Olivé and Llorenç Torrado, eds., *Boqueria: 150 Aniversari*. Barcelona: Ajuntament de Barcelona, 1986.

Grau i Fernández, Ramon. "La Metamorfosi de la ciutat enmurallada: Barcelona, de Felip V a Ildefons Cerdà." In *Evolució Urbana de Catalunya*, edited by Miquel Tarradell et al. Barcelona: Edicions de la Magrana, Institut Municipal de Barcelona, 1983.

Graves, Tomás. *Volem Pa Amb Oli*. Palma de Mallorca: J. J. de Olañeta, 1998.

Greci, Roberto. "Donne e corporazioni: La fluidità di un rapport." In Angela Groppi, ed., *Il lavoro delle donne*. Roma: Laterza, 1996.

Grewe, Rudolf, Amadeu J. Soberanas, and Joan Santanach i Suñol. *Llibre de Sent Soví. Llibre de totes maneres de potages de menjar. Llibre de totes maneres de confits*. Barcelona: Barcino, 2004.

Grigg, David. "Food Consumption in the Mediterranean Region." *Tihdschrift voor economische en sociale geografie* 90, no. 4 (1999): 391–409.

Groppi, Angela, ed. *Il lavoro delle donne*. Roma: Laterza, 1996.

Grupo de Estudios de Asociacionismo y Sociabilidad (GEAS). *España en Sociedad: Las Asociaciones a Finales del Siglo XIX*. Vol. 22, *Colección Humanidades*. Cuenca: Ediciones de la Universidad de Castilla-La Mancha, 1998.

Guàrdia, Manuel, and Albert García Espuche. "1888 y 1929: Dos Exposiciones, Una Sola Ambición." In *Barcelona, 1888–1929: Modernidad, Ambición y Conflictos de Una Ciudad Soñada*, directed by Alejandro Sánchez. Madrid: Alianza Editorial, 1992.

Guàrdia, Manuel, and José Lluis Oyón, eds. *Fer ciutat a través dels mercats: Europa, segles XIX i XX*. Barcelona: Museu d'Història de la Ciutat de Barcelona, 2010.

——— (with Xavier Creus). "La formació del modern sistema de mercats de Barcelona." X

*Congrés d'Història de Barcelona-Dilemes de la fi de segle, 1874–1901.* Accessed 20 July 2013. http://w110.bcn.cat/ArxiuHistoric/Continguts/Documents/Fitxers/guardiatext.pdf.

———. "Los Mercados Públicos en la Ciudad Contempránea: El Caso de Barcelona." *Revista Bibliográfica de Geografía y Ciencias Sociales* 12, no. 744 (August 2007). Accessed 20 December 2013. http://www.ub.edu/geocrit/b3w-744.htm.

Guàrdia, Manuel, José Luis Oyón, and N. Fava, "El sistema de mercats de Barcelona." In *Fer ciutat a través dels mercats: Europa, segles XIX i XX,* edited by Manuel Guàrdia and José Luis Oyón, 263–98. Barcelona: Museu d'Història de la Ciutat de Barcelona, 2010.

Guy, Koleen M. *When Champagne Became French: Wine and the Making of a National Identity.* Baltimore: Johns Hopkins University Press, 2007.

Haba, Juan Piqueras. "La filoxera en España y su difusión espacial, 1878–1926." *Cuadernos de Geografía* 77 (2005): 101–36.

Hames, Gina. *Alcohol in World History.* New York: Routledge, 2012.

Hanawalt, Barbara. *Women and Work in Preindustrial Europe.* Bloomington: Indiana University Press, 1986.

Hargreaves, John. *Freedom for Catalonia? Catalan Nationalism, Spanish Identity and the Barcelona Olympic Games.* Cambridge: Cambridge University Press, 2000.

Harris, Richard L., and Jorge Nef, eds. *Capital, Power, and Inequality in Latin America and the Caribbean.* Lanham: Rowan & Littlefield, 2008.

Helstosky, Carol F. *Garlic and Oil: Food and Politics in Italy.* Oxford: Berg, 2004.

Heywood, Paul. *Marxism and the Failure of Organised Socialism in Spain, 1879–1936.* Cambridge: Cambridge University Press, 2003.

Hobsbawm, E. J. *Primitive Rebels: Studies in Archaic Forms of Social Movement in the 19th and 20th Centuries.* New York: W. W. Norton, 1965.

———. *Revolutionaries: Contemporary Essays.* New York: Pantheon Books, 1973.

Hodson, D. "The Municipal Store: Adaptation and Development in the Retail Markets of Nineteenth-Century Urban Lancashire." In *The Emergence of Modern Retailing, 1750–1950,* edited by N. Alexander and G. Akehurst. London: Frank Cass, 1999.

Hohenberg, Paul M., and Lynn Hollen Lees. *The Making of Urban Europe: 1000–1994.* Rev. ed. Boston: Harvard University Press, 1995.

Holguín, Sandie. *Creating Spaniards: Culture and National Identity in Republican Spain.* Madison: University of Wisconsin Press, 2002.

Holt, Mack P., ed. *Alcohol: A Social and Cultural History.* Oxford: Berg Publishers, 2006.

Honeyman, Katrina. "Doing Business with Gender: Service Industries in British Business History." *Business History Review* 81 (2007): 471–93.

Horowitz, Roger. *Putting Meat on the American Table: Taste, Technology, Transformation.* Baltimore: Johns Hopkins University Press, 2006.

Horrell, Sara, and Jane Humphries. "Women's Labour, Work Participation and the Transition to the Male Breadwinner Family, 1790-1865." *Economic History Review* 48 (1995): 89–117.

Hughes, Robert. *Barcelona.* New York: Alfred A. Knopf, 1992.

Hughes, Sarah, and Brady Hughes. *Women in Ancient Civilizations*. Washington: American Historical Association, 1988.

Humphrey, Kim. *Shelf Life: Supermarkets and the Changing Cultures of Consumption*. Cambridge: Cambridge University Press, 1988.

Ibero, Alba, Antonio Gil, Eva Carrasco de la Fuente, Isabel Pérez Molina, and Marta Vicente Valentín. *Las Mujeres en el Antiguo Régimen: Imagen y Realidad*. Barcelona, Icaria Editorial, 1994.

Iglesies, Josep. *El llibre de cuina de Scala Dei*. Barcelona: Fundació Francesc Blasi Vallespinosa, 1963.

Institución Milá y Fontanals, Únidad Estructural de Investigación de Estudios Medievales. *Alimentació i Societat a la Catalunya Medieval*. Anuario de Estudios Medievales 20. Barcelona: Consell Superior d'Investigacions Científiques, 1988.

Iradiel, Paulino. "Familia y function de la mujer en actividades no agrarias." In *La condición de la mujer en la Edad Media: Actas del Coloquio celebrado en la Casa de Velázquez del 5–7 de noviembre de 1984*. Madrid: Universidad Complutense-Casa de Velázquez, 1984.

Isaevich, Abraham. "Corporate Household and Eco-centric Kinship Group in Catalonia." *Ethnology* 20 (1981): 227–90.

Jacobson, Stephen. *Catalonia's Advocates: Lawyers, Society, and Politics in Barcelona, 1759–1900*. Chapel Hill: University of North Carolina Press, 2009.

———. "Law and Nationalism in Nineteenth-Century Europe: The Case of Catalonia in Comparative Perspective." *Law and History Review* 20, no. 2 (June 2002): 307–47.

Jeffreys, J. B. *Retail Trading in Britain: A Study of Trends in Retailing with Special Reference to the Development of Co-operative, Multiple Shop and Department Store Methods of Trading*. Cambridge: Cambridge University Press, 2011.

Jepson, Jill Christine. *Women's Concerns: Twelve Women Entrepreneurs of the Eighteenth and Nineteenth Centuries*. New York: Peter Lang, 2009.

Jimenéz-Landi, Antonio. *A First Look at a City in Spain*. New York: Franklin Watts, 1961.

Johnston, Hank. *Tales of Nationalism: Catalonia, 1939–1975*. New Brunswick: Rutgers University Press, 1991.

Jones, Geoffrey, and Mary B. Rose. "Family Capitalism." *Business History* 35 (October 1993): 1–16.

Jonnes, Jill. *Eiffel's Tower and the World's Fair Where Buffalo Bill Beguiled Paris, the Artists Quarreled, and Thomas Edison Became a Count*. New York: Viking, 2009.

Jutglar, Antoni. *Historia Crítica de la Burguesía en Cataluña*. Barcelona: Anthropos Editorial, 1984.

Kaplan, Steven L. *Provisioning Paris: Merchants and Millers in the Grain and Flour Trade during the Eighteenth Century*. Ithaca: Cornell University Press, 1984.

Kaplan, Temma. *The Anarchists of Andalusia, 1868–1903*. Princeton: Princeton University Press, 1977.

———. "Female Consciousness and Collective Action: The Case of Barcelona, 1910–1918." *Signs: Journal of Women in Culture and Society* 7, no. 3 (1982): 545–66.

———. *Red City, Blue Period: Social Movements in Picasso's Barcelona*. Berkeley: University of California Press, 1992.

———. "Social Movements of Women and the Public Good." In *Dones en Moviment(s), segles XVIII–XXI*, edited by Cristina Borderías and Mercè Renom, 19–47. Barcelona: Icaria Editorial, 2008.

———. "Women and Communal Strikes in the Crisis of 1917–1922." In *Becoming Visible: Women in European History*, edited by Renate Bridenthal, Claudia Koontz, and Susan Mosher Stuart, 429–49. 2nd ed. Boston: Houghton Mifflin, 1987.

Kay, Alison C. *The Foundations of Female Entrepreurship: Enterprise, Home and Household in London, c. 1800–1870*. New York: Routledge, 2009.

Kearns, Gerry, and Chris Philo, eds. *Selling Places: The City as Cultural Capital, Past and Present*. Oxford: Pergamon, 1993.

Kiernan, Victor Gordan. *The Revolution of 1854 in Spanish History*. Oxford: Clarendon Press, 1966.

Kipple, Kenneth F. *A Moveable Feast: Ten Millennia of Food Globalization*. Cambridge: Cambridge University Press, 2007.

Kurlansky, Mark. *Cod: A Biography of the Fish That Changed the World*. New York: Walker and Company, 1987.

*La Cuynera Catalana: Reglas útils, fácils, seguras y económicas per a cuynar bé*. 1851. Reprint, Barcelona: Alta Fulla, 1996.

Laforet, Carmen. *Nada*. Translated by Edith Grossman. New York: Modern Library, 2008.

*La Mediterrània, Àrea de convergència de sistemas alimentaris, segles V–XVIII*. Palma de Mallorca: Institut d'Estudis Baleàrics, 1996.

Landes, David S. *The Wealth and Poverty of Nations: Why Some Are So Rich and Some So Poor*. New York: W. W. Norton, 1999.

Lanström, H. *Pioneers in Entrepreneurship and Small Business Research*. New York: Springer Science and Business Media, 2005.

Lasuén, José Ramón, and Ezequiel Baró. "Sectors Quinaris: Motor de Desenvolupament de l'Àrea Metropolitana de Barcelona." In *Pla Estratègic Metropolità de Barcelona*. Accessed 20 December 2013. *http://www.bcn.es/plaestrategicdecultura/pdf/Sectors_Quinaris.pdf*.

Laurioux, Bruno. "Les livres de cuisine italiens à la fin du XVe et au début du XVIe siècle: Expressions d'un syncrétisme culinaire méditerranéen." In *La Mediterrània: Àrea de Convergència de Sistemes Alimentaris, Segles V–XVIII: XIV Jornades D'Estudis Històrics Locals*, 73–88. Palma de Mallorca: Institut d'Estudis Baleàrics, 1996.

Lee, Andrew Hamilton. "Mothers without Fathers, or Nothing More Than a Woman: Gender and Anarchism in the Work of Federica Montseny, 1923–1929." PhD dissertation, New York University, 2012.

Lemoine, Bertrand. *L'architecture du fer: France XIXe siecle*. Seyssel: Champ Vallon, 1986.

Lennard, Suzanne H. Crowhurst, and Henry L. Lennard. *Public Life in Urban Places: Social and Architectural Characteristics Conducive to Public Life in European Cities*. Southhampton, N.Y.: Gondolier Press, 1984.

Lerner, Gerda. *The Creation of Patriarchy*. New York: Oxford University Press, 1986.

*Les Festes de Primavera: Recull de Tradicions i Custums de l'Equinoçi de Primavera*. Barcelona: Caixa de Barcelona, Obra Social, 1983.

Lévi-Strauss, Claude. *The Raw and the Cooked*. New York: Harper and Row, 1969.

Lida, Clara E. *Anarquismo y Revolución en la España del XIX*. Madrid: Siglo XXI de España Editors, 1972.

Lindenfeld, Jacqueline. *Speech and Sociability in French Urban Marketplaces*. Amsterdam and Philadelphia: J. Benjamins Publishing Co., 1990.

Lladonosa i Giró, Josep. *La Cuina Catalana Més Antiga*. Barcelona: Editorial Empúries, 1998.

Lladonosa i Giró, Josep, and Jaume Fàbrega. *El Gran Llibre de la Cuina Catalana*. Barcelona: Salsa Books, 2005.

Lladonosa i Vall·llebrera, Manuel. *Catalanisme i Moviment Obrer: El CADCI entre 1903 i 1923*. Barcelona: Publicacions de l'Abadia de Montserrat, 1988.

Llobera, Josep R. *Foundations of National Identity: From Catalonia to Europe*. New York: Berghahn Books, 2004.

López Guallar, Marina, ed. *Cerdà and the First Barcelona Metropolis, 1853–1897*. Barcelona: Museu d'Història de Barcelona, 2010.

López Guallar, Marina. "L'administració municipal del proveïment del pa (1714–1799)." In Museu d'Història de Barcelona, Institut de Cultura, *Alimentar la ciutat: El proveïment de Barcelona del segle XIII al segle XX*. MUHBA Llibret de Sala, 12. Barcelona: Ajuntament de Barcelona, Institut Municipal de Mercats, Museu d'Història de Barcelona, Institut de Cultura, 2013.

López González, Palmira. *Los Inicios del Cine en España, 1896–1909: La llegada del cine, su expansión y primeras producciones*. Barcelona: Liceus, 2005.

Luján, Nestor. *Historia de la Gastronomia*. Esplugues de Llobregat: Plaza & Janés, 1988.

———. "Pequeña historia de los mercados barceloneses." *Especial para La Vanguardia*, 26 October 1983, 5.

———. *Veinte Siglos de Cocina en Barcelona: De las Ostras de Barcino a los Restaurantes de Hoy*. Translated by Sofía de Ruy-Wamba Guixeres. Barcelona: Ediciones Folio, 1993.

Luján, Nestor, Xavier Domingo, and Llorenç Torrado. *Mil Anys de Gastronomia Catalana*. Barcelona: Generalitat de Catalunya, 1989.

Luján, Nestor, Luigi Bettonica, et al. *Teoría y Anectoda de la Gastronomia*. Pamplona: Salvat, 1974.

Luna-Garcia, Antonio. "Just Another Coffee! Milking the Barcelona Model, Marketing a Global Image, and the Restoration of Local Identities." In *Consuming the Entrepreneur-*

*ial City: Image, Memory, Spectacle*, edited by Anne M. Cronin and Kevin Hetherington, 143–60. London: Routledge, 2007.

Madaria, José María García. *Estructura de la Administración Central, 1808–1930*. Madrid: Instituto Nacional de Administración Pública, 1982.

Madoz Ibáñez, Pascual. *Articles Sobre el Principat de Catalunya, Andorra i Zona de Parla Catalana del Regne d'Aragó al "Diccionario geográfico-estadístico de España y sus Posesiones de Ultramar."* Barcelona: Curial Edicions Catalanes, 1985.

Maddox, Richard Frederick. *The Best of All Possible Islands: Seville's Universal Exposition, the New Spain, and the New Europe*. Albany: State University of New York Press, 2004.

Maluquer de Motes, Jordi. "Consumo y Precios." In *Estadísticas Históricas de España*, ed. Albert Carreras and Xavier Tafunell, vol. 2. 2nd ed. Bilbao: Fundaciòn BBVA, 2005.

———. "El Turismo, motor fundamental de la economic de Cataluña." Unitat d'Història Econòmic (UHE) Working Paper 2011_12, Universitat Autònoma de Barcelona, 29 March 2011. Accessed 15 July 2012. http://www.h-economica.uab.es/wps/2011_12.pdf.

Maluquer de Motes i Bernet, Jordi. *Història Econòmica de Catalunya: Segles XIX i XX*. Barcelona: Proa, 1998.

Maranges, Isidra. *La Cuina Catalana Medieval: Un Festí per als Sentits*. Barcelona: Rafael Dalmau Editor, 2006.

Marín Silvestre, Dolors. *La Semana Trágica: Barcelona en llamas, la revuelta popular y la Escuela Moderna*. Madrid: La Esfera de los Libros, 2008.

Marshall, Tim, ed. *Transforming Barcelona*. London: Routledge, 2004.

Martí Escayol, Maria Antònia. *El plaer de la xocolata: La història i la cultura de la xocolata a Catalunya*. Valls: Cossetània Edicions, 2004.

Martí Ramon, Marc, coord. *Ramon Casas i el Cartell*. València: Museu Valencià de la Il·lustració i de la Modernitat, Diputació de València Àrea de Cultura, Caja de Ahores del Mediteráneo Obras Sociales, 2005.

Martínez, Guillem. *Barcelona Rebelde: Guía Historica de una Ciudad*. Barcelona: Debate Editorial and Random House Mondadori, 2009.

Marx, Karl, and Friedrich Engels. *Collected Works*. Vol. 23. New York: International Publishers, 1988.

Mas, Jordi, and Òscar Ubide. *Boqueria Gourmand*. Barcelona: Viena Edicions, 2010.

McDonogh, Gary W. *Good Families of Barcelona: A Social History of Power in the Industrial Era*. Princeton: Princeton University Press, 1986.

———. "Monserdà's Barcelona: Women and the City at the Turn of the Century." *Ideas '92* 7 (Fall 1990): 59–60.

McDowell, Linda. *Gender, Identity, and Place: Understanding Feminist Geographies*. Minneapolis: University of Minnesota Press, 1999.

McNerney, Kathleen, ed. *On Our Own Behalf: Women's Tales from Catalonia*. Lincoln: University of Nebraska Press, 1988.

McRoberts, Kenneth. *Catalonia: Nation Building without a State*. Oxford: Oxford University Press, 2001.

Mennell, Stephen. *All Manners of Food: Eating and Taste in England and France from the Middle Ages to the Present*. Oxford: Blackwell, 1985.

Michonneau, Stéphane. *Barcelona: Memòria i Identitat. Monuments, Commemoracions i Mites*. Translated by Rosa Martinez. Vic: Eumo, 2001.

Miller, Daniel. *A Theory of Shopping*. Ithaca: Cornell University Press, 1998.

Miller, Francesca. "Women in the Social, Political, and Economic Transformation of Latin America and the Caribbean." In *Capital, Power, and Inequality in Latin America and the Caribbean*, edited by Richard L. Harris and Jorge Nef, 174–95. Lanham: Rowan & Littlefield, 2008.

Miller, Maria Teresa. "Un Grapat d'Anecdotes Autobiogràfiques, 1930–1945." Unpublished manuscript in the author's possession. Huntington, W.V., 2007.

Miller, Michael B. *The Bon Marché: Bourgeois Culture and the Department Store, 1869–1920*. Princeton: Princeton University Press, 1981.

Miller, Montserrat M. "Les Reines dels Mercats: Cultura municipal i gènere al sector del comerç al detall d'aliments de Barcelona." In *Fer ciutat a través dels mercats: Europa, segles xix i xx*, edited by Manuel Guàrdia and José Luis Oyón. Barcelona: Museu d'Història de Barcelona, 2010.

——. "Mercats noucentistes de Barcelona: Una interpretació dels seus orígens i significant cultural." *Revista de l'Alguer: Anuari Acadèmic de Cultura Catalana* 4 (December 1993): 93–106.

Mintz, Sydney W. *Sweetness and Power: The Place of Sugar in Modern History*. New York: Penguin Books, 1986.

Molas i Ribalta, Pere. *Comerç i Estructura Social a Catalunya i Valencia als segles XVII i XVIII*. Barcelona: Curial, 1977.

——. *Los Gremios Barceloneses del siglo XVIII: La estructura corporativa ante el comienzo de la revolución industrial*. Madrid: Confederación Española de Cajas de Ahorros, 1970.

Molinero, Carme, and Pere Ysàs. *Patria, Justicia y Pan: Nivell de Vida i Condicions de Treball a Catalunya, 1939–1951*. Barcelona: La Magrana, 1985.

Monserdà de Macià, Dolors. *La Fabricanta: Novel·la de costums barcelonins, 1860–1875*. Barcelona: Edicions l'Eixample, 1992.

Montanari, Massimo. *Food Is Culture*. New York: Columbia University Press, 2006.

Morant, Isabel, M. Ortega, A. Lavrin, and P. Pérez Cantó, eds. *Historia de Las Mujeres en España y América Latina*. Vol. 3, *Del Siglo XIX a Los Umbrales del XX*. Madrid: Ediciones Catedra, 2006.

Morcillo, Aurora G. *The Seduction of Modern Spain: The Female Body and the Francoist Body Politic*. Lewisburg: Bucknell University Press, 2010.

——. "Shaping True Catholic Womanhood: Francoist Educational Discourse on Women." In *Constructing Spanish Womanhood: Female Identity in Modern Spain*, edited by Victoria Lorée Enders and Pamela Beth Radcliff, 51–69. Albany: State University Press of New York, 1999.

———. *True Catholic Womanhood: Gender Ideology in Franco's Spain*. Dekalb: Northern Illinois University Press, 2000.

Moreno Luzón, Javier, ed. *Alfonso XIII: Un Político en el Trono*. Madrid: Marcial Pons Historia, 2003.

Moreu-Rey, E. *Revolució a Barcelona el 1789*. Barcelona: Institut d'Estudis Catalans, 1967.

Morris, Jonathan. "Making Italian Espresso, Making Espresso Italian." *Food and History* 8, no. 2 (2010): 155–83.

———. *The Political Economy of Shopkeeping in Milan, 1886–1922*. Cambridge and New York: Cambridge University Press, 1993.

Muñoz, Ángela Fernández, and Cristina Segura, eds. *El Trabajo de las mujeres en al Edad Media Hispana*. Madrid: Al-Mudayna, 1988.

Muñoz Navarro, Daniel, ed. *Comprar, Vender y Consumir: Nuevas aportaciones a la historia del consumo en la España moderna*. València: Publicaciones de la Universitat de València, 2011.

Museu d'Història de Barcelona, Institut de Cultura. *Alimentar la ciutat: El proveïment de Barcelona del segle XIII al segle XX*. MUHBA Llibret de Sala, 12. Barcelona: Ajuntament de Barcelona, Institut Municipal de Mercats, Museu d'Història de Barcelona, Institut de Cultura, 2013.

Nadal i Oller, Jordi, Jordi Maluquer de Motes, Carles Sudirà i Triay, and Francesc Cabana i Vancells, dirs. *Història Econòmica de la Catalunya Contemporània s. XX*. Barcelona: Fundació Enciclopèdia Catalana, 1989.

Nash, Mary. *Defying Male Civilization: Women in the Spanish Civil War*. Denver: Arden Press, 1995.

———. "Identidad de género, discurso de la domesticidad y la definición del trabajo de las mujeres de España del siglo XIX." In *Historia de las Mujeres en Occidente*, directed by Georges Duby and Michelle Perrot. Vol. 4. Madrid: Taurus, 1993.

———, ed. *Més Enllà del Silenci: Les Dones a la Història de Catalunya*. Barcelona: Comissió Interdepartmental de Promoció de la Dona, 1988.

———. *Mujer, Familia, y Trabajo en España (1875–1936)*. Barcelona: Anthropos, 1983.

———. "Towards a New Moral Order: National Catholicism, Culture and Gender." In *Spanish History since 1808*, edited by José Alvarez Junco and Adrian Shubert, 289–302. London: Arnold, 2000.

———. "Un/Contested Identities: Motherhood, Sex Reform and the Modernization of Gender Identity in Early Twentieth-Century Spain." In *Constructiong Spanish Womanhood: Female Identity in Modern Spain*, edited by Victoria Loreé Enders and Pamela Beth Radcliff. Albany: State University of New York Press, 1999.

Nicolas, Jean. *La Rébellion Française: Mouvements Populaires et Conscience Sociale, 1661–1789*. Paris: Éditions du Seuil, 2002.

Nicolau i Martí, Antoni, and Albert Cubeles i Bonet. "El 150è aniversari de l'enderrocament de les muralles: Repensant la ciutat contemporània." In *Abajo las Murallas!!! 150 Anys de l'Enderroc de les Muralles de Barcelona*, edited by Orial Bohigas et al. Barcelona: Museu d'Història de la Ciutat, 2004.

Nicolau-Nos, Roser, and Josep Pujol-Andreu. "Urbanization and Dietary Change in Mediterranean Europe: Barcelona, 1870–1935." In *Food and the City in Europe since 1800*, edited by Peter J. Atkins, Peter Lummel, and Derek J. Oddy. Aldershot, Eng.: Ashgate, 2007.

Nord, Philip G. *The Politics of Resentment: Shopkeeper Protest in Nineteenth-Century Paris.* Princeton: Princeton University Press, 1986.

Obiols, Isabel i Pere Ferrer. *El Mercat de la Boqueria.* Barcelona: Grup 62, 2004.

Olivé, Xavier, and Llorenç Torrado, eds. *Boqueria: 150 Aniversari.* Barcelona: Ajuntament de Barcelona, 1986.

Oliver, Joan. *Fam.* Barcelona: Institució de les Lletres, 1938.

Olives Puig, Jose. "Deterioración Urbana e Inmigración en un Barrio de Casco Antiguo de Barcelona: Sant Cugat del Rec." *Revista de Geografia* 3, nos. 1–2 (1969):40-72.

Ollé Romeu, Josep Maria. *Les Bullange de Barcelona durant la Primera Guerra Carlina (1835–1837).* Tarragona: Edicions El Medol, 1993–94.

Ortí Gost, Pere. "Protegir i controlar el mercat alimentari: De la fiscalitat reial a la municipal (segles XII–XIV)." In Museu d'Història de Barcelona, Institut de Cultura, *Alimentar la ciutat: El Proveiment de Barcelona del segle XIII al segle XX.* MUHBA Llibret de Sala, 12. Barcelona: Ajuntament de Barcelona, Institut Municipal de Mercats, Museu d'Història de Barcelona, Institut de Cultura, 2013.

Ortiz de Orruño Legarda, José María, and Santiago Castillo Alonso, coords. *Estado, protesta y movimientos sociales: Actas del III Congreso de Historia Social en España. Vitoria-Gasteiz, julio de 1997.* Bilbao: Universidad del País Vasco, 1998.

Orwell, George. *Homage to Catalonia.* New York: Harcourt, 1952.

O'Shea, H. *A Guide to Spain.* London: Longmans, Green and Co., 1865.

Oyón, José Luis. *La quiebra de la ciudad popular: Espacio urbano, inmigración y anarquismo en la Barcelona de entreguerras, 1914–1936.* Barcelona: Edicions del Serbal, 2008.

Oyón, José Luis, José Maldonado y Fernández del Torco, and Eulàlia Grifol. *Barcelona 1930: Un Atlas Social.* Barcelona: Edicions UPC, 2001.

Pallol, Rubén. "Mujer, familia y trabajo en el Madrid de la segunda mitad del XIX." Paper presented at the XIII Coloquio Internacional de la Asociación Española de Investigación de Historia de las Mujeres, Barcelona, 19–21 October 2006, CD-Rom edition.

Pareja, Arantza. "Pequeños negocios femeninos, grandes aportaciones para la familia: Las mujeres bilbaínas a principios del S. XX." Paper presented at the XIII Coloquio Internacional de la Asociación Española de Investigación de Historia de las Mujeres, Barcelona, 19–21 October 2006, CD-Rom edition.

Pascual i Rodríguz, Viçens. *El Baró de Maldà: Materials per a una Biografia.* Barcelona: Publicacions de l'Abadia de Montserrat, 2003.

Pavlovic, Tatjana, Rosana Blanco-Cano, Inmaculada Alvarez, Anitra Grisales, Alejandro Osorio, and Alejandra Sánchez. *100 Years of Spanish Cinema*. Malden: Wiley Blackwell, 2009.

Paz Torres, Olga. *Los Obreros del Comercio: Un Análisis histórico-jurídico de la dependencia mercantil catalana*. Madrid: Dykinson, 2011.

Pendergrast, Mark. *Uncommon Grounds: The History of Coffee and How It Transformed Our World*. Rev. ed. New York: Basic Books, 2010.

Pérez Baró, Albert. *Història de les Cooperatives a Catalunya*. Barcelona: Editorial Crítica, 1989.

Pérez-Bastardas, Alfred. *El Govern de la Ciutat de Barcelona 1249–1986*. Barcelona: Ajuntament de Barcelona, 1986.

Pérez Samper, María de los Ángeles. "Alimentació i Societat a la Catalunya Moderna." *Pedralbes* 31 (1991): 36–37.

———. "Cullera de fusta, forquilla de plata." *Catálogo de la Exposición Seure a taula? Una història del menjar a la Mediterrània*. Andorra and Barcelona: Govern d'Andorra, Diputació de Barcelona, Museu d´Arqueologia de Catalunya, Ajuntament de Gavà, Museu de Gavà, 1996.

———. "El Pan Nuestro de Cada Día en la Barcelona Moderna." *Pedralbes* 22 (2002): 29–72.

———. "Espacios y prácticas de sociabilidad en el siglo XVIII: Tertulias, refrescos y cafés de Barcelona." *Cuadernos de Historia Moderna* 26 (2001): 11–55.

———. "La alimentación catalana en el paso de la edad media a la edad moderna: La mesa capitular de Santa Ana de Barcelona." *Pedralbes* 17 (1997): 79–120.

———. "Los Recetarios de Mujeres y para Mujeres: Sobre la Conservación y transmission de los saberes domésticos en la época moderna." *Cuadernos de Historia Moderna* 19 (1997): 121–54.

Pérez-Fuentes, Pilar. "El trabajo de las mujeres en la España del los siglos XIX y XX: Consideraciones metodológicas." *Arenal: Revista de Historia de las Mujeres* 2, no. 2 (1995): 219–45.

———. *Ganadores de pan y amas de casa: Otra mirada sobre la industrialización vasca*. Bilbao: Servicio Editorial Universidad del País Vasco, 2004.

———. *Vivir y morir en las minas: Estrategias familiars y relaciones de género en la primera industrialización vizcaína, 1877–1913*. Bilbao: Servicio Editorial Universidad del País Vasco, 1993.

Pérez Molina, Isabel, et al. *Las Mujeres en el Antiguo Régimen: Imagen y Realidad (S. XVI-XVIII)*. Barcelona: Icaria Editorial, 1994.

Perinat, Adolfo, and María Isabel Marrades. *Mujer, Prensa y Sociedad en España*. Madrid: Centro de Investigaciones Sociológicos, 1980.

Permanyer, Lluís. *Establiments i Negocis que han fet Història*. Barcelona: Edicions La Campana, 1990.

Petrie, Charles. *King Alfonso and His Age*. London: Chapman and Hall, 1963.

Phillips, William D., Jr., and Carla Rahn Phillips. *A Concise History of Spain*. Cambridge: Cambridge University Press, 2010.

Pi i Vendrell, Núria. *Bibliografia de la Novel·la Sentimental Publicada en Català entre 1924 i 1938*. Barcelona: Diputació de Barcelona, 1986.

Pilcher, Jeffrey M. *Food in World History*. New York: Routledge, 2006.

———. *The Sausage Rebellion: Public Health, Private Enterprise, and Meat in Mexico City, 1890–1917*. Albuquerque: University of New Mexico Press, 2006.

Pirenne, Henri. *Medieval Cities: The Origins and Revival of Trade*. Princeton: Princeton University Press, 1980.

Pla, Josep. *Llagosta i pollastre: Sobre la cuina catalana*. Barcelona: Editorial Selecta, 1952.

———. *Un Señor de Barcelona*. Barcelona: Destino, 1945.

Pla, Josep, and Francesc Català-Roca. *El que hem menjat*. Barcelona: Ediciones Destino, 2005.

Polanyi, Karl. *The Great Transformation: The Political and Economic Origins of Our Time*. Boston: Beacon Press, 2001.

Polska, Allyson. "How Women's History Has Transformed the Study of Early Modern Spain." *Society for Spanish and Portuguese Historical Studies Bulletin* 36, no. 1 (2008): 5–19.

Prats, Llorenç. *La Catalunya Rància: Les condicions de vida materials de les classes populars a la Catalunya de la Restauració segons les topografies mèdiques*. Barcelona: Editorial Alta Fulla, 1996.

Provansal, Danielle, and Melba Levick. *Els Mercats de Barcelona*. Barcelona: Ajuntament de Barcelona, 1992.

Puigvert i Solà, Joaquim M. "De manescals a veterinaris: Notes per a una sociología històrica de la profesió veterinària a Catalunya." *Estudis d'Història Agrària* 17 (2004): 729–50.

Pujol, Anton. "Cosmopolitan Taste: The Morphing of the New Catalan Cuisine." *Food, Culture, & Society* 12, no. 4 (2009): 437–55.

Pujol-Andreu, Josep, M. Gónzalez de Molina, L. Fernández Prieto, D. Gallego, and R. Garrabou. *El Pozo de Todos los Males: Sobre el Atrazo de la Agricultura Española Contemporánea*. Barcelona: Crítica, 2001.

Pujol i Puigvehí, Anna. *Arrels Clàssiques de la Cuina de la Catalunya Vella: D'Apici, segle 1, a Josep Pla, Segle XX*. Barcelona: Icaria Editorial, 1997.

Quevado, Francisco. *La Vida del Buscón Llamado don Pablos*. Edited by Carolyn Nadeau. Newark, Del.: European Masterpieces, 2007.

Radcliff, Pamela Beth. "The Emerging Challenge of Mass Politics." In *Spanish History since 1808*, edited by José Alvarez Junco and Adrian Shubert. London: Arnold, 2000.

———. *Making Democratic Citizens in Spain: Civil Society and the Popular Origins of the Transition, 1960–1978*. Basingstoke and New York: Palgrave Macmillan, 2011.

———. "Women's Politics: Consumer Riots in Twentieth-Century Spain." In *Constructing Spanish Womanhood: Female Identity in Modern Spain,* edited by Victoria Loreé Enders and Pamela Beth Radcliff. Albany: State University of New York Press, 1999.

Ràfols Casamada, Joan. "La innovación tecnológica como factor de reubicación de la producción lacteal." *Scripta Nova: Revista Electrónica de Geografía y Ciencias Sociales* 69 (1 August 2000). Accessed 2 January 2014. http://www.ub.edu/geocrit/sn-69–14.htm.

Raurell i Torrent, Anna. "Avaluació de la incidència de diversos productes làctics en la variació de les característiques organolèptiques i reològiques de la xocolata." PhD diss., Universitat de Vic, 1999.

Ravetllat i Mira, Pere Joan, and Carme Ribas. "El mercat de Sant Antoni: Quatre nous espais." *D'UR* 01/2-10 (October 2010): 86–93. Accessed 27 December 2013. http://hdl.handle.net/2099/10222.

Rebagliato, Joan. "L'evolució demogràfica i dinàmica social al segle XIX." In *Història Salvat de Catalunya,* edited by J. Salrach. Vol.5. Barcelona: Salvat, 1978.

Reher, David S. *La Familia en España: Pasado y Presente.* Madrid: Alianza, 1996.

Rekas i Mussoms, Salomé, and Ramon Arús i Masramon. "El Bornet: De la realidad a la tela." *Informe 8 B.MM* 66, October 2005, www.bcn.es/publicacions/b_mm/ . . . /o8-17.pdf. Accessed 2 January 2014.

Renom, Mercè. *Conflictes socials i revolució: Sabadell, 1718–1823.* Vic: Eumo Editorial, 2009.

———. "Les Dones en els Moviments Socials Urbans Preindustrials: Catalunya en el Context Europeu." In *Dones en Moviment(s), segles XVIII–XXI,* edited by Cristina Borderías and Mercè Renom, 49–75. Barcelona: Icaria Editorial, 2008.

———. "Les formes i el léxic de la protesta a la fi de l'Antic Règim." *Recerques* 55 (2007): 5–33.

Resina, Joan. *Barcelona's Vocation of Modernity: Rise and Decline of a Modern Image.* Stanford: Stanford University Press, 2008.

———. "From Rose of Fire to City of Ivory." In *After-Images of the City,* edited by Joan Ramon Resina and Dieter Ingenschay. Ithaca: Cornell University Press, 2003.

———, ed. *Iberian Cities.* New York: Routledge, 2001.

*Revolución de Barcelona, Proclamando la Junta Central: Diario de los Acontecimientos de que ha sido teatro esta cuidad durante los meses Setiembre, Octubre, y Noviembre de 1843. Redactado por un testigo de vista.* Barcelona: Imprenta D. Manuel Saurí, 1844.

Reventós, Joan i Jacint. *Dos Infants i la Guerra: Records de 1936–39.* 2nd ed. Barcelona: Club Editor, 1978.

Riera i Melis, Antoni. "Documentació notarial i història de l'alimentació." *Estudis d'Història Agraria* 13 (1999): 41–42.

———. *Senyors, Monjos i Pagesos: Alimentació i identitat social als segles XII i XIII.* Barcelona: Institut d'Estudis Catalans, 1997.

Ringrose, David. *Spain, Europe, and "The Spanish Miracle," 1700-1900.* New York: Cambridge University Press, 1996.

Risques, Manel, Angel Duarte, Borja de Riquer, and Josep M. Roig Rosich. *Història de la Catalunya Contemporània*. Barcelona: Pòrtic, Biblioteca Universitària, 1999.

Robert, Mestre. *Libre del Coch: Tractat de cuina medieval*. Edited by Veronika Leimgruber. Barcelona: Curial Edicions Catalanes, 1996.

Roberts, Mary Louise. "Gender, Consumption, and Commodity Culture." *American Historical Review* 103, no. 3 (June 1998): 817–44.

Robinson, William H., Jordi Falgàs, and Carmen Belen Lord, eds. *Barcelona and Modernity: Picasso, Gaudí, Miró, Dalí*. New Haven: Cleveland Museum of Art in association with Yale University Press, 2006.

Roche, Daniel. *A History of Everyday Things: The Birth of Consumption in France, 1600–1800*. Cambridge and New York: Cambridge University Press, 2000.

Rodoreda, Mercè. *La Plaça del Diamant*. Barcelona: Club Editor, 2004.

———. *The Time of the Doves*. Translated by David H. Rosenthal. New York: Taplinger Publishing, 1980.

Romero Marín, Juanjo. "Artisan Women and Management in Nineteenth-Century Barcelona." In *Women, Business, and Finance in Nineteenth-Century Europe: Rethinking Separate Spheres*, edited by R. Beachy, B. Craig, and A. Owens, 81–95. Oxford: Berg, 2006.

———. "La Força d'una Cadena Descansa Sobre l'Anella més Dèbil: Mestresses Artesanes Barcelonines al segle XIX." In *La Ciutat i les Revolucions, 1808–1868*. Vol. 2, *El Procés d'Industrialització: Barcelona Quaderns d'Història*, edited by Ramon Grau, 11. Barcelona: Ajuntament de Barcelona, 2006.

———. "La Maestría Silenciosa: Maestras Artesanas en la Barcelona de la Primera Mitad del siglo XIX." *Arenal: Revista de Historia de las Mujeres* 4, no. 2 (1997): 275–94.

———. "Presència femenina a la gestió dels negocis artesanes barcelonins: 1823–1860." *Recerques: Història/Economia/Cultura* 56 (2008): 165–80.

Rondissoni, José. *Culinaria Exprés: Selección de Recetes para preparer con la Olla a Presión*. Barcelona: Bosch, 1960.

———. *Culinaria: Nuevo Tratado de Cocina. Mil Recetas de Cocina, Pastelería, i Repostería*. Barcelona: Bosch, ca. 1946.

———. *Recetario para la parilla eléctrica Setur*. Publisher unknown, no date.

———. *Rondissoni Culinaria: El Recitario de un gran maestro*. 6th ed. Barcelona: Bon Ton, 1999.

Rose, Sonya. *Limited Livelihoods: Gender and Class in Nineteenth-Century England*. Berkeley: University of California Press, 1992.

Roure, Alfons. *La Reina del Mercat: Sainet en tres actes*. Barcelona: La Escena Catalana, no. 220, Archivo Teatral Moderno, n.d.

Rowe, Peter G. *Building Barcelona: A Second Renaixença*. Barcelona: Barcelona Regional, Actar, 2006.

Rumbau, Montserrat. *La Barcelona de fa 200 anys*. Barcelona: Tibidabo Edicions, 1990.

———. *La Barcelona de Principis del Segle XIX*. Barcelona: Tibidabo Edicions, 1993.

Rundell, Maria Eliza Ketelby. *A New System of Domestic Cookery: Formed upon principles of economy, and adapted to the use of private families*. London: John Murray, 1808.

Russinyol, Santiago. *La Auca del Senyor Esteve*. Barcelona: Edicions 62, 1989.

Sala, Teresa-M. *La vida cotidiana en la Barcelona de 1900*. Madrid: Silex, 2005.

Salrach, J., ed. *Història Salvat de Catalunya*. Barcelona: Salvat, 1978.

Sánchez, Alejandro, dir. *Barcelona 1888–1929: Modernidad, ambición y conflictos de una ciudad soñada*. Madrid: Alianza Editorial, 1994.

Sánchez, Alicia, and María Pomés. *Historia de Barcelona: De los Orígenes a la Actualidad*. Barcelona: Editorial Optima, 2000.

Sánchez Martínez, Manuel. "Vi i tavernes a la Barcelona medieval." In Museu d'Història de Barcelona, Institut de Cultura, *Alimentar la ciutat: El Proveiment de Barcelona del segle XIII al segle XX*. MUHBA Llibret de Sala, 12. Barcelona: Ajuntament de Barcelona, Institut Municipal de Mercats, Museu d'Història de Barcelona, Institut de Cultura, 2013.

Santamaria i Puig, Santiago. *La cocina al desnudo: Una vision renovadora del mundo de la gastronomía*. Madrid: Temass de Hoy, 2008.

Santanach i Suñol, Joan, and Robin M. Vogelzang. *The Book of Sent Soví: Medieval Recipes from Catalonia*. Woodbridge: Tamesis; Barcelona: Barcino, 2008.

Sarasúa, Carmen, and Lina Gálvez-Muñoz, eds. *Mujeres y Hombres en los mercados de trabajo: ¿Privilegio o eficiencia?* Alicante: Publicaciones de la Universidad de Alicante, 2003.

Saurí, Manuel, and José Matas. *Guía General de Barcelona*. Barcelona: Imprenta de Manuel Saurí, 1849.

Scarpellini, Emanuela. "Shopping American-Style: The Arrival of the Supermarket in Postwar Italy." *Enterprise & Society* 5, no. 4 (2004): 625–68.

Schama, Simon. *The Embarrassment of Riches: An Interpretation of Dutch Culture in the Golden Age*. New York: Vintage Books, 1987.

Schmiechen, James, and Kenneth Carls. *The British Market Hall: A Social and Architectural History*. New Haven: Yale University Press, 1999.

Schultz, T. Paul, ed. *Investment in Women's Human Capital and Economic Development*. Chicago: University of Chicago Press, 1995.

Scott, Joan Wallach. *Gender and the Politics of History*. Rev. ed. New York: Columbia University Press, 1999.

Scranton, Philip. "Introduction: Gender and Business History." *Business History Review* 72 (Summer 1998): 185–87.

Segura i Marta Selva, Isabel. *Revistes de Dones, 1846–1935*. Barcelona: Edhasa, 1984.

Seidman, Michael. *Republic of Egos: A Social History of the Spanish Civil War*. Madison: University of Wisconsin Press, 2002.

———. "Social History and Antisocial History." *Common Knowledge* 13, no. 1 (2007): 40–49.

———. "Women's Subversive Individualism in Barcelona during the 1930s." *International Review of Social History* 47 (1992): 161–76.

Sagarra, Josep Maria de. *Obres Completes: Prosa*. Vol. 2. Barcelona: Editorial Selecta, 1967.

Seligmann, Linda J. *Peruvian Street Lives: Culture, Power, and Economy among Market Women of Cuzco.* Urbana: University of Illinois Press, 2004.

Seminario de Estudios de la Mujer de la Universidad Autonoma de Madrid, ed. *Las mujeres medievales y su ámbito jurídico: Actas de la II Jornadas de Investigación Interdisciplinaria.* Madrid: Universidad Autónoma, 1983.

Serra, Daniel, and Jaume Serra. *La Guerra Quotidiana: Testimonis d'una Ciutat en Guerra (Barcelona 1936–1939).* Barcelona: Columna, 2003.

Serrahima Balius, Pol. "Les interferències de la Catedral en el proveïment del pa." In Museu d'Història de Barcelona, Institut de Cultura, *Alimentar la ciutat: El Proveiment de Barcelona del segle XIII al segle XX.* MUHBA Llibret de Sala, 12. Barcelona: Ajuntament de Barcelona, Institut Municipal de Mercats, Museu d'Història de Barcelona, Institut de Cultura, 2013.

Serrano, Vincenç. *Manuel del boletaire catalá.* Barcelona: Editorial Barcino, 1959.

Serratosa, Albert, et al. *Semiòtica de l'Eixample Cerdà.* Barcelona: Edicions Proa, 1995.

Sert, Lluís. *Can Our Cities Survive? An ABC of Urban Problems, Their Analysis, Their Solutions.* Cambridge: Harvard University Press, 1942.

Shammas, Carole. *The Pre-Industrial Consumer in England and America.* Oxford: Oxford University Press, 1990.

Shore, Elliot. "Dining Out: The Development of the Restaurant." In *Food: The History of Taste,* edited by Paul Freedman. Berkeley: University of California Press, 2007.

Shubert, Adrian. *A Social History of Modern Spain.* London: Unwin Hyman, 1990.

Simpson, James. *Spanish Agriculture: The Long Siesta, 1765–1965.* Cambridge: Cambridge University Press, 1995.

Smith, Angel, ed. *Red Barcelona: Social Protest and Labour Mobilization in the Twentieth Century.* London: Routledge, 2002.

Smith, Eliza. *The Compleat Housewife: Accomplish'd Gentlewoman's Companion.* London: J. Pemberton, 1727.

Sobrer, Josep Miquel, ed. and trans. *Catalonia: A Self-Portrait.* Bloomington: Indiana University Press, 1992.

Sorribas, Sebastià. *Barri Xino: Una Cronica de Postguerra.* Barcelona: Editorial Base, 2008.

Sobrequés Callicó, Jaime. *Barcelona: Aproximació a Vint Segles d'Història.* Barcelona: La Busca, 1999.

———. "El Precio y la Reglamentación de la Venta de Carne en Barcelona Durante el Siglo XIV." In *Divulgación histórica de Barcelona,* edited by Pedro Voltes Bou. Vol. 12, *Los Abactecimientos de la ciudad: Oficios y Técnicas, Índice Analítico de los Tomos I-XII, Textos del Boletín Semenal radiado desde la emisora "Radio Barcelona" por el Instituto Municipal de Historia de la Ciudad.* Barcelona: Ayuntamiento de Barcelona, Instituto Municipal de la Historia, 1965.

Solà, Àngels. "Impressores i llibreteres a la Barcelona dels segles XVIII i XIX." *Recerques: Història/Economia/Cultura* 56 (2008): 91–129.

————. "Las Mujeres como productoras autónomas en el medio urbano (siglos XIX y XX)." In *La Historia de las Mujeres: Perspectivas Actuales*, edited by Cristina Borderías. Barcelona: Asociación Española de Investigación de Historia de las Mujeres and Icaria Editorial, 2009.

————. "Las Mujeres y Sus Negocios en el Medio Urbano." In *Historia de Las Mujeres en España y América Latina*. Vol. 3, *Del Siglo XIX a Los Umbrales del XX*, directed by Isabel Morant, and coordinated by M. Ortega, A. Lavrin, and P. Pérez Cantó. Madrid: Ediciones Catedra, 2006.

————. "Negocis i identitat laboral de les dones." *Recerques: Història/Economia/Cultura* 56 (2008): 5–18.

Solà Parera, Teresa, and Àngels Solà Parera. "El creixament urbà de Gràcia en les dècades de 1820 i 1830: Anàlisi de la urbanització Trilla." In *El Pla de Barcelona i la Seva Història: Actes del 1er Congrés d'història del Pla de Barcelona, celebrat a l'Institut Municipal d'Història el dies 12 i 13 de novembre del 1982*, 389–410. Barcelona: Edicions La Magrana, Institut Municipal d'Història de l'Ajuntament de Barcelona, 1984.

Solé Sabarís, L. *Geografia de Catalunya*. Barcelona: Editorial Aedos, 1958.

Sopeña i Nualart, Assumpta. "La publicitat com a font documental per la història contemporànea: *El Hogar y La Moda* (1913–1931)." *Gazeta: Actes de les Primeres Jornades d'Història de la Premsa* 1 (1994): 367.

Sòria i Ràfols, Ramon, ed. *Diccionari Barcanova d'Història de Catalunya*. Barcelona: Barcenova, 1989.

Soria Puig, Arturo, and Ildefonso Cerdá. *Cerdá: The Five Bases of the Theory of Urbanization*. Madrid: Electa, 1999.

Spang, Rebecca L. *The Invention of the Restaurant: Paris and Modern Gastronomic Culture*. Cambridge: Harvard University Press, 2000.

Spitzer, Theodore Morrow, Hilary Baum, Urban Land Institute and Project for Public Spaces, et al. *Public Markets and Community Revitalization*. Washington: Urban Land Institute, and New York: Project for Public Spaces, 1995.

Sponsler, Lucy A. "The Status of Married Women under the Legal System of Spain." *Journal of Legal History* 3 (1982): 125–82.

Spufford, Peter. *Power and Profit: The Merchant in Medieval Europe*. New York: Thames & Hudson, 2002.

Standage, Tom. *An Edible History of Humanity*. New York: Walker and Company, 2009.

————. *A History of the World in Six Glasses*. New York: Walker and Company, 2005.

Stearns, Peter N. *Gender in World History*. 2nd ed. New York: Routledge, 2006.

————. "Stages of Consumerism: Recent Work on the Issues of Periodization." *Journal of Modern History* 69, no. 1 (March 1997): 102–17.

Steele, Carolyn. *Hungry City: How Food Shapes Our Lives*. London: Chatto and Windus, 2008.

Stoddard, Charles Augustus. *Spanish Cities*. New York: Charles Scribner's Sons, 1892.

Strasser, Susan, Charles McGovern, and Matthias Judt, eds. *Getting and Spending: European and American Consumer Societies in the Twentieth Century.* Cambridge and New York: Cambridge University Press, 1998.

Sudarkasa, Niara. *Where Women Work: A Study of Yoruba Women in the Marketplace and in the Home.* Ann Arbor: University of Michigan Press, 1973.

Sudrià, Carles. "La modernidad de la capital industrial de España." In *Barcelona 1888–1929: Modernidad, ambición y conflictos de una ciudad soñada*, directed by Alejandro Sánchez, 44–56. Madrid: Alianza Editorial, 1994.

Tangires, Helen. "Lliçons d'Europa: La reforma del mercat public als Estats Units derant el Període Progressista, 1894–1922." In *Fer ciutat a través dels mercats: Europa, segles XIX i XX*, edited by Manuel Guàrdia and José Luis Oyón. Barcelona: Museu d'Història de Barcelona, 2010.

———. *Public Markets and Civic Culture in Nineteenth-Century America.* Baltimore: Johns Hopkins University Press, 2003.

Tarr, Joel, and Gabriel Dupuy, eds. *Technology and the Rise of the Networked City in Europe and America.* Philadelphia: Temple University Press, 1988.

Tarradell, Miquel, et al. *Evolució Urbana de Catalunya.* Barcelona: Edicions de la Magrana, Institut Municipal de Barcelona, 1983.

Tarragó i Balagué, Marçal. *PECAB: Pla especial de l'equipament comercial alimentari de la ciutat de Barcelona.* Barcelona: Ajuntament de Barcelona, Àrea de Proveïments i Consum, 1990.

Taylor, Lynne. "Food Riots Revisited." *Journal of Social History* 30, no. 2 (Winter 1996): 483–96.

TenHoor, Meredith. "The Architecture of the Market: Food, Media and Biopolitics from Les Halles to Rungis." PhD dissertation, Princeton University, 2012.

Termes, Josep. *Anarquismo y Sindicalismo en España, 1864–1881.* Barcelona: Editorial Crítica, 2000.

———. *De la Revolució de Setembre a la fi de la Guerra Civil (1868–1939).* Vol. 6, *Història de Catalunya*, directed by Pierre Vilar. Barcelona: Edicions 62, 1987.

Teuteberg, Hans J. "El Nacimiento de la Era del Consumidor." In *Gastonomía: Historia del paladar*, edited by Paul H. Freedman. València: Publicaciones Universitat de València, 2009.

Thibaut-Comelade, Eliane. *La Table Médiévale des Catalans.* Montpellier: Les Presses de Languedoc, 1995.

Thirsk, Joan. *Food in Early Modern England: Phases, Fads, Fashions 1500–1760.* London: Hambleton Continuum, 2006.

Thompson, E. P. "The Moral Economy of the English Crowd in the Eighteenth Century." *Past and Present* 50 (February 1971): 76–136.

Thompson, Victoria E. "Urban Renovation, Moral Regeneration: Domesticating the *Halles* in Second-Empire Paris." *French Historical Studies* 20, no. 1 (Winter 1997): 87–109.

———. *The Virtuous Marketplace: Women and Men, Money and Politics in Paris, 1830–1870.* Baltimore: Johns Hopkins University Press, 2000.

Thomson, J. K. J. *A Distinctive Industrialization: Cotton in Barcelona, 1728–1832.* Cambridge: Cambridge University Press, 1992.

Thorne, R. *Covent Garden Market: Its History and Restauration.* London: Architectural Press, 1980.

Tilly, Louise A., and Joan W. Scott. *Women, Work, and Family.* New York: Routledge, 1989.

Toboso Sánchez, Pilar. *Pepín Fernández, 1891–1982: Galerías Preciados, el pionero de los grandes almacenes.* Madrid: LID Editorial Empresarial, 2001.

Torra Fernández, Lídia. "Las 'botigues de teles' de Barcelona: Aportación al estudio de la oferta de tejidos y el crédito al consumo (1650–1800)." *Revista de Historia Económica* (2nd Series) 21 (2003): 89–105.

———. "Les xarxes de crèdit en el desevolupament comercial tèxtil a la Barcelona del setcents." In *El segle de l'absolutisme, 1714–1808,* edited by Ramon Grau, 221–34. Barcelona: Ajuntament de Barcelona, 2002.

———. "Pautas del Consumo Textil en la Cataluña del Siglo XVIII: Una Visión a Partir de los Inventarios *Post-Mortem.*" In *Consumo, Condiciones de Vida y Comercialización: Cataluña y Castilla, siglos XVII-XIX,* directed by J. Torras and B. Yun, 89–106. Valladolid: Junta de Castilla y León, 1999.

Torras, J., and B. Yun, dirs. *Consumo, Condiciones de Vida y Comercialización: Cataluña y Castilla, siglos XVII-XIX.* Valladolid: Junta de Castilla y León, 1999.

Torras, Jaume, Montserrat Duran, and Lídia Torra. "El Ajuar de la Novia: El Consumo de Tejidos en los Contratos Matrimoniales de una Localidad Catalana, 1600–1800." In *Consumo, Condiciones de Vida y Comercialización: Cataluña y Castilla, siglos XVII-XIX,* directed by J. Torras and B. Yun, 61–70. Valladolid: Junta de Castilla y León, 1999.

Tortella, Gabriel. *The Development of Modern Spain: An Economic History of the Nineteenth and Twentieth Centuries.* Cambridge: Harvard University Press, 2000.

Toussaint-Samat, Maguelonne. *A History of Food.* Translated by Anthea Bell. Cambridge: Wiley Blackwell, 2004.

Townson, Nigel. "The Second Republic, 1931–1936: Sectarianism, Schisms, and Strife." In *Spanish History since 1808,* edited by José Alvarez Junco and Adrian Shubert. London: Arnold, 2000.

———. *Spain Transformed: The Franco Dictatorship, 1959–1975.* New York: Palgrave Macmillan, 2007.

Trenc, Eliseu. "Modernista Illustrated Magazines." In *Barcelona and Modernity: Picasso, Gaudí, Miró, Dalí,* edited by William H. Robinson, Jordi Falgàs, and Carmen Belen Lord. New Haven: Cleveland Museum of Art in association with Yale University Press, 2006.

Trenc, Eliseu, and Pilar Vélez. *Alexandre de Riquer: Obra gràfica.* Barcelona: Caixaterrasa, Marc Martí, 2006.

Tribó, Gemma. "La ramaderia a les portes de Barcelona: El cas del Baix Llobregat (1850–1930)." *Estudis d'Història Agrària* 13 (2000): 107–26.

Trubeck, Amy B. *Haute Cuisine: How the French Invented the Culinary Profession.* Philadelphia: University of Pennsylvania Press, 2000.

———. *The Taste of Place: A Cultural Journey into Terroir.* Berkeley: University of California Press, 2008.

Turner, Jack. *Spice: The History of a Temptation.* New York: Knopf, 2004.

Tusell, Javier, Ángeles Lario, and Florentino Portero, eds. *La Corona en la Historia de España.* Madrid: Biblioteca Nueva, 2003.

Tusell, Javier, and Genoveva G. Queipo de Llano. *Alfonso XIII: El Rey Polémico.* Madrid: Taurus, 2001.

———. "The Dictatorship of Primo de Rivera, 1923–1931." In *Spanish History since 1808*, edited by José Alvarez Junco and Adrian Shubert. London: Arnold, 2000.

Ucelay da Cal, Enric. *La Catalunya Populista: Imatge, Cultura i Política en l'etapa Republicana (1931–1939).* Barcelona: La Magrana, 1982.

———. "The Restoration: Regeneration and the Clash of Nationalisms, 1875–1914." In *Spanish History since 1808*, edited by José Alvarez Junco and Adrian Shubert. London: Arnold, 2000.

Ulianova, Galina. *Female Entrepreneurs in Nineteenth-Century Russia.* London: Pickering & Chatto, 2009.

Ullman, Joan Connelly. *The Tragic Week: A Study of Anticlericalism in Spain, 1875–1912.* Cambridge: Harvard University Press, 1968.

Universitat Politécnica de València, Escuela de Arquitectura Técnica, Asociación de Vendedores del Mercado Central de València. *El Mercado Central en Papel.* València: Universitat Politécnica de València, 1998.

U.S. Department of Commerce and Labor. *Municipal Markets and Slaughterhouses in Europe.* Special Consular Reports, Vol. 42, Part 3. Washington: Government Printing Office, 1910.

Utrecht-Friedel, Louise Béate. *Le Petit Cuisinier habile, ou l'art d'apprêter les Alimens avec délicatese et économie: Suivi d'un petit Traité sur la conservation des Fruits et Légumes les plus estimés. Par Madame Fr. Nouvelle edition corrigée et augmentée.* Paris: L'auteur, 1814.

van dern Heuvel, Danielle. *Women and Entrepreneurship: Female Traders in the Northern Netherlands, c. 1580–1815.* Amsterdam: Aksant, 2007.

Vásquez Montalban, Manuel. *Carvalho Gastronómico: La Cocina de los Mediterráneos. Viaje por las cazuelas de Cataluña, Valencia y Baleares.* Barcelona: Zeta, 2008.

———, et al. *La Boqueria: La Catedral dels Sentits.* Barcelona: Ajuntament de Barcelona, 2001.

Veblen, Thorstein. *The Theory of the Leisure Class: An Economic Study of Institutions.* New York: Macmillan, 1899.

Venero Maximiano, García. *Historia del nacionalismo catalán.* Madrid: Editora Nacional, 1944.

Verdés-Pijuan, Pere. "Fiscalitat i proveïment: Dues cares de la mateixa moneda?" In Museu d'Història de Barcelona, Institut de Cultura, *Alimentar la ciutat: El Proveiment de Barcelona del segle XIII al segle XX.* MUHBA Llibret de Sala, 12. Barcelona: Ajuntament de Barcelona, Institut Municipal de Mercats, Museu d'Història de Barcelona, Institut de Cultura, 2013.

Vernon, James. *Hunger. A Modern History.* Cambridge: Belknap Press of Harvard University Press, 2007.

Vicente, Marta. *Clothing the Spanish Empire: Families and the Calico Trade in the Early Modern Atlantic World.* New York: Palgrave Macmillan, 2006.

———. "'Comerciar en Femení': La identitat de les empresàries a la Barcelona del segle XVIII." *Recerques: Història/Economia/Cultura* 56 (2008): 47–59.

———. "El Treball de la Dona dins els Gremis a la Barcelona del segle XVIII (una aproximació)." *Pedralbes: Revista d'Història Moderna* 8, no. 1 (1988): 267–76.

———. "El Treball de les Dones en els Gremis de la Barcelona Moderna." *L'Avenç* 142 (1990): 36-40.

———. "Mujeres Artesanas en la Barcelona Moderna." In *Las Mujeres en el Antiguo Régimen: Imagen y Realidad,* edited by Alba Ibero, Antonio Gil, Eva Carrasco de la Funte, Isabel Pérez Molina, and Marta Vicente Valent. Barcelona: Icaria Editorial, 1994.

———. "Textual Uncertainties: The Written Legacy of Women Entrepreneurs in Eighteenth-Century Barcelona." In *Women, Texts and Authority in the Early Modern Spanish World,* edited by Marta Vicente and Luis Corteguera, 183–95. Aldershot: Ashgate, 2003.

Vicente, Marta, and Luis Corteguera, eds. *Women, Texts and Authority in the Early Modern Spanish World.* Aldershot: Ashgate, 2003.

Vilar, Pierre. *Catalunya dins l'Espanya Moderna: Recerques Sobre els Fonaments Econòmics de les Estructures Nacionals.* 4 vols. Barcelona: Edicions 62, 1964–68.

———, dir. *Història de Catalunya.* Barcelona: Edicions 62, 1987.

———. *La Catalogne dans l'Espagne moderne: Recherches sur les fondements économiques des structures nationales.* Paris: S.E.V.P.E.N., 1962. Vol. 2.

Villarroya i Font, Joan. *Els Bombardeigs de Barcelona durant la Guerra Civil, 1936–1939.* Barcelona: Publicacions de l'Abadia de Montserrat, 1999.

Villiers-Wardell, Mrs. *Spain of the Spanish.* New York: Charles Scribner's Sons, 1915.

Vinyoles i Vidal, Teresa Maria. "La mujer bajomedieval a través de las ordenanzas municipales de Barcelona." In *Las mujeres medievales y su ámbito jurídico: Actas de la II Jornadas de Investigación Interdisciplinaria,* edited by Seminario de Estudios de la Mujer de la Universidad Autonoma de Madrid, 137–54. Madrid: Universidad Autónoma, 1983.

Viñas y Campi, *El Indicador de España y de Sus Posesiones Ultramarinas: Inscripción General de todas las clases comprendidas en el Subsidio Industrial y de Comercio, las de la Magistratura y Administración y las casas estranjeras que faciliten antecedentes al efecto. Año económica 1864 á 1865.* Barcelona: Imprenta de Narciso Ramírez, 1865.

Voltes Bou, Pedro, ed. *Divulgación histórica de Barcelona*. Vol. 12, *Los Abactecimientos de la ciudad: Oficios y Técnicas, Índice Analítico de los Tomos I-XII, Textos del Boletín Semenal radiado desde la emisora "Radio Barcelona" por el Instituto Municipal de Historia de la Ciudad*. Barcelona: Ayuntamiento de Barcelona, Instituto Municipal de la Historia, 1965.

———. *La Semana Trágica: Días de historia*. Barcelona: Espasa Calpe, 1995.

Walker, Juliet E. K. *The History of Black Business in America: Capitalism, Race, Entrepreneurship*. Chapel Hill: University of North Carolina Press, 2011.

Warwick, Joe. *Where Chefs Eat: A Guide to Chefs' Favorite Restaurants*. London: Phaidon, 2013.

Wason, Betty. *The Art of Spanish Cooking*. Garden City, N.Y.: Doubleday, 1963.

Watts, Sydney. *Meat Matters: Butchers, Politics, and Market Culture in Eighteenth-Century Paris*. Rochester: University of Rochester Press, 2006.

Weatherhill, Lorna. *Consumer Behavior and Material Culture in Britain, 1660–1760*. London: Routledge, 1996.

Whitaker, Jan. *The Department Store: History, Design, Display*. London: Thames and Hudson, 2011.

Wiesner-Hanks, Merry. *Gender in History: Global Perspectives*. 2nd ed. Chichester: Blackwell Publishing, 2011.

Wilk, Richard R. *Fast Food/Slow Food: The Cultural Economy of the Global Food System*. Lanham, MD: Altamira Press, 2006.

Winstanley, Michael J. *The Shopkeepers World, 1830–1914*. Manchester, Eng.: Manchester University Press, 1983.

Wynn, Martin G. "Peripheral Urban Growth in Barcelona in the Franco Era." *Iberian Studies* 7, no. 1 (Spring 1979): 13–28.

———, ed. *Planning and Urban Growth in Southern Europe*. London: Mansell Publishing Limited, 1984.

Zdatny, Steven M. *The Politics of Survival: Artisans in Twentieth-Century France*. Oxford: Oxford University Press, 1990.

Zimmerman, M. M. *The Super Market: A Revolution in Distribution*. New York: McGraw Hill, 1955.

Zimmerman, M. M., Antonio Pérez-Ruiz Salcedo, and Rafael Cremades Cepa. *Los Supermercados*. Madrid: Rialp, 1959.

## NEWSPAPERS

*ABC Edición de Andalucía*
*Diario de Barcelona*
*El Correo Catalan*
*El Destino*

*El Noticiero Universal*
*Gaceta Municipal de Barcelona*
*L'Opinió*
*La Prensa*
*La Publicitat*
*La Unión: Órgano de la Unión de Vendedores de Pescado de Barcelona y su Provincia*
*La Vanguardia de Barcelona*
*La Vanguardia Española*
*Le Veu dels Carnissers*
*Solidaridad Nacional*
*Solidaridad Obrero*


## INTERVIEWS WITH AUTHOR

Barceló Duran, Francesc, 25 May 1992.
Cararach Vernet, Maria, 5 May 1992
Colera Magrans, Isabel, 1 June 1992.
Colominas Aluja, Semi, 11 May 1992.
Colominas Aznar, Francesc, and Joana Calvet Carrado, 22 May 1992.
Conejero Moreno, Asunción, 27 March 1992.
Esteba Esteve, Joaquim, 13 May 1992.
Fernández Mitjans, Maria Teresa, 27 March 1992.
Giner Folch, Carme, 10 May 1992.
González Morales, Carmen, 11 May 1992.
Grillé Fornell, Joana, 1 June 1992.
Jover Barceló, Antoni, 3 June 1992.
Malla Vila, Pere, 25 May 1992.
Manadé Ginestà, Núria, 20 March 1992.
Mani Burgada, Joan, 8 April 1992.
Marqués Ruiz, Maria, 19 May 1992.
Martí Fiol, Rafel, 11 May 1992.
Miró García, Mercè, 13 March 1992.
Noguerolas Casas, Josefa, and Tomàs Sancho Roman, 19 May 1992.
Palmada, Francesca Orriols, and Lluís Casals, May 18, 1992
Peña Martín, Antonia, 21 May 1992.
Sanaluja Cot, Rosa, 14 May 1992.
Valls Roig, Carmen, 18 July 1990, 19 June 1992.

# Index

For alphabetization purposes, definite and indefinite articles in English, Spanish, and Catalan are ignored.

wine, 44, 92, 154, 290n1

women, x–xi; in associations and guilds, 156–
57, 291n10, 291n12; biological essentialism
toward, 259n47; in consumer protests, 7,
41–42, 187–89, 258n39; and cooking, 99,
103–5; domestic responsibilities of, 23,
99, 103, 178, 214; and food consumerism,
98–107, 154–56; and gendered division
of labor, 12, 78, 153–54, 181, 183, 214; and
gender ideologies, 50, 151–52, 157, 166, 172,
214–15, 248; legal status of, 161–63; middle
class and affluent, 127, 154; and shopping,
23, 100, 153–54, 225, 245; and sociability,
x–xi, 152, 154–55, 178–79; and taverns, 86,
155, 176; working-class, 7, 127, 155, 285n89

women vendors, xii, 151–52, 223, 248, 292n20;
in 1700s, 49–50, 269n106; codification of
female entrepreneurship, 156–63; depictions and stereotypes of, 10–12, 78, 157,
168–71, 247, 258–59n43; as embedded in
neighborhoods, 171–72; as entertainers and
counselors, 167–68; under Franco dictatorship, 213–15; and gender identity, 166–67;

municipal regulation of, 49–50, 78, 161–62;
orality traditions of, 99–101, 167–68; scholarship on, 260n52; and stall-acquisition patterns, 163–65; statistics on, 11–12, 157–58,
292n18; widows as, 12, 259–60n51. *See also*
female entrepreneurship; vendors

working class, 24, 56, 87, 97, 156; categories
of, 259n48; diet of, 90–92; housing for, 91;
market vendors seen as part of, 11, 259n48;
protests and uprisings by, 63, 67, 68; wages
of, 90–91, 93; women shoppers from, 127,
155, 285n89

World War I, 111

Xocolata Amatller, 96

Yagüe, Juan, 208–9
yogurt, 95
Ysàs, Pere, 205

Zapatero, José Luis, 252
Zona Franca, 249